How to Build a Business Rules Engine

EXTENDING APPLICATION FUNCTIONALITY THROUGH
METADATA ENGINEERING

Malcolm Chisholm

AMSTERDAM • BOSTON • HEIDELBERG
LONDON • NEW YORK • OXFORD
PARIS • SAN DIEGO • SAN FRANCISCO
SINGAPORE • SYDNEY • TOKYO

Morgan Kaufmann is an imprint of Elsevier

MORGAN KAUFMANN PUBLISHERS

SENIOR EDITOR   Lothlórien Homet
PUBLISHING SERVICES MANAGER   Simon Crump
EDITORIAL ASSISTANT   Corina Derman
PROJECT MANAGER   Sarah Manchester
TEXT DESIGN & COMPOSITION   SNP Best-set Typesetter Ltd., Hong Kong
COVER DESIGN   Juan Carlos Morales
COVER IMAGES
COPYEDITOR   Kristin Landon
INDEXER   Michael Ferreira
PRINTER   The Maple-Vail Book Manufacturing Group
COVER PRINTER   Phoenix Color

Designations used by companies to distinguish their products are often claimed as trademarks or registered trademarks. In all instances in which Morgan Kaufmann Publishers is aware of a claim, the product names appear in initial capital or all capital letters. Readers, however, should contact the appropriate companies for more complete information regarding trademarks and registration.

Morgan Kaufmann Publishers
An Imprint of Elsevier
500 Sansome Street, Suite 400
San Francisco, CA 94111
www.mkp.com

2007   2006   2005   5   4   3   2

Library of Congress Control Number: 2003107473
ISBN: 1-55860-918-0

This book is printed on acid-free paper.

COVER IMAGES   Artville LLC. Illustration by Johnathan Evans.

How to Build a Business Rules Engine

EXTENDING APPLICATION FUNCTIONALITY THROUGH
METADATA ENGINEERING

*To my wife, children, and parents for their
unconditional love and support.*

CONTENTS

FOREWORD

I like to say business rules are *inevitable*. Every organization has them—thousands of them—and every organization needs to be able to manage them far better today. I believe it's no exaggeration to say that many organizations' very survival depends on it.

In this book, Malcolm Chisholm makes an important contribution to the business rule movement. His is a very practical approach that blends best practices of the database field with new techniques based on rules. It's an approach that I can relate to well because my own work with business rules shares much of the same origin and trajectory.

To many in the IT world, especially those whose technical coming of age, started with object orientation and/or web services, the notion that rules should be tied to databases may seem novel or even heretical. Not at all! Localization of logic and control of "state" are both intimately related to the issue of data and databases. To see it otherwise is frankly an aberration. I fully understand that this represents a broad indictment of the kinds of technical architectures prevalent over the last decade. In these architectures, databases have played a largely passive role—in many cases coming into existence almost as an afterthought as the need for persistence is inevitably recognized.

I don't want to steal any of Malcolm's thunder, so I will let his work in this book show you how to achieve the powerful business (and technical) advantages that rule-oriented data-based architectures can provide. I do want to applaud Malcolm's candor in explaining that his build-it-yourself approach is not for everyone. For a more generalized rule environment, or for inference-oriented problems, a commercial rule engine is generally a better choice.

But business rules are literally everywhere in operational business processes, and there are huge opportunities for rule-oriented development on a smaller scale. Admittedly I'm biased, but the question I would be asking is why *not* take a rule-oriented data-based approach for most of the problems where in-house development is the best option?

At the risk of oversimplifying, the problem with applications today is that they are generally *black boxes* with respect to rules. That simply means the rules are not visible to business workers—or even accessible in any meaningful way.

The opposite of "black box" is *white box* (or *glass box* if you prefer). Think of the business rules approach as a "white box" solution with respect to rules. The rules are never to be hidden from (authorized) business workers. Instead, every possible effort is made to ensure the rules are visible, accessible and understandable. If you want your organization's business processes and practices to be highly adaptive—and what company doesn't these days?!—it's almost painfully obvious that this must be the case.

There's more to it of course than simply wishing it to be so. Success demands pragmatic, proven techniques. For one thing, as Malcolm explains in Chapter 6, even business rule applications must overcome "black box" *mindset* problems.

I have followed Malcolm's work for many years—his work on reference data, for example, is world-class. If I had to choose a leader to follow in this "new" area of do-it-yourself business rules, it would be Malcolm. Congratulations, Malcolm, on an important work. Well done!

Ronald G. Ross
Principal, Business Rule Solutions, LLC
Executive Editor, www.BRCommunity.com

INTRODUCTION

Business rules is a term that is becoming increasingly common across the spectrum that makes up today's information technology (IT) industry. Many of the issues that IT professionals face in a variety of specialized fields seem to have a business rules component, and this has probably helped to gain the term such widespread acceptance. Yet, it is very difficult to find common ground on a detailed definition of business rules. Different people tend to see business rules through the prism of their own particular specializations. Some emphasize analytical aspects of business rules, while others think of the nuts and bolts of how business rules can be implemented in computer applications. Even business users with responsibilities outside IT are becoming aware of business rules and are adding a new set of viewpoints to the debate.

The central idea behind the concept of business rules is that any organization has logic that it uses to carry out its operational and managerial tasks. The individual pieces of this logic are termed business rules, and if they are properly defined it should be possible to implement them in computerized applications. This, of course, sounds rather obvious and seems to describe what has been happening in IT for several decades. It is true that every computer application contains logic that represents the tasks of the organization that the application supports. However, this logic is usually described in textual documents used to design such an application without being formally itemized as individual rules. In reality, such documents may be missing, incomplete, outdated, or just wrong. Little effort is typically devoted to documentation, compared with activities such as programming.

Within the program code of an application, it is usually very difficult to even recognize what pieces of the code make up any particular rule. Indeed, there is a major disconnect between any written or verbal understanding of the business logic that is used to run an organization, and the program logic in the applications that carry out so many of the organization's tasks. This disconnect has been recognized for a very long time and is known to be a source of potentially severe problems. It tends to come to the fore when large-scale changes need to be made to applications, and people suddenly realize that they do not know in sufficient detail how these applications work. The concept of business rules seems to offer a way of packaging the logic used by an organization, so that as each item of logic that is used or referenced anywhere in the organization can be immediately recognized and understood. This applies in particular to applications. With a business rules approach, it should be possible to know in which applications any piece of logic—a business rule—is implemented, where to find it within these applications, how it is implemented in each application, who has responsibility for the implementation, and so on.

It should be pointed out that business rules are not a topic simply for computer applications. There are often many issues that an organization confronts with business rules that have little to do with IT. For instance, staff in one area of an organization may not understand certain rules or may not be able to correctly operationalize them. Some staff may simply not know what the rules are. It is also possible to find staff in one area of an organization who use different rules than staff in another area to perform the same tasks. To many, business rules approaches hold the promise of preventing these situations from arising in an organization, or at least mitigating them to a great extent.

These are only a fraction of the different perspectives on business rules that may be met within any organization. There are also many different, even competing, views about how business rules should support these perspectives. Every interested party naturally wants his or her problems solved first. It is against this background that business rules engines tend to be discussed. Quite simply, a business rules engine is a piece of software that can execute a business rule that is defined within it. The degree to which this can actually be done varies according to many factors, such as how well the rules can be defined, the availability of information needed by the rules, and the capacity of the software to put into effect what the rule dictates.

Business rules engines are only one aspect of a much larger business rules approach that reaches out to many different communities within an organization. Indeed, a better way of looking at the term *business rules* is that it covers a multi-faceted and multidisciplinary approach to organizing the logic needed to run an organization. The business rules approach attempts to bring order to this logic by decomposing it into individual business rules. If this can be done, it becomes easier to know, understand, and manage the logic at many different levels and in many different situations.

In today's economy, the business rules approach is meeting requirements generated by enterprises that are engaged in ever more complex undertakings in a general environment of increasing change. The degree to which organizations do not understand, or are not able to manage, the business rules that drive their operations is increasingly seen as a factor that will affect future success, or even survival. Business rules engines are being looked at by many organizations for their promise in several areas:

- **Increased speed of implementation**. It can take a long time to change some computerized applications. A business rules engine can permit new business rules to be implemented immediately. This increases organizational agility.

- **Management of diversity**. Many enterprises have operations that are increasingly diverse, or even customized. They find that no one set of business rules meets any particular situation. Creating individual applications specifically for these situations can be prohibitively expensive and impossible to manage. Organizations are looking for ways where new sets of rules can quickly be implemented for specific, perhaps even transient, situations. Business rules engines can meet these requirements. They permit organizations to expand their portfolio of operations and quickly take advantage of new opportunities.

- **Auditability**. Many organizations are unsure of exactly what their computerized applications are doing, which leaves them exposed to adverse events. This may be compounded by regulatory requirements demanding proof that operations are being carried out in an approved manner. Business rules engines have the capability to provide the level of assurance required. Thus, organizations can manage, and even reduce, their overall risk profiles.

- **Engineering compliance**. This is very similar to the need for auditability. Many organizations want to forward engineer computerized applications from sets of specifications. In traditional systems development approaches, testing is the primary means of determining whether what has been implemented matches what has been specified. Business rules engines hold out the promise of being able to directly implement specifications, or at least match what is executing within them with a set of original specifications.

Such promises makes business rules engines very appealing, but decision makers want to know whether rules engines can actually deliver on such promises. One of the major questions is whether it is possible to build a rules engine in-house, or whether the organization should look for a commercially available solution.

This book is intended to show what is required to build a rules engine. It describes the components that a rules engine must have, and how these may be implemented. The book has been written based almost entirely on the experience of the author in building rules engine functionality over a period of 12 years. During this period the author has worked in a variety of organizations and used a variety of software environments to implement the rules engines.

The primary focus of the book is design. A myriad of design decisions have to be met when building a rules engine, and many of these may not be obvious at the outset. Some design decisions involve choices that can lead to grave errors. Other design decisions involve more balanced options, and a choice can only be made with a good understanding of the requirements for the rules engine. The book discusses these design options and provides a general architecture for a rules engine. However, after the design of a piece of functionality is finalized, it is also legitimate to ask whether it can be implemented. Many people want to see that something is capable of working before they are prepared to invest anything in implementing their specific requirements. Therefore, the book also provides a sample application in which all the concepts that are discussed are implemented.

A business rules engine is not necessarily a monolithic application. Like business rules in general, it is more of an approach. It is a set of functionalities that can be implemented to a greater or lesser degree in any number of situations to meet a precise set of requirements. This book strongly advocates taking advantage of using whatever components of rules engine design apply to specific circumstances.

Audience

The intended audience for this book is professionals who have some degree of interest in understanding what might be involved in building a business rules engine. Many will be IT professionals who have been involved in systems development to some extent, either from managing it, or from actually doing the work to implement it. Others will be from the business side of organizations that may need to take advantage of rules engines to support core business activities.

Certain readers will only be interested in understanding what the components of a rules engine are, what level of effort may be involved in building such components, and whether it appears that these components will meet the business requirements the readers must deal with. The term *rules engine* is fairly generic and can hide a lot of complexity. Since this book provides a roadmap to building an actual application, all the components of a rules engine are described. Readers do not necessarily need to follow in great detail how to implement all the functionality described, but can appreciate what it is, and how easy or difficult it may be for their organization to build it. They should also be able to determine whether this functionality matches the challenges facing their organization. The book also describes a number of organizational issues that may determine the success of a business rules engine after it has been built and implemented. These may be of particular interest to nontechnical readers, although some of these issues can be mitigated by building the right kind of functionality into the rules engine.

Other readers will be interested in how it is possible to implement rules engine functionality. Some may already have built rules engine functionality and may want details about a few areas that are new to them. Others may be looking for a general architecture, but may only be interested in implementing parts of it. A different set of readers may be looking for a checklist, perhaps at a very detailed level, to make sure that they have not missed anything in their rules engine. The book offers practical advice and guidance on a number of levels across a wide range of rules engine functionality.

It is also hoped that this book will provide other audiences with useful information. In particular, information resource professionals who work with metadata should find a great deal to interest them. Metadata, often described as "data about data," is usually thought of as a form of documentation in many organizations. As such, there are questions about its usefulness and the need to have it complete and up-to-date. It is the primary driver of the business rules engine described in this book, and as such it needs to be complete and up-to-date. Indeed, the approach to business rules engines described here can be viewed as part of what can be called *metadata engineering*—that is, using metadata to create, or drive, components of computer applications.

It is also hoped that the book will be of interest to those trying to develop conceptual approaches that involve business rules and business rules engines. Nearly all of this book has come from the author's direct experience in building and deploying rules engines, rather than from the use and adaptation of theoretical approaches. It would have greatly helped the author's tasks in this area had there been more information available about conceptual approaches to building rules engines and about dealing with business rules in general.

Organization

The book begins with a discussion of business rules and business rules engines. This is followed by an examination of the reasons why organizations may choose to build a business rules engine, or at least build components of a rules engine. It then moves on to a description of some of the concepts behind a rules engine, chiefly rule definition and data modeling. Rule definition is a large area in itself and cannot be adequately covered in a book oriented toward rules engine design, but the issues inherent in it must be appreciated. The data modeling concepts are necessary, because so much of the rules engine design involves designing database tables.

Chapters 4, 5, and 6 introduce factors that affect the operational success of a rules engine and that therefore must be addressed in the design of a rules engine. These factors are not necessarily obvious, but they are important.

Chapter 7 describes the fundamental components of a rules engine. The remainder of the book is oriented toward the detailed design and implementation of these components. Perhaps the most important is the repository of the rules engine that, among other things, captures information about the business area on which the rules engine operates. Chapters 8 through 12 discuss how the repository can be implemented and populated.

With the repository built, Chapters 13 and 14 deal with the requirement to define new business information in a rules engine, and the techniques needed to manage this information. New business rules often imply new business data, and a rules engine must be able to implement new business data.

Chapters 15 through 20 deal with defining business rules and getting them to execute. This is often regarded as the core functionality of a business rules engine, but it cannot be implemented until the infrastructure described in the previous chapters has been built. The final two chapters of the book deal with management issues in the rules engine, such as monitoring its activity.

The chapters of the book are intended to be a progression where functionality and concepts described in earlier chapters are built on in subsequent chapters. A great number of design considerations are involved in building a rules engine, and it is not possible to present all of them at the outset. Nor is it easy to appreciate many of these considerations in the absence of detailed examples of the functionality they affect. Thus, design considerations are presented in the context of concepts and functionality where they apply. The simpler and more fundamental design considerations are presented in earlier chapters, and the more complex ones in later chapters. The reader should also be aware that there are some design themes that occur repeatedly in different areas of rules engine design. These themes are important and are stressed in the different contexts where they apply. This repetition is also needed because some of the concepts dealt with are not commonly discussed, even by IT professionals. Rather than assume that the reader will remember the details of such concepts from earlier chapters, they may be briefly restated where they have special relevance to a particular section.

Readers who are not interested in the details of implementation should simply skip the parts within each chapter where programming constructs are discussed. However, these chapters also contain observations on rules engine design, operation, and management that emerge from design decisions concerning individual pieces of functionality. The reader is encouraged to take note of these observations, even though they may arise from implementation detail.

Readers who are interested in the details of how individual pieces of functionality actually work will need to download the sample application, as described in the next section.

The Sample Application

Many readers will want not only to learn more about rules engine design, but also to look more closely at how the design has been implemented. Indeed, it is often not possible to have confidence in, or to fully appreciate, a specific design unless an implemented version of it can also be examined. A sample application has been created for this purpose. It is not practical to present design implementations in a variety of software environments, and to do so would risk losing the coherence that a single sample application can bring. Therefore, Microsoft Access has been chosen as the vehicle for the sample application. However, everything has been done to keep the programming in the application as easy to follow as possible. To this end, functionality that is highly specific to Microsoft Access has been avoided, although this has not always been possible. Similarly, program code has been simplified by restricted use of object-oriented approaches and complex programming constructs. For instance, arrays have been avoided. The objective has been to provide program code that is as easy as possible to follow. The code is functional, but can be viewed almost as pseudocode and, it is hoped, can be adapted to a number of different programming environments. It is a very good idea to use object-oriented approaches and constructs such as arrays to the extent that they are available in a given programming environment. However, the author has had the experience of working in situations where these were not available, and the ways in which they are implemented can differ from one environment to the next. Readers are strongly encouraged to adapt what they see in the sample application to the environment in which they work.

The sample application is intended to illustrate how the design concepts outlined in this book can be implemented. It is not intended to be a rules engine solution that can be implemented in a production setting. The business area covered by the sample application is the management of investments by an investment partnership. It is a very simple business area, with just a couple of business-oriented data-entry screens, and a couple of business processes. However, a thorough review of rules engine functionality is possible even within such a restricted business context.

To download the sample application, the reader should go to the Web site http://www.bizrulesengine.com. On the left-hand side is a link titled "Sample Application." Click on that to go to a page that presents some information about the book and contains a link "Download Sample Application." Readers will have to fill in some information to indicate that they have purchased a copy of the book, and will have to agree to the terms of use of the sample application.

The reader will need a version of Microsoft Access to run the application. Further details on how to install and use the sample application can be found in Appendix A.

1

WHAT ARE BUSINESS RULES AND BUSINESS RULES ENGINES?

As noted in the Introduction, the term *business rules* means different things to different people. The term can be used so widely that it becomes meaningless. For instance, the author has seen the following stated as a business rule in an investment partnership:

> The portfolio shall earn no less than 10% a year.

Simply saying that this is a rule does not bring it any closer to happening, though a lot of people might wish it would. It is also very difficult to imagine a foolproof way that such a "rule" could be implemented. Of course, it is not really a rule, but a goal or a target.

There is similar confusion about business rules engines. If a term such as *business rules engine* is "hot," then it will be used more frequently by anyone who feels that it can advance a particular product or position. The author has seen applications that claimed to be business rules engines, but that did not capture rule definitions, and required programmers to implement all rules functionality. These products could not really be distinguished from applications built using traditional systems development techniques.

Apart from extreme examples, it is important to understand what business rules and business rules engines are, and what can reasonably be expected from approaches that involve them.

Business Rules

A reasonable definition of a business rule comes from GUIDE, an industry user group. It states that a business rule is:

A statement that defines or constrains some aspect of the business. It is intended to assert business structure or to control or influence the behavior of the business.[1]

Although reasonable, this is a fairly broad definition. Since business rules is a term that means different things to different people, it is also unlikely to satisfy a number of points of view. One interesting aspect of the definition, however, is that it does not imply that business rules necessarily have anything to do with a business rules engine. It is very important that anyone thinking about building or using a rules engine be aware of this. Business rules have such a wide scope that a business rules engine cannot satisfy all requirements that have anything to do with business rules.

GUIDE is now defunct, but further information about definitions of the term business rule can be found at the Web site of the Business Rules Group, http://www.businessrulesgroup.org.

Some business rules are oriented purely to organizational behavior. A visit to a coffee station in any organization will reveal many business rules that affect organizational behavior but that will never be considered for a rules engine. Examples the author has seen include:

Do not put fish in the refrigerator.

Do not heat bagels in the microwave if they have butter on them.

Any items left in the refrigerator after 6:00 P.M. on Fridays will be thrown away.

More seriously, rules concerning ethics may be very important to an organization, but are not something that can be operationalized through a business rules engine. *Operationalized* means that the desired effect of the rule can be obtained by having it executed in a rules engine. It is possible for computerized applications to gather information that indicates whether rules about ethics are being followed, but it is not possible for the applications to actually follow these rules.

Recognizing that the term business rules is broad, and that business rules can exist that will never end up in a rules engine, is only part of the problem. Because there is no commonly accepted theoretical basis for many aspects of information management in organizations, the term business rules tends to become appropriated by people to describe activities that they carry out. It is a convenient label because it is self-evident that it describes something important and useful, which is difficult to challenge.

If the definition of business rules is so elastic that it can describe any number of activities, then once again many of these activities will not necessarily involve business rules engines. There are many activities related to business rules that happen only at a general analytical level. For instance, some organizations try to enforce "global" rules that require special, unique interpretations in some units of the organization. A

---

1. T. Morgan. *Business Rules and Information Systems.* Boston: Addison-Wesley Publishing, 2002.

rules engine cannot directly help with such interpretations. In other cases, staff in one area of an organization may not know that certain rules have been implemented, or that others have become obsolete. A rules engine by itself cannot solve this kind of communication problem. Significant efforts are being made in many organizations to extract business rules from knowledgeable users, such as through facilitated workshops. A rules engine cannot take the place of a facilitator.

Of course, it is an exaggeration to say that rules engines can play no role at all in these kinds of activities. The ability to capture the definitions of business rules in a rules engine can be a valuable aid in many situations. What is important to realize is that a business rules engine simply cannot perform many tasks that fall under the term business rules, or solve many business rules issues.

It is possible to come up with a more restrictive definition of business rules that applies to a business rules engine. However, before that can be done it is first necessary to look at what is meant by a business rules engine.

Business Rules Engines

Business rules engines are software applications that contain definitions of business rules. However, there is a great deal of variation among business rule engines, and Ronald Ross has classified them as those that primarily deal with databases, and those that are used to make inferences.[1]

Computer applications are primarily used by organizations to manage information. This is why the overwhelming majority of them are connected to data storage facilities. Today, most of these data storage facilities are relational databases, although flat or indexed "files" can still be found on mainframe computers. This book uses the term *database* to refer to all data storage mechanisms, and it uses relational databases in the implementation approaches it describes. The overwhelming majority of computer applications not only read data from databases, they update data as well. Therefore, data—the stored representation of facts in databases—is a fundamental component of information technology. Indeed, that is why it is called *information* technology, and why it was formerly known as *data* processing.

The importance of data in computer applications is reflected by the amount of logic in these systems that processes this data in ways that the business requires. This logic reflects business rules, but there is often a lot of other logic that is used to manage the applications themselves. Obviously, business rules engines are prime candidates for dealing with business rules in these situations. However, this is not the only kind of rules engine that there is.

Some rules engines are primarily used to make inferences. A user may want to know something, and the rules engine can generate an answer to the user's question

---

1. Ronald G. Ross, *Principles of the Business Rule Approach*, Addison-Wesley, 2003. Available via www.BRSolutions.com

based on rules definitions that it possesses and data that it can access. Alternatively, a user may simply wish to know what can be inferred from a given set of data based on the rules contained in the engine without necessarily posing a specific question to the engine. Rules engines oriented to inference in this way are related to applications that are called expert systems or artificial intelligence. These applications have a fairly long pedigree and are very useful. However, they are far less common than the kinds of applications oriented to data management.

This book takes an unashamedly data-oriented view of business rules engines. This is where the greatest number of requirements are, and thus the greatest number of opportunities for rules engines to make a difference. The rules engines that are used for inferences are very interesting, and indeed for the requirements they satisfy it is difficult to think of an approach that would work that did not involve a rules engine. However, they are not the kind of rules engine that is built in this book.

Business Rules in Business Rule Engines

Given that we are considering business rules engines that will apply organizational logic to manage stored information, it becomes a little easier to find a more specific view of business rules. In this instance, a business rule can be defined as an atomic package of business logic that uses data constructs. A data construct is a level of data stored in a database, that is, an individual data value, or a record (row), or a column (field), or a table. Most of the time, these business rules will operate on an individual data construct, for example, to calculate a value or to constrain a change in a value or values within the construct. However, this is not true all of the time. Perhaps a business rule will cause emails to be sent to clients who have not paid their telephone bills within the past 60 days. What is important is that for business rules engines oriented to data management, the business rules implemented in them are driven by data stored in a database.

This more specific view of a business rule helps to more clearly define the role of the kind of business rule engine that will be built in this book. Yet, all rules engines must fit within the greater context of the much wider spectrum covered by business rules. It is very unwise to try to build a rules engine without some idea of how this wider context will affect it. In particular there must be an appreciation of where the business rules that will end up in the engine come from.

Where Do Business Rules Come From?

It is fairly obvious that business rules should come from the business, as opposed to coming from IT personnel responsible for applications that support the business.

In theory this is what should happen, although it is not always very easy to get to specific rule definitions. In reality, there may be more involvement by IT staff than is warranted.

What cannot be disputed is that IT professionals should not define business rules. Defining a business rule implies making a business decision, and business decisions are the responsibility of the personnel who have direct responsibility for running a particular business area. IT staff who look after applications that support a business area cannot be expected to have the business understanding that is required to make business decisions, and should not be placed in a position where they are responsible for doing so. Of course, analysts and programmers have always tended to do things that make their lives easier, and they may occasionally try to implement business rules in a way that seems to fit better with a particular technical architecture. Such compromises usually become visible to users, and if they have a negative business impact they tend to be corrected. However, compromises of this kind are quite different from analysts and programmers actually making business decisions.

Ideally, there should be a seamless chain of operationalization flowing from high-level business strategy to a coherent set of business rules that are well defined and easy to implement in a rules engine. Yet, this model is rarely seen in practice, and in any case it does not fit the way many organizations want to use business rules. A major problem is that there can be difficulties in getting well-defined business rules from the personnel who are supposed to know what the rules are. Organizational disconnects can lead to arguments between different groups about what the rules are. There may be no coherent set of documentation describing the rules, and it may be difficult to create one by harvesting rules from a variety of disparate sources. Users may be reluctant to be forthcoming about rules because they fear that their roles will be misunderstood, or that they will be punished for interpreting rules in ways that may differ from the spirit behind higher-level rules. Even arriving at good rule definitions when all parties are cooperative and the necessary information is available can be surprisingly difficult.

These are factors that someone building a rules engine cannot control. They mean that it cannot be assumed that if a rules engine is built, the rules will come to it. Thus, the construction of a business rules engine must fit into a larger organizational context where there is a reasonable assurance that rules will be formulated with a reasonable degree of specificity, and that sufficient rules will be formulated so that the rules engine can actually carry out operations of value to the organization.

The linear sequence flowing from business strategy to rule operationalization mentioned above is also too simple a model for many organizations. Many enterprises undertake activities that cannot be described by a monolithic set of rules. For instance, investment partnerships may manage many investments and have one distinct set of rules around each investment. These rules are not central to the running of the partnership, but they certainly govern the administration of each investment.

An even more extreme example can be seen in the portfolio management of private client asset management. In this rapidly growing area of finance, institutions manage the assets of wealthy individuals. These individuals often demand that the institution managing their money follow any set of rules that they may come up with. One individual may not want to invest in tobacco-related stocks; another may want 67% of her assets invested in bonds; and yet another may want all his money invested in U.S. corporations. Situations where a set of rules applies to one and only one client of an enterprise are growing. The IT infrastructure to manage it is not well developed, but rules engines are having an increasing impact. Just as an earlier generation of computer applications enabled enterprises to manage volumes of transactions well beyond the capacity of humans to keep track of, so rules engines hold the promise of being able to permit organizations to manage hugely complex relationships each with their own set of rules. In such environments the idea of a single set of business rules that an enterprise runs by is simply outmoded.

In the traditional scenario of a single set of rules that is responsible for running an enterprise, there may be considerable difficulty in eliciting all the rules from all the parties. This is due to the kind of organizational difficulties mentioned above. A great deal of analysis may be required to get to the point where these rules are well defined. In instances where an enterprise has special relationships with many parties, and each relationship tends to be governed by a distinct set of rules, there are typically contracts, deals, or other written documents that contain the rules. These documents can be reverse engineered to obtain the rules. In fact, in certain areas of modern finance, reverse engineering rules out of deals is already quite an industry.

The factors that control how many rules can be defined, and how good these definitions are, can therefore vary widely from situation to situation. These factors are nearly always outside of the control of the personnel building the rules engine, but they certainly affect how successfully the rules engine will be adopted.

It was mentioned above that it is difficult to imagine that IT professionals would intentionally make business decisions that affect the definition of business rules. However, this can happen indirectly. An obvious way is reverse-engineering from program code. Where the documentation defining business rules is missing or unreliable, it may be necessary to reverse-engineer rule definitions from the source code of computerized applications. Business users are somewhat at the mercy of IT staff in this situation and are forced to rely on how well the staff perform the task of reverse-engineering. More importantly, in building a business rules engine there can be design decisions that effectively foreclose the capacity to define certain kinds of business rules, or to define business rules in a way that has true business meaning. As we shall see in later chapters, building business rules with great specificity can be enormously helpful to an organization. By contrast, building a rules engine that limits the kinds of rules that can be specified can seriously limit the success of the rules engine.

Conclusion

This chapter has shown something of the diversity that lies behind the term business rule and the different understandings that arise from this diversity. The definitions of business rules and business rules engines have been narrowed to the area of data-driven approaches, which will be the focus of the remainder of this book. Building a business rules engine can be a complex task, but a rules engine fits into a larger picture that must be understood. This larger picture includes the processes by which business rules are discovered and defined. Although often beyond the control of anyone building a rules engine, these processes can ultimately determine how successful the rules engine will be.

2 WHY BUILD A BUSINESS RULES ENGINE?

There are a number of business rules engines on the market at the present time, and they fill several different kinds of niches. Broadly speaking, they fall into two main groupings. The first are basically inference engines, which can read information from a database and operate rules in order to find answers to questions that users ask. The second group is more concerned with deriving results that can be stored in a database after the results have been calculated. All these rules engines are to some extent generic and have some degree of acceptance in the current market. No doubt there will be changes in the coming years as the market matures, and there is likely to be increased product sophistication and differentiation.

There is another category of software on the market that can also be considered to be rules engines. These products are not marketed as business rules engines, but rather as targeted applications that meet specific business needs. One of the most important business domains for which such products are designed is accounting. In accounting it is important to recognize flows of money and categorize them correctly. Operational systems of an enterprise typically process and settle transactions such as orders. The accounting applications are designed to integrate with the databases of the operational systems, or intercept electronic messages that flow between them, and post the information about financial activity to the correct accounts. This is only feasible using a business rules approach because each enterprise has an individual way of accounting, and a unique information systems architecture. However, the accounting packages are sold as such, and not specifically as rules engines. In addition to accounting applications there are a number of other kinds of applications that contain rules engines functionality, but are not marketed as such. Instead they are marketed as solutions for a specific business area—as indeed they should be. It is not clear which economic sector is currently making the most use of these applications, but they are clearly heavily used in the financial sector.

Therefore, if there are already generic business rules engines on the market, or specific applications that are in fact rules engines, why would anybody consider building a rules engine? Surprisingly, there are a number of reasons why build rather than buy can be a good idea.

Cost and Scale

A major reason for building a business rules engine is cost. Commercial business rules engines can cost hundreds of thousands of dollars to purchase or license. Even after that, they must be integrated into the enterprise's IT environment. In particular, they need to be configured to acquire the data they need to process. This can add significantly to the overall cost.

In large-scale operations where many transactions are processed, or where extremely large monetary values are involved, purchasing a commercial rules engine should be seriously considered. This is also true where there are potentially highly damaging risk factors that need to be mitigated. If the costs and risks involved in a particular business area are high, it is easier to justify the purchase of a business rules engine. Sometimes the job that the rules engine is expected to perform is very specific and is recognizably something that requires a rules engine. In these situations there is likely to be greater acceptance of the need to purchase a rules engine. A good example is an enterprise processing credit card transactions. There may be many hundreds of thousands of transactions per day, each with a relatively high value. The consequences of incorrectly approving transactions that should be declined (and vice versa) can be costly. Yet the logic to decide whether to approve or decline a particular transaction can be involved and can change over time. In this kind of situation a rules engine immediately jumps to mind as a solution, and the costs and risks involved suggest that a commercial product should be considered. Of course, another advantage is that the buyer will also have the company that provides the rules engine available for support and maintenance.

Rules engines that are marketed as specific applications are a little different from general rules engines, although they too are often very expensive. They are usually not pure rules engines, but include components that are unique to the business area they are addressing, such as a module to build a Chart of Accounts in the case of accounting packages. Like the commercial rules engines, the integration of these packages into the enterprise's IT environment may be very costly and may push up the total cost of acquisition of the software. It may even be necessary to employ high-priced consultants to configure the software. Again, therefore, these packages tend to make sense only for situations where the business is so lucrative or critical in nature that the large costs involved can be justified.

However, for every one instance of an operation that can justify the cost of acquiring a business rules engine (both the purchase price and the cost of integration) there are many smaller operations that simply do not have the funds required. For these operations the only choice is to build a rules engine or do without. Smaller organizations, and even larger ones, tend to have simpler applications, or even complex ones that are not mission critical. If these applications require rules engine functionality, it is very difficult to make a case to purchase a commercial rules engine, even if there are funds available. There are just too many higher priorities for these funds in any organization. Obviously, there are many more smaller applications than larger ones, and many more nonmission-critical applications than mission-critical ones. Thus, there is a large scope for considering building rules engine functionality.

Beyond this, there are situations where the nature of an application requires the presence of some kind of rules engine functionality, but only for one or a few areas of the application, perhaps covering only a couple of business requirements. It makes little sense to buy a commercial rules engine solution and go through the cost and technical difficulty required to integrate it into the application. Furthermore, even if integration is achieved at one point in time, there may be a cost to ensuring that it is maintained over time. Building the rules engine functionality to meet these marginal requirements, if it can be done reliably with reasonable cost and effort, is likely to be a more acceptable alternative. Such situations where regular applications have some marginal need for rules engine functionality may be far more common than many IT professionals think.

Building Software for Diverse Environments

Today there is an explosive proliferation of software products for all kind of niche applications. While most organizations are happy to buy such packages, they are also aware that there can be issues in getting them to work properly. Vendors also understand that although they may have a great product, they can never know in advance all the details about the exact needs of their future clients. Each client has its own unique set of business practices, and its own peculiar mix of computer hardware, software, personnel, and procedures that may have been evolving for decades.

Once a software package has been purchased, it usually has to be integrated into the client's IT environment. Often teams of consultants are hired to perform the integration, which can dramatically increase the total cost of acquisition to the client. This alone can significantly limit sales for the vendor. Furthermore, clients almost always have specific, detailed requirements beyond what the package was designed to deal with. These two forces—the cost of integration and specific client requirements—continually place pressure on vendors to keep their clients satisfied. Figure 2.1 illustrates the problem.

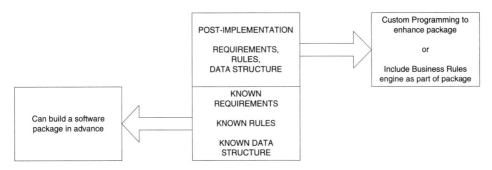

FIGURE 2.1
Issues in Building Software Packages for Use in Diverse Organizations

If vendors respond to these challenges by undertaking custom programming work after selling the package to a client, they risk limiting their capacity to sell their products. This is because the vendor will inevitably only have the staff resources to focus on a few clients at any one time. Such a situation can also be a long-term trap for the vendor, since the support burden will increase with sales, and may ultimately consume all of the vendor's development resources. Having a business rules approach can get vendors out of this trap by helping with both integration and the specific client needs. The package can be configured more quickly and with less skilled staff, and additional detailed requirements can be met by implementing rules engine functionality.

However, should the approach be to use the software package in conjunction with a business rules engine, or to build a business rules engine within the software package itself?

Vendors have to consider the proprietary nature of their products, and for this reason may not wish to include software that does not belong to them. This can also be a sensitive point when selling software products. Some clients have less trust in products that were not fully developed by the vendor they are dealing with.

Furthermore, vendors of software packages do not want to require their clients to purchase additional products, such as rules engines, to make the packages they are selling work in the client's particular environment. From the vendor's perspective this will reduce sales because it effectively increases the cost of acquisition (the client now has to buy something additional) and the money involved goes to the provider of the rules engine, not the package vendor. Also, clients often have reduced confidence in software packages that require the purchase of something else to make them work fully. A much better approach is to have a business rules engine, perhaps with limited functionality, as part of the software package itself. This can then address the needs of integration and customization.

Another reason for not buying a business rules engine is that if it is used to augment a package that is being purchased, management headaches increase. The client now has to deal with the vendor of the new system, and also with the vendor of the business rules engine. Clients would much rather have only one vendor to deal with. When two different entities are supplying software for a single business need, this often more than doubles the management required compared to dealing with a single entity. Clients are also aware that they are likely to encounter integration problems if the rules engine and software package have never worked together before. This is a risk that most clients would prefer to avoid.

The coupling between a commercial rules engine and a software application can be so tight that the developer of the application is in fact responsible for all aspects of the application, and the clients only have to deal with the vendor. This mitigates some of the problems mentioned above, but the vendor must have a great deal of confidence in the rules engine that they are embedding in their software.

Many of these issues can also surface within organizations developing software for their own use, where the software has to be deployed in a range of different environments that may have their own specific requirements. The target software environments and detailed business requirements where the application will reside are rarely going to be known in advance. In these situations, a software development team in an organization can easily find themselves in a similar position to a package vendor.

Total Integration of Software

In the case where a business problem domain requires a specific software application plus some degree of business rules engine functionality, there are significant advantages that can come from building a rules engine as part of the overall software application.

The first advantage is that the look and feel of the rules engine functionality can be similar to that of the application. This increases user acceptance of the rules engine and makes it easier for users to work with the engine's functionality. For package vendors, this is an important consideration. Vendors usually want to present an integrated solution to their client, and having a business rules component that looks and feels completely different from the rest of the package usually is not considered a good thing.

The next advantage is that a business rules engine must obtain information from the application's database and will usually have to write data back into that database. Figure 2.2 illustrates this point.

The business rules engine must be able to access the application's database, read from it, and very often write to it as well. More importantly, the engine must "understand" the data model from which the database has been built so it can work with the data that the database contains. In other words, before the rules engine can work

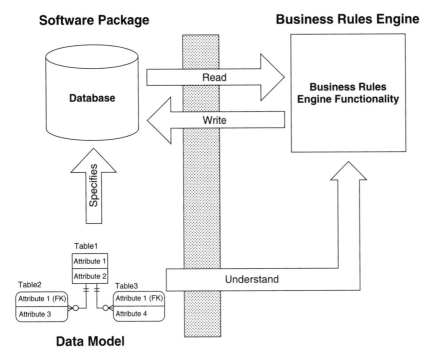

FIGURE 2.2
Relationship between Business Rules Engine and Database of a Software Application

it must be "trained" to understand the data model and connected to the database.

The data model and the database are not the same thing, and the data model cannot simply be derived from the database by automated reverse engineering—something that is often postulated as a solution where no data model exists. For instance, the database contains only physical column names, but the rules engine will inevitably need the business names of these columns. Also, it is difficult to infer relationships from the database. If the database has no declared foreign keys, this cannot be done automatically. Even if the database has declared foreign keys, the relationship may only really apply to a subset of records in the parent table and another subset in the child table. This is information that cannot be captured from foreign key declarations.

If a rules engine is built as part of the application from the start, the rules engine is much more likely to be kept up-to-date with the data model information it requires. This is particularly important if the data model contains denormalized design elements. These inevitably require additional functionality in the rules engine for when data is read from or written to the database. In addition, the possibility exists to implement the database of the engine within the database of the application. This achieves the data integration needed for the engine to read from and write to the application's data tables. It also eliminates the need to manage two separate databases.

Another point to remember is that if a commercial rules engine is acquired, the work to connect the rules engine to the application's database, and to make the rules engine understand the application's data model, will have to be done after the rules engine is implemented. This could be a large task, it may have to be done in a relatively short period of time, and it must be completed before rules can be defined. It may be necessary to wait until the application is substantially completed. By contrast, if a rules engine is built as part of an application, there is a greater opportunity to update it incrementally, for example, to define rules gradually for one business process at a time. Furthermore, rule definition can be completed before the application is implemented, rather than being something that has to be done post-implementation.

Even if the separate rules engine is implemented and trained to understand the application's data model, the data model may change over time. The business rules engine will have to reflect these changes, in a timely fashion—which may be difficult. Another point to remember is that it may be necessary to extend the database, such as to implement business rules that calculate values which must be stored in new columns. This will be much easier if the rules engine is part of the application.

Specificity of Rules

If a rules engine is purchased to address a set of business requirements, the engine will inevitably begin from a very generic standpoint. The types of rules that are available to the user may be so generalized that they may only be described in technical terms, such as *constraints* or *calculations*. In some software packages (not commercial rules engines) this is taken to an absurd extreme. The users are expected to learn a scripting language that is specific to the package and is required "to define business rules." This attempts to turn users into a species of programmer, and it inevitably leads them into writing procedural code (or its equivalent) rather than declaring business rules. Not surprisingly, users are quite resistant to this approach and will only take it if it is forced on them, or if there is no alternative.

Users are often able to recognize the different types of business rules they deal with, and to categorize them in business terms. They would like business rules engines to do the same thing. For instance, in many investment partnerships there is a rule type called *Pay Pro-Rata*. This involves a sum of money that has to be allocated to the partners belonging to the partnership, based on a participation percentage—a percentage at the partner level that sums to 100 for all qualified partners. The participation percentage defines the portion of the money that the partner is to receive. In a partnership there are many monetary amounts that have to be distributed to partners from time to time. From a user's perspective it is very nice to see a rule definition interface for a Pay Pro-Rata rule type. This would identify the monetary amount to be distributed, what qualifies a partner to receive any of it, and the participation percentage. By contrast, more generic rules definition interfaces require the users not only to declare rules, but also to specify how the rules execute, such as the arithmetic operations of a Pay Pro-Rata rule.

Even if a generic rules engine permits a specific rule definition interface such as Pay Pro-Rata to be built (which is questionable for some of them), work is needed to actually build the template, and there may be restrictions on how it can be used. Worse yet, it may not fully implement what the user wants, in terms of what it can do, error conditions that it traps, or additional business-related metadata that it permits to be captured. By contrast, building a rules engine permits the designers to go straight to creating rule-type definition interfaces that are specific to the business area covered by the application. The need for general rule-type definition interfaces is reduced, and the result is much easier for users to work with. Also, it is conceptually easier to handle from the designer's viewpoint. A designer with a sound understanding of the business area covered by the application will be aware of what rule types exist, and can thus design the rules definition interfaces that have to be built with a great deal of specificity. This specificity can include such things as the terminology that appears on the screen of the rule template, and the way the generated rules connect to the underlying database. Another advantage is that rule types that are not needed for the underlying business are not present, so users do not have to choose from a pool of rule types that includes a subset they will never use.

Users in general prefer to work with specific rule types rather than generic ones, and to the extent that such a set can be provided, the application will be more successful. Building the rules engine increases the chances that this specificity will be achieved.

Extension of Applications

Building a business rules engine need not be an "all-or-nothing" undertaking, in the sense that it is not necessary to build an engine that can do anything, versus hand-coding all software in a traditional systems development approach. As described above, there is often a need to expand the functionality of an application so it can meet new requirements when it is introduced into new environments, or when new requirements are encountered over time within one environment. This contrasts with building a generic business rules engine that can generate entire systems or be used as a major system component.

The capacity to extend systems in this way is at the heart of what this book is about. Although it is true to say that building a "do-all" business engine is not described here, what is described are designs (and program code) that can be ported from application to application. Thus, designers should not worry that if they build some business rules engine components for one application, they will have to start from scratch when they encounter another application that also requires some business rules engine functionality. There will always be some specificity that cannot be replicated, such as certain rule-type definition interface screens, or programming implementation constructs that work in one programming language but not another. However, there is a great deal that the designer and programmer can reuse.

What is important to think about are the aspects of the business operation under consideration that require a business rules approach. These requirements, if they can be correctly articulated, should be the most important drivers for implementing a business rule approach. Again, an application may only require certain elements of a business rules engine. In such situations there is little point in acquiring a rules engine with extensive functionality, of which much will remain unused. Thus, an application can be divided into one part that is known with near certainty and can be coded by hand, and another part that is variable and requires business rules to be defined after implementation. If the designer can determine the extent to which an application needs rules engine functionality, it is much easier to estimate the effort required to build the functionality. This estimate can then be compared with that required to purchase and integrate a commercial business rules engine.

How Easy Is It to Build a Rules Engine?

The answer to this depends on the requirements at hand. To build a generic rules engine is extremely difficult, and even the commercial products available tend to address different needs. None of them is truly generic, and they all fill different market niches. To build a business rules engine that extends a particular application or addresses a set of specific business requirements should always be much easier. This book provides a methodology that can be followed for developing such a rules engine. Designers are encouraged to apply this methodology to their sets of requirements and then estimate the effort required in their particular situations.

The rules engine designer should also attempt to keep the focus of the development team firmly on business requirements. It is these that should drive design, and ultimately what is built. Developers may be tempted to enhance something like a business rules engine to make it do clever but unnecessary things. This can add both cost and risk to the project. The designer should go no further than is necessary in building rules engine functionality for the application at hand.

One encouraging fact is that a great many successful software applications have some degree of a business rules approach implemented within them. This functionality may not be described in terms of business rules, but that is what it is. Even Microsoft Outlook, a well-known application for managing email, permits users to define business rules that can then process email messages in various ways. Anyone contemplating building rules engine functionality should take heart from this and be encouraged to consider a business rules approach as a valid design alternative for specific application components. The choice is not between building a monolithic multipurpose business rules engine or hand-coding every part of an application. It is really about including business rule-based functionality into an application wherever this makes sense.

Still, many people need to have a feel for the time and effort involved in building a rules engine. An extremely rough guide can be provided based on the author's experiences. However, readers should realize that this may not translate to any set of requirements that they are considering.

The author developed the sample application over a period of 2 1/2 months, working about one-third of the time on it. Everything in the sample application was developed completely from scratch. However, the general designs were based on more than 12 years of experience in the field.

It is the author's experience that in working with a small team of two or three persons in a new situation, it takes about a month to create a general design for rules engine functionality. This is mainly taken up by determining the correct strategy to generate program code in the software being used. It also assumes that there is a good data model of the underlying business area. It takes about another month to create the basic repository. The author tends to use the same design concepts, but adapt them to different situations. Thereafter, it takes about a week to create each rule type to be implemented. At this point the basic rules engine functionality is developed. The remaining effort, which may be considerable, is to define rules, test the functionality, and develop management tools such as reports. How long this takes depends on the complexity of the underlying business. Analyzing the business to determine what the rules are and to define them can take a lot longer than building the rules engine functionality.

There is no guarantee that the author's experiences will ever translate to any particular situation that a reader has in mind; these experiences should be treated with great caution.

Conclusion

The preceding discussion has shown that there can be a role for building a business rules engine instead of buying one. However, there are circumstances when the best decision is to purchase a commercial business rules engine. It all depends on business requirements and the environmental constraints that interact with these requirements. Generally, for projects where there are high volumes of data or transactions, where large sums of money are involved, or where risk to the organization (or its clients) is high, a commercial business rules engines may be needed. One may also be needed where an entire system, or a large component of it, has to be quickly generated. There is, however, no simple set of criteria that determine whether to buy or build, and judgment will be needed. The enterprise has to make such decisions on a case-by-case basis. What this book attempts to do is to show what is involved in one general approach to building rules engines, so the enterprise can attempt to make a reasonable estimate of effort required to build one. The full set of functionality that is presented may not be relevant to any particular set of requirements. In such cases, only the relevant functionality, and the design approaches that lie behind it, should be considered.

3 DATA MODELING AND DATABASE DESIGN

The approach taken to building a business rules engine in this book relies heavily on utilizing metadata that exists for application databases. Such databases contain business-relevant data, and this data represents much of the raw material that a rules engine must utilize. The overwhelming use of information technology in the modern era is to mange data, rather than to perform tasks that do not deal with stored information. Thus, databases occupy a central role in rules engine design. In particular, the structure of application databases must be understood by the rules engines that use them.

Database design itself is a major field in information technology, and it will not be covered here. However, it is necessary to review a little of the methodology that is used to create data models. A data model is designed as a blueprint for a database, and it is then used to create the physical database. Today, most data models are created using special software applications, called data modeling tools. These tools provide a visual representation that enables designers to see what a database looks like before it is physically implemented. They also contain a good deal of the metadata needed for a rules engine. *Metadata* is a term that is often defined as "data about data," but this is a rather unsatisfactory definition. In practice, metadata is data that is something other than business data. Business data is data that is directly used in business operations and would be used even in the absence of computerized systems. Metadata is additional data that describes what these computerized systems contain and how they work, or describes the business data, such as definitions of business terms. A large component of the metadata that systems designers work with is the metadata that describes the structure of an application database. It is very important for a rules engine designer to understand and be able to work with this kind of metadata, which is captured in data models that exist at the physical level (also known as the "implementation level").

Data models are typically built using database design practices based on concepts of relational database theory. In practice this means that each piece of information belongs in only one place in a database, that similar pieces of information are grouped together, and that these groupings may be related by sharing common pieces of information. These objects are discovered, recorded, and structured into a design by a process called *data modeling*, which is part science and part art. It is part science because there are rules that constrain how a database should be built, and it is part art because it requires extracting complete and correct information about data from business users (not an easy task). Even so, a data modeler may produce a sound database design, only to have other parties—particularly programmers—ask for changes to improve system performance, or simply to make their lives easier. Thus, the physically implemented database design may end up being different from the logical database design that truly represents the structure of the enterprise's business. In addition, databases that require fast responses to queries require a different design than those that process individual transactions. Hence, data warehouses and data marts typically have designs that are quite different from those of the databases of more traditional information systems. In this book we will consider more traditional operational systems, rather than data warehouses and marts.

The best approaches to data modeling use visual techniques to record database design. There are a number of excellent alternatives available, and the one used in this book is IDEF1X. Again, it is not necessary to get into a detailed discussion of this notation, but it is important to understand the basics of what it has to offer, and the metadata that it permits to be captured.

Attributes and Entities

The basic, atomic unit of data can be called a number of things. In physical implementations of databases it can be called a *field* or *column*. In a database design, and hence in IDEF1X, it is called an *attribute*, and each attribute must have a unique definition, different from every other attribute in the database. After all, an important principle of database design is that one piece of information should be stored in only one place in a database.

Attributes can be grouped together by discovering something they have in common. They form sets, each of which is called an **entity** in a database design, and is called a **table** in a physically implemented relational database. A better way of looking at this from a design viewpoint is that an entity is something of interest to the enterprise for which information has to be stored, and the different pieces of information that pertain to an entity are called attributes. In data modeling, it is usual

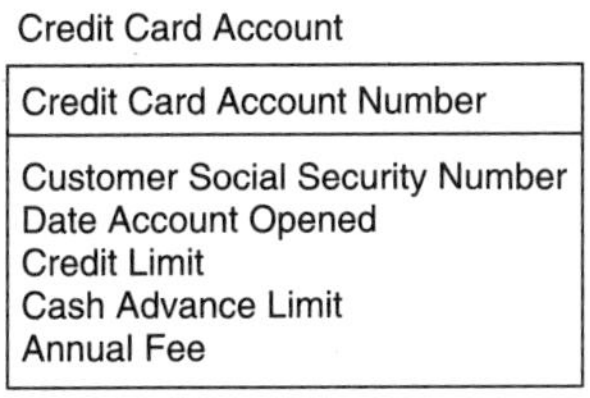

Credit Card Account

Credit Card Account Number
Customer Social Security Number Date Account Opened Credit Limit Cash Advance Limit Annual Fee

FIGURE 3.1
Credit Card Account Entity in IDEF1X

to first figure out what the entities are, and then the attributes that belong to them, rather than coming up with a list of attributes and trying to group them.

Entities that are represented in a database design are not individual instances of things, but are the information that describes these things. For instance, a bank may issue several million private label credit cards, but the kind of information that is used to describe each cardholder's account is identical.

Entities are represented by boxes in IDEF1X, and attributes are lines of text within them. Figure 3.1 gives an IDEF1X example of an entity called **Credit Card Account**, which has the following attributes (of course it could have many more):

- *Credit Card Account Number*
- *Customer Social Security Number*
- *Date Account Opened*
- *Credit Limit*
- *Cash Advance Limit*
- *Annual Fee*

The name of the entity is placed just above the box in IDEF1X. Within the box there is a line that separates the attribute *Credit Card Account Number* from all the other attributes in the entity. This is because *Credit Card Account Number* is the *primary key attribute* of **Credit Card Account**. The primary key of an entity is the attribute or attributes that are needed to uniquely identify real world instances of the entity. Thus, every **Credit Card Account** is identified by a *Credit Card Account Number*, which must have a different value for every **Credit Card Account** that exists. In IDEF1X the primary key attributes are shown above the line, and the nonkey attributes are listed below it.

Relationships

Entities that have certain attributes in common have a *relationship*. Two kinds of relationship can be described in IDEF1X: an *identifying relationship* and a *nonidentifying relationship*. In both of these kinds of relationship there is a parent entity and a

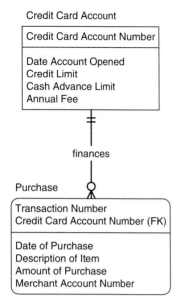

FIGURE 3.2
Identifying Relationship

child entity. Usually, the parent entity is the entity to which the attributes shared with the child primarily belong. Alternatively, the parent entity is more closely related to the entity where these attributes primarily belong than the child is. The entity to which the attributes in question primarily belong is the entity where these attributes are the primary key, but are not foreign keys.

An *identifying relationship* is one where there is a child entity that cannot exist or be uniquely identified without a parent entity. Figure 3.2 shows the parent **Credit Card Account** entity with a child **Purchase** entity (by convention the singular form rather than the plural is used in entity names). The **Purchase** entity is designed to store basic information about each transaction where the customer uses the credit card to buy something.

Notice how the corners of the **Credit Card Account** entity are square, and those of the **Purchase** entity are rounded. These mark the **Credit Card Account** entity as an *independent entity*, and the **Purchase** entity as a *dependent entity*.

The solid line joining the two boxes in Figure 3.2 represents an identifying relationship. In an identifying relationship, the primary key of the parent entity is migrated into the primary key of the child entity, making the child entity a dependent entity. Thus, *Credit Card Account Number* becomes part of the primary key of **Purchase**. It has "(FK)" placed after it to indicate it is a *foreign key*, that is, it has arrived in **Purchase** as a result of a relationship to another table where it is a primary key.

The crow's foot at the end of the relationship line is always on the child side, and so conveys the direction of the relationship. It also indicates that the parent may have many children. This is not "pure" IDEF1X modeling notation—which would replace the crow's foot with a little circular blob. However, it is more frequently encountered than the blob, and perhaps conveys a better sense of "one to many," so it is the convention used in this book.

The relationship has a *verb phrase* that describes the nature of the relationship. In this example it is "finances," so that we can say "Credit Card Account finances Purchase." This describes the relationship from the viewpoint of the parent entity. It is also possible to describe the relationship from the viewpoint of the child entity, for example, "Purchase is financed by Credit Card Account." It is more common to show only the verb phrase describing the parent-to-child view of the relationship on a data model.

It is not easy for data modelers to formulate accurate and precise verb phrases to describe relationships, and they sometimes fall back on more generic statements such as "has" and "belongs to," which do not convey the real nature of the relationship being documented.

A *nonidentifying relationship* is similar to an identifying relationship, except that the child entity does not need to be identified by the parent, so the migrated foreign key goes into the nonkey child attributes. Figure 3.3 shows a nonidentifying relationship between **Customer** and **Credit Card Account**.

This time the relationship line between **Customer** and **Credit Card Account** is dashed instead of being solid.

Relationships also have a property called *cardinality*. This specifies the number of instances of entities that there can be in the relationship. The related property of *optionality* specifies whether the parent, the child, or both must be present in the relationship. In an identifying relationship there must be at least one instance of the parent entity. If there is an "O" just before the crow's foot at the end of the relationship line, this means that there can be *zero or more* instances of the child entities. If instead of an "O" there is a little bar crossing the relationship line, this means there must be *one or more* instances of the child entity. Other cardinalities/optionalities that may apply to the child are *zero or one* (an "O" followed by a little bar that replaces the crow's foot, and *exactly N* (a little bar followed by a crow's foot). On the parent side, cardinality and optionality are represented by two little bars crossing the relationship line, the one closest to the parent entity representing optionality. In nonidentifying relationships the little bar farther away from the parent entity (optionality) is often replaced by an "O" meaning that the child does not need to have a parent, and that the foreign key column in the child may contain null values.

This can all be rather confusing at first, but it is important. Fortunately, the most common cardinality by far is the one where a parent entity has zero or more children. This is often described loosely by IT professionals as a "one-to-many"

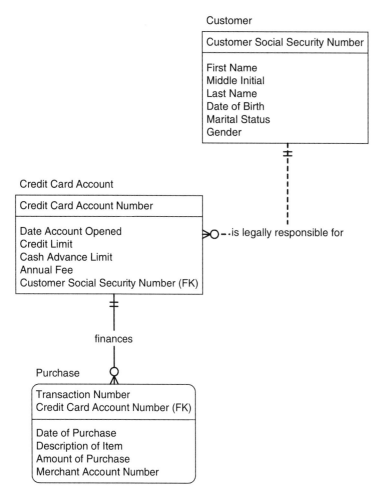

FIGURE 3.3
Nonidentifying Relationship

relationship. When used like this, "one-to-many" is probably more often intended to convey which is the parent entity and which is the child entity in the relationship, rather than what cardinality or optionality apply.

Subtype Relationships

Another important concept implemented in IDEF1X is the subtype relationship. This models a situation where an entity exists as a number of different categories, all of which are somewhat different in terms of the nonkey attributes they can contain. Figure 3.4 further refines the example in Figure 3.3.

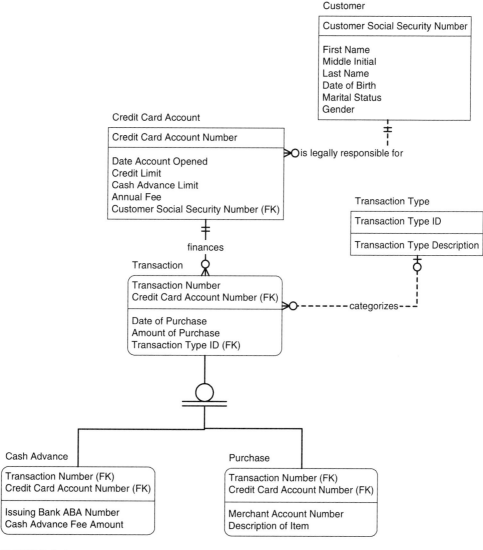

FIGURE 3.4
Subtype Relationship

A **Credit Card Account** now finances a **Transaction**, which can either be a **Cash Advance** or a **Purchase**. **Transaction** is called the *supertype* and contains the attributes all *subtypes* (i.e., **Cash Advance** and **Purchase**) have in common. The subtypes have exactly the same primary key attributes as the supertype and contain nonkey attributes that are not shared with other subtypes. Thus, **Purchase** has *Merchant*

Account Number and *Description of Item*, attributes that only apply to purchases. Likewise, **Cash Advance** has the unique attributes *Issuing Bank ABA Number* and *Cash Advance Fee Amount.*

Figure 3.4 shows the **category** symbol—the circle with the two lines underneath—which indicates we are dealing with a subtype relationship. There has to be an attribute in the supertype to distinguish between the different subtypes. This attribute is called *category discriminator,* and in Figure 3.4 it is *Transaction Type ID.* It is listed next to the category symbol. This attribute comes from the entity **Transaction Type** where it is the primary key, and this entity is linked to the **Transaction** entity by a nonidentifying relationship. In all subtypes there is a similar situation— a category discriminator that comes from a related table.

Conclusion

This brief tour of IDEF1X has only touched on the basic components of the notation needed to provide a framework for the discussion of the metadata we must manage in order to build a rules engine. For those who wish to know more—and there is a great deal more to know—a complete treatment can be found in *Designing Quality Databases with IDEF1X Information Models* by Tom Bruce.[1] As noted at the beginning of this chapter, there are other notations for representing database designs, and it is not intended to suggest that IDEF1X is better than any other notation. It is simply the one that is used to represent database designs and data models in this book.

---

1. T. Bruce. *Designing Quality Databases with IDEF1X Information Models.* New York: Dorset House Publishing, 1992.

4 WHO DEFINES BUSINESS RULES AND WHEN DO THEY DO IT?

Anyone involved in designing and building a business rules engine will have plenty to think about from the technical perspective. Yet, it is important to keep in mind that there will be many other parties involved in the implementation and operation of the rules engine after it is built. Designing and building the rules engine is, therefore, only a part of a larger picture, but it is critically important that the rules engine designer be able to clearly understand what that picture is. In particular the designer needs to think about who is going to define the business rules and when this will be done. These considerations can strongly influence the design of the rules engine, and indeed they should. There are many different actors who can be involved in rule definition, and rule definition can occur at different points in the implementation cycle of a business rules engine, and indeed in the life cycle of a business. A rules engine should match its operational environment in a way that makes sense to the people who use it at the time they use it.

The Actors

The different types of actors who may be involved in defining business rules typically have rather different capabilities, which may in turn influence the design of a business rules engine. For instance, one group of actors may be less conversant with the business domain on which the rules engine operates, and so may not be able to reliably use screens for specifying rules that contain a lot of business jargon they are unfamiliar with. These users will need extra help features in the rule definition screens.

Although business rules engines are a somewhat new concept, it does seem possible to identify several categories of actors that are, or may be, involved in business rule definition. As more information becomes available on the usage of rules engines in practice, it is very likely that the ways these actors deal with rules engines will be better understood. For now, however, it is possible to understand some of the perspectives that these actors have, and which may influence rules engine design.

Each of these categories of actors is dealt with from the perspective of the actor's function—actual job titles will vary from organization to organization. Although designing and building a rules engine is the responsibility of the rules engine designer, business users and their management also have responsibilities. Anyone thinking about implementing a business rules engine should think about whether they have staff, or can hire consultants, with sufficient capabilities to define the business rules. There comes a point where a rules engine designer cannot compensate for lack of user staff capabilities through implementing different design options. After all, business rules engines are usually utilized in complex business areas. If there are not sufficient human resources available, then the implementation of the rules engine may not be successful.

Business Analysts

Business analysts are sometimes professionals whose sole function is to provide an interface between a business area and IT professionals. At other times, the role is filled by business users who volunteer, or are drafted, to provide this interface for a specific system or project. Business analysts can be expected to be very intelligent, have good communication skills, and have an intimate knowledge of the business domain they represent. They often have some of the skills of a systems analyst. These include the capacity to decompose problems into their component parts and to provide high-quality descriptions of business requirements. Sometimes they are able to do design work to a certain level, which can be useful for developing prototypes.

Business analysts are excellent candidates for translating business requirements into business rules. For them, rule definition screens should be very specific and attuned to the underlying business. Business analysts will also be good at thinking in detail. This supports the implementation of atomic rules, which must inevitably result in more rules being defined than may at first be supposed.

Business analysts will expect to have tools to support rule definition, such as an array of management reports that show, for example, what rules have been defined and in what sequence these rules fire. If they have prior experience with system development or systems integration, they will have come to expect such supporting tools.

One other role that business analysts can play is helping in the design of the screens to define rules. This only happens once, during development of the business rules engine, whereas rule definition will happen repeatedly after the engine has been implemented. It is worthwhile for designers to consider involving business analysts when designing rule-type definition screens.

System Operators

System operators are generally not good candidates for assisting in rules definitions. They are usually employed to make sure an application keeps running from day to day. As such, they are often more familiar with the eccentricities of the system they look after in a production setting than the business concepts that underlie it. Unfortunately, IT professionals frequently think that system operators are their best interfaces with the business community, merely because the operators are in close contact with computerized systems. This is not the case.

System operators should generally be thought of as administrators of production systems, not partners in development activities, though there may sometimes be exceptions. Definition of business rules is a development activity since it consists of bringing new functionality into being. System operators typically lack a sufficient level of understanding of the business to do this. In addition, the typical system operator lacks experience in designing and implementing systems. This, too, tends to make them poor candidates for defining business rules.

Sometimes client decision makers who sponsor the building, or purchase, of a business rules engine (or an application which contains one) assume that systems operators will be able to define business rules. It is certainly true that someone will be needed to operate the live system, but definition of business rules is different. It is not in the interests of the builder, or vendor, of the business rules engine to let decision makers go down this track. It ultimately jeopardizes the success of the implementation of the rules engine.

Consultants

An organization that wishes to implement an application containing a business rules engine often employs consultants for such projects. A consultant is not an employee of the organization, but is rather an outsider hired for a specific task. In this, consultants differ from business analysts and systems operators who are employees. Consultants are expected to have a knowledge of the underlying business which is at least as good as that of business analysts. This is usually the case, but not always, and finding well-qualified consultants can be difficult. Even if consultants have a good knowledge of the business, they usually have less understanding of the organization (i.e., its structure and internal politics) that is hiring them than employees who are business analysts.

On the other hand, consultants are usually highly motivated to complete their tasks and can typically be relied on to get the job done. Where there are shortfalls in the consultants' knowledge, they can usually find out what they need to know, and they are rarely shy about asking questions. A big advantage of using consultants is that they can work on short-term, one-time-only tasks. It may simply be impossible to reassign employees to such tasks as rule definition if they are already fully occupied in their regular jobs. Another advantage of using consultants is that they may be familiar with the rules engine in general, something that is unlikely to be the case for employees. Thus, they can be expected to understand the overall processes involved in rule definition.

Consultants, therefore, are very good candidates for defining business rules. Even in situations where an organization is building its own rules engine, consultants may be required to undertake rules definition. This is particularly true if the rules engine is to be deployed to a number of sites in a short time period.

Business Knowledge Workers

System operators may run a production system, but they are not usually the persons who use the outputs of the system. These persons are business knowledge workers, who are usually in more senior positions than system operators and need the outputs to run business operations or make management decisions. Business knowledge workers will need to be convinced of the utility of a rules engine if they are to accept it, because it directly affects their work, and they often have a veto in the decision to build or purchase a rules engine.

The extent to which business knowledge workers are willing or able to assist in the rules definition process seems to be variable. In some circumstances, business knowledge workers are too busy. In other circumstances they may be temperamentally indisposed to getting too close to "technology." If they are able and willing to be involved, business knowledge workers are good candidates for assisting in rules definition. However, they sometimes lack the methodological depth and attention to detail that are expected from business analysts. For instance, they may not realize the need to carefully review rule dependencies or the need for testing. Furthermore, they may be less successful in learning the interface of the rules engine—particularly if they have had limited experience in operating applications.

What business knowledge workers do have is knowledge of the rules that underlie the business domain in which they work. It may be a good idea to have a consultant or business analyst obtain this knowledge from them and then define the rules, rather than having the knowledge worker define the rules.

One thing that should be avoided is for business knowledge workers to nominate the system operators they work with to define business rules. Knowledge workers often have a close relationship with system operators and think of them as being able to get systems to do the things they want. It may be quite natural for them to suppose that rule definition is just another administrative task, and to suppose that the system operators can undertake it.

Business Senior Management

Senior management in the business ultimately determine whether a rules engine is needed for a particular business area. They will take advice from others in the organization, some of whom may be able to veto the building or acquisition of the rules engine. However, senior management cannot be expected to become involved in the minutiae of rule definition.

In terms of rules definition, what business senior management needs is an assurance that it is going to be feasible. In other words, will the rules engine permit definition of the specific rules that exist in the business domain that the rules engine is intended to support? Senior management will also need to know who will define the rules, how long this process will take, and what impact, if any, there will be on normal business operations.

The builder of a rules engine must be able to answer these questions. Once again we see that building a business rules engine is not just a question of a technical approach, but also requires consideration of how the rules engine can be successfully implemented in a given business environment.

Information Technology Staff

Even when an organization decides to build a business rules engine there may be issues with its information technology (IT) staff. Today, IT staff tend to be administrators of the organization's hardware and software resources and often have limited understanding of information resource management. They may even be inexperienced in systems development. Many of their tasks are oriented to implementing new software and installing upgrades from time to time.

A business rules engine may not fit into this pattern, especially during the periods when rules are being defined. Depending on the strategy for rules implementation, rule definition may cause changes to the environment in which the rules engine is implemented. For instance, a rules engine may generate new files containing program code when new rules are defined. If the IT staff have placed too much security in the environment in which the rules engine is implemented, there may be problems—for example, it may not be possible to generate the required files. Thus, although IT staff do not define rules, there is often a need to work with them so that rules definition can proceed smoothly.

Programmers

Programmers are a special kind of IT staff, and programmers will be needed to build a rules engine. Despite this, they are not ideal candidates to define business rules.

They typically know little of the underlying business and tend to want to solve problems by introducing new procedural code.

Some older software applications that claim to have rules engine functionality require programmers to actually write new blocks of code to implement the rules. These applications have some degree of flexibility, but they can hardly be considered as rules engines. Having programmers involved in this way defeats many of the goals of using a rules engine.

One of the big advantages of building a business rules engine is to avoid having programmers involved when new rules are to be defined. Anyone building a rules engine should be careful not to depend on programmers during rule definition.

When Are Rules Defined?

We have looked at the roles of the major actors in rule definition, but another important consideration is the time at which rules are defined. When people think of rules engines in general, they sometimes imagine that rules are defined all the time during the life of the underlying application. In reality there are a number of different schedules within which rules can be defined.

Rules Known in Advance

Sometimes, a rules engine can be called upon to generate an entire system, or a large component of a system, where the rules are all known in advance. Thus, the rules can be "baked in" before the system is deployed. At deployment the system is installed and goes into production with no further rule definition. This is rather like traditional systems development, except that a rules engine is used instead of a programming environment. Perhaps the biggest advantage of using a rules engine in these cases is that it can increase the speed with which the process can be completed.

In such scenarios, it is doubtful that building a rules engine is the best alternative, since it may take more time than is available. Purchasing a commercially available rules engine may be a more viable approach. However, the author has built and implemented one rules engine that did generate an entire system, so the requirement does sometimes arise. Of course, a traditional systems development approach is also an alternative worth considering in these situations.

Rules Defined at Implementation

Business rules approaches are very good at meeting requirements where business rules are not known until an application is implemented. This is often the case with software packages for niche applications, where the way the underlying business works varies from client to client. It is also a common requirement where any software package has to be integrated into a client's IT environment. A similar situation exists for an organization developing an application that must be implemented in several different locations within the organization. In these cases, the software application generally does what the users want, but it does not do everything exactly as the users want. Business rules are not known to the rules engine designer in advance, so a "system generation" approach, like that referred to in the previous section, is not practical.

By *implementation* it is not meant that a software application is put into production and then rules are gradually added. The application will probably not work properly until after the rules are defined in any case. What usually happens is that an application is implemented in a particular IT environment and the application is then configured—that is, the business rules are defined. When this is complete, the application is moved to production, or simply goes live as a production system in the environment in which it was configured.

This is rather different from the traditional systems development life cycle that moves though design, program, unit test, QA test, and production. People more familiar with this life cycle think that software applications either are developed in this way, or are purchased and implemented immediately in production with no changes. It can be quite difficult to deal with people who have this mindset. If they see changes being made in an application, such as rule definition, they may sometimes want development, test, quality assurance, and production environments to be set up. This is hardly needed if most rule definition is undertaken in a discrete pre-production phase. All that needs to be done is to implement the software, define the rules, test them in this setting, and then go live. The developer of the rules engine may need development, test, quality assurance, and production environments, but these are for the rules engine software itself. The personnel using the engine usually do not need these environments, though they may wish to have them if they plan to bring in new versions of the rules engine software.

Sometimes additional environments are needed for the rules engine for purely business reasons. A business may be based on multiple contracts, each of which is like a mini-business that can be completely different from the next contract. A business rules engine can be used to quickly automate each contract, but the engine may have to be implemented in one environment per contract. Organizations in the financial sector sometimes want to use a business rules engine to operate a core business, and also have the rules engine to generate financial forecasts. Implementing the rules engine in a separate environment is one way in which this requirement can be met.

Thus, if anyone is developing a business rules engine as part of a software application where rules are defined at implementation time, they must think carefully about their rule definition methodology, so the users understand in advance how the software will be brought into a live production setting. This will avoid misunderstandings that could cause problems for all parties involved.

Business Changes in Production Systems

Once an application is live in production, a business rules approach provides a means for implementing changes to the business. Rules engines developers should be careful not to make too much of this, or they may get into trouble. After all, the natural rate of change of many businesses is not very fast most of the time. Suggesting that it is may cause credibility problems for the rules engine developer. It may also give the impression that the rules engine is designed to meet requirements that are only rarely encountered. There are also limitations to what can be done with a business rules engine in terms of managing changes to the business, as will be described below.

It is important for anyone developing a rules engine to think carefully about what new rules can be introduced after production implementation. Generally speaking, rules engines can cope with the following types of postimplementation changes:

- New rules are possible if they use the existing database, or permissible extensions to the existing database
- The database can safely be extended by adding new nonprimary-key columns to existing tables. Adding new tables, or new relationships between tables, is typically beyond the capabilities of most business rules engines.

Some commercial business rules engines, which are more general and flexible, may be able to go beyond this and accommodate radical business changes. In the end, however, even they have limits. Anyone building a rules engine should be guided by the above limitations. On the other hand, it is not that difficult to go beyond these boundaries to meet certain specific requirements. For instance, a rules engine could be built to allow the introduction of new tables in the underlying database to categorize other tables. Nevertheless, the rules engine developer must not mislead potential users about what can be changed in the application after it is in production.

If the business user does need to introduce or change rules, what precautions should be taken? At one extreme, a quality assurance (QA) environment can be set up that mimics production. The new rules can be implemented in this and can be tested to see if they work correctly, say by running parallel to production. At the other extreme, the new rules can simply be implemented in production. This latter approach poses some risk. However, a rules engine should have reporting that will show how the new rule interacts with other rules and columns. This may enable the risk to be quantified, and thus to justify direct implementation in production. Also, the new rule may be totally isolated—for example, if it simply calculates a new column that is only used in reporting or is an additional constraint for some data entry field. This makes it a safer candidate for direct implementation in the production setting.

Of course, if an entire process is to have its rules rewritten, the only safe way to proceed may be to make the changes in a quality assurance environment and test them there. However, the need to rewrite the rules for an entire business process should be comparatively rare. Indeed, why this would ever need to be done is a good question. If the original set of rules were incorrect, why were they allowed into production? If the business has changed radically, we will probably need changes to the underlying database that are beyond what the rules engine was designed for. Therefore, the capability to restructure entire sets of rules may not be a realistic requirement for a rules engine, and designers should consider carefully whether they wish to support this requirement at all.

What Kinds of Organizations Need a Business Rules Approach?

Earlier in this chapter the main actors involved in defining business rules were described. However, at another level, it is worth considering what kinds of organizations are more likely to need a business rules approach in the first place. It is not necessarily the organizations themselves that dictate whether they need a business rules approach, but rather the type application that needs to be run. Nevertheless, there are certain kinds of organization that are well suited to a business rules approach, and there are others for which it is doubtful that a business rules engine could provide any great benefit.

Invariant Transactions

The activities of many organizations are rather simple in structure. For instance, a company may make one or more products. The rules for selling each product will be well known in advance and may never vary. Indeed, nobody in such an organization may even think that there are "rules" about their sales process. These kinds of transactions are *invariant*—they consist of one rule set that applies to all instances of the type (or class) of transaction implemented by the enterprise. The rule set will be known to the organization before it processes any transaction, and there is no reason to expect that the rule set will vary for any particular transaction. It is possible that the rule set may change very slowly over time, such as if a local jurisdiction introduces a sales tax, but this is a very rare event.

Invariant transactions are not good candidates for business rules engines that are part of an application. Once built, an application that processes invariant transactions rarely needs to have its rules changed, and so it is probably better to develop a system in the traditional way. A major exception is software packages that can be implemented in enterprises that have invariant transactions, but where each enterprise is different. This is discussed in the next section.

Software Packages

Software packages have already been mentioned as good candidates for having a rules engine component. They may not only be applications created by a vendor for sale in the general market, but also applications created by an organization for use in multiple locations within the organization. Packages typically provide functionality for a specific business area and are designed to be implemented at sites about which little, if anything, is known when the package is being developed. When the package is to be implemented in a new location, there are two questions that the package developer must confront:

- What are the variations in the fundamental business that are specific to this client, and that the package does not address?
- How will the package integrate with the target IT environment? Some packages are truly stand-alone, but many do need some degree of integration.

Users of the rules engine may be dealing with what they see as an application that is governed by invariant transactions. However, the package developers are dealing with many somewhat different versions of a business area in every place where the package is implemented. Thus, the package needs to have more generalized capabilities that can be tailored at implementation time. For this reason, software packages designed to be implemented in multiple sites are ideal candidates for business rules approaches.

Contract-Based Businesses

Many organizations have businesses that are built up of invariant transactions. However, in the modern economy, more and more businesses run based on many contracts with different counterparties. Service providers such as logistics organizations (e.g., transportation companies) may need to negotiate quite different contracts with different kinds of counterparties. For instance, a contract to transport gold bullion is likely to be quite different from a contract to haul medical waste. Thus, each contract can be expected to have different terms and conditions. The organization's whole business is based on a portfolio of these contracts, and the only thing that can be certain is that no two contracts will be identical.

The approach of hand-crafting an application for each contract is fine if the business has only relatively few contracts. The alternative of trying to force clients to accept identical or near-identical contracts is not much better and is hardly suited to the flexibility expected in the modern economy. Both approaches will limit the growth and success of the business.

The only real answer in this instance is a rules-based approach. Contract-based businesses are an exciting area for business rules engines, because they are a key piece of infrastructure that can really enable the business to change and grow.

One-to-One Marketing

The term *one-to-one marketing* has been growing in importance over the past few years. A great deal of it is concerned with components that do not really have anything to do with business rules, such as data warehousing and customer relationship management. Also, this term often means a lot more than just marketing; it may encompass a great deal more of the relationship between an organization and its customers. As mentioned in Chapter 1, private client banking arrangements often permit very rich clients to define rules about how their portfolios can be managed. A particular client may not want to invest in liquor stocks, may want no more that 33% of the portfolio to be in bonds at any one time, and may specify that any stocks invested in be U.S.-based companies.

In the future, many organizations will need to move in this direction if they are to remain competitive. Business rules engines are the only way that these kinds of requirements can be accommodated, and rules engines hold the potential to revolutionize the way in which organizations interact with the customers.

Intensively Rules-Based Activities

There are some activities that are almost completely based on business rules. Accounting is "hog heaven" for anyone wishing to get involved in a rules-based approach because it is nearly all rules. For instance, an organization may sell many products and will probably have several operational systems to manage these sales. For accounting purposes, funds flowing through these systems have to be recognized for what they are and assigned to the correct accounts. An accounting application designed in this way has to "understand" the databases it is looking at and then have rules that operate on them to perform the accounting functions. Many commercial accounting packages work in this way and require what they term *rules writers* (typically consultants) to define the accounting rules for each client.

Credit scoring is another business activity that happens to be highly rules-based. When a person or organization applies for a loan, a set of rules is invoked to determine whether the applicant should be approved. The chain of rules that fires for one applicant may be quite different from that which fires for another client. Not only credit scoring but all kinds of activities where "things" are being selected from a general pool of "things" require a business rules approach. Thus, there are some applications that are inherently rules-based, and there cannot be an alternative to implementing a business rules engine for them.

Conclusion

In this chapter we have reviewed the actors involved in defining business rules, the times at which business rules may be defined, and different kinds of applications that are relevant to business rules. The rules engine developer needs to think carefully about all of these factors, because they may affect the functionality that is built into the rules engine, and they will certainly influence the way the rules engine is presented to different clients. In addition, these factors affect the way in which the rules engine is used, and the ways that users will have to plan to adopt it.

5 THE ATOMICITY OF BUSINESS RULES

A principle of data modeling is that every attribute in a data model (every column in a physical database table) must store one kind and only one kind of information. A corollary is that one kind of information is stored in only one place in a database. The situation for business rules is very similar. One business rule should encapsulate logic that consists of only one logical statement. It should not encapsulate many different logical statements. A corollary is that a unique piece of logic in a business is represented by one and only one business rule. This does not mean that a business rule cannot contain components that are themselves the *products* of other business rules. In fact, this is quite common, as we shall see in later chapters.

Although this definition of atomicity is fairly easy to state, it is not always easy to appreciate the implications. However, without an understanding of these implications, the rules engine designer can accidentally end up forcing the user to build procedural code (or its equivalent), or to use a single column in a database to store different pieces of information. This chapter explores how atomicity applies to business rules, and how atomicity affects both the rules engine designer and the business users who define business rules.

What Is Atomicity?

It is not necessarily easy to precisely define atomicity from the viewpoint of the logic of a business rule. In general, a business rule should not include the logic of other business rules, and no two business rules in an application should replicate the same logic. This may not be easy to enforce from the rule engine designer's standpoint, precisely because it is rather general. The truth is that what constitutes duplication of logic varies from one type of rule to the next, so there is no simple formula or checklist that identifies duplication. Yet, enforcement of atomicity is important, and there is little point in making a statement such as "business rules should be atomic" if there is nothing practical that can be done about it. Fortunately, if the rules engine designer thinks in terms of different types of rules and the way they work, it is possible to conceive of some strategies for ensuring atomicity.

In the following chapters, a number of different business rule types will be considered. Techniques to guard against rule duplication will be described for all of them. However, all rule types can be placed into higher-level categories, and these categories tend to behave similarly in terms of rule atomicity. Three main categories of business rule types are constraints, calculations, and inferences. It is worth looking at how atomicity applies to these categories because they cover many rule types. For each of these rule types, the starting point for managing atomicity is the way that it is managed in the more general category to which the rule type belongs.

Constraints

If a rule acts as a constraint it typically operates on an item of data so that only certain values can be used to populate the data item. Usually, the data item ends up being stored as a single column in a database. In rare circumstances a constraint rule may operate on an item of data that has no representation in a database. However, the most common case in business applications is where there is a field on a data entry screen that is used to update a column in a database. Thus, the great majority of constraint rules have database columns as their targets. For any one such column there can be many constraint rules, but for a given column no two constraint rules should replicate each other's logic. Ensuring atomicity becomes easier to implement if there is a fixed set of rule types for constraints, such as required fields or permitted ranges for field values. If a business rules engine is built using this approach, then it is possible for the engine to print out reports on rules, sorting them by target column. Users can then read the reports to determine whether any are duplicates. Beyond this, it is possible to construct screens for defining rules that permit only one target column per rule type. For instance, one rule type could be to ensure that required fields are entered on screens, and a rule type definition interface could be built for this rule type. Within this interface it is an easy matter to detect if a selected database column already has this kind of rule defined for it. Thus, the rules engine can prevent duplicate rules being formulated. It is also possible to prevent constraint rules from including many other business rules by creating rule type definition interfaces that permit a rule to operate on only one target column at a time.

It is possible for constraints to act on objects other than columns, such as firing of events. However, the same mechanisms for ensuring atomicity can be applied that were used for columns. Each instance of the object should have only one instance of each piece of constraint logic operating on it per rule type, and no constraint rule should contain multiple rules.

One lesson for design that flows from this approach is that rule types should be as specific as possible. They cannot be too generalized—for example, constraints are a category of rule types and are not a rule type. If rule types are too generalized it is simply impossible to build rules engine functionality that can detect the formulation of duplicate rules, and it can only then be done through human intervention.

Calculations and Derivations

Calculations (including derivations) are another major class of business rule. A calculation should yield only one result, and this is nearly always stored in a column in a database. A calculation rule is atomic if it populates the value in one and only one column in a database. It might be expected that one column should have one and only one calculation rule to populate it, but this is not always true.

Database columns that are based on lookup-type reference data tables require multiple rules to populate them. A lookup-type reference data table contains a set of records that represent discrete values, and any computerized application often has many such tables. There are other kinds of tables that are called reference data tables by IT professionals, but there is a common understanding that lookup-type reference data tables are the kind that have discrete values. For the purposes of this book, *reference data tables* refers only to the lookup type of reference data tables.

The discrete values in a reference data table are typically represented by codes and descriptions. For instance, a credit card company may have the column *Customer Preference Code* in the **Customer** table. This column is related to a lookup-type reference data table called **Customer Preference**, as shown in Figure 5.1.

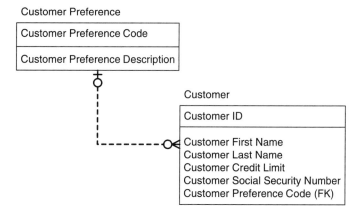

FIGURE 5.1
Customer Preference Code

CUSTOMER PREFERENCE CODE	CUSTOMER PREFERENCE DESCRIPTION
GOLD	Gold Preference Customer
SILVER	Silver Preference Customer
BRONZE	Bronze Preference Customer

TABLE 5.1 Records in Customer Preference Table

The table **Customer Preference** may have three records, as shown in Table 5.1.

Thus, the column *Customer Preference Code* in the **Customer** table can contain only the values GOLD, SILVER, and BRONZE. In the reality of the business, how a customer gets assigned any one of these values depends on factors such as how much the customer has spent in the past 12 months, and how quickly bills have been paid. There will be one business rule for how a **Customer** can be assigned each of these values. Thus, there will be three business rules for the population of *Customer Preference Code* in the **Customer** table.

For other kinds of columns in a database we can assume that there should be only one business rule to update them, until proven otherwise. Generally speaking, if there is more than one business rule that results in the population of a column, this implies that there is more than one kind of data in the column, and this violates the data modeling rule of atomicity. Of course, columns containing reference data code values, as we have just seen, can be updated through more than one business rule.

A business rules engine should be able to create rules reports that show whether any rules update the same target column. Such rules should be allowed only for columns that utilize reference data code values. It is possible that a rules engine designer may encounter other kinds columns where more than one business rule is required. The theory behind this part of data modeling is not well developed, so it is not possible to say that only columns associated with reference data code values can be populated through multiple business rules.

However, most calculations and derivations really do target columns that can only be populated through one rule. In these situations, the rules engine designer must create rule type definition interfaces that ensure users cannot create different rules to update the same column.

Sometimes data is calculated that is not stored in a database, such as totals and subtotals on reports. However, these can be considered to be system objects with unique definitions. Thus, the same approach can be taken as for columns—the only problem is in identifying the targets of these rules. In principal, system objects that are targets of rules should be identifiable. For a subtotal on a report, the report has a physical name that identifies it within the system, and the subtotal also has a physical name. Thus, it becomes possible to create a rule type definition screen that calculates one subtotal on one report and that can determine whether any other rule exists that targets the same subtotal on the same report.

Of course, rule type definition screens for calculations and derivations should ensure that users cannot actually define multiple rules within what should be one rule. There is always a temptation to create rule definition interfaces that permit very complex logic to be entered. The danger is that this complex logic actually includes intermediate results that need to be stored and reused somewhere else. Such intermediate results should be broken out into additional rules, or atomicity of business rules is surely being violated.

Inferences

Inferences are somewhat like calculations that do not populate any values in the database. They provide an answer to a question of some kind with some level of certainty. However, they are a little more difficult to deal with, because they do not typically target some preexisting system object whose value they update. The best that can be done in these circumstances is to report on inference rules by themselves, perhaps looking at any source columns they use, to determine whether duplicates exist. The screens for defining these rules should be constructed in such a way as to keep them from actually defining multiple rules within one rule.

Levels of Abstraction of Business Rules and Rule Dependencies

An issue that is sometimes confused with atomicity of business rules is their level of abstraction. Many problems, including business rules, can be expressed at different levels of abstraction. Higher levels are very useful for understanding the concepts that underlie a particular area of knowledge. However, they are often not concrete enough to be implemented in information systems as they stand. For instance, a credit card company can have "rules" such as "We will not tolerate fraud" or "Our customers are our first priority." As statements they are fine, but they are nowhere nearly atomic enough to be implementable in a business rules engine. Nevertheless, as rules become more and more specific, a point is reached where they can be implemented.

Let us consider one example taken from the world of asset securitization, whereby debts are turned into securities (usually bonds) that are purchased by investors. Suppose that we set up a company that buys a large number of individual automobile leases (a *pool* of these leases) worth $1 billion from an automobile manufacturer that issues leases. Our company now issues bonds based on these leases. The bonds are worth $1 billion face value for a term of 5 years, and we are able to successfully sell all our bonds to investors. The details of the exact terms of this deal will be quite complex and are always laid out in legal documents that must be followed.

In the legal documents we find that every month, we must pay interest to the investors, and that this interest is calculated as follows:

> Monthly interest due to investors is calculated by multiplying the outstanding principal balance by the prevailing interest rate.

We can attempt to make a business rule out of this statement and give it the business rule number "R1":

> **R1:** *Monthly Interest Due*
>
> = *Prevailing Interest Rate* * *Outstanding Principal Balance*

This is fairly easy to understand and is quite useful to use in conversations. If we have the columns *Prevailing Interest Rate* and *Principal Balance* in our database, we could even implement a rule to calculate *Monthly Interest Due* in a business rules engine that could access the database. We might even include the rule R1 in certain documents. However, the rule statement does not tell the whole story. It may be *atomic* in the sense that it encapsulates a single piece of logic that is not found elsewhere, but it is not *elementary* because it includes terms that are themselves calculated by, or derived from, other business rules, which are:

- The term *Prevailing Interest Rate*
- The term *Outstanding Principal Balance*
- The term *Monthly Interest Due*

What this means is that we can implement the rule R1 in our application, but it is going to be dependent on other business rules. We could find out exactly what these terms mean by looking at the legal documents that define the deal. Let us suppose that they are defined as follows:

- *Prevailing Interest Rate* is the LIBOR interest rate on the day that interest is calculated, plus an additional 2.0000%.

- *Outstanding Principal Balance* is the sum of the principal amount yet to be paid for all the leases in our pool. It is calculated as last month's *Outstanding Principal Balance* minus the sum of this month's *Principal Payments*, *Prepayments*, and *Defaults*.

- *Monthly Interest Due* is the result of the calculation. It is the interest to be paid to the investors. It is to be calculated on the last Monday of each month. It is calculated for the days from the 16th calendar day of the previous month and includes the 15th calendar day of the current month.

From these definitions we can see that our original business rule was atomic, but also has components that are represented by data calculated by other business rules. Yet, even these components of the original business rule are themselves dependent on other rules. For instance, *Prevailing Interest Rate* requires us to determine the day on which monthly interest paid to investors is calculated. We see that there is one *Interest Calculation Date* per month and that this is the last Monday of the month. Hence we need:

- A business rule to calculate *Prevailing Interest Rate*
- A business rule to calculate *Interest Calculation Date* for every month

These can be expressed as business rules as follows:

R2: *Prevailing Interest Rate* = LIBOR on *Interest Calculation Date* + 2.000%

R3: *Interest Calculation Date for Month* = *Date of Last Monday in Month*

When we get down to R3 we are finally at an elementary level—this rule cannot be further decomposed into components that are dependent on other business rules. What we have ended up with therefore is a hierarchy of business rules that feed into each other. Figure 5.2 shows this hierarchy.

Rule dependencies and hierarchies are very significant in building business rules engines. They determine the sequence in which rules can be fired. From the point of view of atomicity, however, there is no problem at all with a rule that utilizes the

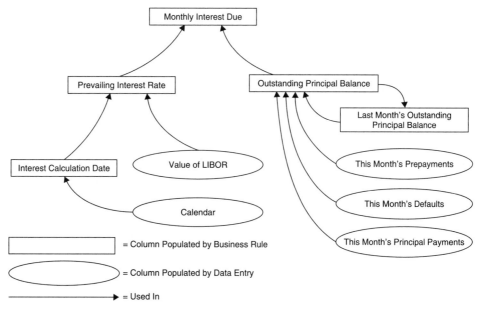

FIGURE 5.2
Example of Hierarchy of Business Rule Dependencies

products of other rules. Atomicity means that a rule does not actually contain logic that makes it more than one rule, and that no two rules have the same logic.

Is Atomicity Important?

Atomicity is important, but some programmers and others are always tempted to take shortcuts that compromise atomicity for some perceived benefit. There is little point in building a business rules engine in order to enable the creation of a Tower of Babel within an enterprise. Having different rules that replicate exactly the same logic is pointless. What is a lot worse is having business rules that try to replicate the same logic but have differences. For instance, suppose we have two rules that update *Interest Charged*:

> **R1:** *Interest Charged*
>
>   = *Average Daily Balance for Calendar Month* $*18.5\% *(30/360)$
>
> **R2:** *Interest Charged*
>
>   = *Average Daily Balance for Past 30 Days* $*18.5\% *(30/360)$

This situation is dangerous because we can get different values in the same column depending on which rule fires.

Another issue is the when a business rule contains more than one business rule. This can happen all too easily in rules engines that rely on expressing rules in scripting languages. Such languages can allow "rules" like the following to be written:

```
If Client.UnpaidBalanceDays > 180 then
    Client.PreferredStatus = "PLUTONIUM"
    Client.DefaultIndicator = "Y"
    Client.AssignToCollectionDate = Now()
End if
```

This is simply procedural code that is like anything a programmer may have produced. The fact that it can be created by a user in a post-implementation environment may be useful, but so much is lost. It is very difficult to parse such a script to produce a report that shows what logic results in what columns being updated, or to show rule dependency hierarchies. It is also difficult to separately report on the target columns and the source columns. The *target* column is the column that gets updated; the *source* columns are columns that are used in the rule logic that leads to the update of the target column. In general, the capacity for metadata engineering or even metadata management is severely limited. In contrast, having atomic rules enables us to see more accurately, via more easily produced reports, what rules update which columns, in which rules a particular column is used as a source, and how rules are interrelated.

Implications of Atomicity—More Columns

There are implications when business rules are atomic, particularly for rules that are calculations or derivations. Leaving aside the special case of columns populated by reference data code values, atomicity implies the following principle for calculated or derived columns in a database:

A calculated or derived column can only be populated by one business rule.

At first glance this seems perfectly reasonable, and one might assume that even when programmers build systems with traditional hand-crafted techniques they would follow it. After all, we have all heard for many years, if not decades, about practices and methodologies such as structured programming and object-oriented programming. A particular emphasis in these approaches is the need to avoid the duplication of program logic.

However, from a database perspective, there can still be a subtle kind of loss of atomicity that the principle of business rule atomicity will expose. Let us suppose there is a bank that charges its customers monthly fees for their account, as illustrated in the data model fragment in Figure 5.3. This bank charges fees based on what type of customer owns the account, as described in Table 5.2.

What we see in Table 5.2 are three rules for calculating *Current Month Fees Charged* in the **Account** table. This violates the principal of rule atomicity. Programmers used to procedural code might feel that there is no problem here and that all three rules could be combined into one "super rule" that could be visualized in program code by something like the following pseudocode:

```
If Customer Type ID = "INDIVIDUAL" then
  If Current Month Average Balance > 500.00 then
    Current Month Fees Charged = 0
  Else
    Current Month Fees Charged =
```

CUSTOMER TYPE	RULE FOR CHARGING MONTHLY ACCOUNT FEES
Individual	For average daily balances of up to $500, charge 3% of the average daily balance. Charge no fees for average daily balances over $500.
Corporation	3% of the current month's average balance. Fees cannot exceed $40.00 in any month.
Not-for-Profit	There is no charge.

TABLE 5.2 Rules for Calculating Bank Fees

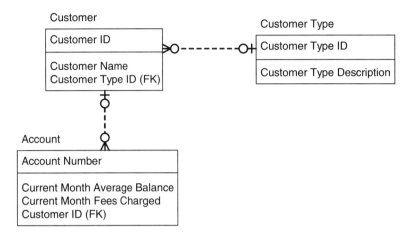

FIGURE 5.3
Data Model Fragment for Bank Account Fees

```
        Current Month Average Balance * 0.03
    End if
  Elseif Customer Type ID = "CORPORATION" then
    Current Month Fees Charged =
      Min(Current Month Average Balance * 0.03, 40.00)
  Elseif Customer Type ID = "NOTFORPROFIT" Then
    Current Month Fees Charged = 0.00
  End if
```

This is procedural code that can only be input through a scripting interface in a business rules engine. If the rules engine designer goes in this direction, he or she might as well let programmers write the rule logic. The real problem here is that we have three rules because we really have three different subtypes of **Customer**, each of which behaves differently—and probably not just in the way they are charged monthly fees. The truth of the matter is closer to that shown in Figure 5.4, where three subtypes of **Customer** each have their own **Account** tables.

Some designers might implement subtypes in this way, but in general it is not done because it tends to multiply entities within the data model, and it requires a lot of resources to be devoted to subtypes that are relatively unimportant. For instance, in addition to the three customer types, there may also be:

- **Customer Domicile Status**: United States or abroad—this affects tax processing

- **Customer Preferred Status**: Gold, Silver, or Bronze—this affects discounts given to the customer

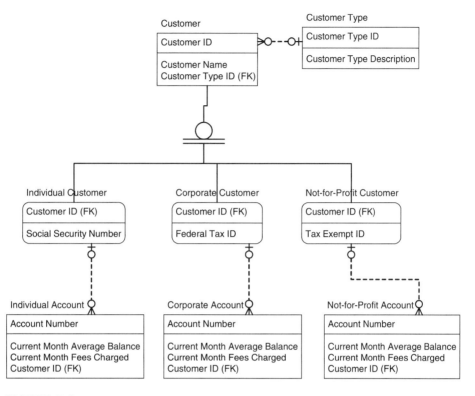

FIGURE 5.4
Implementing Customer Subtypes

- **Customer Target Category**: High Value, Medium Value, or Low Value—reflecting the likely value of the lifetime relationship with the customer, and the products the bank offers to the customer

There can be many other ways of slicing and dicing **Customer** into groups that behave differently from each other. **Account** may similarly have inherent categories. If the database designer uses subtypes for these purposes, the result would be perhaps tens of **Account** tables, which would be a nightmare to implement. Is this worth doing, just because there are a few columns, and a few rules that differ from one subtype to the next (which is generally the case)? Of course not. Thus, database designs tend to look like that in Figure 5.3. Tables such as **Customer** are surrounded by reference data tables, such as **Customer Type**, that are essentially used to define subsets of records within **Customer**, which are really hidden subtypes integrated into what should be their parent supertype table.

A result of adopting rule atomicity is that it makes these hidden subtypes apparent. In hand-crafted systems the programmer can get around the logic needed to deal with the hidden subtypes. Looking again at the banking example, suppose that for individuals any *Current Month Fees Charged* in a given year are reimbursed at the end of the year if the *Annual Average Balance* (as opposed to the *Monthly Average Balance*) exceeds $750.00. A programmer is assigned to create the functionality to send reimbursement checks to the relevant customers. The *Current Month Fees Charged* column contains values for all kinds of customer, but the programmer must retrieve values only for individual customers. The programmer has to select **Account** records only for **Customers** where **Customer Type ID** = "INDIVIDUAL" to do this. In other words, the programmer has to know in advance that there is a trick involved in *how* to do this. For a business rules engine this is impossible. The rules engine must assume that a column contains only one kind of information.

The way out of this problem for a rules engine is to add more columns to deal with the hidden subtypes. In the current example we would need to add these columns to the **Account** table:

- *Individual Customer Current Month Fees Charged*
- *Corporate Customer Current Month Fees Charged*

There is no need to add a *Not-For-Profit Current Month Fees Charged* since they are not charged fees (unless there is a real possibility that they could be charged fees in the future).

This enables us to easily use these two columns in different business rules where only one or the other applies. This contrasts with trying to use *Current Month Fees Charged* and trying to figure out if is for an **Account** record that belongs to an individual, corporation, or not-for-profit. It makes reporting a lot easier, too.

It is worthwhile keeping *Current Month Fees Charged* and making it the sum of *Individual Customer Current Month Fees Charged* and *Corporate Customer Current Month Fees Charged*. The column is then available for business rules (or reporting) where there is a need to process **Accounts** in general (the supertype) rather than for any particular *Customer Type ID* (the subtypes).

Thus, an inevitable result of implementing business rule atomicity is that there will be an increase in the number of columns in database tables as columns that pertain to particular hidden subtypes are implemented. This may surprise even experienced data modelers. However, it should come as no surprise. A data modeler may have placed the attribute *Current Month Fees Charged* in a data model with a definition such as "The money the bank charges in the current month for administering the account on behalf of the customer." This is true, but it is at too high a level, and it fails to recognize the fact that different types of customer are essentially charged different monthly fees. Data models are often filled with such columns, and it may not be until business rules are being defined that the need for additional columns is discovered. That is why it is so important to allow the database to be extended in a business rules engine—a topic we shall cover more in subsequent chapters.

Implications of Atomicity—Intermediate Results

A second implication of atomicity is the need to preserve intermediate results. A business rule that is a calculation may use several source columns and do calculations that perhaps should contain intermediate results that need to be preserved. Let us revise the way in which our bank in the previous section charges corporations for monthly account fees. *Corporate Customer Current Month Fees Charged* is now charged as:

3% of the current month's average balance plus $0.25 for every check cleared.

Let us suppose that we have a column *Number of Checks Cleared this Month* in the **Account** table. We could implement this as a business rule and end up with the business rule engine creating code that looks like the following pseudocode:

$$Corporate\ Customer\ Current\ Month\ Fees\ Charged = (Current\ Month\ Average$$
$$Balance * 0.03) + (0.25 * Number\ of\ Checks\ Cleared\ this\ Month)$$

However, suppose we need to use the portion of the fees derived from clearing checks for some other purpose, such as reporting, or in another business rule. Our business rule now looks distinctly unatomic. It is also a waste of effort (and risks introducing bugs) to recalculate the sum each time it is used. Also, what happens if the calculation changes, say if we charge 20 cents per check? We will have to find all the places where the calculation is performed and change it. This kind of "impact analysis" problem is very troublesome in hand-coded systems and is something we want to avoid in a business rules approach.

A better way of dealing with this issue is to introduce a new column into the **Account** table, *Current Month Check Clearance Fees*. A new business rule can be formulated to populate the column:

$$0.25 * Number\ of\ Checks\ Cleared\ this\ Month$$

There is another reason why we may want intermediate results spun off as new columns and rules. This is for auditability of our business rules. Suppose we have a complex rule involving seven columns, A, B, C, D, E, F, G, that looks like:

$$A = B + (C * D * (E * (F + G) * 0.25))$$

A user may wonder how a particular value got into A. To check it the user will need to shadow the business rule by hand. This may be tricky and time-consuming to do, and there may be factors such as rounding that play a role within the calculation. For instance, the user may calculate E * (F + G) * 0.25 and find it to have a value of 2,715,644.03, but there is no way of knowing what number the business rule has obtained for this portion of its calculation. In such circumstances, there is no alternative but to introduce a new column, say H, and a rule to populate it, so we end up with:

$$H = E*(F+G)*0.25$$

$$A = B+(C*D*H)$$

Thus, complex calculations implemented as business rules may not be atomic from the perspective of auditability, and there is a need to decompose them into simpler rules. Again, this means that there is a way to extend the database by adding columns to it after the rules engine has been implemented.

When Are Calculations Atomic?

In these past two sections we have focused on the implications of atomicity for business rules that are calculations or derivations. Complex calculation business rules should always be examined to determine whether they are atomic, but how *do* we determine that? This depends on the usage of the information used in the rule by the overall application. Basically a business rule is not atomic if:

- Some subset of it is reused in other business rules
- Some subset of it specifies a value that is used in reporting
- Some subset of it is needed for audit trail purposes
- Another rule duplicates its logic
- If the rule populates a column with a value and another rule populates the same column unless the column contains reference data code values

Conclusion

Atomicity of business rules enables more effective management of rules and opens up metadata engineering possibilities that do not exist in traditional hand-coded applications. By contrast, deviating from atomicity inevitably leads back to the need for procedural logic and may result in a loss of auditability of business rules. The price paid for atomicity is the need for more columns in a database and a greater number of simpler business rules, rather than fewer, more complex ones. However, this is more than offset by the reduced need for programming complexity that inevitably exists in traditional applications.

6 THE BLACK BOX PROBLEM

There is a great deal of enthusiasm surrounding the business rules approach to systems development and the advent of using business rules engines more widely. Because of this there is the perception that business rules engines will be well received by most user communities, even though there may need to be some advocacy and education about the benefits of the business rules approach. This perception seems to be justified when users are engaged in discussions about business rules management. Many users are genuinely interested in being able to define and implement rules within the information systems they work with. In particular, they often want to implement incremental enhancements, or change their systems to match gradual evolution of their businesses. It seems to these users that the difficulties of dealing with IT departments to have such changes implemented in the traditional way outweigh the benefits to be gained, and such users would welcome any mechanism to implement their own business rules. Beyond incremental changes to systems, users and major software vendors are also looking for ways to make systems integration easier. Everyone seems to agree that it would be much more efficient and probably a lot cheaper to allow users to implement rules that enable packaged software products to be successfully integrated with the business processes and existing systems of an enterprise. This goal may still be some way off, but it no longer seems to be unattainable.

If there is so much genuine interest and demand for business rules automation, could there possibly be any resistance to it on the part of users? Unfortunately, those users who have actually participated in business rules engine implementation projects can experience a distinct unease that is sometimes manifested as resistance. This reaction occurs as a result of what can be called the *Black Box Problem*, and it is a problem that deserves close attention from anyone that wants to build a business rules engine.

The problem arises when users have to work with a piece of software into which they enter business rules, and which then receives inputs that are transformed into outputs. To the users, this software is like a black box—they can see rules they have created, the outputs that are produced, and perhaps the inputs. However, they cannot *see* the execution of the rules inside the black box, which may lead to feelings of uncertainty and loss of control. Problems like this can lead to resistance to, or even outright rejection of, the use of a rules engine. Indeed some users are now demanding that any rules engine they have to use not be a black box, and in some instances they are actually using the term *black box*—so awareness of this problem may be more extensive than many IT professionals suspect.

User Resistance to Business Rules Engines

For more than 12 years the author has been building software applications for structured finance. A large part of this has involved building interfaces that allow users to define their own business rules, which then run as part of the application. The world of finance is extremely ripe for business rules automation because it consists of many complex deals. These deals fall into many classes ranging from real estate partnerships to the securitization of automobile leases. Within each class of deal there is a considerable similarity, but not all related deals are identical. These slight differences arise as a result of financial innovation, different goals of the parties involved, changing legal and regulatory environments, and other factors. It is simply impossible to build one system that can manage a family of similar deals without making allowances for the variations between them—and these variations cannot be known in advance. The author's experience has been that the only real way to overcome this problem (and prevent an impossible support burden) is to allow users to define their own business rules that run as part of the system.

However, the author also found early on that although users recognized the value of this approach, and used it, they behaved in ways that indicated they did not trust it. The Black Box Problem had manifested itself.

User Duplication of Rules

One very surprising finding was that users who eagerly adopted a business rules automation solution would also run a shadow set of spreadsheets that replicated the rules they input into the system. When a particular business process ran, the users would then repeat the entire process in their spreadsheet models. This generated a great deal of extra work for the users involved, although they kept quiet about what they were doing, and their senior management was not fully aware of it. When the users were asked why they were doing this large amount of extra work, they said it was to be sure that the results they were getting from the rules-based software were accurate, and to double-check the calculations that were going on inside it.

The author has found that this experience has been shared by other colleagues who build software applications that have rules engine functionality. They, too, found that users duplicated what the rules automation software was doing in order to check the results it was providing.

How, Not What

A second symptom of the Black Box Problem also manifested itself early on in the author's business rules career. I found that I was called in on a number of occasions to explain how certain numbers were calculated based on rules that the users themselves had defined. For these users it was important to understand how the rules were working. They were not interested in the technical architecture of the rules engine as such, but the processes at work within the rules themselves.

In such circumstances it was not helpful to tell users that the rules executed whatever it was that the users themselves had instructed the rules to do. It turned out that the users had varying degrees of uncertainly about whether they had written the rules correctly. Even though the application demanded that the rules were highly atomic, and they were expressed in English terms, the users had the following concerns:

- When a user selected a database column to be included in a rule, was this column really the one they meant? Even when the application displayed agreed logical names for the data, they worried that they could be choosing the wrong column.

- Where the rule was a calculation (which many of the rules were), what was the order of operations within the rule?

- What was the order in which rules fired? This was particularly important where a result produced by one rule became an input into another rule.

These problems manifested themselves by users trying to correlate the rules they had written in the business rules automation software with the spreadsheets they had built to shadow the rules application. It was only when the users could see exactly how a particular output number was derived from the inputs they had provided that they agreed with the rule.

Significant problems arose when the users felt that there was a discrepancy between a number they calculated in their spreadsheets and the number the rules engine generated. These problems sometimes required a great deal of research and fell into four classes:

- The expected result had been incorrectly calculated by whatever means the users used to shadow the rules application, so there was really no problem.

- There were data quality problems with the input data.
- The users had written the rule incorrectly when they input it into the application.
- There was a bug in the rules engine itself.

It was very rare to find a bug in the rules engine. This is because by its very nature rules engine software is highly leveraged—that is, the same code is used repeatedly to generate the executable forms of many different rules. Thus, any bugs that may exist become apparent in a very short time. The most common issues were that there was not a problem, or that the users had written a rule incorrectly.

What Are the Rules?

There is another problem that can become bound up with the Black Box Problem, even though it is not really part of it. This is the issue that users may not be fully able to articulate and define the rules they use in their business processes, and hence cannot include them in the rules they define in the business rules engine. In the financial world, this is usually manifested when the users observe that the business rules engine is producing a number that they consider to be incorrect. Once again, the question is asked—"How is this number being produced?" It is not unusual, after all the steps in the production of the number are retraced, to find that a rule is missing. This is often because a rarely encountered condition has not been taken into account and one or more rules need to be included to deal with it.

Unfortunately, in a production scenario, all problems seem to be viewed by users through the prism of the Black Box Problem, and the complaint is that if they could only "see" what is happening inside the rules engine, they would have increased confidence in its use.

Inflexibility Beyond Rules

If a user forgets to define a rule, it is not really the fault of the rules engine designer. However, there is also a danger that the designer may, perhaps unwittingly, include inflexible hard-coded rules in the rules engine itself. For anyone building a rules engine there is always the temptation to include certain functions "to make things easier for the user." However, these functions may not always be quite what the user wants, and in trying to employ these functions the user may never be able to write a particular rule to work in the way that he or she wants. For instance, in some financial rules it is necessary to determine the number of days between two dates. Sometimes the dates are inclusive while under other circumstances they are not. Thus, a simple date difference function is insufficient.

If the users are constrained by functions to only be able to do things in a certain way, they again feel that the business rules automation software is behaving like a black box that they cannot control. This is a particularly devastating criticism for software that is designed to provide users with the flexibility to write their own rules. The only way to avoid it is to try to anticipate how users may want to override the working of each function and make sure that this is built in. In reality, especially with fixed deadlines, this can be a very difficult goal to meet, but it is essential for building a successful business rules engine.

Support for the Users

People who are building a business rules engine, or who are participating in the decision to implement one, will do well to put themselves in the place of the users who will have to use the engine. Because building and implementing a business rules engine is not like a traditional systems development project, users will need to be more self-reliant, and the rules engine should help them as much as possible.

Reliance on IT Personnel

Now, it may be argued that any piece of software put into production is a black box from a user's perspective. However, in traditional systems development, users typically have developers as partners. The principal responsibilities of the users are usually to confirm that their business requirements have been gathered, perhaps to validate that a proposed design will meet these requirements, and to undertake user acceptance testing. If something goes wrong with the implemented system, the users may need to confirm that there is a genuine problem, but they will call in IT staff, or equivalent technical resources, to diagnose the bug and to fix it.

With a rules engine, the users are placed in a position where they must be more self-reliant. By using such software the users avoid the problems of dealing with IT staff to build and implement a solution. However, there is usually no IT support available in the same way as there would be for a traditional systems development project. Even when there is such support, programmers may find it difficult to understand what the rules engine is doing, because they do not understand the business context that gave rise to the rules that were defined. From the programmer's perspective, the users created the logic.

The perception that there is not a partner who must take responsibility for technical support can be very unsettling to users. This is true even if the support they have received from IT staff has traditionally been very poor, and even if the rules engine builder is prepared to provide some degree of support. The fact is that the users understand that they will have to be responsible for the rules they write. Users everywhere tend to shy away from having responsibilities for anything that is technical—and for good reason. Yet, if they are dealing with a rules automation black box, they are never quite sure of where the boundary between technology and business lies. The result can be a feeling that the users have acquired additional responsibilities that they are not equipped to deal with.

Seeing Is Believing

It is important for anyone building a business rules engine to understand just how real the Black Box Problem is, and to design features into their engine that will mitigate it. Failure to appreciate this problem and to add the required functionality can destroy the investment made in building a rules engine. There are several components that can be added to the rules engine:

- The first component is to provide reports of the rules themselves. These reports should state in English what operations the rules are carrying out.

- It is also necessary to supply a well-documented data model of the overall business area on which the rules engine operates. If the users are to understand the rules, they must understand the data they are dealing with. In complex financial transactions this approach does seem to work. Users in this arena are often highly educated and quick to adapt to new techniques. They are use to modeling deals, and they welcome the representation of their data.

- Even good documentation of individual rules and a clear description of a data model are not sufficient to explain how rules have been set up in a business rules engine—users also demand to know the sequences in which rules fire. It is not very productive to explain to users that the rules engine can itself determine the sequence in which rules fire by working out dependencies—they want to actually have it described to them. Thus, this is another kind of report that has to be produced.

Auditability

Producing reports about how rules are structured and how they will run goes only so far. Users typically demand to be able to audit the results that are produced by the business rules engine. This means that as each rule fires, information about it must be recorded. The information is typically the name of the rule, the values that are input to it, and the outputs that are produced. This can be derived from knowing which database records the rule operates on. Other information about these database records can also be provided if the records are known. After all the rules in a business process have been run, a report can be printed containing this information, and the users can then see how any numbers or other data values they may question were produced.

Including such auditability may come at a price. It often slows down the execution process of the rules software and generates a great deal of output. This can be mitigated by making the running of the audit functionality a user option. Another problem is that it may be quite difficult to provide this audit functionality for certain types of rule, such as those that aggregate data. However, implementing this approach can make an enormous difference for users and can greatly reduce support requirements on the part of the rules engine builders. It provides the transparency that is required to really overcome the Black Box Problem.

Conclusion

The Black Box Problem is something that should be taken seriously by anyone building a business rules engine. Users who opt for implementing business rules engines should not be put in a position where they feel they are dealing with something whose inner workings are mysterious, and for which they have limited or no support. The best ways to mitigate this problem are to provide detailed and useful reports on the rules the users have written and the sequence in which they fire. Sequence may be especially important to certain users whose rules involve specifying precedence. Beyond this, it is necessary to provide users with an optional audit trail of what the rules do as they fire in the execution of a business process. Additional support materials may be useful, especially a data model accompanied by an explanation that is thorough enough to allow users to understand what they are doing when they work with data in writing their rules.

7
THE COMPONENTS OF A BUSINESS RULES ENGINE

The kind of business rules engine built in this book is oriented to working with data. This dictates the general architecture to some extent. Many of the components of this architecture are applicable to other kinds of business rules engine, but not all. For instance, business rules engines that make inferences do not necessarily need to update the underlying database. However, the type of rules engine described in this book must be able to update the database. In this chapter, the various components will first be introduced and then examined in more detail. Subsequent chapters will describe how they can be built and managed.

The Rules Engine Components

Figure 7.1 gives an overview of the components of the type of business rules engine that is described in this book.

At the heart of the rules engine is the *Business Rules Repository*. This is a special set of database tables that contains information about the application database, definitions of business rules, and definitions of the business processes that the application performs. Users can define business rules through a special set of screens called the *Rule Definition Interface*. The rules definitions are captured in the Business Rules Repository. They are utilized by *Code Generation Routines* that create *Executable Business Rules*. The Code Generation Routines are essentially programs that write program code containing the logic of the business rules. This generated code represents the Executable Business Rules and is componentized so that rules that must run together in a single step are associated. A *Rule Invocation Interface* allows the user to run the steps involved in a business process, although the system itself can also fire business

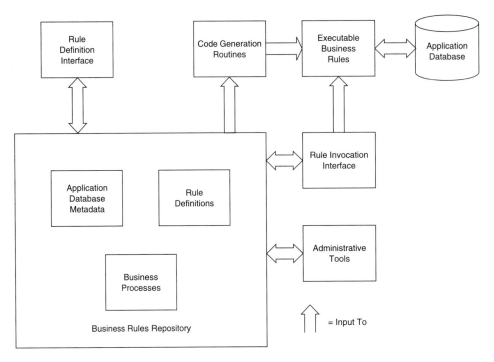

FIGURE 7.1
Overview of Components of the Business Rules Engine

rules, such as via a task scheduler. When the rules fire, they read from and update the application database—the database tables that contain the information about the underlying business area. Lastly, there is a set of *Administrative Tools*. These include management reports about the rules that have been defined, and audit functions that permit the tracing of rule execution.

These components are what must be built in order to create a functioning business rules engine. Each component consists of several subcomponents, and any subcomponent may be quite complex in its own right. Furthermore, there are many design alternatives for each component and subcomponent. These need to be evaluated carefully because they can affect the functionality of the overall rules engine and the ease with which it can be built, operated, and managed. The following sections provide a more detailed description of the components, review their design alternatives, and explore in more depth the alternatives chosen for the rules engine described in this book.

The Business Rules Repository

A repository is a database that stores metadata. Metadata is loosely defined as "data about data." As noted in Chapter 3, this definition is rather poor, but is very widely accepted. Unfortunately, there is not an easy distinction between *data* and *metadata*. The reality is that metadata is any data that the user of the system does not manage. In other words, a business application manages a set of data, which would in fact exist in the absence of any computerized system. Metadata exists for this business data, such as definitions of business terms. Again, a lot of this kind of "business" metadata exists even in the absence of a computerized system. This metadata may be needed by staff in order to manipulate the business data, but the metadata is not itself processed. When a computerized application is introduced there is a great deal more metadata to contend with. This new kind of metadata is everything that describes the computerized application and how it works. Again, this metadata may be needed to understand how to run the application, but is not actually processed by the application—or, at least, processing it is not directly relevant to the business area covered by the system. Only the processing of data is relevant to the business area. So very roughly, information that a user needs to manipulate is data, and all the other information that a system stores and manipulates is metadata. The data is stored in the application's database. Metadata is stored in a database that is by convention called a repository.

The distinction between metadata and data can get confusing when dealing with business rules engines because a rules engine intimately entwines the two.

The type of business rules engine described in this book has at its heart a Business Rules Repository that contains several different kinds of metadata. In the sample application presented here the Business Rules Repository is a set of tables that exists in a single database along with other tables that make up the application database which contains the business data. It may be more appropriate in other circumstances to separate the Business Rules Repository into a distinct database. For instance, there may be a requirement that the Business Rules Repository be a proprietary component of an application, and security can be implemented to prevent unauthorized access to it. In other situations there may be other needs that dictate that the Business Rules Repository and business data must reside in the same single database. In general, from the perspective of the rules engine, either design will work. A convention adopted here is that all tables that belong to the Business Rules Repository have physical names that end with "_M" (for "metadata"). The tables containing business data have different suffixes. This makes it easy to distinguish the tables of the Business Rules Repository in the database of the sample application.

Let us now consider the subcomponents of the Business Rules Repository.

Application Database Metadata

Perhaps the most fundamental part of the Business Rules Repository is the application database metadata. This is metadata that describes the structure of the application database. A database has a structure that consists primarily of tables containing columns. The business rules engine has to understand this structure so that it can access data in the database and update relevant data as required. There are also relationships between tables. These are extremely important for a rules engine, because they dictate how the database must be navigated.

Beyond this, there are more subtle aspects of the application database that are necessary for the rules engine. Subtypes are extremely important. These are subsets of records and columns in a table that behave in a specific way. They are not always recognized as such either in data modeling techniques or in application development. Yet they are critical for rules engines because many business rules apply only to one or a very few subtypes. Closely related to subtypes is the area of reference data. This has been mentioned in earlier chapters and consists of lookup tables such as **Country**, **Customer Type**, or **Order Status**. Reference data tables usually consist of a single primary key column that is a code and a single nonkey column that is a description—for example, a *Country Code* of "CAN" that goes with a *Country Name* of "Canada" may be found in a **Country** table. Reference data tables are primary drivers of business rules because they identify the subtypes that the rules operate on. Up to 50% of the tables in an application database can be reference tables of this kind. Here we see how reference data, which is always considered to be application data, can also be viewed as a kind of metadata, an example of how the boundary between data and metadata can be blurred.

Business Processes

Simply defining a big stack of business rules for an entire business area is not going to be enough to make a business rules engine work successfully. It is true that a rules engine can determine the sequence between rules to some extent. However, it has to be recognized that different rules are combined into sets and are executed within these sets. These sets of rules should correspond to business processes.

A business process is a stand-alone logical unit of work. Ideally, it should consist of end-to-end processing that begins with an event of some kind and ends in the production of the outputs that respond to that event. Less ideally, business processes can be split into other processes where work piles up at the end of one process, and then is processed in batches by the next process. An example of one of these less ideal business processes is the way in which stock trades are cleared by stockbrokers. A customer may buy some stock during the day, perhaps through an online broker. What usually happens is that the trades of all customers that occur during the day are saved, and at night batch processing occurs which actually clears the transactions (e.g., matches buy and sell transactions, does the accounting, and sends out confirmations). Actually, all of this can, and usually does, take a couple more days. The ideal business process in this case would be for the customer's order to be immediately matched with a counterparty, and for all the accounting and other processing to be done in real time. This approach is also known as *straight-through processing*, or STP.

Business reality will dictate to an application what the business processes are, and they may often be less than the ideal state of straight-through processing. There is not much that a rules engine per se can do to change this. Within each process however, there will be a number of steps. These do fit together in an STP-like manner. Each step involves a different set of coherent actions that usually involve a different set of *actors* (the term given to participants in a process step, whether they be human, organizational, or systematic). These process steps are important for a rules engine because they are closer to logical units of work that utilize well-defined sets of rules.

Business process steps are an important construct in the approach to building business rules engines described in this book. They are used to define sets to rules that are executed together. Therefore, the Business Rules Repository needs to capture the business processes that are run by the application upon which it operates. These in turn must be decomposed into business process steps, each of which represents a set of business rules. Within these sets of rules, the rules engine must have the capability to overcome a problem that is seen repeatedly in rules engines—rules dependency.

Table 7.1 shows that *Today's Opening Balance* is computed using *Yesterday's Closing Balance*. However, *Yesterday's Closing Balance* is computed using *Today's Closing Balance*. Rules engines try to deduce the sequence in which rules should fire by seeing what data items created by a rule are used as inputs to other rules. In general, the rules engine will fire the rules that create a data item before the rules that use it. The problem in Table 7.1 is that the outputs of one rule are used as inputs to another, in a kind of "which came first: the chicken or the egg" scenario. It is impossible for the rules engine to decide which rule to fire first. One way out of the problem is to split the processing into different steps. The first step can be to compute all opening balances, the next step can be to calculate the current day's activity, and the third step can be to compute all closing balances. These three steps run in this sequence, and the rules engine is expected only to determine the sequence in which rules fire *within* each step.

The kind of problem illustrated in Table 7.1 is always found in computer systems that process periodic information—and such systems are very common. The method of breaking the processes up into distinct steps is a good one. It is also something

RULE NUMBER	RULE
1	*Today's Opening Balance* = *Yesterday's Closing Balance*
2	Today's Closing Balance = Today's Opening Balance + *Today's Credits* − *Today's Debits*
3	*Yesterday's Closing Balance* = *Today's Closing Balance* on record for this account from prior day

TABLE 7.1 Example of Rule Dependency

that makes sense to users. For instance, anyone familiar with accounting will probably agree that in processing daily financial activity, the first thing to do is to calculate opening balances, and after that current account activity can be computed.

There is some resistance to this approach in theoretical writings about business rules. There is a thought that any specification of procedure runs counter to the business rules approach. Proceduralization, in terms of telling a system exactly how to execute rules logic, is certainly counter to the business rules approach. However, specifying the sequence in which business process steps should run is not. In fact, even within an individual business process step it may sometimes be necessary for users to specify the sequence in which rules fire. For instance, when a company is liquidated, rules govern the precedence of creditors. All the assets of the company are sold and the money received is distributed according to legal rules. Some classes of creditor get paid before other classes. Creditors toward the end of the line often get nothing at all, since the money goes to pay debts to creditors with higher priority. These rules are clearly defined in law, specific contracts, and other binding agreements that companies enter into, and they are ideal material for implementation via a business rules approach.

Business processes, therefore, need to be captured in the Business Rules Repository and nearly always need to be decomposed into steps that fire consistent sets of rules. The sequence of these steps inevitably needs to be defined. The rules engine should be capable of determining the sequence in which rules fire within each step, but sometimes sequence itself is a business rule and must be defined by users.

Rule Definitions

The remaining subcomponent of the Business Rules Repository is the rule definitions. These are what the rules engine is designed to manage and execute. Historically, application designers have had several approaches to the definition of business rules, but these have often involved programmers writing program logic. In some cases, analysts, consultants, or even business users have been expected to write procedural logic to define business rules. This general design approach means that rule definition is no different from rule implementation. The rule definition is really the definition of an executable form of the rule in some form of programming language, which may be a commercial language, or a special "scripting language" developed for the rules engine involved.

This "one-step" approach of going straight from the user's understanding of a business rule to its executable form has no drawbacks if viewed from the perspective of a programmer. This is, after all, what programmers do. However, it has significant disadvantages from just about every other perspective that can be imagined.

Program logic is a black box to everyone except programmers. Even for programmers it is pretty much a black box, which is why they spend so much of their professional lives reverse-engineering program code to "see what it does." Program logic cannot be related to other metadata, so there is no way in which its management can be systematized. Getting answers to questions such as "What edit validations do we have on this screen?" or "How does this number get calculated?" require programmer intervention, to review and parse the program code. Even then, the answers the programmers provide can be less than complete or reliable, or even understandable. The information is typically never documented. Thus, if the same question is asked again, the whole process has to be repeated. It is true that from time to time commercial products appear that claim to parse program logic to reveal business rules, and to some extent they can perform this function. However, there are severe limitations on what they can do, and they tend not to provide anything approaching the solutions that are required to manage an enterprise's business rules.

Therefore, the "one-step" approach of going from the user's understanding of a business rule to its implementation in executable form is not good enough for any business rules engine in today's world. What is required is that the rules engine capture the definition of each business rule—and executable program logic is not a definition.

The definition of a business rule consists of structured metadata that describes the rule. More than this, if the rule refers to other objects in the computerized application, metadata about these objects must also be captured in the rule definition. If this is done, the rules can be related to other information that is held about these objects elsewhere in the Business Rules Repository. The principal objects that business rules refer to are tables and columns—since these contain the business data on which the rules operate. Metadata about tables and columns is stored in the application database metadata discussed above. Thus, at a minimum, business rules definitions must be stored in repository tables that are related to the tables of the application database metadata. This means that a "two-step" approach is required to managing business rules in the rules engine. The first step is to capture the rules definition as metadata in tables of the Business Rules Repository. This opens up the business rules to a whole host of extremely valuable management techniques. The second step is to use the rule definitions to create an executable form of each business rule.

This book makes a strong case for using a business rules approach in order to allow general applications to meet new or different requirements without the need for programming. However, a justification of equal weight is that the business rules approach provides the potential for management of rules logic that is simply missing in the traditional "black box" of hand-crafted program code. In any situation that demands visibility of the business rules, such as to prove regulatory compliance, the two-step approach to rules management gives the enterprise the additional capabilities required. Unfortunately, the somewhat higher level of abstract thought required to appreciate metadata and the permeation of traditional systems development blind many enterprises to these possibilities.

There is one other enormously important aspect that must be understood about the Business Rules Repository. Rule definitions are not just relevant to business rules engines. They are also critically important for many aspects of rules management that have nothing to do with rule execution. This could include understanding what rules exist in an organization, who has responsibility for them, and what policies or other governing documents they originated from. A repository is required to meet these requirements, and the Business Rules Repository could be a starting point for such a repository. However, a great deal of additional metadata is also required, which is beyond the scope of what is needed for a business rules engine. Such a repository must also be available to many other actors beyond those involved in building and using a rules engine, such as business analysts and systems analysts with roles in rules management. It is possible to create a repository that is distinct from any rules engine that can be used for these additional rules management needs, and which can also contain the metadata needed for a rules engine. This may be a distinct advantage for many organizations. General rules management, and the repository metadata it requires, are topics that are far too broad to be dealt with in this book. Therefore, only the repository functionality required to support the rules engine will be considered. The rules engine designer must, however, be aware of the broader scope in which a Business Rules Repository can be utilized.

The Business Rules Repository will therefore contain tables that hold rule definitions and will relate rule metadata to other metadata that is held in the Repository.

At this point the major subcomponents of the Business Rules Repository have been considered. There is a need for some other metadata to be held in the Repository, chiefly for application objects such as screens. However, this other metadata is rather limited in scope and specialized. It is dealt with in subsequent chapters where it directly bears on the construction of the rules engine.

Rule Definition Interface and Executable Business Rules

The Business Rules Repository can hold metadata that defines business rules, but how does rule metadata get in there? The answer is that an interface must be created that allows rules to be defined. This interface consists of a set of screens that allows a user to define rules.

At this point it is necessary to introduce the concept of *business rule types*. There are many similarities between different business rules, and it is possible to group similar rules together into categories. These categories are termed business rule types. Different people have created different categories of rules. For instance, computation rules may be considered to be one rule type. A computation rule can be considered to be any kind of business rule that involves a calculation. Another commonly discussed rule type is a derivation. This is held to be any business rule where a value is derived from other values. For example, *Customer Preferred Status* can be "Platinum," "Gold," or "Silver," and "Platinum" is derived as follows:

> If Customer has borrowed more that $100,000 in the past 2 years
> And Customer has been late with payments no more than once in the past 2 years
>> Then Customer Preferred Status = "Platinum"

Rule types such as calculations and derivations are often mentioned where business rules are discussed. Unfortunately, these "rule types" are rather general and are not derived from any particular business. More ominously, they seem to be very natural categories to programmers. This is because such rule types closely resemble programming constructs. However, in building a business rules engine it is a mistake to take a programming perspective as the main point of reference. It is the business that should be taken as main point of reference. If this is the case, is it really useful to categorize business rules into rule types that are primarily a reflection of how they would be represented in hand-crafted program code? It has to be admitted that there is some utility to this, as we shall see in later chapters. However, if designers go down this path they will end up creating a rules definition interface where there is one rule type for calculations, another for derivations, etc. Such an interface could be equally used in an application for a hospital, or a hedge fund, or a hat manufacturer. The more oriented someone is to IT, the more likely they are to see this as an advantage rather than a drawback.

It is a drawback because in any particular business domain there are very often types of business rules that are specific to that domain. There are certainly specific business terms that describe what the rules are doing, and there are certainly names for the business processes (and their component steps) that need to be executed to run the business. Given this wealth of specificity among business users, why should rules be categorized in a way that makes most sense to IT professionals, and why should the way that users see the rules be ignored? Clearly, a successful business rules approach will cater for the business users first.

The problem with starting from a business perspective is that it is not clear what rule types exist at the outset. Both analysis and design are required. The analysis seeks to understand what the users are doing and what vocabulary they use to describe their work. The design uses this information to construct screens for defining rule types in ways that make sense to the users. Ideally, a given rule type will apply to different organizations that do the same kind of work, but they cannot be relevant for every business.

Let us consider an example of a rule type in some detail. There is a rule type that exists among investment partnerships that at least some companies call "Pay Pro-Rata" and which was introduced in Chapter 2. Rules of this type are used to distribute

ITEM	NAME	DESCRIPTION
1	Distribution Amount	The amount of money at the Partnership level that has to be distributed
2	Participation Percentage	The percentage of the Distribution Amount to which an investor is entitled
3	Investor Proceeds	The amount of the Distribution Amount that the investor receives

TABLE 7.2 Elements of Rule Type **Pay Pro-Rata**

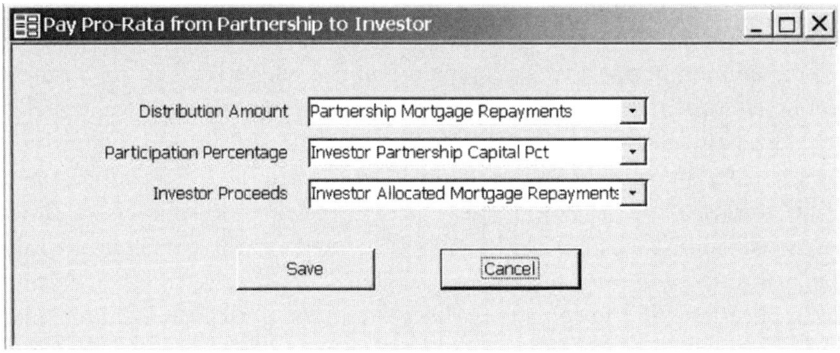

FIGURE 7.2
Screen Prototype for Definition of **Pay Pro-Rata** Rules

income, or other monies that the partnership receives, to investors in the partnership. How much each investor receives depends on their Participation Percentage. This is the percentage of the money that an investor is entitled to receive. Often it is the amount of money that the investor invested in the partnership divided by the total amount of money in the partnership. The elements of the rule type **Pay Pro-Rata** have now been described and are listed in Table 7.2.

The **Pay Pro-Rata** rule type may be used for many different rules in an investment partnership. In a real-estate partnership there may be one rule to allocate income from mortgages, another to allocate income from management fees, another to allocate income from sales of buildings, another to allocate income for professional services, and so on. All these rules will use the **Pay Pro-Rata** rule type.

Given the elements of the rule type in Table 7.2, it is fairly easy to sketch out a design for a screen where the rule type can be defined, as shown in Table 7.3.

It is now possible to create a prototype of the screen to enter definitions of rules for this rule type, as shown in Figure 7.2.

ITEM	NAME	DESIGN APPROACH
1	Distribution Amount	The user should select a column from the table where Partnership information is stored. This will be the field where the Distribution Amount is stored. The Distribution Amount will be data-entered on one of the application screens. Only numeric fields should be displayed to the user—fields of other datatypes do not make sense for Distribution Amount.
2	Participation Percentage	The user should select a column from the table where Investor information is stored. This will be the field where the Participation Percentage is stored. Only columns that represent percentages should be displayed to the user. Participation Percentages are calculated by other business rules.
3	Investor Proceeds	The user should select a column from the table where Investor information is stored. This will be the field where the Investor Proceeds is stored. Investor Proceeds is the result calculated by the **Pay Pro-Rata** rule type. Only numeric fields should be displayed to the user—fields of other datatypes do not make sense for Investor Proceeds.

TABLE 7.3 Design Considerations for **Pay Pro-Rata** Rule Type

The screen shown in Figure 7.2 captures the basic metadata required for the rules that are **Pay Pro-Rata** rules. Although more work will need to be done on the screen, it is already very specific for this rule type, yet fairly simple. As shown in Figure 7.2 the screen does require knowledge of what a **Pay Pro-Rata** rule type is, but any user who is familiar with the **Pay Pro-Rata** rules will easily adapt to it.

There is a good deal more metadata that should be captured in the rule definition screen shown in Figure 7.2, such as a rule number, a rule note, and the date and time that the rule was created and last updated. However, what is presented in Figure 7.2 contrasts sharply with what would have to be built if rules types were approached from the IT perspective. In this case, **Pay Pro-Rata** would never be defined as a rule type. Instead there would probably be a **Calculation** rule type. This rule type definition screen would probably have to look something like what is shown in Figure 7.3.

Figure 7.3 accomplishes much of what Figure 7.2 does in terms of capturing metadata, but the user has to tell the system how to perform the calculation as well. In actual fact, it traps less metadata than is done in Figure 7.2. For instance in Figure 7.2 the fields are clearly assigned to their roles in the **Pay Pro-Rata** rule—for example, the topmost field is the Distribution Amount. There is no equivalent of this in Figure 7.3.

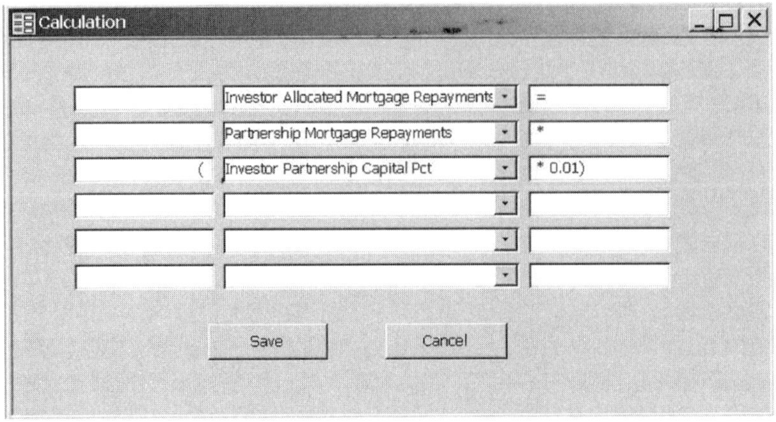

FIGURE 7.3
Screen for Definition of Calculation Rules

The screen in Figure 7.2 will have a code generation routine associated with it that is specific to the **Pay Pro-Rata** rule type. However, the screen in Figure 7.3 handles calculations in general, and its code generation routine does not contain (or require) any special intelligence to handle the **Pay Pro-Rata** rule type.

The approach of designing an interface that consists of rule types that are specific to the underlying business is possible for the kind of business rules engine described in this book. This kind of rules engine is based on extending a more general application. Rules engines designed to generate entire applications, or that work with any set of data, cannot easily adopt such an approach. They tend to have more generalized rules definition interfaces. It is true that additional work is required to analyze, design, and build interfaces for business-specific rule types, but the result is an engine that is closely tied to the underlying business, and thus much easier for users to work with. This kind of specialization tends to outcompete more general designs, which have to achieve the required specificity by demanding more of the user.

This is not to say that there is no place for general rule types, like that shown in Figure 7.3. Most applications will have a need for simple calculations or derivations that truly do not belong to a business-specific rule type. However, the designer must be certain that this is the case and avoid reusing general rule types simply because they have already been built.

Code Generation Routines

Capturing business rules metadata is one thing, but having executable forms of these rules is quite another. There are three main approaches to executing business rules:

- The user defines the rule in an executable format. Essentially, the user inputs some kind of program code that can be executed with little or no transformation.

- The rules engine captures rule metadata. When the rules are executed, the engine interprets the metadata and executes the logic of the rules.

- The rules engine captures rule metadata and uses this to generate program code. When the rules are invoked the program code is executed.

The first design has considerable drawbacks, as discussed in previous sections in this chapter. It places the metadata of the business rules immediately in a black box of procedural code (or its equivalent) that makes it impossible to relate this metadata to the rest of the Business Rules Repository. This has adverse implications for the capacity of the rules engine to manage business rules. Also, this approach means that the user has to learn some kind of scripting language or perhaps even a true programming language. Users are highly averse to being placed in such a position.

The other two design alternatives are better suited to building a business rules engine and are discussed in more detail below.

Direct Interpretation of Rules

The second design approach builds from what was discussed in the previous section. The Business Rules Repository captures rules metadata that the rules engine can interpret sufficiently to create executable code. In this approach, the rules engine has one routine for each rule type per programming language in which executable rules are created. In the previous section an interface was built to define rules for a rule type called **Pay Pro-Rata** (see Figure 7.2). It is not too difficult to conceive of a function that the rules engine designer could build to create executable code for this rule. The basic processing of this function is shown in the steps in Table 7.4.

The design shown in Table 7.4 could be implemented as shown in Listing 7.1, in an environment where the database tables involved are already known.

Thus, whenever the rules engine needs to execute a **Pay Pro-Rata** business rule, it can pass the rule metadata to the function shown in Listing 7.1. The code in Listing 7.1 will execute the rule globally, and in practice it may perhaps need to be enhanced to restrict it to certain investors or certain partnerships.

This design approach means that the rules engine designer is building a rules interpreter. In the rules engine, there will be one function like that shown in Listing 7.1 for each rule type. These functions directly interpret the rule metadata to interpret the code. A major drawback to this approach occurs if the designer wants to let the user define rule types that themselves contain functions. This is illustrated in Figure 7.4, which shows a less specific way of defining a **Pay Pro-Rata** rule type, first introduced in Figure 7.3.

STEP	DESCRIPTION
1	The function is passed the physical names of the columns that hold Distribution Amount; Participation Percentage; and Investor Proceeds.
2	The function opens the Partnership and Investor tables. These are the only two tables that play a role in the **Pay Pro-Rata** rule type.
3	The function relates the two tables. An investor is associated with one and only one partnership.
4	For each investor, the function finds the appropriate partnership information. The function retrieves the column that holds the Distribution Amount from the Partnership record. It multiplies this by the value in the column that holds the Participation Percentage on the Investor record. The result is stored in the column that holds the Investor Proceeds on the Investor record.

TABLE 7.4 Design of Function to Directly Execute **Pay Pro-Rata** Rule Type

LISTING 7.1
Function to Directly Execute **Pay Pro-Rata** Rule Type

```
    Public Function FirePayProRata(strDistCol as string, strPartPctCol
as string, _
                        StrInvProcCol as string) As String
'****************************************************************
' Executes the Pay Pro-Rata rule.
'
' Parameters:
'   strDistCol = Name of column with Distribution Amount.  This is
'   in the Partnership table
'   strPartPctCol = Name of column for the Investor's Participation
'   Percentage.
'                   This is in the Investor table
'   strInvProcCol = Name of column for the Investor's Proceeds.
'                   This is in the Investor table
'
' Returns: "Y" indicates successful completion
'****************************************************************

Dim rstRule As ADODB.Recordset, strSQL As String, lngAffected As
Long
Dim cmd As ADODB.Command, dblDist as double, dblPct as double
```

```
        FirePayProRata = "Y"
        Set rstRule = New ADODB.Recordset
        Set cmd = New ADODB.Command
        cmd.ActiveConnection = CurrentProject.Connection
        cmd.CommandType = adCmdText

        strSQL = "SELECT * FROM PARTNERSHIP A, INVESTOR B" _
              & "WHERE A.PARTNERSHIP_ID = B.PARTNERSHIP_ID "

        rstRule.Open strSQL, CurrentProject.Connection, _
              adOpenKeyset, adLockOptimistic, adCmdText
        Do While Not rstRule.EOF
           dblDist = rstRule(strDistCol)
           dblPct = rstRule(strPartPctCol)

           strSQL = "UPDATE INVESTOR SET " & strInvProcCol _
                 & " = " & Cstr(dblDist * dblPct * 0.01) _
                 & " WHERE INVESTOR_ID = '" & rstRule("INVESTOR_ID") &
"'"
           cmd.CommandText = strSQL
           cmd.Execute lngAffected
           rstRule.MoveNext
        Loop
        rstRule.Close
        Set rstRule = Nothing
        Set cmd = Nothing

End Function
```

In Figure 7.4, the rule definition includes a Maximum() function. This function is designed to return the greater of two values, and its use in Figure 7.4 is to make sure that Investor Allocated Mortgage Repayments can never be populated with a value less than zero (in the unlikely event that Partnership Mortgage Repayments ever contained a negative value, i.e., a value that is less than zero). In rule definitions it is necessary sometimes to permit users to use functions such as Maximum(). Admittedly, in the example of **Pay Pro-Rata** this would be better handled by enhancing the screen shown in Figure 7.2 to give the user the option of whether the Investor Proceeds column could contain a value less than zero. Indeed, it should be pointed out that the overall recommendation of this book is to create specific rule definition inter-

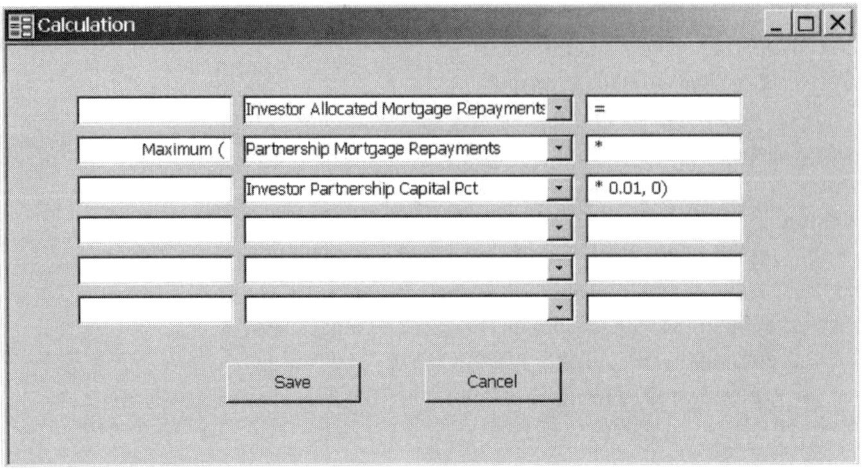

FIGURE 7.4
A Rule Definition Containing a Function

faces that avoid the need to include functions such as Maximum(). However, in the end, there is always the possibility that there are cases where the user has to directly include a function in a rule definition, like Maximum() in Figure 7.4.

The problem for a rules engine that directly interprets rules metadata is that if there are more than a few functions that can be used in more than a few rule types, the design of the interpreter becomes very complex. Inevitably, the interpreter has to be made to parse the rules definition. If a new function has to be introduced, a great deal of the rules interpreter has to be enhanced—and this is a major change. None of this may be apparent to the designer at the outset of building a rules engine, but if these considerations are not appreciated they can lead to severe problems later on when the complexity has to be dealt with.

Another issue for the rules interpreter approach is that there is sometimes a need to work in a variety of environments. For instance, the rules engine may be implemented in a particular programming language and work with a certain database. This database may be capable of handling stored procedures, and stored procedures often work very nicely with business rules approaches. In particular, they are very useful for executing long-running processes involving database activity. They usually execute such processes much faster than can be done with other techniques. However, it is a lot of work to write one rules interpreter for the main rules engine, and a second rules interpreter for the stored procedure environment. In fact, without a great deal of staff and budgetary resources this may be impossible.

A third issue with the rule interpreter is that it may not be easy to find what rules are fired for a particular business process step. It is rather difficult to include debugging functionality in a rules interpreter. The rules interpreter has to interpret the rule definition metadata (where something can go wrong) and then execute what it has interpreted (where something else can go wrong). Even if everything works correctly, the results may not be correct from a business viewpoint, so there is a third level at which things can go wrong. It is covering all these possibilities that makes adding debugging functionality to a rule interpreter so difficult. This contrasts sharply with the next approach to rules execution that will be considered—code generation.

Code Generation: Interpretive versus Compiled Programming Languages

Rather than have one routine that interprets rule metadata for each rule type, it is possible to have a routine that generates executable code based on the rule type metadata. This code is then invoked to execute the rule logic.

Many designers are not familiar with building programs that themselves write other programs, and they wonder if such a thing is possible. In the majority of programming environments it appears to be fully supported. However, if this approach is to be adopted, the designer is immediately faced with a major decision: Is the programming environment to be used one where program code is interpreted, or one where program code is to be compiled?

Interpreted languages, such as Visual Basic for Applications (VBA) and Cold Fusion, require the programmer to create source code. The source program code is "interpreted" at run time to execute it. Actually, it is usually a lot more complicated than this, but the bottom line is that the programmer can create source code and run it without taking any other actions. Compiled languages, in contrast, require the source code to be run through a compiler (and perhaps other tools such as a linker) to produce an executable form of the code. The source code itself cannot be run without being processed in this way. Again, this is a simplification of what actually happens, but the point is that the source code itself cannot be executed.

Obviously, interpretive programming languages are easier to work with than compiled languages for a business rules engine that generates code to execute rules. There are fewer steps that need to be implemented. However, many programmers are suspicious of interpretive languages and prefer to work with compiled languages. A major reason that is stated for this is "performance." Some programmers feel that interpretive languages work more slowly than compiled ones. It can be astonishing to see how programmers influence enterprise architectures by objecting to design alternatives simply by raising the specter of performance. If this happens in the context of building a business rules engine, it is worth asking a few questions:

- Is performance in general being discussed, or is there a specific issue? General performance issues may not be issues at all, and the rules engine designer should only deal with specifics. If performance is likely to be an issue there need to be agreed response times for the outputs that the rules engine is expected to produce. There also needs to be an estimate of the volumes of data to be processed and the number of rules to be fired. It is only on this factual basis that the design of the rules engine can factor in performance, such as for the use of compiled versus interpretive languages.

- Are the supposed performance issues material? Does it really matter if an output is produced in an additional millisecond, or second, or ten seconds, or even ten minutes? Is it worth sacrificing the advantages of an interpretive language for something that is irrelevant to the users, to achieve a purity of design that perhaps only a programmer can appreciate?

- If performance is an issue, is the answer really to adopt a compiled language instead of an interpreted one? This may be a false choice. For instance, if large volumes of data are involved, the real answer may be to use stored procedures so that all processing occurs on the database server, and use of a compiled language is irrelevant. Just because a programmer correctly diagnoses a performance issue does not mean that they have the right prescription to correct it.

Another issue with using a compiled language is that it may be difficult to regenerate rules. The compile and link steps may not be easy to perform in a particular environment. If this is the case, the tendency is to avoid the problem by building a rules interpreter rather than generating code, and, as noted in the previous section, this may not be able to cope with certain levels of complexity.

One further problem with compiled languages is error detection. If users are allowed to define rules using syntactic constructs such as functions (e.g., the Maximum() function discussed in the previous section) the possibility exists that the user can make a syntax error. It may not be easy to detect this in a compiled language until the source code is compiled. However, in an interpretive language there may be ways in which syntax errors can be detected more quickly.

The author has built rules engines with both compiled and interpretive languages with good results. However, it is definitely easier to use an interpretive language, and this is the design alternative followed in this book.

Code Generation: What Does It Mean?

If a rules engine is designed to generate program code for executable rules, and the engine is built using an interpretive programming language, how does this process work?

The approach used in this book is to build one code generation routine for each rule type, for each programming language environment in which rules have to be

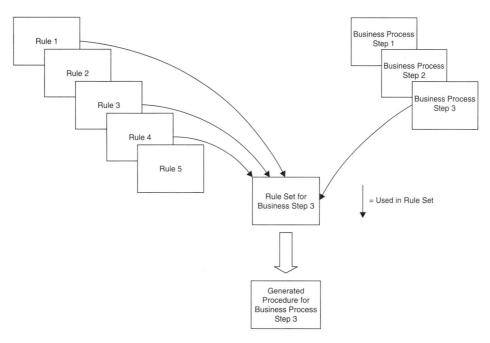

FIGURE 7.5
Example of Code Generation of Procedures for Business Process Steps

implemented. When the rule metadata is created, or when it changes, the code generation routine is called and creates the source code for the required programming language environment. However, rather than having individual pieces of program code for each business rule, the source code is grouped into rule sets. Each business process step is considered to be a rule set and is implemented as a distinct routine. Thus, even if just one rule changes, the rules engine regenerates the program code for all business process steps in which the changed rule participates. A major reason for doing this is that if a rule's definition is changed, it may affect the sequence in which rules run within a business process step. Thus, it is necessary to resequence all the rules in the rule sets (i.e., business process steps) in which the changed rule participates. This really cannot be avoided, and thus regenerating only the program code for the changed rule is not an option. Figure 7.5 illustrates this approach.

In Figure 7.5, Rules 1, 3, and 4 are the rules that are used within Business Process Step 3. Thus, these rules need to be fired when Business Process Step 3 is run. The rules engine generates a routine for Business Process Step 3 that consists of source code representing Rules 1, 3, and 4. When Business Process Step 3 is run this routine is executed. If Rule 1, or Rule 3, or Rule 4 has its definition changed by the user, the entire procedure for Business Process Step 3 is regenerated.

Rules 1, 3, and 4 could also be associated with other business process steps. If this is the case, the routines for these other business process steps have to be regenerated if the definitions change for any of Rules 1, 3, or 4.

There are some big advantages to generating code for entire business process steps rather than for individual rules. The first is that it is very easy to execute a business process step—it is simply a matter of invoking the associated routine. If business rules had source code generated for them as stand-alone routines, the rules engine would have to find all these little routines when Business Process Step 3 was run and execute these individual pieces of code in the correct sequence.

A second advantage is that it is possible for a programmer to look at the routine for a business process step and understand with confidence what happens when the business process step is executed. It is simply a matter of looking at the code that is generated for the routine. This would not be the same if the rules engine called individual routines for the rule belonging to a business process step at run time.

Subsequent chapters will describe how to build routines that generate code, but there are some other considerations that can affect the design of the rules engine. The first is that business process steps usually need some program logic in addition to what is defined by the rules. For instance, a business process step that processes daily account activity for a bank will require some program logic to insert new records in the Account table for the current day—one new record for each account that is open on the day being processed. Once this has been done, the logic that executes the rules for this business process step can be invoked. There may also be some "cleanup" code required after the rules have fired, such as to commit updates to the database. Thus, the generated routine for a business process step often has program code beyond that which is needed for business rules that are associated with the business process step. This means that besides creating one code generation routine for each rule type, the

LISTING 7.2
Fragment of Generated Visual Basic for Applications Code, Showing Comments

```
'ScrChkfrmINV_INVESTMENT_S----Start
Public Function ScrChkfrmINV_INVESTMENT_S(frmMe As Form) As String
Dim intErr As Integer, strErr As String
' This Function validates data entry on the screen
' frmINV_INVESTMENT_S
'—Investment Details
' Last Generated: 1/11/2003 9:53:59 PM
' Tables updated by this screen:
'    INV_INVESTMENT_S  Investment

intErr = 0
strErr = ""
```

```
' Section 1: Validate Datatypes of Entered Data
' Rule: R0014 / User Rule: R0014
' Rule Name: Investment Close Date must be a valid date
' Investment Close Date (INV_CLOSE_D)
' This field must have a datatype of date
If Not IsNull(frmMe.INV_CLOSE_D) Then
   If Not IsDate(frmMe.INV_CLOSE_D) Then
      intErr = intErr + 1
      strErr = strErr & "Investment Close Date does not have a
valid date entered " _
               & "for it.   Please check the data and re-enter
it." & Chr(10) & Chr(13)
   End If
End If
' Rule: R0015 / User Rule: R0015
' Rule Name: Investment Total Amount must be a valid number
' Investment Total Amount (INV_TOTAL_A)
' This field must have a datatype of numeric
If Not IsNull(frmMe.INV_TOTAL_A) Then
   If Not IsNumeric(frmMe.INV_TOTAL_A) Then
      intErr = intErr + 1
      strErr = strErr & "Investment Total Amount does not have a
valid number " _
               & "entered for it.   Please check the data and re-
enter it. " _
               & " A minus sign and decimal point can be entered"
& Chr(10) & Chr(13)
   End If
End If
```

rules engine designer must create one code generation routine for each business process step. It is this latter routine that creates the program logic needed for the business process step in addition to what is defined by the business rules it contains.

Another advantage of generating code is that it is possible to generate program comments as well as program logic. Many programmers do not include comments in the program code that they write, making it very difficult to understand. However, the Business Rules Repository contains a great deal of metadata that can be used to create relevant comments when code is generated. An example of comments in generated Visual Basic for Applications code is shown in Listing 7.2. The comments are the lines that start with a single quote.

Rule Invocation Interface

In the previous section the way in which executable business rules are created and packaged as routines representing rules sets was discussed. When an application runs, these routines must somehow be invoked. This is most frequently done by a user selecting an option on a menu or clicking on a button on a screen. These components of an application are built by hand by programmers, and this means that the programmers have to know how to call the routines containing the rules sets.

In order to implement a rules invocation interface, the first requirement is to have a clear process model of the system. This should contain a list of all the business processes within the system and the business process steps that run sequentially within each business process. Such a process model should clearly identify the names of the generated routines that correspond to the business process steps. In addition, any parameters that have to be passed by the programmer to the routines have to be clearly identified. For instance, if a business process step processes daily activity for bank accounts, it will probably have to have the processing date passed to it.

Programmers will also have to know if the routines that execute the business rules return any information that the code the programmer is writing must be aware of. Perhaps a routine can return a status code which means that no further processing must be done. The program code created by the programmer must be able to deal with this appropriately.

Of course, it is more consistent with the business rules approach if parameters and return values can be dealt with by the generated code rather than any logic created by programmers. However, this is not always possible. Nevertheless, it is quite feasible to reduce what programmers have to implement to call executable business rules to just a few simple statements.

Administrative Tools

The components needed to build a business rules engine have now been described. However, there is always going to be a need for tools to administer the rules engine. Indeed, the architecture that a rules engine provides means that a whole host of administrative tools can be implemented that would be impossible in an application hand-crafted by programmers. Here are some examples:

- Reports showing which rules are used in each business process
- Reports showing which columns in a database table are updated by business rules
- Reports showing dependencies between rules in the same business process step
- Reports showing which rules a given database column is used in
- Reports showing all the rules defined for a particular rule type

A great deal more than this is possible in practice. The rules engine designer will be able to see the metadata captured in the Business Rules Repository he or she has created and can potentially use any of this for administrative reporting.

Another important administrative tool is the capacity to audit the execution of business rules. This is rarely done for applications that programmers build. In hand-coded applications, if there are questions about how certain values got into the database, the programmers are usually called in to debug the system. With business rules engines there may not be programming resources available for this kind of activity. However, it is possible to add auditing techniques to the code that is generated for executable business rules. This will be discussed more in subsequent chapters.

Conclusion

This chapter has reviewed the major components of the business rules engine and the most important design alternatives involved in building these components. The design alternatives used in building the kind of rules engine described in this book have been clearly identified. The following chapters will describe how to build these components and will deal with the more detailed design decisions that arise in this process.

8 POPULATING TABLE DATA IN THE REPOSITORY

The essential parts of a data model are entities, attributes, and relationships. These must all be represented in the Business Rules Repository. Entities are conceptually at the highest level. Strictly speaking, the term *entity* applies to a logical data model, and *table* applies to the equivalent physical implementation in a live database. Since business rules have to operate at the physical level, it is necessary to store data about tables in the Repository. However, it is also necessary to store some additional information about tables, which, strictly speaking, exists only at a logical level. For instance, the business definition of the information a table contains can be very helpful for a user when rules are being defined. This is an important consideration, because systems development staff often ignore constructs that exist at the logical level, thinking of them primarily as documentation. They tend to view documentation as something that does not play an active role in computerized systems, and as something that exists only in printed form or its electronic equivalent. Information resource professionals such as data administrators have almost the opposite perspective: they are often uncomfortable dealing with constructs at the physical level. Yet data administrators are often involved in the creation and maintenance of data models, and data models are a primary source of the information that is needed to populate the Business Rules Repository. Any successful business rules approach must take into account both of these perspectives: the logical view of data and the physical view.

The first step in populating the Business Rules Repository is to build the infrastructure that will hold information about logical entities and physical tables. This chapter describes an approach to meeting this requirement, including how relevant metadata can be imported into the Business Rules Repository from data modeling tools. Today, data modeling tools are used in most system development projects. If an application is to be built for a business area, then it is very probable that a data model will be created for it. Such data models contain a great deal of the metadata needed for the Business Rules Repository. Indeed, it is assumed here that a data model of the business area exists, and that the metadata from this model must be imported into the Business Rules Repository.

The Table Entity

The Business Rules Repository is itself a database, and as such it needs to be designed by first building a data model, and then implementing that data model as a physical database. The most basic construct needed in the Repository data model is something to hold information about entities and tables. An entity called **Table** has been created for this purpose. It must hold information about the logical entities and physical tables in the underlying business application upon which the business rules engine will operate. The pieces of information that the **Table** entity must hold are discussed below.

Table Physical Name

This is the physical name of the table in the implemented database; it is not the logical or business name of the table. *Table Physical Name* is also used as the primary key of the **Table** entity. It is assumed that the data model of the business area contains all the tables that exist in the business area upon which the rules engine will operate, and that the data model contains physical names for all these tables.

A full discussion of naming conventions for tables (and other database components) is a topic in itself and is beyond the scope of this book. However, naming conventions can play an important role in metadata engineering and can affect rule engine design.

It is important that *Table Physical Name* have a limit placed on its size. This is because long names are unwieldy, which makes discussing them difficult for the technical staff of a project. Perhaps more importantly, database products sometimes have limitations on the number of characters that can be in a table name. Business rules approaches are very useful when implemented within software applications that are implemented in different environments, such as packages sold to different clients. These environments often dictate the database platform that must be used for the business rules engine. Therefore, any rules engine design should try to accommodate this fact. For *Table Physical Name* this means choosing a maximum size that will be within the limits set by commonly used database management systems. A limit of 30 characters seems to work well and is used in the sample application in this book.

Physical table names are usually assigned when a data model is transitioned from the logical level to the physical level. This is something that is not always done well. In most cases, the only goal is to be descriptive enough that a programmer will have some idea of the data that the table contains. This is a laudable goal, but it is not sufficient for a metadata engineering approach, since so much of what is being dealt with will be metadata and not data. Physical table names (and other metadata) will be used over and over again in tables that hold information about business rules. Their names need to be helpful—they must not require difficult decoding to figure out what they are. In this regard, the best design option is to put intelligence into *Table Physical Name*, something that is called *naming conventions*. *Table Physical Name* must to be understandable to the staff building the rules engine and others who have some role in administration of databases. They need to be able to refer to database tables in a way that not only identifies each table, but also describes what each table contains.

Many enterprises have already created naming conventions for database tables. During a business rules project, consideration should be given as to whether these conventions should be followed. If the business rules project is to develop an application engine that will be used strictly within the enterprise, then there is good reason to follow these standards. Even if the standards are poor, the business rules application will be consistent, which is a virtue in itself. On the other hand, if a package is being developed that will be sold to many different clients, there is no necessity to follow a set established naming conventions for any one client. This means that the rules engine designer may be involved in developing naming conventions for the tables of the business application with which the rules engine works. The naming conventions used in this book are as follows:

- The entire table name cannot be more than 30 characters in length.

- Table name is divided into three nodes, connected by underscores.

- The first node cannot be more than five characters and is a unique acronym for the table. The acronym is formed by abbreviating the second node of the name.

- The second node of *Table Physical Name* is descriptive. It is an abbreviation of *Entity Name* (the business name of the table). There are many methods for abbreviating texts, but it is important that abbreviations be consistent. If the same word is abbreviated to form part of a *Table Physical Name* for one table, then it should be abbreviated the same way when it is used for the names of other tables.

  Some people like to break up the second node by introducing underscores. This is fine if it does not take up too much space.

DATABASE TABLE CLASSIFICATION CODE	DATABASE TABLE CLASSIFICATION DESCRIPTION
M	The table contains metadata
R	The table contains reference data
E	The table contains enterprise structure data
S	The table contains transaction structure data
D	The table contains transaction activity data
A	The table contains transaction audit data

TABLE 8.1 Database Table Classification Codes

- The third and final node of *Table Physical Name* is a single character that defines the classification to which the table belongs. This scheme outlined in Table 8.1 helps anyone looking at a table name to understand what its use is and where it fits in the general information structure. In particular, tables that hold metadata can be easily distinguished from those holding "regular" data. This is especially important if we implement the repository within the same database that holds the "regular" business data.

- Only capital letters, digits, and underscores can be used to construct table names. This tends to make table names stand out. Some technical staff believe strongly that there are other ways of achieving this, such as mixtures of upper and lower cases. Design decisions of this kind are often driven simply by what people feel comfortable with, and what they have been used to working with. It is quite valid to take people's experience into consideration in this way when formulating naming conventions. However, feelings of comfort or familiarity should not be allowed to override good design decisions that have sound reasoning behind them. The cases of the letters used to construct *Table Physical Name* is a relatively minor decision, and some flexibility can be allowed.

In the data model of the Business Rules Repository, **Table** entity itself must be given a physical name. This is **TAB_TABLE_M**.

Issues with Table ID as the Primary Key

In the previous section, the physical name of the table was chosen as the primary key. However, some IT staff are more comfortable with primary keys that are unique codes or sequence numbers. These are technically known as surrogate keys, but are commonly referred to as *IDs* (meaning "identifiers"). A surrogate key is an attribute that has no business meaning, but that can be used to identify instances of an entity. Thus, it might be natural to assume that a surrogate key such as *Table ID* could be used as the primary key of the **Table** entity. Sometimes database products have functionality that supports surrogate keys—for example, the database engine can automatically populate them with values without the need for programmer intervention.

As it happens, a number of data modeling tools do have internal codes to describe entities (i.e., tables), and these codes are surrogate keys. It is certainly tempting to use these codes, but it is better not to. Even if they can be extracted from the modeling tool there is no guarantee that the data modeling tool will keep them constant. This may be a problem if metadata has to be imported from the data modeling tool into the Repository multiple times.

There is still the possibility that sequence numbers can be assigned automatically. However, automatically assigned sequence numbers seem to vary widely from database product to database product. For instance, Microsoft Access has the autonumber datatype, Microsoft SQL Server 7.0 has an Identity datatype, and Oracle 8 has a record number concept. If a Repository is built to take advantage of what is offered by one of these products, then it will not work with any of the others.

Table Physical Name is also a better candidate as the primary key of the **Table** entity than trying to implement a *Table ID* because it is a "natural" key. It matches a unique identifier for a table in the data model, which is something that cannot be guaranteed for a *Table ID*. Furthermore, it is assumed that all tables have been identified in the data model, so there will never be a need to add any more through functionality in the business rules engine.

One other advantage of using *Table Physical Name* as the primary key of the **Table** entity is that, as we shall see, it is used heavily as a foreign key in other tables of the Business Rules Repository. The functionality of the rules engine requires *Table Physical Name* when working in the context of these other tables. By having *Table Physical Name* as the primary key of **Table**, and thus as the foreign key in the related tables, a lot of the functionality required for the rules engine is easier to build. This is also the reason why a surrogate key in general is not used as the primary key of **Table**.

Entity Name

This is the English language (or other human language) name by which the entity is known in the enterprise. It is a logical-level construct, rather than a physical-level one, and is information gathered by analysts or data modelers rather than by programmers or database administrators (DBAs). It is very important to have the correct and complete name. Sometimes these names can be long. In these situations, there may be a need to store an "official" long name, and an unofficial "short" or "working" name. To accommodate this, a separate attribute called *Entity Short Name* could be added to the **Table** entity, though this has not been done in the sample application.

The word *short* is particularly significant in this context because if the length is kept within a standard maximum size, then it will be possible to use this attribute on screens and reports, where space is always an issue. As we shall see later this is something that can be useful.

Entity Definition

This is the business definition of the entity. It is often neglected, even in many data modeling exercises. The reason is probably that it is regarded as "just documentation" or that it has no obvious connection to program logic or business rules. The reality is otherwise. The definitions of certain entities have a very direct connection with business rules and must be completely clarified. For instance, is a "Customer" someone who has purchased something from the enterprise? If so, a person should only be included in the **Customer** table after he or she has made a purchase. What exactly is a "Purchase"? Is it when an order is placed, or when payment for an order clears? This will affect reporting of sales figures.

Entity definitions are therefore vital for the understanding of analysts, programmers, and also business users. They should be constructed carefully and should be as clear as possible. Examples should be included to help readers better understand their meaning. They may also have to be kept up-to-date. As an enterprise changes it is possible that the meaning assigned to a particular entity will change, too, and this implies that the business rules involving this entity will also change.

Having *Entity Definition* readily available within an application is useful in other ways. Frequently, entity definitions are placed in documentation, including that which forms the basis of the "Help" functionality of an application. Thus, definitions are often stored and appear in multiple places in an application. As a result the various instances of the definitions tend to become different over time, causing confusion. Having *Entity Definition* in one place—the Repository—where it can be easily accessed can prevent this.

Table Type

The classification scheme for database tables presented in Table 8.1 has been used in *Table Physical Name*. Naming conventions are for ease of use by human beings. They should not be used in processing logic because they are not easily updateable. What is updateable in a database are data values, not names. It is very important that we distinguish each kind of table that needs to be processed by the rules engine. In particular, it is very important to distinguish reference data tables from other types of database tables. This is because reference data tables are used extensively in rules engine functionality. Therefore, a *Table Reference Table Indicator* has been implemented in the **Table** entity.

However, it is possible that the rules engine designer will need to have special rules engine functionality not only for reference data tables, but also for other kinds of table. If this is the case, a *Table Type Code* attribute will need to be implemented in **Table**. A corresponding reference data table called **Table Type** will also need to be implemented. Each record in **Table Type** would be for a different type of table (perhaps following the scheme suggested in Table 8.1). This is not required in the sample application, so neither *Table Type Code* nor **Table Type** are included in the Business Rules Repository.

Data Model Entity ID

The section "*Issues with Table ID as the Primary Key*" discussed reasons why **Table** should not be identified with an internal entity id imported from a data modeling tool. Even if this is agreed upon, there may still be pressure to include *Data Model Entity ID* as a nonkey attribute of the **Table** entity.

The question that needs to be asked is what value can be gained from doing this. In reality it will probably not be of any use in a business rules engine. It may be useful as an audit trail back to the data model, and it may be useful for other data administration needs. If adding *Data Model Entity ID* to the **Table** entity serves no purpose in terms of the business rules engine, it should not be done. The problem is that once a project begins to build a repository, it quickly becomes clear that the repository can serve a number of other functions, none of which has anything to do with building a business rules engine. This can result in scope creep and attempts to satisfy incompatible goals. The problem is not just confined to *Data Model Entity ID*; it affects a whole host of other metadata as well.

If scope creep involves issues of general metadata management, the best course of action is to resist expanding the role for the repository. If an enterprise wants to build a repository in order to administer metadata, that is an exercise which is completely different from building a rules engine. Unless a compelling reason in terms of business rules can be found for adding *Data Model Entity ID* to the **Table** entity, it should not be done. Building a business rules engine is difficult enough. Such a project cannot be turned into providing a general metadata solution for an enterprise.

However, there may be a desire to expand the repository for the administration of business rules in general. That is a different issue. As noted earlier, much of the metadata in the Business Rules Repository can be used in general rules administration. Of course, a great deal of additional metadata is also required. It makes very little sense to have one Repository for administration of business rules and another Repository for a rules engine. Nevertheless, discussions about how to expand the role of a rules engine repository during its construction indicate a lack of planning. In the end, expansion of the Repository to cover general rules management is hard to argue with.

ATTRIBUTE LOGICAL NAME	COLUMN PHYSICAL NAME	COLUMN DATATYPE
Table Physical Name	TAB_PHYSNAME_T	Character (30)
Entity Logical Name	TAB_ENTLOGNAME_T	Character (250)
Entity Definition	TAB_ENTDEFN_M	Memo
Table Reference Table Indicator	TAB_REFTAB_I	Character (1)

TABLE 8.2 Structure of **TAB_TABLE_M** (Table) Table

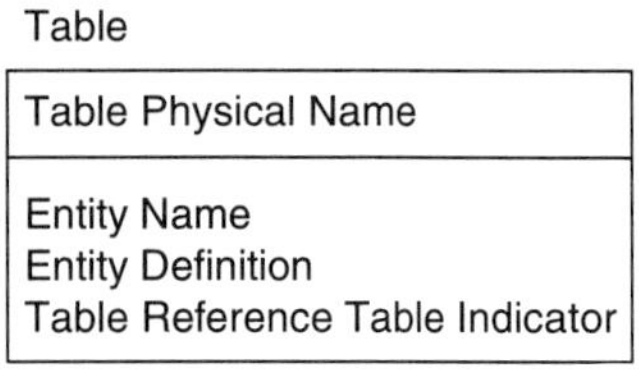

Table

Table Physical Name
Entity Name
Entity Definition
Table Reference Table Indicator

FIGURE 8.1
Logical Design for **Table** Entity

Summary of Design for Table Entity

The basic design of the **Table** entity in our repository is now complete. It is shown at the logical level in Figure 8.1. The design in Figure 8.1 is a starting point, not a completed design that will support all business rules implementations. It represents a minimum of what is needed to support these implementations, but there are certain kinds of business rules that will require more attributes to be added to **Table**, and these will be discussed more in subsequent chapters. The reader should remember that this book is not an encyclopedia of business rules, nor can it be. Every enterprise has unique rules that will be structurally different from anything encountered in this book. When these rules are encountered, the reader will have no alternative but to expand the **Table** entity to meet the needs of these rules.

The physical version of the Table entity can now be implemented in the sample application's business rules engine. This has already been done in the sample application, where the table has been given the physical name **TAB_TABLE_M**. The structure of **TAB_TABLE_M** is shown in Table 8.2.

Extracting Table Data from the Data Modeling Tool

Having designed the **Table** entity and implemented it as **TAB_TABLE_M**, we are ready to populate it. The first step in this process is to extract metadata from the data modeling tool. There are many different data modeling tools, and some enterprises use related tools such as data dictionaries. What is important is that there is a source for the data with which we need to populate **TAB_TABLE_M**. If there is no such source, it is very doubtful whether a business rules engine can be built correctly, since it must operate on an application's database.

Given that there are so many different data modeling tools, we will concentrate on one example and try to use the most general features of it that are likely to work with other tools. The example is Computer Associate's ERWin tool. Although this tool does have special mechanisms to extract the metadata it contains, it is also possible to do this through its report generator. Other data modeling tools, and data dictionaries, have similar report interfaces, so the mechanism we create to extract metadata from ERWin may be applicable—in a general way—in these other environments. Ideally, readers can adapt what follows to their particular circumstances.

Two versions of ERWin are commonly used, Version 3.5.2 and Version 4.1 (also known as AllFusion ERWin Data Modeler). The approach required for each is somewhat different, as described in the following sections.

Create ERWin 3.5.2 Extract Report File

Open the data model with ERWin 3.5.2 and ensure that it is in logical view.

1. Click on **Tasks** in the main menu and then on **Generate Reports . . .** in the popup that appears. The ERWin Report Browser appears. A tree control like that shown in Figure 8.2 appears and shows all the categories of reports that ERWin contains. Click on Entity Reports. We will need to create a new report.

2. Click on **File** in the main menu of the ERWin Report Browser and then on **New ERWin Report**. The ERWin Report Editor window appears. Provide a name for the new report—"TAB_TABLE_M Extract" has been used in this example. Select the report category "Entity" and click **OK**. The new report will have been added to the list under the Entity Reports node of the tree control in the main window.

3. Right-click on the newly added TAB_TABLE_M Extract report and select the option **Edit ERWin Report "TAB_TABLE_M Extract"**. The ERWin Report Editor opens again. The main window of the editor is a tree control called **Options** showing all the metadata that ERWin manages. We need to select the metadata we are going to use to populate **TAB_TABLE_M**. Click the following check boxes on the **Options** tree control:

   Under the Entity node, click the check boxes for *Name* and *Definition*

   Under the Tables node, click the check box for *Name*

   Click **OK** to close the window

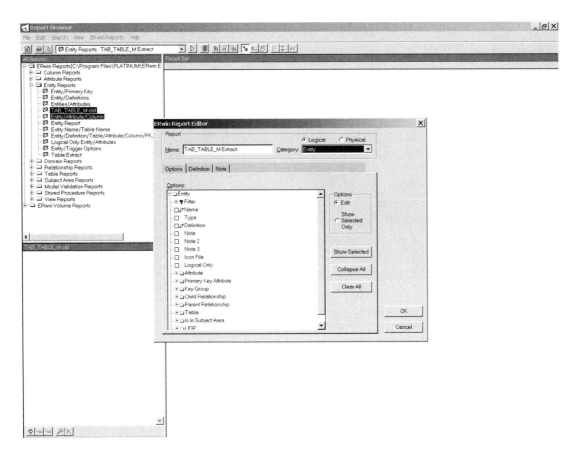

FIGURE 8.2
Defining a New Report in ERWin 3.5.2

4. Right-click again on the newly added TAB_TABLE_M Extract report and
   select the option **Execute ERWin Report "TAB_TABLE_M Extract"**. The
   ERWin Report executes and places the results set in the right-hand side of the
   screen. A new entry appears in the tree control underneath the
   TAB_TABLE_M Extract node indicating that we have produced this results
   set, as shown in Figure 8.3.

5. Right-click on the new entry that has appeared in the tree control underneath
   the TAB_TABLE_M Extract node and select the option to export the results
   set as shown in Figure 8.4.

6. A new window now appears with some options for the exported results set, as
   shown in Figure 8.5. Select HTML for the **Export format**, Tabular with
   Duplicates for the **Presentation**, and File for **Export to**. Then click the **Export**

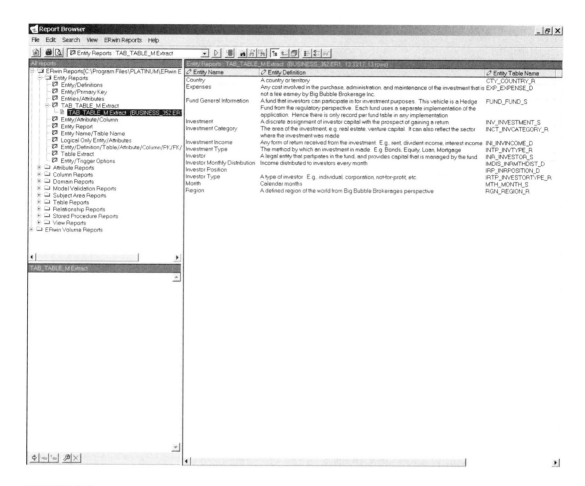

FIGURE 8.3
Generated Report for TAB_TABLE_M Extract in ERWin 3.5.2

button. You will be asked for a location to store the file containing the results set. Make sure it is saved as an HTML file. We have now created the report extract file. The next step is to get import it into Microsoft Access and populate the **TAB_TABLE_M** table.

Create ERWin 4.1 Extract Report File

Open the data model with ERWin 4.1 and ensure that it is in logical view.

1. Click on **Tools** in the main menu and then on **Report Builder** and then on **Report Builder . . .** in the popups that appear. The ERWin Report Templates window appears, as shown in Figure 8.6.

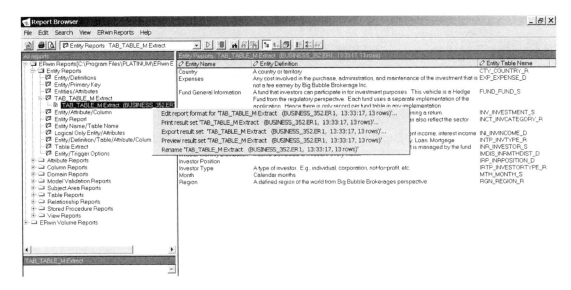

FIGURE 8.4
Export Results Set in ERWin 3.5.2

2. Click on the **New . . .** button in the Report Templates window. The Report Template Builder window now appears, as shown in Figure 8.7.

3. On the left of this window is a tree control called "Available Sections:" with the objects in the data model. Click on the Entity node and press the arrow button to add it to the Report Layout area on the right.

4. Right-click on Entity in the Report Layout area and click on **Properties** in the popup that appears. A window like that shown in Figure 8.8 appears.

5. On the Properties window, reveal the entire tree structure and check the boxes for *Name* and *Definition* below *Entity*.

6. Find the *Table* node and reveal the tree structure below it. Check the box for *Name* under *Table*.

7. Close the Properties window. Back on the Report Template Builder window, right-click on the top line of the Report Layout area (i.e., the text "Document Untitled"). Select **Properties** on the popup that appears. The Report Properties window now appears, as shown in Figure 8.9.

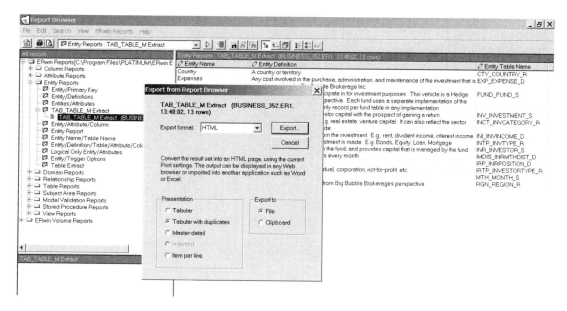

FIGURE 8.5
Results Set Export Options in ERWin 3.5.2

8. In the Report Properties window, select the Export tab. Select TEXT as the export type, and "Duplicates" in the Format section. Select "Comma Delimited" in the Delimiters section, and double quotes in the Text Qualifier section.

   Select the Title tab and provide a report title, such as "Entity Report".

   Close the Report Properties window.

9. Back on the Report Template Builder window, run the report by pressing the button with the downward-pointing arrow.

10. A file with the extension ".CSV" will be created for this report. Excel may be invoked to display the contents of this file.

    Save the new report template. This will also save the ".CSV" file. It will be placed in the directory specified in the ERWin Report Templates window shown in Figure 8.6.

    The next step is to get import it into Microsoft Access and populate the **TAB_TABLE_M** table.

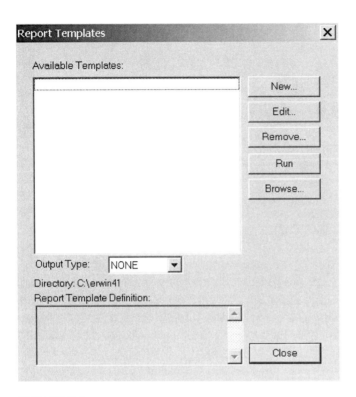

FIGURE 8.6
Report Templates Window in ERWin 4.1

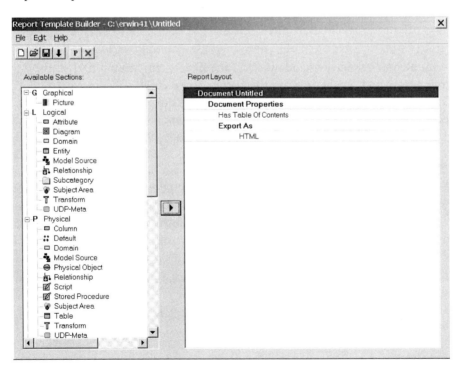

FIGURE 8.7
Report Template Builder Window in ERWin 4.1

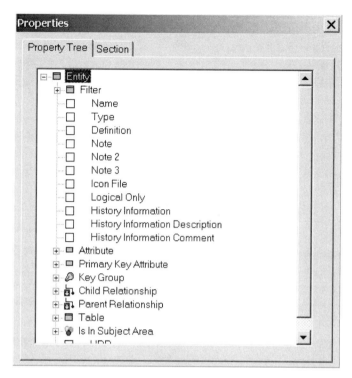

FIGURE 8.8
Object Properties Window in ERWin 4.1

Importing ERWin 3.5.2 Table Metadata into the Repository

If the report extract was produced using ERWin 3.5.2, it can now be imported into the repository of the sample business rules application, bizengine.mdb. Follow these steps:

1. Open up the Microsoft Access file bizengine.mdb. Go to the Tables tab. Right-click in this area and select the **Import** option. This starts the Access import wizard.

2. A file selection dialog now appears. At the bottom is a combo box entitled "Files of type". Select the value for HTML files. Navigate to where you saved the report extract file form ERWin and select it.

3. The next screen that appears in the Access import wizard asks if the first row contains column headings. It does, check this box, as shown in Figure 8.10. Then click **Next**.

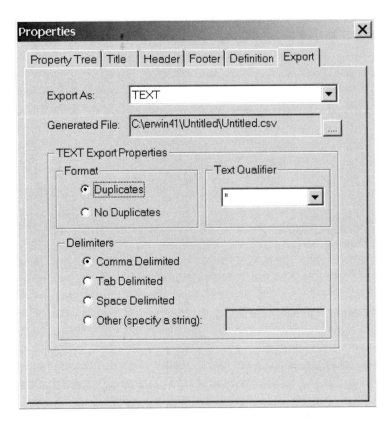

FIGURE 8.9
Report Properties Window in ERWin 4.1

4. The next screen asks if the file should be brought into a new table. Indicate that it should be, and click **Next**.

5. The next screen is where you specify the datatypes for the data that is being imported. Access provides a default of Text (255) for all text fields. This is sufficient for most fields, but the *Entity Definition* may be longer than this. Highlight the *Entity Definition* field by clicking on it. Then select a datatype of Memo, as shown in Figure 8.11. Then press **Next**.

6. The next screen that appears asks whether you want to let Access add its own primary key, or whether you want to specify it. Choose the option to let Access add its own primary key and press **Next**.

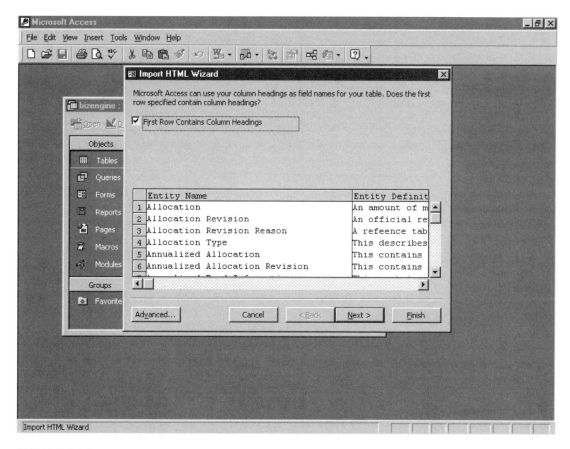

FIGURE 8.10
Specify Column Headings in Access Import Wizard (Import from ERWin 3.5.2)

7. The final screen of the import wizard now appears. It asks you to provide the name of the table. Give it a name of IMPT_IMPORTTAB_M. Then press **Finish**. Access will now import the data. Access will report any errors to you. The most frequent one that happens is due to forgetting to make the *Entity Definition* a memo field, which results in data truncation.

If you need to repeat this process, delete the table **IMPT_IMPORTTAB_M** and start again. Alternatively, delete all records from **IMPT_IMPORTTAB_M**, and when the data is re-imported specify **IMPT_IMPORTTAB_M** as the destination table instead of specifying that the data will go into a new table.

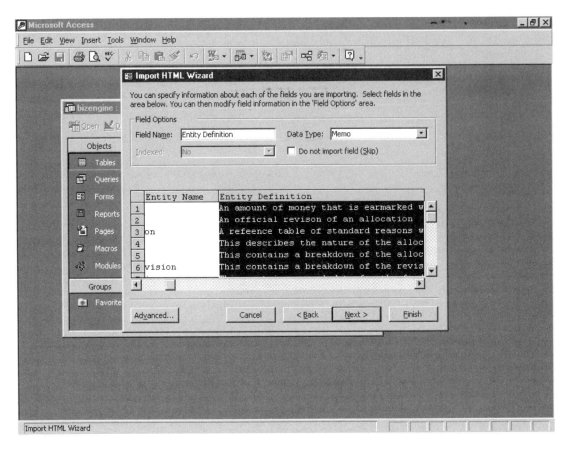

FIGURE 8.11
Specify Entity Definition with a Datatype of Memo (Import from ERWin 3.5.2)

Importing ERWin 4.1 Table Metadata into the Repository

The procedure to import the report extract produced from the ERWin 4.1 data model into the repository is a little different from that for the ERWin 3.5.2 extract. Follow these steps:

1. Open up the Microsoft Access file bizengine.mdb. Go to the Tables tab. Right-click in this area and select the **Import** option. This starts the Access import wizard.

2. A file selection dialog now appears. At the bottom is a combo box entitled "Files of type". Select the value for Text files (which will include ".CSV" files). Navigate to where you saved the report extract file from ERWin 4.1 and select it.

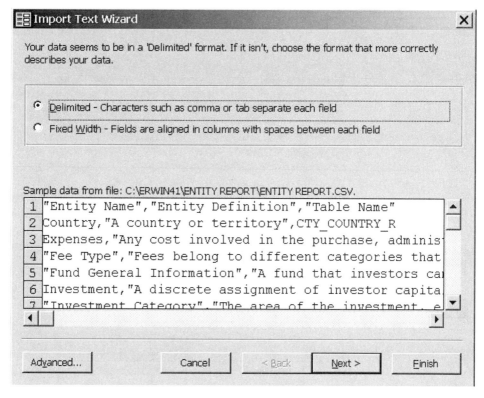

FIGURE 8.12
Specify Delimiter Type (Import from ERWin 4.1)

3. The next screen that appears in the Access import wizard is shown in Figure 8.12. This requires the type of file format to be specified. Select the "Delimited" type. Then click **Next**.

4. The next screen, shown in Figure 8.13, requires that the delimiter character be specified. Choose "comma" and make sure the Text Qualifier is set to double quotes. Then click **Next**.

5. The next screen asks whether the file should be brought into a new table. Indicate that it should be, and click **Next**.

6. The next screen is where you specify the field names and datatypes for the data that is being imported.

   The field names that are provided are *Field1*, *Field2*, and *Field3*. Replace these names with *Entity Name*, *Entity Definition*, and *Table Name*.

   Access provides a default of Text (255) for all text fields. This is sufficient for most fields, but, the *Entity Definition* may be longer than this. Highlight the

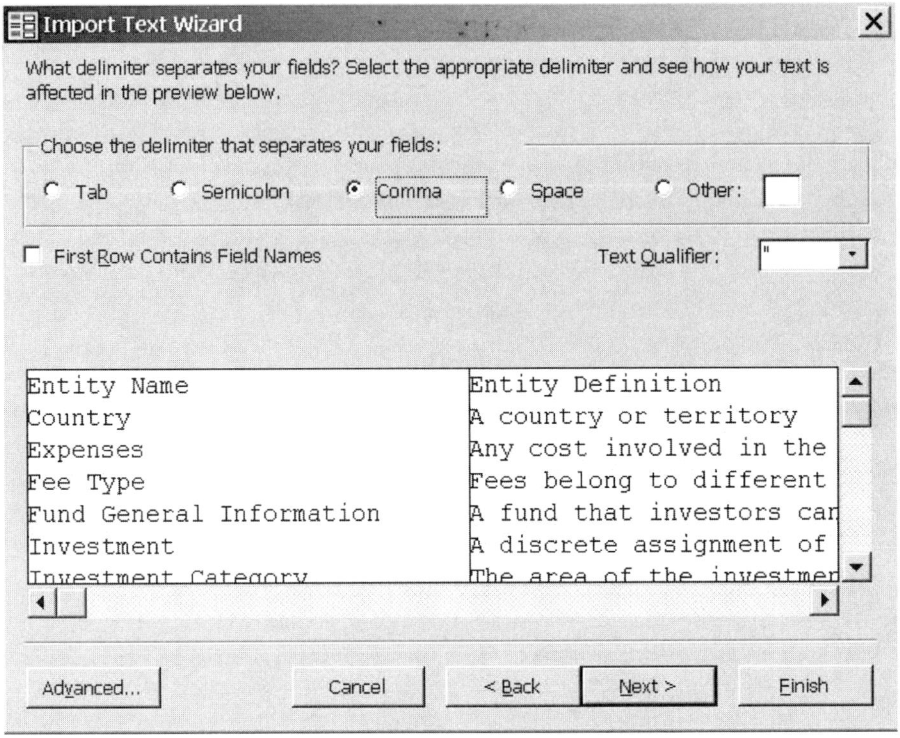

FIGURE 8.13
Specify Delimiter Characters (Import from ERWin 4.1)

Entity Definition field by clicking on it. Then select a datatype of Memo and press **Next**.

7. The next screen that appears asks if you want to let Access add its own primary key, or if you want to specify it. Choose the option to let Access add its own primary key and press **Next**.

8. The final screen of the import wizard now appears. It asks you to provide the name of the table. Give it a name of IMPT_IMPORTTAB_M. Then press **Finish**. Access will now import the data. Access will report any errors to you. The most frequent one that happens is due to forgetting to make the *Entity Definition* a memo field, which results in data truncation.

If you need to repeat this process, delete the table **IMPT_IMPORTTAB_M** and start again. Alternatively, delete all records from **IMPT_IMPORTTAB_M**, and when the data is reimported specify **IMPT_IMPORTTAB_M** as the destination table instead of specifying that the data will go into a new table.

Updating the TAB_TABLE_M Table

With the metadata for tables now inside the **IMPT_IMPORTTAB_M** table in bizengine.mdb, we need to update **TAB_TABLE_M**. To do this we have to write some simple Access VB code, which is shown in Listing 8.1. This listing shows the function PopTable(), which is implemented in the module ImportMetaData of the sample application.

LISTING 8.1
Load **TAB_TABLE_M** with Entity Metadata

```
Private Function PopTable() As String

' Loads Entity information imported from ERWin

Dim intResp As Integer, strCriteria As String, strMy As String
Dim strGo As String, rsSRC As ADODB.Recordset, strOID As String,
strTxt1 As String
Dim strTxt2 As String, strTxt3 As String, rsTGT As ADODB.Recordset
Dim cmd As ADODB.Command, strText As String, lngAffected As Long

    PopTable = "Y"
    Set cmd = New ADODB.Command
    cmd.ActiveConnection = CurrentProject.Connection

    cmd.CommandType = adCmdText
    Set rsSRC = New ADODB.Recordset
    Set rsTGT = New ADODB.Recordset

    ' Clean out all existing records from TAB_TABLE_M
    strText = "DELETE FROM TAB_TABLE_M"
    cmd.CommandText = strText
    cmd.Execute lngAffected

    ' Clean out all existing subtypes
    strText = "DELETE FROM STP_SUBTYPE_M"
    cmd.CommandText = strText
    cmd.Execute lngAffected

    ' Source table is IMPT_IMPORTTAB_M, Target is TAB_TABLE_M
    rsSRC.Open "IMPT_IMPORTTAB_M", CurrentProject.Connection, _
        adOpenKeyset, adLockOptimistic, adCmdTable
```

```
    rsTGT.Open "TAB_TABLE_M", CurrentProject.Connection, _
        adOpenKeyset, adLockOptimistic, adCmdTable

    rsSRC.MoveFirst
    Do While Not rsSRC.EOF
        If Not IsNull(rsSRC("Entity Table Name")) Then
            rsTGT.AddNew
            rsTGT("TAB_ENTLOGNAME_T") = rsSRC("Entity Name")
            rsTGT("TAB_ENTDEFN_M") = rsSRC("Entity Definition")
            rsTGT("TAB_PHYSNAME_T") = rsSRC("Entity Table Name")
            rsTGT.Update
        End If
        rsSRC.MoveNext
    Loop

    rsSRC.Close
    rsTGT.Close

End Function
```

This program code first deletes all data from **TAB_TABLE_M**. Then it reads all the records in the imported data table **IMPT_IMPORTTAB_M** and, as long as there is a table name, it adds a record to **TAB_TABLE_M**.

We now have successfully imported the entity metadata from the ERWin data modeling tool and populated the first table in our repository, **TAB_TABLE_M**. If you open up **TAB_TABLE_M** you will see the data that has been imported.

It is assumed that when the table data is being imported, no column or relationship data has yet been imported. If such data is present, it should be deleted before table data is imported.

Screen Interface for Updating Table Metadata

Even after the metadata for table data has been imported from the data modeling tool, there may be a need to change it. For instance, an entity may be known by one name in a particular organization, but called something quite different in another organization. Since so much of the flexibility of a rules engine is geared to supporting multiple installations where there are somewhat different business requirements, it is important that changes to metadata can be done quickly and easily. Going back to the original data model and changing it is not an option. First of all, it is time consuming to make a small change and then reimport all the metadata from the

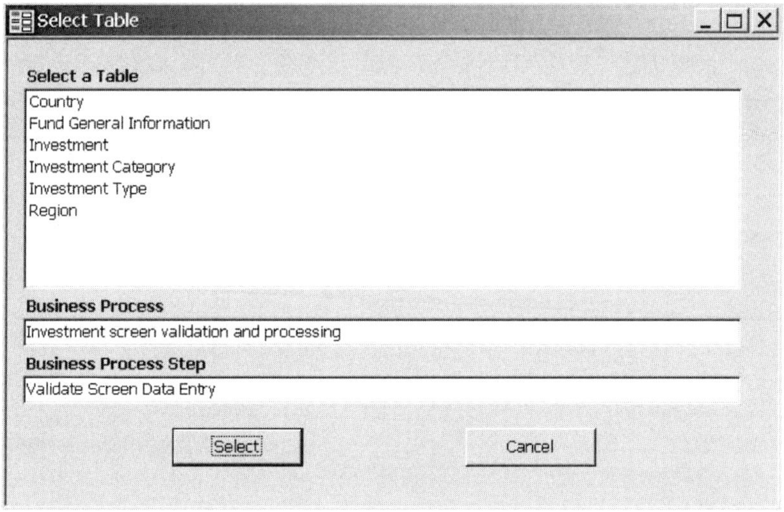

FIGURE 8.14
Select a Table

model. Second, it is not really the data model that is changing in the case of alternate business names being given to entities. In fact, these kinds of aliases are things that many data modeling tools cannot support—they tend to allow only one business name per entity. As we shall see in later chapters, there is a great deal of metadata management functionality that is not supported by data models in general. Therefore, these issues have to be dealt with in the business rules engine itself.

In the sample application, screens have been built to permit table metadata to be edited. If the menu option **Database Maintenance** is selected, and then **Edit Database Tables** from the popup that appears, the user will be asked to select a Business Process and then a Business Process Step. After that, the screen shown in Figure 8.14 will be displayed.

The reasons why Business Process and Business Process Step have to be chosen first is to provide a meaningful drill down for business users, something that will be discussed more in Chapter 12. The screen shown in Figure 8.14 shows all tables associated with a business process step. When the user selects one of these tables, the screen shown in Figure 8.15 appears.

This screen permits users to update the business name of a table (*Entity Name* in the **Table** entity), and the definition of a table (*Entity Definition*). The user can also select whether a table is a reference data table or not (*Table Reference Table Indicator*). The physical name of a table (*Table Physical Name*) cannot be changed on this screen.

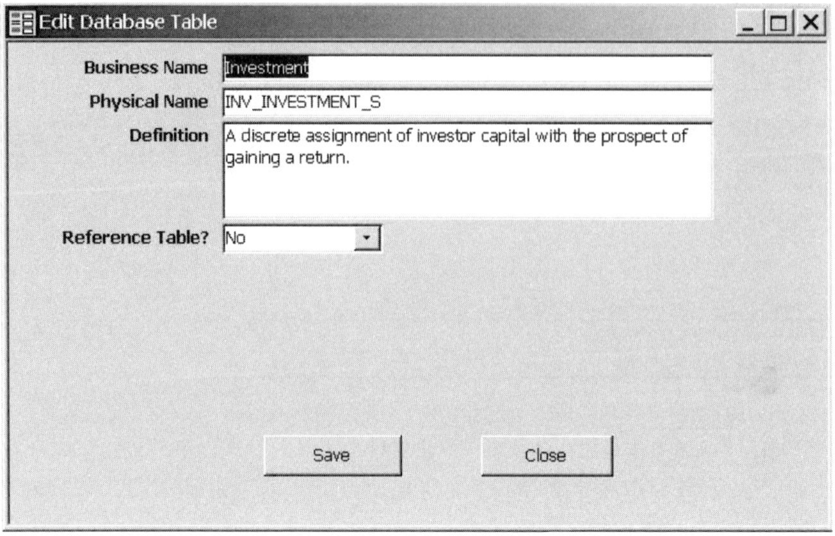

FIGURE 8.15
Edit Table Screen

The screen in Figure 8.15 can be extended to include additional user-defined metadata about tables, as will be seen in subsequent chapters.

Conclusion

At this point, a rather simple Table entity has been created in the Repository data model and implemented as the physical table **TAB_TABLE_M** in the sample application's Business Rules Repository. Relevant metadata about tables has been imported from a data model and used to populate **TAB_TABLE_M**. However, tables are just the beginning, and there is a great deal more metadata that has to be put into the Business Rules Repository before it can be used to define business rules. In the next chapter we shall discuss how column data is treated in the Repository.

9 POPULATING COLUMN DATA IN THE REPOSITORY

In the previous chapter the **Table** entity of the Business Rules Repository was designed, implemented, and populated. It is represented by the table **TAB_TABLE_M** in the physical database of the repository. The next type of metadata that has to be dealt with is the information about the columns that are contained in all database tables. These too must be included in the repository. The Business Rules Repository must be able to hold metadata about the columns that are used to contain business-relevant data.

If any data model is examined at the logical level, it can be seen that each entity has attributes. When a physical database is implemented, the entities are represented by tables and the attributes by columns. In this chapter we will discuss the structure of the entities needed to capture column information. Information at both the logical level, such as names and descriptions, and at the physical level, such as datatypes, needs to be stored and made available to the business rules engine. There tends to be a lot more information about a column than there is for a table. This means that the entities needed to store column data are quite extensive in terms of the number of attributes they contain, and the number of records that will end up in the physically implemented tables is also greater.

The first step is to design the main entity to hold column information in the Business Rules Repository. This entity is called **Column**, and its basic design is covered in the following section. After that, the means by which the physically implemented **Column** table can be populated from a data model are discussed. However, it should be clearly understood that what is discussed in this chapter are the most basic aspects needed to capture column metadata in the Business Rules Repository. The design discussed here must inevitably be extended as the functionality of a business rules engine expands. As we shall see in subsequent chapters, one of the main drivers to extend this design is increasingly complex rule types.

Column Entity

A **Column** entity is required to hold basic information about the columns that contain data relevant to the business. In the sample application it is physically implemented as a database table called **COL_COLUMN_M**. This follows the naming conventions for tables discussed in the previous chapter. An immediate question for the **Column** entity is if it should be a dependent entity of the **Table** entity—that is, should there be an identifying relationship with **Table** as the parent and **Column** as the child? If **Column** were made a dependent entity, this would mean making the primary key of the **Table** entity part of the primary key of the **Column** entity. By contrast, making the relationship from **Table** to **Column** a nonidentifying relationship means that the primary key of **Table** will end up in the nonkey area of **Column**.

There are valid arguments on both sides. Some people say that an attribute depends both for its existence and identification on an entity—it cannot exist without an entity. This favors an identifying relationship between **Table** and **Column**. Other people say that attributes exist by themselves, and we merely classify them into entities. What is undeniable is that it is better if there is a single column primary key for the physically implemented **Column** table (**COL_COLUMN_M**). This makes it much easier to build a business rules engine, because so much of the rules engine's functionality requires manipulating column metadata without needing to refer to the associated table metadata. Thus, for the approach in this book the **Column** entity has a primary key with a single attribute—*Column ID*. The reader may wish to adopt a different design, where the relationship between the two is an identifying one. This may be advantageous in the reader's particular situation, and it is a valid approach.

Column ID

The need to identify each column with a *Column ID* closely parallels the discussion of *Table ID* in the previous chapter. There must be a primary key, which could be the physical name of the column—*Column Physical Name*—which can be retrieved from the data model of the business area. However, if there are problems about knowing all the values of *Column Physical Name* on a timely basis, or if *Column Physical Name* is subject to unpredictable change, then it is best to use a surrogate key—*Column ID*—as an attribute of the **Column** entity and use it as the primary key.

Unfortunately, it is not possible to know about the values of *Column Physical Name* on a timely basis. This is because there has to be a need to permit users to extend the database by adding new columns to it. In this respect, columns differ from tables. It can reasonably be expected that all tables are present in a data model of the business area, and that there will be no reason to add more tables after the business rules engine is running. Columns, by contrast, are associated very closely with business rules, and quite often a new rule requires a new column.

It is therefore necessary to introduce *Column ID* as a surrogate key. It should be a meaningless code and have no intelligence built into the values assigned to it. The internal key of any data modeling tool from which metadata is extracted should not be used either. The business rules engine must be able to add more records to the physical **COL_COLUMN_M** table without having to check for uniqueness of values with a separate data modeling application.

Using *Column ID* implies that there will be only one place in the Business Rules Repository where *Column Physical Name* values can be found—in the **Column** entity. However, in a very few instances in the Business Rules Repository this design is changed so that *Column Physical Name* appears in additional places. These denormalized constructs help with building rules engine functionality.

In the design used here, *Column ID* is the primary key of the **Column** entity. *Column Physical Name* occurs in the **Column** entity as a nonkey attribute. Furthermore, *Column ID* is a simple sequence number. This design approach means that all child entities of **Column** will have *Column ID* migrated into them. It also avoids problems that may arise from having a large number of characters in key fields in the physical tables of the Business Rules Repository. *Column Physical Names* often exceed 30 characters in length, and in some applications may be more than 60 characters in length. This could potentially cause problems for **COL_COLUMN_M**, the physical implementation of the **Column** table, because some databases have problems with key fields of this length. *Column ID* will be implemented with a physical name of COL_C, a datatype of Character and length of 4. This will allow many thousands of attributes to be defined.

Column Physical Name

From a business rules perspective, *Column Physical Name* is perhaps the single most important attribute in the entire Business Rules Repository. It must contain the physical column name used for the column it describes. This immediately leads to the issue of naming conventions for database columns. A complete treatment of naming conventions is beyond the scope of this book, but we do have to pay some attention to the conventions for *Column Physical Name*.

Just as there had to be a size limit for *Table Physical Name*, so one is needed for *Column Physical Name*. It should be constructed so that it does not exceed the size limits of the commonly used database management systems. Long names are unwieldy in any case, especially for programmers and others who actually have to use these names in discussions.

A value of *Column Physical Name* should help the people who use it as much as possible, without causing problems for its usage within a computerized application. Many enterprises already have standards for column names, and it may be a requirement to use them. Obviously, an organization cannot enforce this for software packages that it purchases. However, organizations do like to see that some form of naming convention has been used by these packages.

The standard used in this book is as follows:

- A column name cannot exceed 30 characters.

- A column name consists of three nodes, joined by underscores.

- The first node is the first node of the physical name of the highest-level table where the column is defined. For example, the column INV_C is defined in the table **INV_INVESTMENT_M**. A nonkey column should only be found in one table. However, a primary key column may be migrated into other tables as a result of relationships with them. Thus, even though INV_C is migrated into other tables, the first node is always "INV" in the names of all these foreign key attributes.

- The second node is a description of the information held in the column. It should be an abbreviation of *Attribute Logical Name* (see below). There are many methods for abbreviating texts, but it is important that abbreviations be consistent. If the same word is abbreviated to form part of one *Column Physical Name* for one table, then it should be abbreviated the same way when it is used in other *Column Physical Names*.

  Some people like to break up the second node by introducing underscores. This is fine if it does not take up too much space.

- The third and final node is a single character that identifies what kind of data we are dealing with. This classification is shown in Table 9.1. It is broadly based on datatype, but is considerably extended. Many enterprises have already implemented schemes for classifying columns. These may take up more than the single character used here, and they may be much more detailed. Obviously, if such a standard exists within an enterprise where the repository is being built, then it should be used.

- Only capital letters, digits, and underscores can be used to construct values in *Column Physical Name*. This tends to make column names stand out. Some technical staff feel strongly that there are other ways of achieving this, such as mixtures of upper and lower cases. Such design decisions are fine if they meet defined requirements or overall goals. However, they should not be driven simply by what the designers feel comfortable with.

COLUMN CLASSIFICATION CODE	DESCRIPTION
C	A code used in a primary key, irrespective of datatype—for example, it can be character or numeric. The code can be a surrogate key internally assigned by the system, or it can be an "id" assigned by the enterprise: Account ID could be "ACCT_ID_C".
N	A count of something.
D	A date.
A	A financial amount.
Y	A year.
P	A percentage.
Q	A quantity, that is, an amount that is not financial.
M	A month.
I	An indicator, flag, or Boolean column.
R	A ratio.
T	A name or other descriptive text.

TABLE 9.1 Classification of Column Types

Using these conventions, we can assign a column name to the attribute *Column Physical Name* of the entity **Column**—COL_PHYSNAME_T.

Datatype

The datatype of the column is something that needs to be known in many circumstances for a business rules engine. For instance, it often plays a role in code generation algorithms. Unfortunately, datatypes are somewhat specific to each database management system. If the rules engine being built is only intended to work with one such database product, there is not much of a problem. However, if the rules engine has to work with more than one database product, things can get tricky.

Datatypes have other issues as well. Some datatypes belong to higher-level categories, such as the numeric ones. Others are subtypes with their own special characteristics—for example, character datatypes usually have a length. These issues contribute to the complexity of modeling datatype in the repository.

A basic design for **Datatype** is shown in Figure 9.1.

The designer might question the need to separate *Datatype Code* and *Datatype Name*. They are not necessarily the same thing. The problem is that different database servers use the same value of *Datatype Name* to mean different things. For example, "Text" in Microsoft Access is a character datatype that can be up to 250

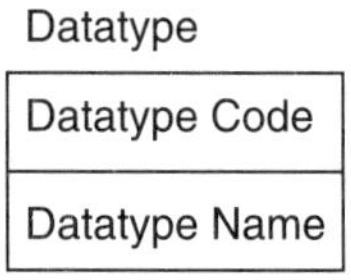

Datatype

Datatype Code
Datatype Name

FIGURE 9.1
Basic **Datatype** Entity

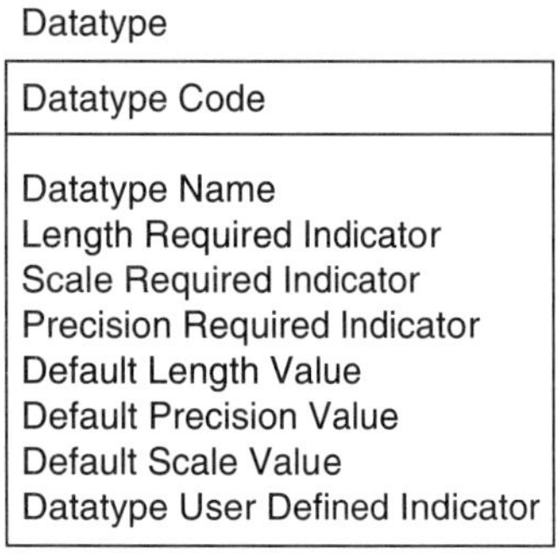

Datatype

Datatype Code
Datatype Name   Length Required Indicator   Scale Required Indicator   Precision Required Indicator   Default Length Value   Default Precision Value   Default Scale Value   Datatype User Defined Indicator

FIGURE 9.2
Fully Attributed **Datatype** Table

characters long, whereas in Microsoft SQL Server 2000, "Text" represents a memo-type datatype that can hold much larger blocks of textual information. Another reason for taking this design approach is that it will also permit user-defined datatypes, something quite useful for a business rules engine.

The design in Figure 9.1 needs some additional information. For each datatype there is a need to know whether a length, precision, and scale also need to be defined. This information is so that it can be used in functionality that allows users to extend the database, and in rules that validate data entry. Length is a concept for character type fields. Precision applies to numeric datatypes and is the total number of significant digits. Scale is the number of digits (if any) that follow a decimal point in a numeric datatype. Thus, a numeric datatype of 12345.678 has a precision of 8 and a scale of 3.

It may also be necessary to put into the **Datatype** entity a default length, scale, and precision for each datatype that is defined. Obviously these should only be populated with values if the datatype has a corresponding length, precision, or scale.

One other component needed is to be able to have user-defined datatypes. In this book frequent use is made of indicators—columns that are one character in length and which have a value of "Y" for True or Yes, and "N" for False or No. At a minimum, it is necessary to know whether a particular datatype is user-defined or not. The attribute *Datatype User Defined Indicator* makes this possible.

This yields a design for the **Datatype** entity like that shown in Figure 9.2.

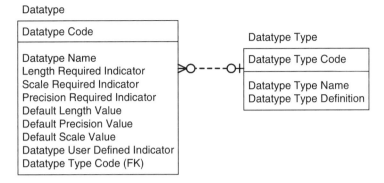

FIGURE 9.3
Datatype Type

Some data modelers may object to this design, saying that datatype is really something that is specific to a database server such as Access or Oracle. This would argue for making **Datatype** a child of a **Database Server** entity. It would solve the problem of identically named datatypes being different things in different databases (like "Text" in Access and SQL Server). However, it would also make the repository design presented here more complex, and it would be unnecessary unless there is a need to deal with multiple different database servers. It is therefore not used in the design presented here. Nevertheless, designers may find that they have to introduce a **Database Server** entity and make **Datatype** a child of it.

One other issue that needs to be dealt with is the requirement to classify datatypes into groupings that are needed for the rules engine. Figure 9.3 shows the introduction of the entity **Datatype Type** for this purpose.

Datatype Type is implemented as a lookup-type reference table called **DTTP_DTPTYPE_R**. Its primary purpose is to categorize datatypes to simplify processing for the rules engine. For instance, Microsoft Access has datatypes with names such as "integer," "long integer," "single," and "decimal." These are all numeric datatypes, capable of being used in arithmetic expressions. From the rules engine's perspective it is simpler to classify them with a *Datatype Type Code* of "numeric," and then deal with columns on the basis of **Datatype Type** rather than **Datatype**. Table 9.2 shows the values that are used to populate **Datatype Type**.

The next consideration for the Business Rules Repository design is how to relate **Datatype** and **Datatype Type** to the **Column** entity. Figure 9.4 shows the design.

Figure 9.4 has a denormalized construct in it—**Datatype Type** has been related to **Column**. The reason for this is that, as we will see in later chapters, the business rules engine often cares much more about **Datatype Type** than about **Datatype**, and it is necessary to have this information readily available when the rules engine accesses **Column** data.

DATATYPE TYPE CODE	DATATYPE TYPE NAME	DATATYPE TYPE DEFINITION
CHAR	Character	All character type datatypes, such as "Char" or "Varchar". These can hold any character, but require a maximum length to be specified.
DATE	Datetime	Any datatype that holds date or date plus time data.
INDICATOR	Indicator	A special datatype that we define. It is a one-character datatype, with possible values of "Y" for Yes (or True) or "N" for No (or False).
MEMO	Memo	Any datatype that can hold an unlimited amount of text (or an amount that is very large and subject only to some maximum defined by the database server).
NUMERIC	Numeric	Any datatype that holds only numbers and can be used to perform arithmetic.

TABLE 9.2 Records in Physical Implementation of **Datatype Type**

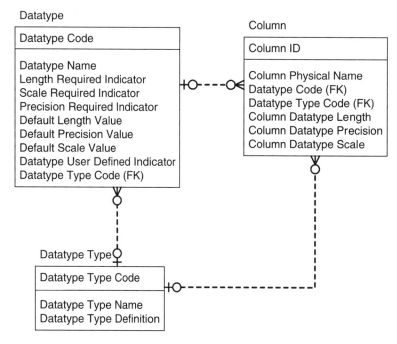

FIGURE 9.4
Column and Datatype

Column Datatype Length

Column Datatype Length is something that should be included in the **Column** entity. It is the length that is specified when a column is created in the database. Only certain datatypes need to have a value for datatype length. The attribute *Length Required Indicator* in the **Datatype** entity specifies whether *Column Datatype Length* should be populated. For example, in Microsoft Access it is not necessary to specify *Column Datatype Length* for a "Memo" datatype.

Column Datatype Length may also mean different things for different datatypes. In Microsoft SQL Server, the *Column Datatype Length* for a "Varchar" datatype means the maximum number of characters that can be stored in a column, not the actual length of the column in bytes (even when a string of the maximum size is stored). Although this is a fact, it does not appear to be relevant for business rules, and it is not considered further. However, it is not impossible that this could be an issue for some designers, and if so they will have to accommodate it.

The reason that *Column Datatype Length* should be included in the **Column** entity is that it may be necessary for users to create additional columns, and this may be one of the required pieces of information.

Precision and Scale

Precision and scale only apply to numeric columns. Precision is the total number of digits that can be found on both sides of the decimal point, which really defines the biggest number that the column can hold. Scale is the number of digits to the right of the decimal point. Thus, *Column Datatype Precision* and *Column Datatype Scale* have been introduced into the **Column** entity.

The value of these items of metadata is that they can be used in business rules—for example, to control the maximum values entered into a field on a screen.

Attribute Logical Name

Attribute Logical Name is the business name for the column. It is a logical-level construct, rather than a physical-level one, and is information gathered by analysts or data modelers rather than by programmers or DBAs. This attribute is extremely important in any business rules application, because the *Attribute Logical Names* identify data in business rules. Sometimes these names can be long, and there may be a need to store both an "official" long name, and an unofficial "short" or "working" name. In these cases, a separate attribute called *Attribute Short Name* can be added to the **Column** entity. The word *short* is particularly significant in this context because if the length is kept within a standard maximum size, then it may be possible to use this attribute on screens and reports where space is always an issue.

It is very important to have a complete and accurate value for *Attribute Logical Name.* It should be what the column is called by business users. If designers deviate from this, then users will not be able to recognize what the column is when they come across it or try to search for it. This can conflict somewhat with the desire to have standard *Attribute Logical Names.* For instance, a common approach is to prefix every attribute with the name of the entity to which it belongs. Thus, every attribute of the **Customer** entity would start with the word "Customer"—for example, *Customer ID, Customer First Name, Customer Last Name, Customer Date of Birth.* This kind of naming convention is very helpful to data administrators, DBAs, programmers, and other IT staff. Most of the time it is no problem to users, and indeed it can often help them. Occasionally, however, it may be confusing. This is particularly true for an attribute that is technical in business terms, that is, it consists of business jargon. If such an attribute is called something by users, this may be the only name they have ever used to identify it. Renaming it to conform to some data administration standard may cause a problem. Even if the user-given name is inconsistent, it is better to preserve it rather than substitute something that is theoretically more accurate, but unfamiliar to users.

There can, of course, be another extreme where users have really confusing names for things, such as when they use homonyms—one name that can refer to two or more completely different columns, depending on the context in which it is used. In such cases, there may need to be an insistence on using clearer names. If this is not done, users may be unable to distinguish different meanings of the homonyms when they encounter them in the rules engine. This is quite common for columns such as currency codes. Sometimes database tables can have many financial amount columns, and each financial amount column has an associated currency. To the extent possible, the name of each currency column should indicate which financial amount column it is associated with. It should not be just "Currency."

Attribute Definition

Attribute Definition is another important piece of information needed for the **Column** entity. It is often neglected, perhaps because the effort to collect it seems too great, or perhaps because no role can be seen for it at the programming level. Yet *Attribute Definition* is very useful. Users can look at it to decide whether they have correctly identified the column they were looking for. *Attribute Definitions* can also contain information that is very useful in understanding the limits of business rules that can be built around the columns they represent.

Although they are necessary, compiling good *Attribute Definitions* can be a daunting task. In many organizations the data administration function is responsible for *Attribute Definitions* and may already have a repository containing them. In fact, it can be a real problem for a business rules implementation project if *Attribute Defin-*

itions are not available in this way. Collecting *Attribute Definitions* can be very time consuming and even controversial. Enterprises often have difficulty agreeing on such things as when a *Customer ID* can be assigned so that a person is formally recognized as a customer—and this is only one aspect of the definition of *Customer ID*. The reality is that a project to implement a business rules engine must be able to handle *Attribute Definition* within a reasonable period of time. This can be done by:

- Obtaining *Attribute Definitions* from another source, such as a repository maintained by data administration.

- Working in a business area where there are a limited number of attributes.

- Not going into great depth to collect *Attribute Definitions*.

As noted above, the last option is risky. The need to deal with *Attribute Definitions* highlights the fact that a project to build a business rules engine is more likely to be successful in an enterprise that has a mature data administration function. Such a project cannot be simply regarded as another "programming" project.

Not only must *Attribute Definitions* be complete and accurate, they must also be kept up to date. It is possible for *Attribute Definitions* to change as enterprises grow and develop. Monitoring this kind of change may be the responsibility of the data administration function in an organization. It should be noted that if the semantic meaning of an attribute changes, the business rules built around the attribute may also need to change.

Having *Attribute Definition* readily available within the Repository can also be useful when implementing "Help" functionality, or for producing documentation. The definitions often appear in multiple places in traditional systems, and are frequently different in each location, which causes confusion. Having *Attribute Definition* in one place can prevent this.

Primary Key Indicator

It is very important for rules engines that interact with databases to know which columns of a table make up the primary key. For instance, this is needed when data is moved between tables, such as in rules that calculate aggregate data. Therefore, the Repository must track whether a particular column is used as a primary key in the table where it occurs. This information is housed in *Column Primary Key Indicator* (COL_PK_I) in the **Column** table. COL_PK_I is a Text (1) column in the sample application with a value of "Y" if the column is a primary key column, and a value of "N" if it is not.

Foreign Key Indicator

Similarly, it is important for rules engines to know if a column is a foreign key. This, too, must be stored in the Business Rules Repository. It is placed in *Column Foreign*

Key Indicator (COL_FK_I) in the **Column** table. COL_FK_I is a Text (1) column in the sample application with a value of "Y" if the column is a foreign key column, and a value of "N" if it is not.

User-Defined Column Indicator

Business rules engines inevitably require that users must be able to extend the database by adding columns, as we shall see in later chapters. This means that there must be a way to distinguish columns defined by users from those that come from a data model produced by IT professionals. It is always possible that the data model can be updated after users have defined new columns. If this is done there will be a need to reimport data model data, and it is important not to lose any information about user-defined columns when this happens. A reasonable design approach is to create a *Column User Defined Indicator* in the **Column** table. This has a column name of COL_USERDEFINED_I and a datatype of Text (1) in the sample application. A value of "Y" means that the column has been defined by the user and does not come from the data model.

Table Physical Name

Every column is found in one table. It is necessary to identify this table, which is done by including *Table Physical Name* (TAB_PHYSNAME_T) in the **Column** entity. This is, of course, a foreign key from the **Table** entity.

Foreign Key Parent Table

If a column is a foreign key, the rules engine will need to know what the parent table is from which the foreign key has been migrated. This can be done by having another relationship with the **Table** entity to introduce the column *Foreign Key Parent Table* (TAB_FKPARENT_T).

Foreign Key Parent Column ID

If a column is a foreign key, then there must be a corresponding column in the parent table. The rules engine will need to know what this is. This requires knowing the *Column ID* of the corresponding column in the parent table. The column *Foreign Key Parent Column ID* holds this information and requires a recursive nonidentifying relationship for the **Column** entity.

Foreign Key Parent Column Physical Name

Foreign Key Parent Column ID contains the value of *Column ID* for the parent column of a foreign key. Yet the rules engine will often need the physical name of the column

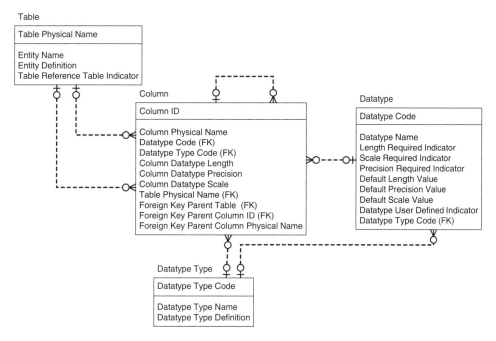

FIGURE 9.5
Review of Design for the **Column** Entity

as well. For efficiency, the *Column Physical Name* of the *Foreign Key Parent* Column is also stored as a distinct column called *Foreign Key Parent Column Physical Name.* This is a denormalized design construct, but is needed to aid rules engine functionality.

Design Review

Figure 9.5 shows the design for the part of the Business Rules Repository that centers on the **Column** entity.

Table 9.3 shows the structure of **COL_COLUMN_M**, the physical implementation of the **Column** entity.

Table 9.4 shows the structure of **DTP_DATATYPE_M**, the physical implementation of the **Datatype** entity.

Table 9.5 shows the structure of **DTTP_DTPTYPE_M**, the physical implementation of the **Datatype Type** entity.

At this point the basic design of the entities that hold column information is complete. The next step is to import data from a data model to populate the physical tables that represent these entities.

ATTRIBUTE LOGICAL NAME	COLUMN PHYSICAL NAME	COLUMN DATATYPE
Column ID	COL_C	Character (4)
Column Physical Name	COL_PHYSNAME_T	Character (30)
Datatype Code	DTP_C	Character (10)
Datatype Type Code	DTTP_C	Character (10)
Column Datatype Length	COL_DTPLEN_N	Integer
Column Datatype Precision	COL_DTPPRECISION_N	Integer
Column Datatype Scale	COL_DTPSCALE_N	Integer
Table Physical Name	TAB_PHYSNAME_T	Character (30)
Foreign Key Parent Table	TAB_FKPARENT_T	Character (30)
Foreign Key Parent Column ID	COL_PARCOLUMN_C	Character (4)
Foreign Key Parent Column Physical Name	COL_PARPHYSNAME_T	Character (30)

TABLE 9.3 Structure of **COL_COLUMN_M (Column)** Table

ATTRIBUTE LOGICAL NAME	COLUMN PHYSICAL NAME	COLUMN DATATYPE
Datatype Code	DTP_C	Character (10)
Datatype Type Code	DTTP_C	Character (10)
Datatype Name	DTP_NAME_T	Character (50)
Length Required Indicator	DTP_LENREQ_I	Character (1)
Scale Required Indicator	DTP_SCALEREQ_I	Character (1)
Precision Required Indicator	DTP_PRECISIONREQ_I	Character (1)
Datatype Default Length	DTP_DFTLEN_N	Integer
Datatype Default Scale	DTP_DFTSCALE_N	Integer
Datatype Default Precision	DTP_DFTPRECISION_N	Integer
Datatype User Defined Indicator	DTP_USERDEFINED_I	Character (1)

TABLE 9.4 Structure of **DTP_DATATYPE_M (Datatype)** Table

ATTRIBUTE LOGICAL NAME	COLUMN PHYSICAL NAME	COLUMN DATATYPE
Datatype Type Code	DTTP_C	Character (10)
Datatype Type Name	DTTP_DESC_T	Character (80)
Datatype Type Definition	DTTP_DEFN_M	Memo

TABLE 9.5 Structure of **DTTP_DTPTYPE_M (Datatype Type)** Table

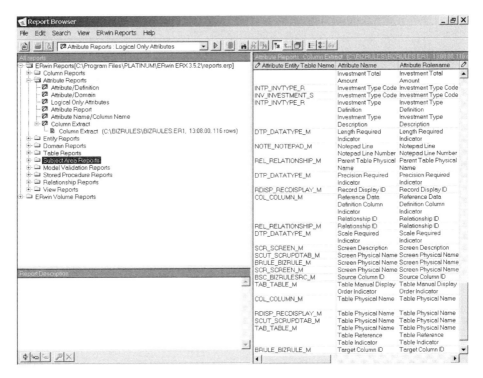

FIGURE 9.6
Generated Column Report in ERWin 3.5.2

Extracting Column Data from a Data Modeling Tool

As with table data in the previous chapter, we will base our example on Computer Associate's ERWin tool. Again, we will be using its report generator. Other data modeling tools and data dictionaries have similar report interfaces, so the mechanism we use to extract metadata from ERWin may be applicable—in a general way—in these other environments. Ideally, readers will be able to adapt what follows to their particular circumstances.

Two versions of ERWin are commonly used, Version 3.5.2 and Version 4.1 (also known as AllFusion ERWin Data Modeler). The approach required for each is somewhat different, as described in the following sections.

Create ERWin 3.5.2 Extract Report File

Open the data model with ERWin 3.5.2 and ensure that it is in logical view.

1. Click on **Tasks** in the main menu and then on **Generate Reports** . . . in the popup that appears. The ERWin Report Browser appears. A tree control like

that shown in Figure 9.6 appears and shows all the categories of reports that ERWin contains. Click on "Attribute Reports". We will need to create a new report.

2. Click on **File** in the main menu of the ERWin Report Browser and then on **New ERWin Report**. The ERWin Report Editor window appears. Provide a name for the new report— "Column Extract" has been used in this example. Select the report category "Attribute" and click **OK**. The new report will have been added to the list under the Entity Reports node of the tree control in the main window.

3. Right-click on the newly added Column Extract report and select the option **Edit ERWin Report Column Extract'**. The ERWin Report Editor opens again. The main window of the editor is a tree control called **Options** showing all the metadata that ERWin manages. We need to select the metadata we are going to use to populate **COL_COLUMN_M**. Click the following check boxes on the **Options** tree control:

    Under the Attribute node, click on the Entity node, click the Table node and then the check boxes for *Name*. This is the physical name of the table to which the attribute belongs.

    Back under the Attribute node, click the check boxes for *Name*, *Rolename*, *Definition, IS PK, IS FK*.

    Click on the Column node. Click the check box for *Name*. This is the physical column name. Also, click the check box for *Datatype*.

    Click **OK** to close the window.

4. Right-click again on the newly added Column Extract report and select the option **Execute ERWin Report Column Extract'**. The ERWin Report executes and places the results set in the right-hand side of the screen. A new entry appears in the tree control underneath the Column Extract node indicating that we have produced this results set, as shown in Figure 9.6.

5. Right-click on the new entry that has appeared in the tree control underneath the Column Extract node and select the option to export the results set.

6. A new window now appears with some options for the exported results set, as shown in Figure 9.7. Select HTML for the Export Format, Tabular with Duplicates for the Presentation, and File for Export to. Then click the **Export** button. You will be asked for a location to store the file containing the results set. Make sure it is saved as an HTML file. We have now created the report extract file. The next step is to import it into Microsoft Access and populate the **COL_COLUMN_M** table.

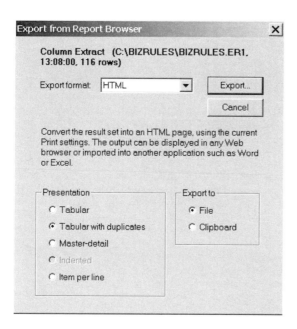

FIGURE 9.7
Results Set Export Options in ERWin 3.5.2

Create ERWin 4.1 Extract Report File

Open the data model with ERWin 4.1 and ensure that it is in logical view.

1. Click on **Tools** in the main menu, then on **Report Builder**, and then on **Report Builder** . . . in the popups that appear. The ERWin Report Templates window appears, as shown in Figure 9.8.

2. Click on the **New** . . . button in the Report Templates window. The Report Template Builder window now appears, as shown in Figure 9.9.

3. On the left of this window is a tree control called "Available Sections:" with the objects in the data model. Click on the Attribute node and press the arrow button to add it to the Report Layout area on the right.

4. Right-click on "Attribute" in the Report Layout area and click on **Properties** in the popup that appears. A window like that shown in Figure 9.10 appears.

5. On the Properties window, reveal the entire tree structure, then click the check boxes for *Name, Rolename, Definition, IS PK, IS FK.*

> Click on the Column node. Click the check box for *Name*. This is the physical column name. Also, click the check box for *Datatype*.

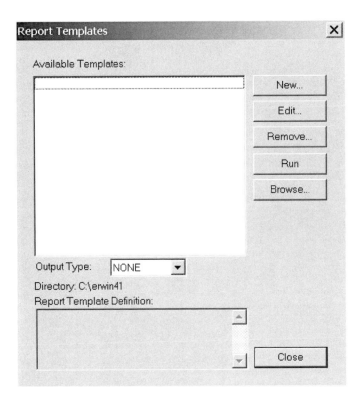

FIGURE 9.8
Report Templates Window in ERWin 4.1

Click on the Table node. Click the check box for *Name*. This is the physical table name.

6.   Close the Properties window. Back on the Report Template Builder window, right-click on the top line of the Report Layout area (i.e., the text "Document Untitled'). Select **Properties** on the popup that appears. The Report Properties window now appears, as shown in Figure 9.11.

7.   In the Report Properties window, select the Export tab. Select TEXT as the export type, and "Duplicates" in the Format section. Select "Comma Delimited" in the Delimiters section, and double quotes in the Text Qualifier section.

Select the Title tab and provide a report title, such as "Attribute Report".

Close the Report Properties window.

8.   Back on the Report Template Builder window, run the report by pressing the button with the downward-pointing arrow.

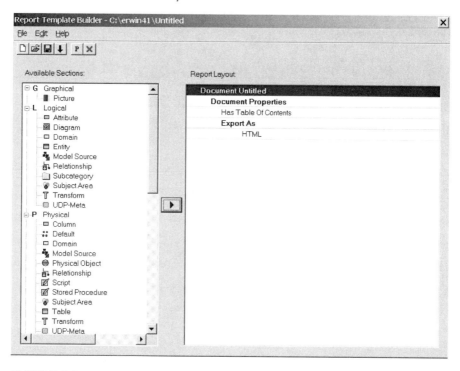

FIGURE 9.9
Report Template Builder Window in ERWin 4.1

9. A file with the extension ".CSV" will be created for this report. Excel may be invoked to display the contents of this file.

> Save the new report template. This will also save the ".CSV" file. It will be placed in the directory specified in the ERWin Report Templates window shown in Figure 9.8.

> The next step is to import it into Microsoft Access and populate the **COL_COLUMN_M** table.

Importing ERWin 3.5.2 Column Metadata into the Repository

If the report extract was produced using ERWin 3.5.2, it can now be imported into the Repository of the sample business rules application, bizrules.mdb. We will create a table called **IMPC_IMPORTCOL_M**. The very first time that the import is performed, this table is created. Afterward, we will always import the column metadata into this table. This process closely parallels that described in the previous chapter for database tables. See that chapter for more details on the Access screens that appear in the import process.

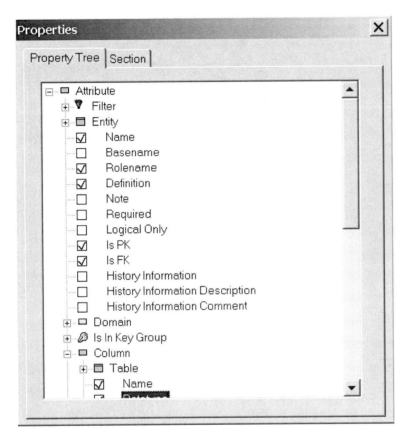

FIGURE 9.10
Object Properties Window in ERW 4.1

1. Open up the Microsoft Access file bizrules.mdb. Go to the Tables tab. Right-click in this area and select the **Import** option. This starts the Access import wizard.

2. A file selection dialog now appears. At the bottom is a combo box entitled "Files of type". Select the value for HTML files. Navigate to where you saved the report extract file form ERWin and select it.

3. The next screen that appears in the Access import wizard has a check box at the top of the screen that asks whether the first row contains column headings. It does, so check this box. Then click **Next**.

4. The next screen asks whether the file should be brought into a new table. For the very first time the import is done, indicate that it should be, and click **Next**.

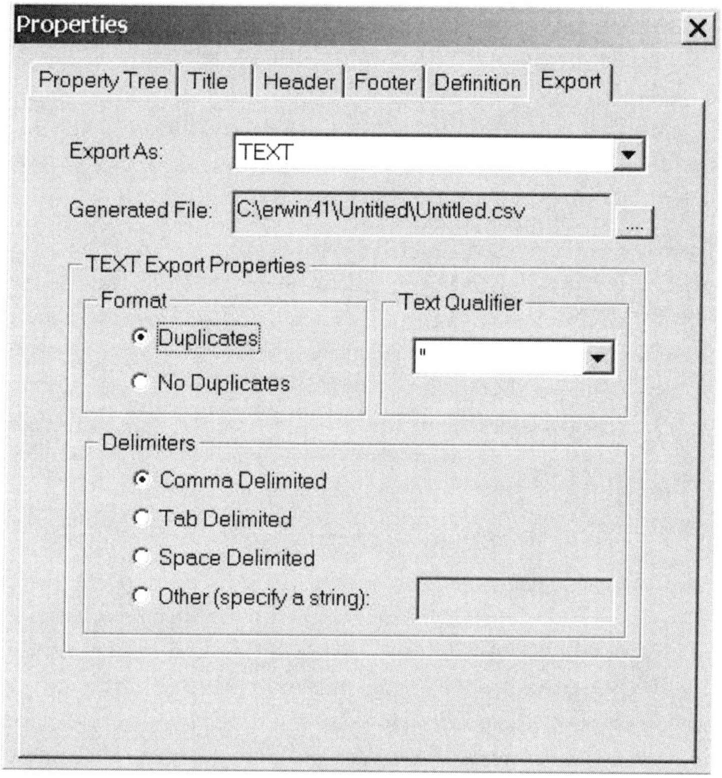

FIGURE 9.11
Report Properties Window in ERWin 4.1

For every time afterward that the import is done, indicate that the data will be imported into the table **IMPC_IMPORTCOL_M**. The import will then complete. The following steps only apply to the very first import.

5. The next screen is where you specify the datatypes for the data that is being imported. Access provides a default of Text (255) for all text fields. This is sufficient for most fields, but the *Attribute Definition* may be longer than this. Highlight the *Attribute Definition* field by clicking on it. Then select a datatype of Memo for it and press **Next**.

6. The next screen that appears asks if you want to let Access add its own primary key, or if you want to specify it. Choose the option to let Access add its own primary key and press **Next**.

7. The final screen of the import wizard now appears. It asks you to provide the name of the table. Give it a name of IMPC_IMPORTCOL_M. Then press

Finish. Access will now import the data. Access will report any errors to you. The most frequent one that happens is due to forgetting to make the *Attribute Definition* a memo field, which results in data truncation.

8. We need an extra field in this table. Go into **IMPC_IMPORTCOL_M** in design mode and add the column IMP_PROCESSED_I Text(1). This will be used when we import data to record which fields are processed.

After this first import is complete, subsequent imports are much simpler because we have set up **IMP_IMPORT_M**. When you perform subsequent imports, delete data from the table **IMPC_IMPORTCOL_M** and perform the import process again. Once you get to the point where you indicate to Access whether you want to import into a new or existing table, choose **IMPC_IMPORTCOL_M** as the target table. The import process will then be completed.

Importing ERWin 4.1 Column Metadata into the Repository

If the report extract was produced using ERWin 4.1, it can now be imported into the Repository of the sample business rules application, bizrules.mdb. We will create a table called **IMPC_IMPORTCOL_M**. The very first time that the import is performed, this table is created. Afterward, we will always import the column metadata into this table. This process closely parallels that described in the previous chapter for database tables. See that chapter for more details on the Access screens that appear in the import process.

1. Open up the Microsoft Access file bizengine.mdb. Go to the Tables tab. Right-click in this area and select the **Import** option. This starts the Access import wizard.

2. A file selection dialog now appears. At the bottom is a combo box entitled "Files of type". Select the value for Text files (which will include ".CSV" files). Navigate to where you saved the report extract file from ERWin 4.1 and select it.

3. The next screen that appears in the Access import wizard requires the type of file format to be specified. Select the "Delimited" type. Then click **Next**.

4. The next screen requires that the delimiter character be specified. Choose "comma" and make sure the Text Qualifier is set to double quotes. Then click **Next**.

5. The next screen asks whether the file should be brought into a new table. Indicate that it should be, and click **Next**.

6. The next screen is where you specify the field names and datatypes for the data that is being imported.

The field names that are provided are *Field1*, *Field2*, etc. Replace these names with *Attribute Entity Table Name*, *Attribute Name*, *Attribute Rolename*, *Attribute Definition*, *Attribute Is PK*, *Attribute Is FK*, *Attribute Column Name*, and *Attribute Column Datatype*.

Access provides a default of Text (255) for all text fields. This is sufficient for most fields, but the *Attribute Definition* may be longer than this. Highlight the *Attribute Definition* field by clicking on it. Then select a datatype of Memo. Then press **Next**.

7. The next screen that appears asks whether you want to let Access add its own primary key, or whether you want to specify it. Choose the option to let Access add its own primary key and press **Next**.

8. The final screen of the import wizard now appears. It asks you to provide the name of the table. Give it a name of IMPC_IMPORTCOL_M. Then press **Finish**. Access will now import the data and will report any errors to you. The most frequent error that happens is due to forgetting to make the *Attribute Definition* a memo field, which results in data truncation.

9. We need an extra field in this table. Go into **IMPC_IMPORTCOL_M** in design mode and add the column IMP_PROCESSED_I Text(1). This will be used when we import data to record which fields are processed.

After this first import is complete, subsequent imports are much simpler because we have set up **IMP_IMPORT_M**. When you perform subsequent imports, delete data from the table **IMPC_IMPORTCOL_M** and perform the import process again. Once you get to the point where you indicate to Access if you want to import into a new or existing tables, choose **IMPC_IMPORTCOL_M** as the target table. The import process will then be completed.

Updating the COL_COLUMN_M Table

With the metadata for tables now inside the **IMPC_IMPORTCOL_M** table in bizrules.mdb, we need to update **COL_COLUMN_M**. To do this we have to write some simple Access VB code, which is shown in Listing 9.1. This function does several things:

- It removes unnecessary spaces that may surround data from the import file.

- It determines whether any of the information that is being imported is for columns that the user has defined. This should never happen, and if it is detected, the process stops.

- Next, the imported data is examined to see if it contains duplicates. This can sometimes happen, depending on how data is extracted from the data

LISTING 9.1
Function to Populate Table **COL_COLUMN_M**

```
Private Function PopColumn() As String
'********************************************************************
' Populates the table COL_COLUMN_M with metadata imported from an
' external source and places it in the table IMPC_IMPCOLUMN_M.
'
' Parameters: None
'
' Returns: "Y" indicates successful completion
'********************************************************************

Dim rstCol As ADODB.Recordset, strSQL As String, lngAffected As
Long
Dim cmd As ADODB.Command, strLastTab As String, strLastCol As
String
Dim intError As Integer, strCol As String, strText As String
Dim strNextCol As String

    PopColumn = "Y"
    Set rstCol = New ADODB.Recordset
    Set cmd = New ADODB.Command
    cmd.ActiveConnection = CurrentProject.Connection
    cmd.CommandType = adCmdText

    ' Get rid of spaces that may surround data in the import file
    ' and set the Import Processed Flag to N
    strSQL = "UPDATE IMPC_IMPORTCOL_M SET " _
          & " [Attribute Entity Table Name] = Trim([Attribute
Entity Table Name]) " _
          & ", [Attribute Column Name] = Trim([Attribute Column
Name])  " _
          & ", IMP_PROCESSED_I = 'N' "
    cmd.CommandText = strSQL
    cmd.Execute lngAffected

    ' Make sure we are not trying to import columns that have
    ' already been defined by a user.  Abandon import if there are
    ' any such columns
```

```
    strSQL = "SELECT A.* FROM IMPC_IMPORTCOL_M A, COL_COLUMN_M B" _
        & " WHERE A.[Attribute Entity Table Name] =
B.TAB_PHYSNAME_T " _
        & " AND A.[Attribute Column Name] = B.COL_PHYSNAME_T " _
        & " AND B.COL_USERDEFINED_I = 'Y' "
    rstCol.Open strSQL, CurrentProject.Connection, _
        adOpenKeyset, adLockOptimistic, adCmdText
  If Not rstCol.EOF Then
    MsgBox "There are columns that are user-defined which are
replicated by " _
        & "the metadata being imported from the data model.  " _
        & "These issues must be resolved before the import can
proceed. " _
        & "The columns will now be listed."
    Do While Not rstCol.EOF()
      MsgBox rstCol("Attribute Entity Table Name") & " / " _
          & rstCol("Attribute Column Name")
      rstCol.MoveNext
    Loop
    MsgBox "Import Abandoned."
    rstCol.Close
    PopColumn = "N"
    Exit Function
  End If
  rstCol.Close

  ' Errors in the production of the import file may lead to
  ' contain duplicate records.  Detect these.  If they exist stop
    the import.
  strSQL = "SELECT * FROM IMPC_IMPORTCOL_M " _
        & " ORDER BY [Attribute Entity Table Name], " _
        & " [Attribute Column Name]   "
  rstCol.Open strSQL, CurrentProject.Connection, _
        adOpenKeyset, adLockOptimistic, adCmdText
  strLastTab = "!"
  strLastCol = "!"
  intError = 0
  Do While Not rstCol.EOF()
    ' You could delete the duplicates instead of issuing a
    ' warning message
```

```
    If strLastTab = rstCol("Attribute Entity Table Name") _
        And strLastCol = rstCol("Attribute Column Name") Then
      MsgBox "Duplicate Column in Import data.  Please resolve. " _
          & strLastTab & " / " & strLastCol
      intError = intError + 1
    End If
    strLastTab = rstCol("Attribute Entity Table Name")
    strLastCol = rstCol("Attribute Column Name")
    rstCol.MoveNext
  Loop
  rstCol.Close
  If intError <> 0 Then
    MsgBox "Import Abandoned."
    PopColumn = "N"
    Exit Function
  End If

  ' Update columns that are already recorded in COL_COLUMN_M
  strSQL = "SELECT A.*, B.COL_C FROM IMPC_IMPORTCOL_M A, 
COL_COLUMN_M B" _
        & " WHERE A.[Attribute Entity Table Name] = 
B.TAB_PHYSNAME_T " _
        & " AND A.[Attribute Column Name] = B.COL_PHYSNAME_T "
  rstCol.Open strSQL, CurrentProject.Connection, _
        adOpenKeyset, adLockOptimistic, adCmdText
  Do While Not rstCol.EOF
    strSQL = "UPDATE COL_COLUMN_M SET " _
          & " TAB_PHYSNAME_T = '" & rstCol("Attribute Entity 
Table Name") & "', " _
          & " COL_PHYSNAME_T = '" & rstCol("Attribute Column 
Name") & "', " _
          & " DTP_C = '" & TransImpDType(rstCol("Attribute Column 
Datatype"), "D") _
          & "', " _
          & " DTTP_C = '" & TransImpDType(rstCol("Attribute 
Column Datatype"), "T") _
          & "', "
    ' If Attribute Rolename is different from Attribute Basename,
    ' use it
    strText = Trim(rstCol("Attribute Name"))
    If strText <> Trim(rstCol("Attribute Rolename")) Then
```

```
        strText = Trim(rstCol("Attribute Rolename"))
      End If
      strSQL = strSQL & "COL_ATTLOGNAME_T = '" & strText & "', "
      strText = ""
      If Not IsNull(rstCol("Attribute Definition")) Then
        strText = Trim(rstCol("Attribute Definition"))
      End If
      If Trim(strText) <> "" Then
        strSQL = strSQL & "COL_ATTDEFN_M = '" & strText & "', "
      Else
        strSQL = strSQL & "COL_ATTDEFN_M = NULL, "
      End If
      strText = TransImpDType(rstCol("Attribute Column Datatype"),
  "L")
      If Trim(strText) <> "" Then
        strSQL = strSQL & "COL_DTPLEN_N = " & strText & ", "
      Else
        strSQL = strSQL & "COL_DTPLEN_N = NULL, "
      End If
      strText = TransImpDType(rstCol("Attribute Column Datatype"),
  "P")
      If Trim(strText) <> "" Then
        strSQL = strSQL & "COL_DTPPRECISION_N = " & strText & ", "
      Else
        strSQL = strSQL & "COL_DTPPRECISION_N = NULL, "
      End If
      strText = TransImpDType(rstCol("Attribute Column Datatype"),
  "S")
      If Trim(strText) <> "" Then
        strSQL = strSQL & "COL_DTPSCALE_N = " & strText & ", "
      Else
        strSQL = strSQL & "COL_DTPSCALE_N = NULL, "
      End If
      strText = "N"
      If UCase(Trim(rstCol("Attribute Is PK"))) = "YES" Then
        strText = "Y"
      End If
      strSQL = strSQL & "COL_PK_I = '" & strText & "', "
      strText = "N"
      If UCase(Trim(rstCol("Attribute Is FK"))) = "YES" Then
        strText = "Y"
```

```
      End If
      strSQL = strSQL & "COL_FK_I = '" & strText & "' "
      strSQL = strSQL & " WHERE COL_C = '" & rstCol("COL_C") & "'"
      cmd.CommandText = strSQL
      cmd.Execute lngAffected

      ' This flags the record so we know we have processed it
      rstCol("IMP_PROCESSED_I") = "Y"
      rstCol.Update

      rstCol.MoveNext
   Loop
   rstCol.Close

   ' Insert records into COL_COLUMN_M for columns
   ' that are not yet recorded in it
   strSQL = "SELECT * FROM IMPC_IMPORTCOL_M WHERE IMP_PROCESSED_I =
'N' " _
         & " ORDER BY [Attribute Entity Table Name]," _
         & " [Attribute Column Name]  "
   rstCol.Open strSQL, CurrentProject.Connection, _
         adOpenKeyset, adLockOptimistic, adCmdText
   Do While Not rstCol.EOF
      ' Get the next available Column ID
      strNextCol = GetNextColID()
      ' Insert a record for the new column
      ' Force the Column User Defined Indicator to be N because
      ' this column came from the data model—it is not user-defined
      strSQL = "INSERT INTO COL_COLUMN_M (COL_C, COL_USERDEFINED_I)
"  _
         & " VALUES ('" & strNextCol & "','N')"
      cmd.CommandText = strSQL
      cmd.Execute lngAffected

      strSQL = "UPDATE COL_COLUMN_M SET " _
         & " TAB_PHYSNAME_T = '" & rstCol("Attribute Entity
Table Name") & "', " _
         & " COL_PHYSNAME_T = '" & rstCol("Attribute Column
Name") & "', " _
         & " DTP_C = '" & TransImpDType(rstCol("Attribute Column
Datatype"), "D") _
```

```
              & "', " _
              & " DTTP_C = '" & TransImpDType(rstCol("Attribute
Column Datatype"), "T") _
              & "', "
     ' If Attribute Rolename is different from Attribute Basename,
     ' use it
     strText = Trim(rstCol("Attribute Name"))
     If strText <> Trim(rstCol("Attribute Rolename")) Then
        strText = Trim(rstCol("Attribute Rolename"))
     End If
     strSQL = strSQL & "COL_ATTLOGNAME_T = '" & strText & "', "
     strText = ""
     If Not IsNull(rstCol("Attribute Definition")) Then
        strText = Trim(rstCol("Attribute Definition"))
     End If
     If Trim(strText) <> "" Then
        strSQL = strSQL & "COL_ATTDEFN_M = '" & strText & "', "
     Else
        strSQL = strSQL & "COL_ATTDEFN_M = NULL, "
     End If
     strText = TransImpDType(rstCol("Attribute Column Datatype"),
"L")
     If Trim(strText) <> "" Then
        strSQL = strSQL & "COL_DTPLEN_N = " & strText & ", "
     Else
        strSQL = strSQL & "COL_DTPLEN_N = NULL, "
     End If
     strText = TransImpDType(rstCol("Attribute Column Datatype"),
"P")
     If Trim(strText) <> "" Then
        strSQL = strSQL & "COL_DTPPRECISION_N = " & strText & ", "
     Else
        strSQL = strSQL & "COL_DTPPRECISION_N = NULL, "
     End If
     strText = TransImpDType(rstCol("Attribute Column Datatype"),
"S")
     If Trim(strText) <> "" Then
        strSQL = strSQL & "COL_DTPSCALE_N = " & strText & ", "
     Else
        strSQL = strSQL & "COL_DTPSCALE_N = NULL, "
     End If
```

```
        strText = "N"
        If UCase(Trim(rstCol("Attribute Is PK"))) = "YES" Then
          strText = "Y"
        End If
        strSQL = strSQL & "COL_PK_I = '" & strText & "', "
        strText = "N"
        If UCase(Trim(rstCol("Attribute Is FK"))) = "YES" Then
          strText = "Y"
        End If
        strSQL = strSQL & "COL_FK_I = '" & strText & "' "
        strSQL = strSQL & " WHERE COL_C = '" & strNextCol & "'"
        cmd.CommandText = strSQL
        cmd.Execute lngAffected

        rstCol.MoveNext
    Loop
    rstCol.Close

    Set rstCol = Nothing
    Set cmd = Nothing

End Function
```

modeling tool. If duplicates are detected, the process stops. An alternative strategy would be to delete the duplicates and continue the process.

- The next step is to determine which columns in the imported data are already present in **COL_COLUMN_M**. These have their metadata updated.

- Last, information for columns not yet recorded in **COL_COLUMN_M** is processed. New records are added to **COL_COLUMN_M** for these columns.

All of this is fairly simple. The only complexity is parsing datatype information. A special function, shown in Listing 9.2, parses datatype information from the import file.

Screen Interface for Updating Table Metadata

As with table metadata, there may be a need to change column metadata after it has been imported into the Business Rules Repository. For instance, a column may be

LISTING 9.2
Function to Parse Datatype Metadata and Return Component Parts

```
 Public Function TransImpDType(strDataType as String, strAction as
String) As String
'********************************************************************
' Parses a datatype from a data model to return the component
' items of information.  What is returned depends on the action
' code strAction
'
' Parameters:
' strDataType = The datatype string
' strAction = Code that determines what will be returned
'               D = Standard datatype
'               L = Length
'               P = Precision
'               S = Scale
'               T = Datatype Type
'
' Returns: string with the requested information
'********************************************************************
Dim strType As String, strCategory As String, strLength As String,
strPrecision As String
Dim strScale As String, intBegin As Integer, intEnd As Integer,
intLen As Integer
Dim strText As String, intComma As String

   TransImpDType = "Unknown"
   strDataType = Trim(UCase(strDataType)) & " "

   strType = ""
   strLength = "0"
   strPrecision = "0"
   strScale = "0"
   strCategory = ""

   If Left(strDataType, 4) = "TEXT" Then
     strType = "TEXT"
     strCategory = "CHAR"
     intBegin = InStr(1, strDataType, "(")
     intEnd = InStr(1, strDataType, ")")
     intLen = intEnd-intBegin-1
```

```
      strLength = Mid(strDataType, intBegin + 1, intLen)
   End If

   If Left(strDataType, 4) = "MEMO" Then
      strType = "MEMO"
      strCategory = "MEMO"
   End If

   If Left(strDataType, 3) = "INT" Then
      strType = "INTEGER"
      strCategory = "NUMERIC"
   End If

   If Left(strDataType, 4) = "LONG" Then
      strType = "LONG"
      strCategory = "NUMERIC"
   End If

   If Left(strDataType, 6) = "DOUBLE" Then
      strType = "DOUBLE"
      strCategory = "NUMERIC"
   End If

   If Left(strDataType, 7) = "DECIMAL" Then
      strType = "DECIMAL"
      strCategory = "NUMERIC"
   End If

   If Left(strDataType, 7) = "NUMERIC" Then
      strType = "NUMERIC"
      strCategory = "NUMERIC"
   End If

   If Left(strDataType, 4) = "DATE" Then
      strType = "DATE"
      strCategory = "DATE"
   End If

   If Left(strDataType, 8) = "DATETIME" Then
      strType = "DATE"
```

```
    strCategory = "DATE"
End If


If Left(strDataType, 9) = "DATE/TIME" Then
  strType = "DATE"
  strCategory = "DATE"
End If


If strType = "DECIMAL" Or strType = "NUMERIC" Then
  intBegin = InStr(1, strDataType, "(")
  intEnd = InStr(1, strDataType, ")")
  intLen = intEnd-intBegin-1
  strText = Mid(strDataType, intBegin + 1, intLen)
  intComma = InStr(1, strText, ",")
  If intComma = 0 Then
    strPrecision = strText
  Else
    intLen = intComma-1
    strPrecision = Mid(strText, 1, intLen)
    intLen = intEnd-intComma-1
    strScale = Mid(strText, intComma + 1, intLen)
  End If
End If


If strType = "" Then
  MsgBox "Function TransImpDType: Cannot process " & strDataType
End If


If strAction = "D" Then      'Datatype
  TransImpDType = strType
End If
If strAction = "P" Then      'Precision
  TransImpDType = strPrecision
End If
If strAction = "S" Then      'Scale
  TransImpDType = strScale
End If
If strAction = "L" Then      'Length
  TransImpDType = strLength
End If
```

```
If strAction = "T" Then      'Datatype Type
    TransImpDType = strCategory
End If

End Function
```

known by one name in a particular organization, but called something quite different in another organization. In the sample application, screens have been built to permit column metadata to be edited. These screens are fully described in Chapter 13, which describes how the database on which the rules engine operates can be extended by the definition of new columns.

Conclusion

In this chapter, the **Column** entity and some related entities have been created to hold column information. These entities have been physically implemented as tables, and functionality has been created to populate them with data extracted from a data modeling tool. In the next chapter we will complete the basic Business Rules Repository by building the components needed to house relationship and subtype data.

10 POPULATING RELATIONSHIP AND SUBTYPE DATA IN THE REPOSITORY

The previous two chapters described how the Business Rules Repository can be designed to hold table and column metadata, and how this metadata can be extracted from a data model and loaded into the Repository. Relationships are the third major component of a data model that need to be dealt with. However, they are not quite as straightforward as tables and columns. Relationships are sometimes missing from data models. This is especially true if the data models are created through reverse-engineering from existing databases without declared foreign keys. Unfortunately, this is a problem for anyone building a business rules engine. As has been emphasized in earlier chapters, it is vital to have a data model of the business area on which the rules engine will operate. The rules engine must be able to navigate the database using metadata—primarily relationships—obtained from the data model.

The **Relationship** Entity

A **Relationship** entity needs to be added to the Business Rules Repository, in order to hold information about relationships. A relationship can be between two and only two entities—a parent entity and the child entity. Therefore, **Relationship** must hold information about these two entities. However, there can be more than one relationship between the same parent and child entities, so the parent and child entities alone cannot uniquely identify a relationship. Something else is required. In this situation a surrogate key such as a simple sequence number is a good candidate to uniquely identify relationships. This has been done in Figure 10.1, where the primary key column *Relationship ID* is a sequence number.

Relationships have names and are traditionally described by verb phrases. There can be one verb phrase for the parent-to-child aspect of the relationship and another

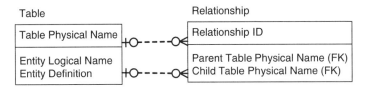

FIGURE 10.1
The Basic **Relationship** Entity

for the child-to-parent aspect. For example, there can be a relationship between **Investor** (the parent) and **Investment Position** (the child) with the parent-to-child verb phrase "purchases". The whole relationship is read as "Investor purchases Investment Position". The child-to-parent verb phrase could be "is held by", and the relationship from the child perspective would be read as "Investment Position is held by Investor". Because this information is captured in the data model, it should be stored in the **Relationship** table.

Frankly, verb phrases are often rather inadequate to describe the relationship. This is not necessarily the fault of the analysts involved. It is simply rather difficult to convey the meaning of a relationship in something that is less than a sentence, and where the names of two entities must be tacked onto the beginning and end. Perhaps because of this, there is a tendency to recycle the same verb phrases, such as "has," "belongs to," "is composed of," and so on. Such verb phrases seem to add so little to the model that they are frequently omitted by data modelers. What is required is a description or definition of the relationship, and in the **Relationship** entity *Relationship Definition* has been added for this purpose. It is this that enables an analyst, or a business user, to understand the purpose and nature of the relationship between the parent and child entities. The relationship should also have a name. *Relationship Name* serves this purpose in the **Relationship** entity. Names are needed for human operators to uniquely identify the relationship. A default *Relationship Name* can be created by using the parent-to-child verb phrase, prefixed by the parent entity name and suffixed by the child entity name. If, as is frequently the case, the verb phrase is missing, the names of the parent and child entities can be used to create a default *Relationship Name*. However, as we shall see, there needs to be a way to update *Relationship Name* in the Business Rules Repository.

One additional attribute that needs to be added to the **Relationship** entity is *Relationship From Data Model Indicator*. It indicates whether a relationship has been extracted from a data model. The purpose of this attribute is discussed more fully later in this chapter, in the sections that cover the manipulation of relationship metadata by users.

Figure 10.2 shows these additional components of the **Relationship** entity.

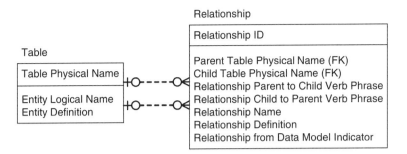

FIGURE 10.2
Relationship Entity with More Attributes

Relationship is physically implemented as the table **REL_RELATIONSHIP_M**. There are some more attributes that must be placed in **Relationship**, and these are discussed in the sections that follow. However, before examining these attributes, it is necessary to consider how to handle attributes that are migrated as part of the relationship.

The **Relationship Key Attribute** Entity

In a relationship the primary key attributes of the parent entity are migrated into the child entity. There is no reason why these attributes should have the same logical or physical names in the child entity, and often they do not. When attribute has a different logical name in the child entity than it has in the parent entity, this is called a *role name*. The name that the attribute has in the entity where it is first defined is the *base name*.

A reasonably easy way to deal with this is to populate *Attribute Logical Name* in the **Column** entity with the role name if one exists and is different from the base name. This is already done in the program logic that loads the **Column** (**COL_COLUMN_M**) table, as described in the previous chapter. This logic also creates a link between a column that is a foreign key and the corresponding column in the parent entity. Unfortunately, this is not sufficient for the management of relationships. What is needed is a design that permits the rules engine to quickly find all the columns that are involved in a particular relationship, and what these columns are called in both the parent and child entities.

This requirement can be met by introducing a new entity to store the information about the primary keys migrated from the parent entity. This new entity is called **Relationship Key Attribute** and has a primary key of *Relationship ID* plus *Parent Column ID*. It is shown in Figure 10.3.

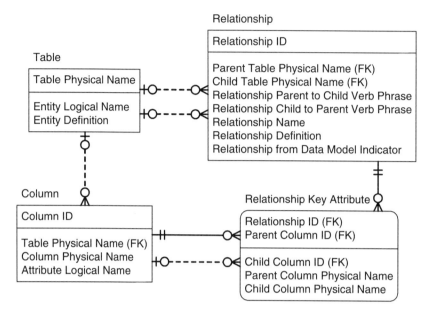

FIGURE 10.3
Relationship Key Attribute

In **Relationship Key Attribute**, *Parent Column ID* is the *Column ID* of the parent column that is migrated from the parent entity into the child entity. *Child Column ID* is the *Column ID* of the corresponding column in the child table, that is, the column that *Parent Column ID* becomes after it arrives in the child table.

One convenience introduced into **Relationship Key Attribute** in Figure 10.3 is two attributes, *Parent Column Physical Name* and *Child Column Physical Name*. These values exist in the **Column** table, in *Column Physical Name* for the two records for the parent column and corresponding child column. The reason for having them in **Relationship Key Attribute** is to have them immediately available for the rules engine when it accesses this table. This is, of course, a denormalized design construct. It is valuable because creating program logic for the rules engine to deal with relationships is rather complex. Having the physical names of the columns readily available in **Relationship Key Attribute** can help to reduce this complexity. Table 10.1 shows the structure of table **RKEY_RELKEYATT_M**, which is the physical implementation of **Relationship Key Attribute**.

Changes to Column Entity for Relationship Information

Two new entities, **Relationship** and **Relationship Key Attribute**, have been introduced to capture relationship information. However, the **Column** table also has to

ATTRIBUTE LOGICAL NAME	COLUMN PHYSICAL NAME	COLUMN DATATYPE
Relationship ID	REL_C	Character (4)
Parent Column ID	COL_PARENT_C	Character (4)
Child Column ID	COL_CHILD_C	Character (4)
Parent Column Physical Name	COL_PARPHYSNAME_T	Character (30)
Child Column Physical Name	COL_CHILDPHYSNAME_T	Character (30)

TABLE 10.1 Structure of Table **RKEY_RELKEYATT_M** (Relationship Key Attribute)

be extended to capture relationship information as well. This is necessary for those columns that are foreign keys, that is, have a corresponding column in a parent table. The rules engine must be able to quickly navigate to the parent table and extract information from it. Since this only applies to foreign keys it only affects metadata for the child entity in a relationship. There is no need to extend **Column** to deal with relationship information that concerns the parent entity of a relationship.

This requirement has already been met in the design described in the previous chapter, where the following attributes were added to the **Column** table.

- *Foreign Key Parent Table.* If a column is a foreign key, then this is the physical name (*Table Physical Name*) of the parent table.

- *Foreign Key Parent Column ID.* If a column is a foreign key, then this is the value of *Column ID* of the corresponding column in the parent table.

- *Foreign Key Parent Column Physical Name.* If a column is a foreign key, then this is the value of physical name (*Column Physical Name*) of the corresponding column in the parent table. Often the physical names are identical, but sometimes they are not.

Relationships and Hidden Subtypes

A major headache of dealing with relationships is that when they are defined in a data modeling tool, it is assumed that all records in the parent are related to all records in the child if they share the same values in the key columns migrated from the parent into the child. This is not always the case, and Figure 10.4 provides an example.

In Figure 10.4, an **Investor** buys into an **Investment** and thus establishes an **Investment Position**. For example, a wealthy individual may pay $2,000,000 to buy an 8% position in a shopping mall. The total contributed by all investors is $25,000,000, and the $2,000,000 represents 8% of this amount. Suppose that the partnership that manages the investment has to calculate taxes for investors at the end of each fiscal year. However, there are three types of **Investor**: Individual Investors,

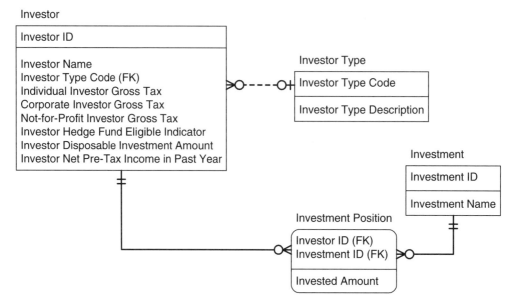

Investor

Investor ID
Investor Name Investor Type Code (FK) Individual Investor Gross Tax Corporate Investor Gross Tax Not-for-Profit Investor Gross Tax Investor Hedge Fund Eligible Indicator Investor Disposable Investment Amount Investor Net Pre-Tax Income in Past Year

Investor Type

Investor Type Code
Investor Type Description

Investment

Investment ID
Investment Name

Investment Position

Investor ID (FK) Investment ID (FK)
Invested Amount

FIGURE 10.4
Hidden Subtypes in Relationships

INVESTOR TYPE CODE (IRTP_C)	INVESTOR TYPE DESCRIPTION (IRTP_DESC_T)
INDIV	Individual Investor
CORP	Corporate Investor
NOTFORPR	Not-for-Profit Investor

TABLE 10.2 Different Types of Investor

Corporate Investors, and Not-for-Profit Investors. The definitions for these three types of investors is captured in three records in the **Investor Type** table (physically implemented as **IRTP_INVESTORTYPE_R**), as shown in Table 10.2.

Each of these types of investor has its gross tax calculated differently. This is reflected by three separate attributes for gross tax in the **Investment** entity. A separate business rule is needed to calculate the values for each of these attributes. Let us suppose that these business rules have to use the information in **Investor Position**. Perhaps for an Individual Investor, the business rules states that *Individual Investor Gross Tax* is 28% of the total of that investor's *Invested Amount*. By contrast, the rule for a Corporate Investor may state that Corporate Investor Gross Tax is only 9% of the total of that investor's *Invested Amount*. Unfortunately, it does not stop there. There will almost certainly be many more attributes in **Investor** that apply uniquely to each of the different types of investor, and business rules that work with these attributes. Yet the single relationship between **Investor** and **Investment Position** does not take any of this into account.

The reality is that there will be a set of business rules that only want to look at the relationship between **Investor** and **Investor Position** in terms of Individual Investors. There will be a similar set of rules that only want to look at this relationship in terms of Corporate Investors, and a third set that only want to look at it in terms of Not-for-Profit Investors. Thus, we are dealing with three subtypes of **Investor**. Yet this subtype has not been formally modeled in Figure 10.4. In fact, formal subtypes are rather rare in data models—in the author's experience nearly all models lack them. The problem is that it is nearly impossible to perform formal subtyping for all the subtypes that actually exist in a data model, because it will spawn an unmanageable set of additional entities (and tables in the physical database). Unfortunately, the reality is that very many subtypes really do exist in most data models. The subtypes only become evident in the physical database when one table has to be related to another. In traditional systems development projects, programmers hand-craft their program code in ways that recognize hidden subtypes. They create SQL statements that restrict the records selected from the parent and child tables to those that are members of the subtypes they wish to process. These SQL statements may have to be reproduced over and over again in the programming of a system. The origin of this complexity is only hazily understood by most participants in the systems development process. They simply think in terms of the need to get to the "right" records to do a certain piece of programming.

The net result is that relationships as they exist in a data model have limited use in describing the way in which the parent and the child behave together, and so have limited use for a business rules engine. The relationships are simply too general to be relevant to a lot of the business rules that a user will want to define.

This area is fraught with other problems. A major issue in the SQL statements used to join parent and child entities for these hidden subtypes is their potential for complexity. Programmers often need to create SQL statements with large WHERE clauses that test the values in several columns so the desired records can be picked out. Often these statements need to be replicated in many parts of a system, and there is always the danger that subtle differences can creep in so two statements may function in slightly different ways and yield different results. This need arises because there is nothing that labels or identifies a particular record in a table as belonging to a particular hidden subtype. Thus, the programmer is forced to repeat the tests that determine if a record does or does not belong to the subtype under consideration, and these tests must be performed on every record in the table.

This is all a considerable challenge for a business rules approach. Both the Business Rules Repository and the rules engine functionality must be designed to cope with it in ways that do not make it difficult for users to understand how to define business rules that work across relationships. The design adopted here is based on the following concepts:

- Every interaction of one hidden subtype in the parent entity with one hidden subtype in the child entity is viewed as a distinct relationship. The general relationships seen in data models are viewed as permitting all records in the parent to interact with all records in the child. If there is a need to restrict the records to those that belong to hidden subtypes, then additional relationships have to be created to deal with each hidden subtype.

- Hidden subtypes must be made explicit in the Business Rules Repository.

- Each hidden subtype must always be identified by one and only one value in one and only one column. This eliminates the need to create many highly complex WHERE clauses in SQL statements associated with many business rules. It also makes the hidden subtypes much more transparent; the records participating in each hidden subtype can easily be identified.

- Each column that identifies a hidden subset either must be the key of a lookup-type reference table or must be an indicator. In the design used here, an indicator is a Character (1) column with a value of "Y" meaning Yes or True, and any other value meaning No or False.

Following these concepts means that the Business Rules Repository must be enhanced to:

- Create a new entity called **Subtype**.

- Add more attributes into the **Relationship** entity in the Business Rules Repository to cope with hidden subtypes.

The Subtype Entity

Hidden subtypes are recorded in the **Subtype** entity in the Business Rules Repository, the structure of which is shown in Figure 10.5.

The **Subtype** entity has a primary key of *Subtype ID*, which is a surrogate key represented by a sequence number. The entity also has *Subtype Name*, which holds a name for the subtype that must clearly identify the subtype to a user. "Individual Investors" would be a reasonable name for a subtype. As noted above, the design calls for there to be one and only one column in the table where the hidden subtype is found that is used to identify the subtype. This column is termed *Subtype Discriminator Column ID*. It can either be a column that is a primary key of a lookup-type reference table, or an indicator column. Having this standard makes it much easier to implement the metadata engineering constructs needed to manipulate subtypes in the rules engine. Our standard for an indicator column is that it is a Character (1)

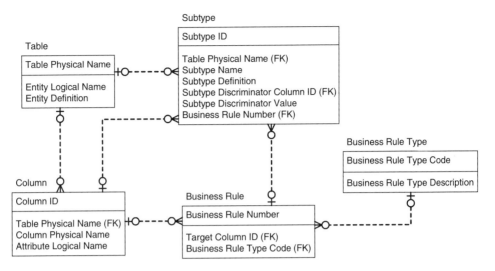

FIGURE 10.5
The **Subtype** Entity

column where "Y" means Yes or True. However, a primary key column of a lookup-type reference data table can potentially have many values. If one of these columns is selected as *Subtype Discriminator Column ID*, it is also necessary to state what value is used to identify the subtype. An example would be the value "INDIV", which corresponds to "Individual Investor," as shown in Table 10.2. The value is recorded in *Subtype Discriminator Value*. Also included in **Subtype** is **Table Physical Name**, which is the table that is being subtyped. This is an admitted denormalization (it can be deduced from *Subtype Discriminator Column ID*), but again makes it a lot easier to build rules engine functionality, as will be seen later.

The final attribute in **Subtype** is *Business Rule Number*. This is the business rule (if any) that is used to populate the column that identifies the subtype with the value that identifies the subtype. We may seem to be getting a little ahead of ourselves here by introducing business rules at this stage, but it is necessary. Each subtype will be identified by a particular value in a particular column that will be populated either (a) by data input by a user on a screen or (b) by logic—that is, by a business rule. Once the value has been populated it is very easy to see which record in a table belongs to which subtype.

Table 10.3 shows the physical implementation of the **Subtype** entity, which is the table **STP_SUBTYPE_M**.

Now let us consider an example of several subtypes that appear in Figure 10.4, all of them in the **Investor** table. The first three subtypes are "Individual Investor," "Corporate Investor," and "Not-for-Profit Investor." Each of these subtypes is

ATTRIBUTE LOGICAL NAME	COLUMN PHYSICAL NAME	COLUMN DATATYPE
Subtype ID	STP_C	Character (4)
Subtype Name	STP_NAME_T	Character (120)
Subtype Discriminator Column ID	COL_C	Character (4)
Subtype Discriminator Column Value	STP_DISCVALUE_T	Character (20)
Subtype Defintion	STP_DEFN_M	Memo
Table Physical Name	TAB_PHYSNAME_T	Character (50)
Business Rule Number	BRULE_NUMBER_C	Character (5)

TABLE 10.3 Structure of Table **STP_SUBTYPE_M** (Subtype)

SUBTYPE ID (STP_C)	SUBTYPE NAME (STP_NAME_T)	SUBTYPE DISCRIMINATOR COLUMN ID (COL_C)	SUBTYPE DISCRIMINATOR COLUMN VALUE (STP_ DISCVALUE_T)	BUSINESS RULE NUMBER (BRULE_ NUMBER_C)
0001	Individual Investor	0005	INDIV	
0002	Corporate Investor	0005	CORP	
0003	Not-for-Profit Investor	0005	NOTFORPR	

TABLE 10.4 Records in **STP_SUBTYPE_M** for the Three Subtypes of Investor Type

identified by different values of *Investor Type Code* (IRTP_C) in the **Investor** table, as shown in Table 10.2. *Investor Type Code* is, of course, a column and is represented by a record in the **Column** table (**COL_COLUMN_C**) in the Business Rules Repository. This record has a *Column ID* (COL_C) with a value of "0005." For each investor, the user determines which subtype the investor belongs to by selecting a value from a combo box on the screen where investor data is entered. Thus, all of these three subtypes are determined by user data entry, and not by the application of business rules. The records for the three subtypes in the **Subtype** table (**STP_SUBTYPE_M**) are shown in Table 10.4.

Now let us consider two other subtypes. An investor may or may not be eligible to participate in hedge funds. In the **Investor** table of the sample application, the column *Investor Hedge Fund Eligible Indicator* is set to "Y" if an investor is eligible, and it is set to "N" if an investor is not eligible. The U.S. government has rules for

SUBTYPE ID (STP_C)	SUBTYPE NAME (STP_NAME_T)	SUBTYPE DISCRIMINATOR COLUMN ID (COL_C)	SUBTYPE DISCRIMINATOR COLUMN VALUE (STP_DISCVALUE_T)	BUSINESS RULE NUMBER (BRULE_NUMBER_C)
0004	Hedge Fund Eligible Investor	0033	Y	R0020
0005	Hedge Fund Ineligible Investor	0033	N	R0020

TABLE 10.5 Records in **STP_SUBTYPE_M** for the Two Subtypes of Investor Hedge Fund Eligibility

who is allowed to be an investor in a hedge fund. Big Bubble Brokers (BBB), the company for which our sample application is being written, has its own rules, too, which are more restrictive than the government's. For BBB, an investor is eligible to invest in a BBB hedge fund if the investor has earned net pre-tax income of $500,000 or more during the past year, and if they have $10,000,000 in disposable assets. On the screen where investor information is recorded there is one field for *Investor Disposable Assets Amount* and another for *Investor Net Pre-Tax Income in Past Year*. The user enters this information and a business rule is fired to populate *Investor Hedge Fund Eligible Indicator*. This rule can be presented as pseudocode as follows:

R0020:
If *Investor Disposable Assets Amount* >= 10,000,000
    and *Investor Net Pre-Tax Income in Past Year* >= 500,000 Then
    Investor Hedge Fund Eligible Indicator = "Y"
Else
    Investor Hedge Fund Eligible Indicator = "N"
End if

The column *Investor Hedge Fund Eligible Indicator* has a value of *Column ID* of "0033" in the **Column** table (**COL_COLUMN_M**). Table 10.5 shows the records in the **Subtype** table for these two subtypes.

As can be seen from this discussion, it becomes tricky to distinguish between data for the business and metadata for the repository when trying to manage the Business Rules Repository. This is a challenge for anyone taking a business rules approach. However, the reality is that even in hand-crafted programming this complexity has to be confronted. In traditional systems development projects, it is simply not dealt

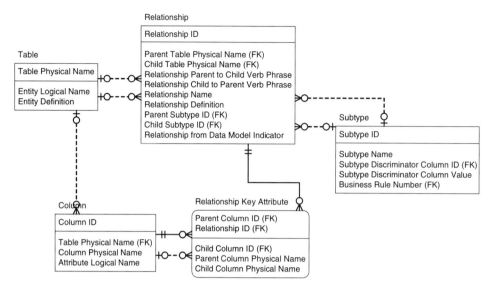

FIGURE 10.6
Relationship Entity with Attributes for Subtypes

with from a conceptual perspective—it is implemented on a redundant piecemeal basis.

Relationships with Subtypes

Figure 10.6 shows the **Relationship** entity enhanced so that it can deal with subtypes.

Relationship now contains *Parent Subtype ID.* If a record in the **Relationship** table has this column populated, it means that the relationship being described is restricted to records in the parent table of the relationship that belong to the subtype being identified. If *Parent Subtype ID* is not populated, it means that all records in the parent table are included in the relationship. Similarly, if *Child Subtype ID* is populated, it restricts the records from the child table that are included in the relationship to those that belong to the child subtype being identified. If *Child Subtype ID* is not populated, then all records in the child table are included in the relationship. Table 10.6 shows the structure of the physically implemented **Relationship** table (**REL_RELATIONSHIP_M**).

Returning to our example, we will have one relationship between **Investor** and **Investor Position** tables shown in Figure 10.4 for each of the three subtypes ("Individual Investor", "Corporate Investor", and "Not-for-Profit Investor"). Table 10.7 shows the three records in the **Relationship** table (**REL_RELATIONSHIP_M**) for these three relationships.

ATTRIBUTE LOGICAL NAME	COLUMN PHYSICAL NAME	COLUMN DATATYPE
Relationship ID	REL_C	Character (4)
Parent Table Physical Name	TAB_PARENT_T	Character (30)
Child Table Physical Name	TAB_CHILD_T	Character (30)
Relationship Parent to Child Verb Phrase	REL_P2CVERB_T	Character (50)
Relationship Child to Parent Verb Phrase	REL_C2PVERB_T	Character (50)
Relationship Name	REL_NAME_T	Character (120)
Relationship Definition	REL_DEFN_M	Memo
Relationship from Data Model Indicator	REL_FROMDM_I	Character (1)
Parent Subtype ID	STP_PARENT_C	Character (4)
Child Subtype ID	STP_CHILD_C	Character (4)

TABLE 10.6 Structure of **REL_RELATIONSHIP_M (Relationship)** Table

Impact of Managing Relationships for Hidden Subtypes

One approach to using hidden subtypes could be to use them to restrict Business Process Steps to dealing with only one subset of information at a time. For instance, there may be many columns in the **Investor** table that are relevant only to Individual Investors and that have to be calculated from data in the **Investor Position** table. A reasonable design might be to place all the business rules for calculating the values of these columns in a Business Process Step that utilizes the relationship between **Investor** and **Investor Position** that is restricted to only Individual Investors. In other words, we could associate a particular relationship with a Business Process Step and force all the rules that fire within that step to operate only on those records that belong to the hidden subtypes that are exposed by the relationship.

Unfortunately, experience suggests that this may not be a fine enough level of control. The need often arises to define individual business rules that are associated with a particular relationship. Thus, no matter what Business Process Steps these rules are associated with, they will always operate only one of the hidden subtypes exposed by the relationship. This is the design approach followed in this book.

One other advantage of the design presented here for managing hidden subtypes is that a single column and value are used to identify records that belong to them. This makes it much easier in general to design rule types. Most importantly, it means that rules that target records belonging to a particular hidden subtype do not redundantly require complex logic to identify the records belonging to these subtypes.

RELATIONSHIP ID (REL_C)	PARENT TABLE PHYSICAL NAME (TAB_PARENT_T)	CHILD TABLE PHYSICAL NAME (TAB_CHILD_T)	PARENT SUBTYPE ID (STP_PARENT_C)	CHILD SUBTYPE ID (STP_CHILD_C)	RELATIONSHIP NAME (REL_NAME_T)
0044	INR_INVESTOR_S	IRP_INRPOSITION_D	0001		Individual Investor purchases Position
0045	INR_INVESTOR_S	IRP_INRPOSITION_D	0002		Corporate Investor purchases Position
0046	INR_INVESTOR_S	IRP_INRPOSITION_D	0003		Not-for-Profit Investor purchases Position

TABLE 10.7 Records in Table **REL_RELATIONSHIP_M** for Relationships of Three Investor Type Subtypes and Investor Position Table

However, there is one important design implication that needs to be understood. Rules that utilize subtypes must always fire after the records that they operate on have been assigned to their subtypes. For instance, **Investor** records all have to be classified as "Individual Investor," "Corporate Investor," etc., before business rules that calculate subtype-specific data, such as *Individual Investor Gross Tax*, can be fired. We shall return to the need to establish the sequence in which rules fire in later chapters.

Unfortunately, as has been pointed out previously, it is impossible to get the metadata needed for managing hidden subtypes from any data modeling tool. This contrasts with metadata about tables and columns, dealt with in earlier chapters. However, the relationship data from the data modeling tool is necessary as a starting point for dealing with hidden subtypes. In the next sections we shall see how this data can be imported from a data modeling tool, and then how it can be augmented to incorporate requirements for dealing with hidden subtypes.

Extracting Relationship Data from the Data Modeling Tool

As with table and column data in the previous chapters, we will base our example on Computer Associate's ERWin tool. Again, we will be using its report generator. Other data modeling tools and data dictionaries have similar report interfaces, so the mechanism we create to extract metadata from ERWin may be applicable—in a general way—in these other environments. Ideally, readers will be able to adapt what follows to their particular circumstances.

One issue that the user may need to deal with in ERWin 3.5.2 is when the ERWin extract file is produced, as described in the next section, there is nothing that uniquely identifies a relationship. ERWin does have an internal *Relationship ID*, but this is not visible in the reporting interface. However, if the user does not put in a parent-to-child verb phrase, then ERWin defaults this value to the *Relationship ID*. Thus, in the ERWin data model for the sample application, no parent-to-child verb phrase has been put in, so this field will be forced to contain *Relationship ID*. The field *Relationship Parent to Child Phrase* is then used as *Relationship ID* to identify unique relationships. It is vital to do this since the same parent and same child may have more than one relationship between them.

Two versions of ERWin are commonly used, Version 3.5.2 and Version 4.1 (also known as AllFusion ERWin Data Modeler). The approach required for each is somewhat different, as described in the following sections.

Create ERWin 3.5.2 Extract Report File

Open the data model with ERWin 3.5.2 and ensure that it is in logical view.

1. Click on **Tasks** in the main menu and then on **Generate Reports . . .** in the popup that appears. The ERWin Report Browser appears. A tree control

appears and shows all the categories of reports that ERWin contains. Click on "Relationship Reports". We will need to create a new report.

2. Click on **File** in the main menu of the ERWin Report Browser and then on **New ERWin Report**. The ERWin Report Editor window appears. Provide a name for the new report— "Relationship Extract" has been used in this example. Select the report category "Relationship" and click **OK**. The new report will have been added to the list under the Entity Reports node of the tree control in the main window.

3. Right-click on the newly added Relationship Extract report and select the option **Edit ERWin Report Relationship Extract'**. The ERWin Report Editor opens again. The main window of the editor is a tree control called Options showing all the metadata that ERWin manages. We need to select the metadata we are going to use to populate **REL_RELATIONSHIP_M**. We will now click several options in the tree.

4. Under the Relationship node, click on the Parent Entity node, click the Table node, and then click the check box for *Name*. This is the physical name of the parent table in the relationship.

5. Again, under the Relationship node, click on the Parent Entity node, the Primary Key Attribute node, and then the Column node. Click the check box for *Name*. This will provide the physical names of the primary key columns of the parent table.

6. Under the Relationship node, click on the Child Entity node, the Table node, and then the check box for *Name*. This is the physical name of the child table in the relationship. Still under Child Entity, click the Column node and then the check box for *Name*. This is the physical name of the migrated key columns from the parent table.

7. Again, under the Relationship node, click on the Migrated Attribute node, click the Primary Key Attribute node, and then the Column node. Click the check box for *Name*. This will provide the physical names of the primary key columns of the parent table.

8. Under the Relationship node, click on the check box for Definition. Then click on the check boxes for Parent to Child Phrase and the Child to Parent Phrase.

9. Click **OK** to close the window.

10. Right-click again on the newly added Relationship Extract report and select the option **Execute ERWin Report Relationship Extract'**. The ERWin Report executes and places the results set in the right-hand side of the screen. A new entry appears in the tree control underneath the Column Extract node indicating that we have produced this results set, as shown in Figure 10.7.

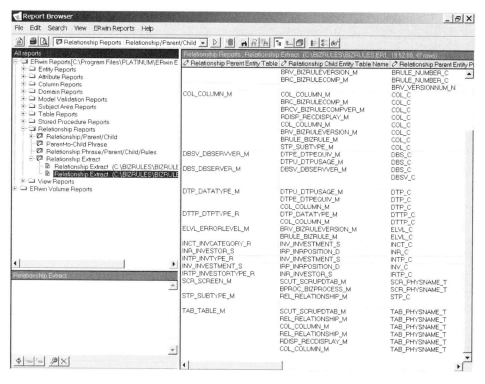

FIGURE 10.7
Relationship Extract Report in ERWin 3.5.2

11. Right-click on the new entry that has appeared in the tree control underneath the Relationship Extract node and select the option to export the results set.

12. A new window now appears with some options for the exported results set, as shown in Figure 10.8. Select HTML for the Export Format, Tabular with Duplicates for the Presentation, and File for Export to. Then click the **Export** button. You will be asked for a location to store the file containing the results set. Make sure it is saved as an HTML file. We have now created the report extract file. The next step is to import it into Microsoft Access and populate the **REL_RELATIONSHIP_M** table.

Create ERWin 4.1 Extract Report File

Open the data model with ERWin 4.1 and ensure that it is in logical view.

1. Click on **Tools** in the main menu and then on **Report Builder** and then on **Report Builder . . .** in the popups that appear. The ERWin Report Templates window appears, as shown in Figure 10.9.

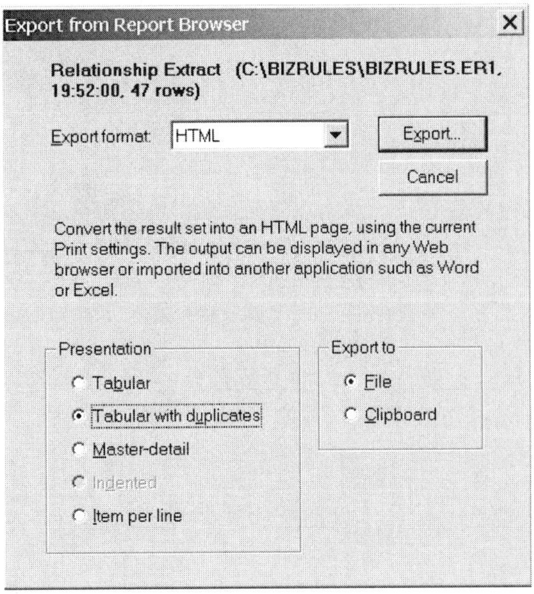

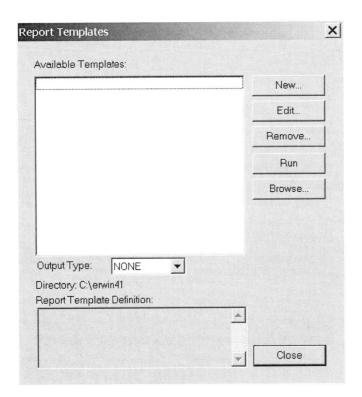

FIGURE 10.8
Results Set Export Options in ERWin 3.5.2

FIGURE 10.9
Report Templates Window in ERWin

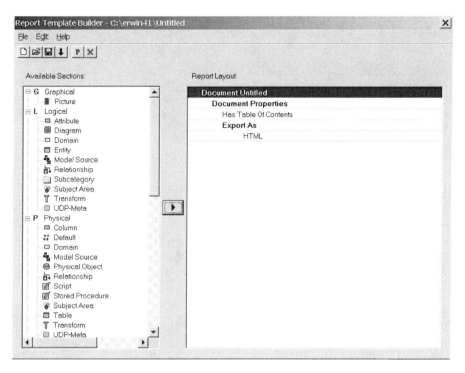

FIGURE 10.10
Report Template Builder Window in ERWin 4.1

2. Click on the **New . . .** button in the Report Templates window. The Report Template Builder window now appears, as shown in Figure 10.10.

3. On the left of this window is a tree control called "Available Sections:" with the objects in the data model. Click on the "Relationship" node and press the arrow button to add it to the "Report Layout" area on the right.

4. Right-click on "Relationship" in the Report Layout area and click on **Properties** in the popup that appears. A window like that shown in Figure 10.11 appears.

5. Under the Relationship node, click on the Parent Entity node, click the Table node, and then click the check box for *Name*. This is the physical name of the parent table in the relationship.

6. Again, under the Relationship node, click on the Parent Entity node, the Primary Key Attribute node, and then the Column node. Click the check box for *Name*. This will provide the physical names of the primary key columns of the parent table.

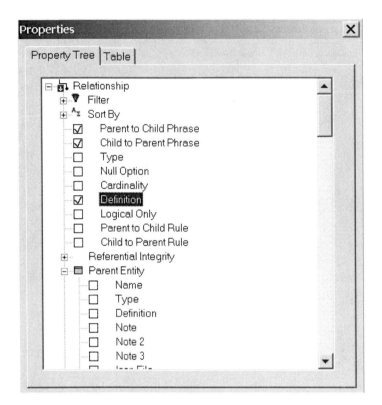

FIGURE 10.11
Object Properties Window in ERWin 4.1

7. Under the Relationship node, click on the Child Entity node, the Table node, and then the check box for *Name*. This is the physical name of the child table in the relationship. Still under Child Entity, click the Column node and then the check box for *Name*. This is the physical name of the migrated key columns from the parent table.

8. Again, under the Relationship node, click on the Migrated Attribute node, the Primary Key Attribute node, and then the Column node. Click the check box for *Name*. This will provide the physical names of the primary key columns of the parent table.

9. Under the Relationship node, click on the check box for Definition. Then click on the check boxes for Parent to Child Phrase and the Child to Parent Phrase.

10. Close the Properties window. Back on the Report Template Builder window, right-click on the top line of the "Report Layout" area (i.e., the text

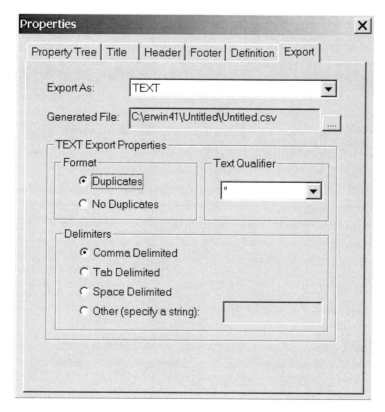

FIGURE 10.12
Report Properties Window in ERWin 4.1

"Document Untitled'). Select Properties on the popup that appears. The Report Properties window now appears, as shown in Figure 10.12.

11. In the Report Properties window, select the Export tab. Select TEXT as the export type, and "Duplicates" in the Format section. Select "Comma Delimited" in the Delimiters section, and double quotes in the Text Qualifier section.

   Select the Title tab and provide a report title, such as "Relationship Report".

   Close the Report Properties window.

12. Back on the Report Template Builder window, run the report by pressing the button with the downward-pointing arrow.

13. A file with the extension ".CSV" will be created for this report. Excel may be invoked to display the contents of this file.

Save the new report template. This will also save the ".CSV" file. It will be placed in the directory specified in the ERWin Report Templates window shown in Figure 10.9.

The next step is to get import it into Microsoft Access and populate the **REL_RELATIONSHIP_M** table.

Importing ERWin 3.5.2 Relationship Metadata into the Repository

If the report extract was produced using ERWin 3.5.2, it can now be imported into the Repository of the sample business rules application, bizrules.mdb. We will create a table called **IMPR_IMPORTREL_M**. The very first time that the import is performed, this table is created. Afterward, we will always import the column metadata into this table. This process closely parallels that described in Chapter 8 for Tables. See Chapter 8 for more details on the Access screens that appear in the import process.

1. Open up the Microsoft Access file bizrules.mdb. Go to the Tables tab. Right-click in this area and select the Import option. This starts the Access import wizard.

2. A file selection dialog now appears. At the bottom is a combo box entitled "Files of type". Select the value for HTML files. Navigate to where you saved the report extract file from ERWin and select it.

3. The next screen that appears in the Access import wizard has a check box at the top of the screen that asks whether the first row contains column headings. It does, so check this box. Then click **Next**.

4. The next screen asks whether the file should be brought into a new table. For the very first time the import is done, indicate that it should be, and click **Next**.

    For every time afterward that the import is done, indicate that the data will be imported into the table **IMPR_IMPORTREL_M**. The import will then complete. The following steps only apply to the very first import.

5. The next screen is where you specify the datatypes for the data that is being imported. Access provides a default of Text (255) for all text fields. This is sufficient for all fields except Relationship Definition, which must be a memo datatype.

6. The next screen that appears asks whether you want to let Access add its own primary key, or whether you want to specify it. Choose the option to let Access add its own primary key and press **Next**.

7. The final screen of the import wizard now appears. It asks you to provide the name of the table. Give it the name IMPR_IMPORTREL_M. Then press

Finish. Access will now import the data. Access will report any errors to you. The most frequent one that happens is due to forgetting to make the *Relationship Definition* a memo field, which results in data truncation.

8. We need an extra field in this table. Go into **IMPR_IMPORTREL_M** in design mode and add the column IMPR_PROCESSED_I Text(1). This will be used when we import data to record which fields are processed

 After this first import is complete, subsequent imports are much simpler because we have set up **IMPR_IMPORTREL_M**. When it is necessary to perform subsequent imports, delete data from the table **IMPR_IMPORTREL_M** and perform the import process again. Once you get to the point where you indicate to Access if you want to import into a new or existing table, choose **IMPR_IMPORTREL_M** as the target table. The import process will then be completed.

Importing ERWin 4.1 Relationship Metadata into the Repository

If the report extract was produced using ERWin 4.1, it can now be imported into the Repository of the sample business rules application, bizrules.mdb. We will create a table called **IMPR_IMPORTREL_M**. The very first time that the import is performed, this table is created. Afterward, we will always import the column metadata into this table. This process closely parallels that described in Chapter 8 for Tables. See Chapter 8 for more details on the Access screens that appear in the import process.

1. Open up the Microsoft Access file bizengine.mdb. Go to the Tables tab. Right-click in this area and select the Import option. This starts the Access import wizard.

2. A file selection dialog now appears. At the bottom is a combo box entitled "Files of type". Select the value for Text files (which will include ".CSV" files). Navigate to where you saved the report extract file from ERWin 4.1 and select it.

3. The next screen that appears in the Access import wizard requires the type of file format to be specified. Select the "Delimited" type. Then click **Next**.

4. The next screen requires that the delimiter character is specified. Choose "comma" and make sure the Text Qualifier is set to double quotes. Then click **Next**.

5. The next screen asks whether the file should be brought into a new table. Indicate that it should be, and click **Next**.

6. The next screen is where you specify the field names and datatypes for the data that is being imported.

The field names that are provided are *Field1*, *Field2*, etc. Replace these names with *Relationship Parent to Child Phrase*, *Relationship Child to Parent Phrase*, *Relationship Definition*, *Relationship Parent Entity Primary Key Attribute Column Name*, *Relationship Parent Entity Table Name*, *Relationship Child Entity Table Name*, and *Relationship Migrated Attribute Column Name*.

Access provides a default of Text (255) for all text fields. This is sufficient for most fields, but the *Relationship Definition* may be longer than this. Highlight the *Relationship Definition* field by clicking on it. Then select a datatype of Memo. Then press **Next**.

7. The next screen that appears asks whether you want to let Access add its own primary key, or whether you want to specify it. Choose the option to let Access add its own primary key and press **Next**.

8. The final screen of the import wizard now appears. It asks you to provide the name of the table. Give it the name IMPR_IMPORTREL_M. Then press **Finish**. Access will now import the data. Access will report any errors to you. The most frequent one that happens is due to forgetting to make the *Relationship Definition* a memo field, which results in data truncation.

9. We need an extra field in this table. Go into **IMPR_IMPORTREL_M** in design mode and add the column IMPR_PROCESSED_I Text(1). This will be used when we import data to record which fields are processed

After this first import is complete, subsequent imports are much simpler because we have set up **IMPR_IMPORTREL_M**. When it is necessary to perform subsequent imports, delete data from the table **IMPR_IMPORTREL_M** and perform the import process again. Once you get to the point where you indicate to Access whether you want to import into a new or existing tables, choose **IMPR_IMPORTREL_M** as the target table. The import process will then be completed.

Updating the REL_RELATIONSHIP_M Table

With the metadata for tables now inside the **IMPR_IMPORTREL_M** table in bizrules.mdb, we need to update **REL_RELATIONSHIP_M**. To do this we have to write some simple Access VB code which is shown in Listing 10.1. This function does several things:

■ It ensures that each record has all needed information. ERWin seems to sometimes leave out certain data, and this is filled in.

■ Unnecessary spaces surrounding values are eliminated.

■ Column and Table data for the columns and tables that participate in each relationship are retrieved from **COL_COLUMN_M** and **TAB_TABLE_T**. If they are not found the update is abandoned.

LISTING 10.1

Function to Populate Table **REL_RELATIONSHIP_M** and **RKEY_RELKEYATT_M**

```
  Private Function PopRelation() As String
'*********************************************************************
' Populates the table REL_RELATIONSHIP_M with metadata imported
' from an external source and placed in the table
' IMPR_IMPORTREL_M.
'
' Parameters: None
'
' Returns: "Y" indicates successful completion
'*********************************************************************

Dim rstRel As ADODB.Recordset, strSQL As String, lngAffected As
Long
Dim cmd As ADODB.Command, strLastTab As String, strLastCol As
String
Dim strText As String, intCt As Integer, strRelNo As String
Dim rstPar As ADODB.Recordset, rstChild As ADODB.Recordset, strName
As String
Dim strParTab As String, strChildTab As String, strRel As String

  PopRelation = "Y"
  Set rstRel = New ADODB.Recordset
  Set rstPar = New ADODB.Recordset
  Set rstChild = New ADODB.Recordset
  Set cmd = New ADODB.Command
  cmd.ActiveConnection = CurrentProject.Connection
  cmd.CommandType = adCmdText

  ' ERWin Seems to not duplicate all information from row to row
  ' so fill in what is missing
  strSQL = "SELECT * FROM IMPR_IMPORTREL_M   " _
        & " ORDER BY ID "
  rstRel.Open strSQL, CurrentProject.Connection, _
        adOpenKeyset, adLockOptimistic, adCmdText
  strParTab = "!"
  strChildTab = "!"
  Do While Not rstRel.EOF
    If strParTab <> "!" Then
```

```
        If IsNull(rstRel("Relationship Parent Entity Table Name")) _
            Or Trim(rstRel("Relationship Parent Entity Table
Name")) = "" Then
          rstRel("Relationship Parent Entity Table Name") =
strParTab
          rstRel.Update
        End If
        If IsNull(rstRel("Relationship Child Entity Table Name")) _
            Or Trim(rstRel("Relationship Child Entity Table
Name")) = "" Then
          rstRel("Relationship Child Entity Table Name") =
strChildTab
          rstRel.Update
        End If
      End If
      strParTab = rstRel("Relationship Parent Entity Table Name")
      strChildTab = rstRel("Relationship Child Entity Table Name")
      rstRel.MoveNext
    Loop
    rstRel.Close

    ' Get rid of spaces that may surround data in the import file
    ' and set the Import Processed Flag to N
    strSQL = "UPDATE IMPR_IMPORTREL_M SET " _
          & " [Relationship Parent Entity Table Name] = " _
          & " Trim([Relationship Parent Entity Table Name]) " _
          & ", [Relationship Child Entity Table Name] = " _
          & " Trim([Relationship Child Entity Table Name]) " _
          & ", [Relationship Parent Entity Primary Key Attribute
Column Name] = " _
          & " Trim([Relationship Parent Entity Primary Key
Attribute Column Name]) " _
          & ", [Relationship Child to Parent Phrase] = " _
          & " Trim([Relationship Child to Parent Phrase]) " _
          & ", [Relationship Migrated Attribute Column Name] = " _
          & " Trim([Relationship Migrated Attribute Column Name])
" _
          & ", IMPR_PROCESSED_I = 'N' "
    cmd.CommandText = strSQL
    cmd.Execute lngAffected
```

```
' Delete all existing relationships
strSQL = "DELETE FROM REL_RELATIONSHIP_M   "
cmd.CommandText = strSQL
cmd.Execute lngAffected
strSQL = "DELETE FROM RKEY_RELKEYATT_M "
cmd.CommandText = strSQL
cmd.Execute lngAffected

' Update relationship data
strSQL = "SELECT * FROM IMPR_IMPORTREL_M   " _
        & " ORDER BY ID "
rstRel.Open strSQL, CurrentProject.Connection, _
        adOpenKeyset, adLockOptimistic, adCmdText
strRel = "!"
intCt = 0
Do While Not rstRel.EOF
  ' Find COL_C value of the parent column
    strSQL = "SELECT A.*, B.TAB_ENTLOGNAME_T FROM COL_COLUMN_M A,
TAB_TABLE_M B " _
          & " WHERE A.TAB_PHYSNAME_T = '" _
              & rstRel("Relationship Parent Entity Table Name")
& "' " _
          & " AND A.COL_PHYSNAME_T = '" _
              & rstRel("Relationship Parent Entity Primary Key
Attribute Column Name") & "' " _
          & " AND A.TAB_PHYSNAME_T = B.TAB_PHYSNAME_T "
    rstPar.Open strSQL, CurrentProject.Connection, _
        adOpenKeyset, adLockOptimistic, adCmdText
    If rstPar.EOF Then
      MsgBox "Function PopRelation: No COL_COLUMN_M data found
for " _
              & rstRel("Relationship Parent Entity Table Name") &
" / " _
              & rstRel("Relationship Parent Entity Primary Key
Attribute Column Name") _
              & "-Import Abandoned"
      PopRelation = "N"
      Exit Function
    End If
    ' Find COL_C value of the child column
```

```
      strSQL = "SELECT A.*,B.TAB_ENTLOGNAME_T FROM COL_COLUMN_M A,
TAB_TABLE_M B" _
            & " WHERE A.TAB_PHYSNAME_T = '" _
                & rstRel("Relationship Child Entity Table Name")
& "' " _
            & " AND A.COL_PHYSNAME_T = '" _
                & rstRel("Relationship Migrated Attribute Column
Name") & "' " _
            & " AND A.TAB_PHYSNAME_T = B.TAB_PHYSNAME_T "
      rstChild.Open strSQL, CurrentProject.Connection, _
          adOpenKeyset, adLockOptimistic, adCmdText
      If rstChild.EOF Then
        MsgBox "Function PopRelation: No COL_COLUMN_M data found
for " _
                & rstRel("Relationship Child Entity Table Name") & "
/ " _
                & rstRel("Relationship Migrated Attribute Column
Name") _
                & "-Import Abandoned"
        PopRelation = "N"
        Exit Function
      End If
      ' Relationship Parent to Child Phrase is used as Relationship
      ' ID
      If strRel <> rstRel("Relationship Parent to Child Phrase")
Then
          ' Create new relationship record
          intCt = intCt + 1
          ' Create Default Relationship Name
          strName = rstPar("TAB_ENTLOGNAME_T") & " has " &
rstChild("TAB_ENTLOGNAME_T")
          strRelNo = Right("0000" & CStr(intCt), 4)
          strSQL = "INSERT INTO REL_RELATIONSHIP_M (" _
              & "REL_C, TAB_PARENT_T, TAB_CHILD_T, REL_P2CVERB_T, "
_
              & "REL_C2PVERB_T, REL_DEFN_M, REL_NAME_T) VALUES(" _
              & "'" & strRelNo & "', " _
              & "'" & rstRel("Relationship Parent Entity Table
Name") & "', " _
              & "'" & rstRel("Relationship Child Entity Table
Name") & "', " _
```

```
                & "'" & rstRel("Relationship Parent to Child Phrase")
& "', " _
                & "'" & rstRel("Relationship Child to Parent Phrase")
& "', " _
                & "'" & rstRel("Relationship Definition") & "',  " _
                & "'" & strName & "') "
        cmd.CommandText = strSQL
        cmd.Execute lngAffected
    End If
    ' Now insert the record in Relationship Key Attribute
    strRel = rstRel("Relationship Parent to Child Phrase")

    ' Insert record in RKEY_RELKEYATT_M
    strSQL = "INSERT INTO RKEY_RELKEYATT_M (" _
            & "REL_C, COL_PARENT_C, COL_CHILD_C, COL_PARPHYSNAME_T,
" _
            & "COL_CHILDPHYSNAME_T) VALUES(" _
            & "'" & strRelNo & "', " _
            & "'" & rstPar("COL_C") & "', " _
            & "'" & rstChild("COL_C") & "', " _
            & "'" & Trim(rstRel("Relationship Parent Entity Primary
Key Attribute Column Name")) & "', " _
            & "'" & Trim(rstRel("Relationship Migrated Attribute
Column Name")) & "') "
    cmd.CommandText = strSQL
    cmd.Execute lngAffected

    rstPar.Close
    rstChild.Close
    rstRel("IMPR_PROCESSED_I") = "Y"
    rstRel.Update
    rstRel.MoveNext
  Loop
  rstRel.Close

  ' Update Relationship From Data Model Indicator
  strSQL = "UPDATE REL_RELATIONSHIP_M SET REL_FROMDM_I = 'Y' "
  cmd.CommandText = strSQL
  cmd.Execute lngAffected
```

```
     Set rstRel = Nothing
     Set rstPar = Nothing
     Set rstChild = Nothing
     Set cmd = Nothing

     MsgBox "Relationship Metadata has been Imported"

   End Function
```

- A relationship name is created. It consists of the parent entity name followed by "has", followed by the child entity name.
- **REL_RELATIONSHIP_M** and **RKEY_RELKEYATT_M** are then updated.

Updating Column Information

Chapter 9 described how the **Column** entity (table **COL_COLUMN_M**) can be enhanced so it can capture information on foreign keys. This information is derived from the relationship metadata imported from the data model. Listing 10.2 shows how **COL_COLUMN_M** is updated using the metadata imported into **Relationship** (**REL_RELATIONSHIP_M**) and **Relationship Key Attribute** (**RKEY_RELKEYATT_M**).

Editing Relationships

Regrettably, importing relationship data into the Business Rules Repository is not sufficient for a business rules engine. As discussed earlier, there is often a need to limit the records visible in a relationship to a subtype in the parent table and/or a subtype in the child table. This can be accomplished by defining new relationships in the Business Rules Repository. These new relationships are termed **subtype relationships** here. The relationships imported directly from the data model are termed **base relationships**.

The screens required for this functionality are not very complex. In the sample application the functionality can be invoked by selecting **Repository Functions** on the main menu and then **Relationship Editor** from the popup that appears. The screen shown in Figure 10.13 is then displayed. It allows the user to select a relationship.

The design elements in this screen are as follows:

- The user can select any relationship to edit.
- The user can create a new **subtype relationship**. This is done by cloning a **base relationship**. The user cannot create a new **subtype relationship** from another **subtype relationship**. If this is attempted an error message appears.

LISTING 10.2
Function to Update Foreign Key Information in Table **COL_COLUMN_M**

```
  Private Function PopColRelData() As String
'*********************************************************************
' Populates COL_COLUMN_M with metadata for foreign keys.  It takes
' this from relationship data.  It sets the Column Foriegn Key
' indicator also.
'
' Parameters: None
'
' Returns: "Y" indicates successful completion
'*********************************************************************

Dim rstRel As ADODB.Recordset, strSQL As String, lngAffected As
Long
Dim cmd As ADODB.Command, strLastTab As String, strLastCol As
String
Dim strText As String, intCt As Integer, strRelNo As String
Dim rstPar As ADODB.Recordset, rstChild As ADODB.Recordset, strName
As String
Dim strParTab As String, strChildTab As String, strRel As String

  PopColRelData = "Y"
  Set rstRel = New ADODB.Recordset
  Set cmd = New ADODB.Command
  cmd.ActiveConnection = CurrentProject.Connection
  cmd.CommandType = adCmdText

  strSQL = "UPDATE COL_COLUMN_M SET TAB_FKPARENT_T = NULL, " _
        & "COL_PARCOLUMN_C = NULL, " _
        & "COL_FK_I = 'N', " _
        & "COL_PARPHYSNAME_T = NULL"
  cmd.CommandText = strSQL
  cmd.Execute lngAffected

  strSQL = "SELECT A.TAB_PARENT_T, A.TAB_CHILD_T, B.* FROM
REL_RELATIONSHIP_M A, RKEY_RELKEYATT_M B " _
        & "WHERE A.REL_C = B.REL_C"
  rstRel.Open strSQL, CurrentProject.Connection, _
        adOpenKeyset, adLockOptimistic, adCmdText
```

```
Do While Not rstRel.EOF
  strSQL = "UPDATE COL_COLUMN_M SET " _
        & "TAB_FKPARENT_T = '" & rstRel("TAB_PARENT_T") & "',
" _
        & "COL_PARCOLUMN_C = '" & rstRel("COL_PARENT_C") & "',
" _
        & "COL_PARPHYSNAME_T = '" & rstRel("COL_PARPHYSNAME_T")
& "', " _
        & "COL_FK_I = 'Y'" _
        & " WHERE COL_C = '" & rstRel("COL_CHILD_C") & "'"
  cmd.CommandText = strSQL
  cmd.Execute lngAffected
  rstRel.MoveNext
Loop
rstRel.Close
Set rstRel = Nothing
Set cmd = Nothing

End Function
```

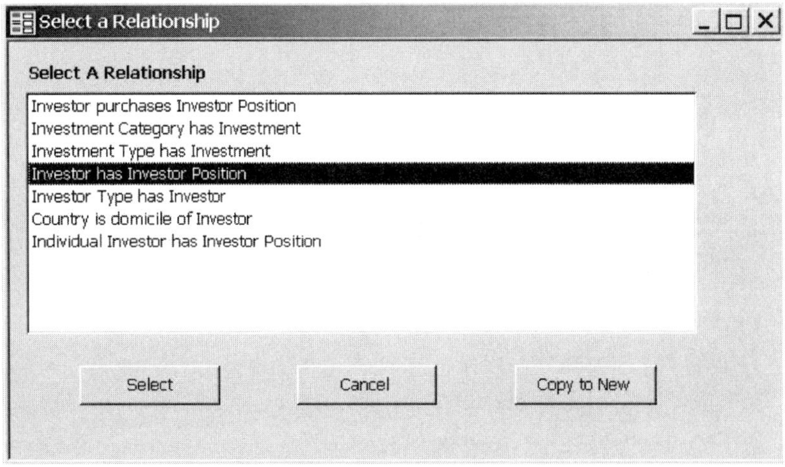

FIGURE 10.13
Screen to Select Relationship

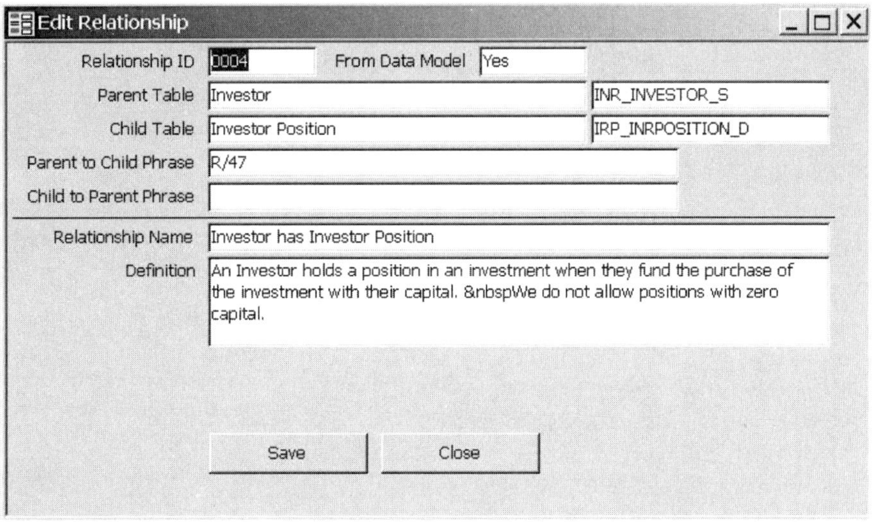

FIGURE 10.14
Screen to Edit **Base Relationship**

When the user selects a **base relationship** to edit, the screen shown in Figure 10.14 appears.

The following design elements apply to the screen to edit **base relationships**:

- The user is not allowed to delete the relationship.

- The user is only allowed to edit the relationship name and relationship definition. Nothing else can be changed.

When the user creates a new **subtype relationship** by cloning a **base relationship**, the screen is a little different, as shown in Figure 10.15.

The design elements for this screen are:

- The user can delete the relationship, but only if the relationship has not been used in any business rules.

- The fundamental relationship data is taken from the selected **base relationship**.

- The user can edit the relationship name and definition.

- When the user defines a new **subtype relationship**, a Parent Subtype and/or Child Subtype must be chosen. Once this has been defined it cannot be edited.

- The user cannot define more than one **subtype relationship** using the same **base relationship** and same subtypes.

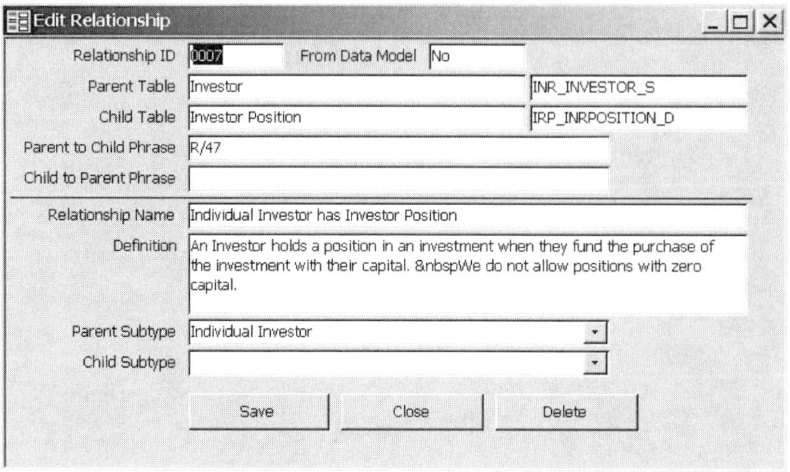

FIGURE 10.15
Screen to Edit **Subtype Relationship**

The reader can look more closely at the objects for this functionality in the sample application. These objects are listed in Table 10.8.

Pathways

Relationship information is necessary, but it is not complete enough for a business rules engine. A business rules engine needs to navigate from one table to another within the database. These tables must be connected by relationships, and it is relatively easy to go from a table to its immediate parent. It is less easy to go from a table to its grandparent or great-grandparent. Furthermore, there may be more than one way to go from a table to any related higher-level table (i.e., parent, grandparent, great-grandparent, etc.). These chains of relationships are termed *pathways* in this book and must be managed in order to build a successful business rules engine. Figure 10.16 illustrates one of the problems with pathways.

In the data model shown in Figure 10.16, there are two possible pathways by which the **Region** table can be reached from the starting point of the table **Investor Position**. One pathway is **Investor Position** to **Investor** to **Country** to **Region**. The other pathway is **Investor Position** to **Investment** to **Country** to **Region**.

When there is only one pathway between two tables, such as from **Country** to **Region**, the business rules engine can determine how to perform the navigation based on the constructs already built in the Business Rules Repository. However, there are usually some tables in a data model that have more than one pathway between them.

ITEM	APPLICATION OBJECT	DESCRIPTION
Menu access		Repository Functions > Relationship Editor
		Select a relationship on the screen that appears, and click on the button **Select** to edit it. Click on the button **Copy New** to create a new subtype relationship.
Relationship Table	REL_RELATIONSHIP_M	
Relationship Key Attributes Table	RKEY_RELKEYATT_M	
Relationship Selection Screen	frmSelRel	This screen is shown in Figure 10.13 and has a class module containing code.
Edit Relationship Screen	frmRel	This screen is shown in Figures 10.14 and 10.15 and has a class module containing code.
Subtype Table	STP_SUBTYPE_M	
Query to find all subtypes for a selected parent table.	qrySTP_SEL_PAR	Used for the Parent Subtype combo box in frmRel
Query to find all subtypes for a selected child table.	qrySTP_SEL_CHILD	Used for the Child Subtype combo box in frmRel

TABLE 10.8 Objects for Editing Relationships in the Sample Application

These can be handled to some extent by limiting the way that users can define rules, and we shall see some of these techniques later on. Nevertheless, in the end the complexity of pathways cannot be escaped. For instance, a user may need to define a business rule that populates a column in **Investor Position**, and this rule needs to use the column Region Business Exclusion Indicator in **Region**. The rules engine simply has to know which pathway to use to navigate from **Investor Position** to **Region**.

Pathway information can be constructed using the relationship information already stored in the business rules repository. Figure 10.17 shows the design of the tables needed to store pathway information.

The **Pathway** entity has one record for each distinct pathway in the data model. The structure of the **Pathway** entity (implemented as the table **PWAY_PATHWAY_M**) is as follows:

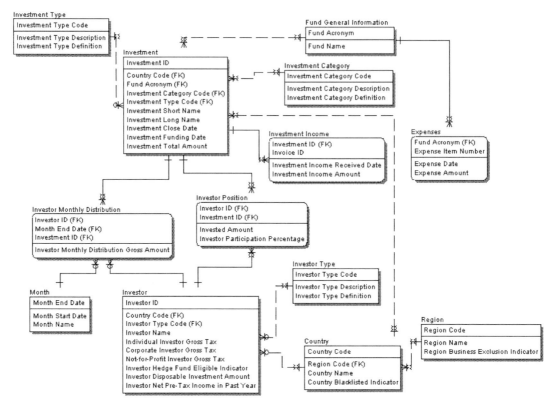

FIGURE 10.16
Pathways from Investor Position to Region

- *Pathway ID*: A unique system-assigned identifier for a pathway
- *Parent Destination Table:* The physical name of the table that is at the parent end of the pathway.
- *Child Destination Table:* The physical name of the table that is at the child end of the pathway.
- *Pathway Name:* A user-assigned name that can be used to distinguish the pathway from other pathways.
- *Number of Levels in Pathway:* The number of relationships in the chain from one end of the pathway to the other.

Each pathway consists of a chain of one or more relationships from one end of the pathway to the other. The **Pathway Level** entity holds one record for each relationship in the chain for each pathway. It is very important that this be based on

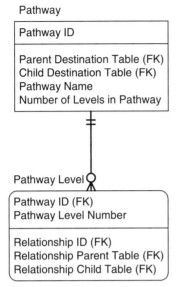

FIGURE 10.17
Entities in Business Rules Repository for Pathway Information

relationships. There is a temptation to only use parent and child tables to identify steps in pathways. However, it must be remembered that there can be more than one relationship between the same parent and child tables. The structure of the **Pathway Level** entity (implemented as the table **PWL_PWAYLEVEL_M**) is as follows:

- *Pathway ID:* A unique system-assigned identifier for a pathway.

- *Pathway Level Number:* Levels are counted going from the Parent Destination Table to the Child Destination Tables. The first relationship in this chain has a *Pathway Level Number* of 1. Subsequent relationships increment this number.

- *Relationship ID:* The unique identifier of the relationship that is recorded in the **Pathway Level** record.

- *Relationship Parent Table:* The physical name of the parent table in the relationship that is recorded in the **Pathway Level** record.

- *Relationship Child Table:* The physical name of the child table in the relationship that is recorded in the **Pathway Level** record.

The physical structures of the **Pathway** and **Pathway Level** tables are shown in Tables 10.9 and 10.10.

The two tables are populated after the relationship information is imported from the data model, and before users define any new relationships. Obviously there will be many more pathways than there are relationships in the data model.

ATTRIBUTE LOGICAL NAME	COLUMN PHYSICAL NAME	COLUMN DATATYPE
Pathway ID	PWAY_C	Character (4)
Child Destination Table	TAB_CHILD_T	Character (50)
Parent Destination Table	TAB_PARENT_T	Character (50)
Number of Levels in Pathway	PWAY_TOTLEVEL_N	Integer
Pathway Name	PWAY_NAME_T	Character (80)

TABLE 10.9 Structure of **PWAY_PATHWAY_M** (Pathway)

ATTRIBUTE LOGICAL NAME	COLUMN PHYSICAL NAME	COLUMN DATATYPE
Pathway ID	PWAY_C	Character (4)
Pathway Level Number	PWL_N	Integer
Parent Table Name	TAB_PARENT_T	Character (50)
Child Table Name	TAB_CHILD_T	Character (50)
Relationship ID	REL_C	Character (4)

TABLE 10.10 Structure of **PWL_PWAYLEVEL_M** (Pathway Level)

Pathway information is derived from relationships. Tables that are parents but that themselves have no parents are the starting point. Pathways are built from them to their children, then their grandchildren, then their great-grandchildren, until child entities are reached that have no children. Then the children of the original tables are selected as a starting point and the process is repeated. Next the grandchildren of the original tables are selected and the process is repeated. This keeps going until the child entities that have no children are reached. This process essentially recurses through all chains of relationships. Thus, there are many more pathways than there are relationships. The function BldPathWay() in the DBExtend module of the sample application performs this processing.

Once the pathway information has been recorded, there is a need to edit it. This is so that the *Pathway Name* in the **Pathway** table can be more meaningful. *Pathway Name* will be needed later on for rule definition purposes and must be readily understandable and unambiguous. The latter is especially important since there can be more than one pathway between the same Parent Destination Table and Child Destination Table. In the sample application, the form frmPWAY is accessed via selecting **Repository Functions** on the main menu and then **Pathway Editor**. This form is shown in Figure 10.18 and can be used to update **Pathway Name**.

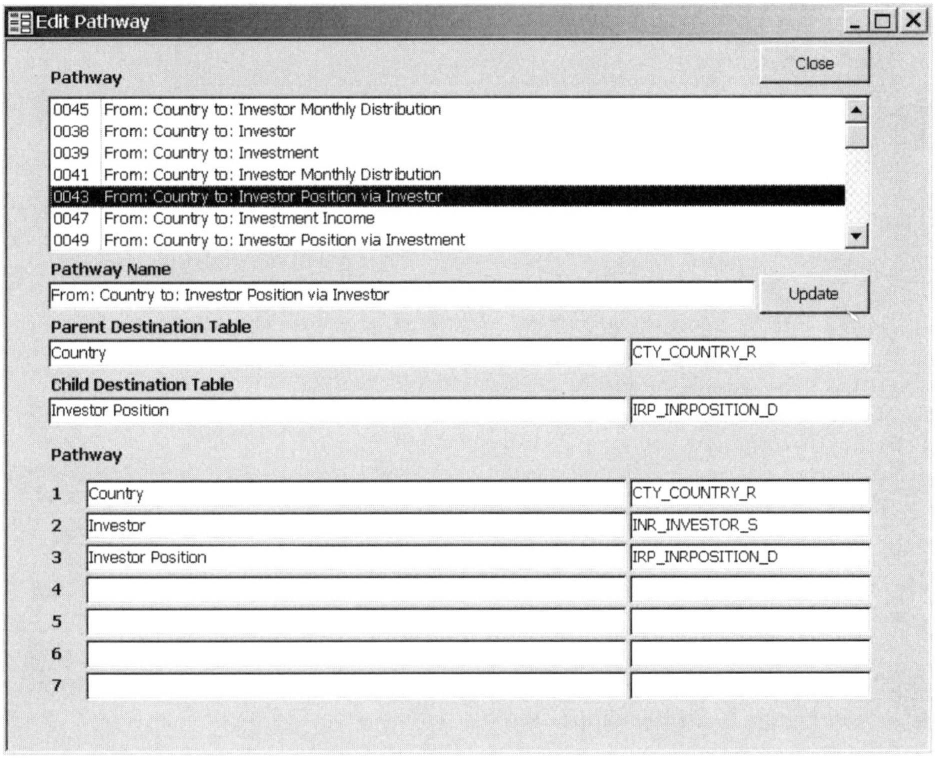

FIGURE 10.18
Edit Pathway Screen

Defining Subtypes

At this point, we have reviewed functionality in the sample application that allows users to manage metadata for relationships and pathways. There is also a need for functionality to manage subtypes. From this point on the term *subtype* is used to refer to what has previously been termed *hidden subtype*. The reality is that hidden subtypes are very common in databases, but formal subtypes of the kind declared in data models are very rare or nonexistent. In the sample application, this functionality can be accessed by selecting the option **Repository Functions** from the main menu and then **Subtype Editor** from the popup that appears. The screen shown in Figure 10.19 is then displayed. This screen allows the user to select a subtype.

The important design elements of this screen are:

- Subtypes are shown using the name of the subtype followed by the name of the table in which the subtype exists.

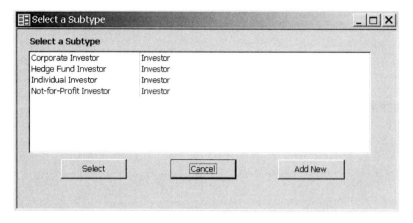

FIGURE 10.19
Select Subtype

- The list is ordered by subtype name within table name.
- The user can click on the **Add New** button to define a new subtype.

When the user selects an existing subtype or decides to add a new one, the screen shown in Figure 10.20 then appears.

This screen has the following design elements:

- The user can delete a subtype, but only if the subtype is not used in any relationship.
- Once a subtype has been defined, the user can only update Subtype Name and Subtype Definition.
- When a new subtype is defined, the user must first select the table in which the subtype exists, via the combo box labeled Table. Then the user must select the Discriminator Column and Discriminator Value for the subtype.
- A Discriminator Column can be any indicator column or any column that is a foreign key of a lookup-type reference data table. This standard is very important as it makes it a lot easier for the rules engine to manipulate subtypes. Only these kinds of columns appear in the combo box for Discriminator Column.
- If a Discriminator Column is chosen that is an indicator column, the Discriminator Value combo box has only two choices: "Yes" and "No".
- If a Discriminator Column is chosen that is a key of a lookup-type reference data table, the Discriminator Value combo box is populated with the contents of the selected table. The program code to do this is interesting, and the user

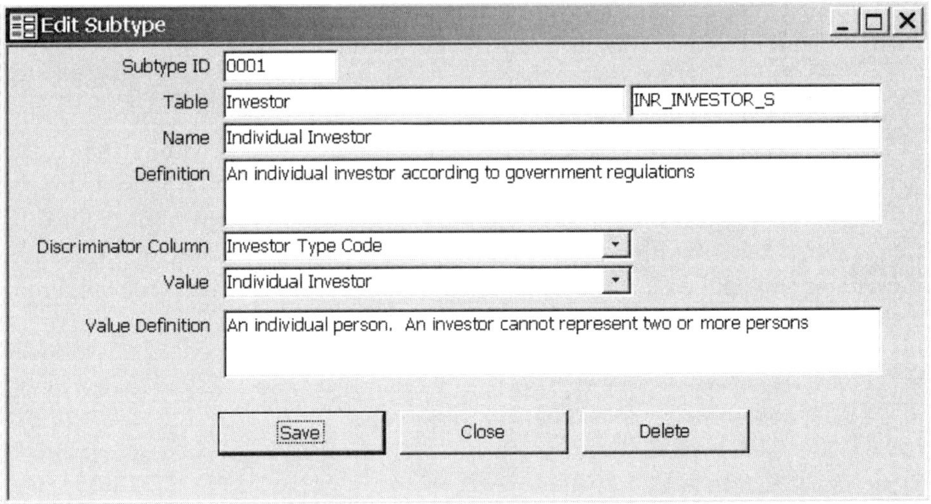

FIGURE 10.20
Screen to Edit Subtypes

may wish to examine it in the sample application. Such program code is possible because of the way that reference data is treated in the Business Rules Repository. This is discussed in detail in the next chapter.

- No two subtypes within the same table can have the same Discriminator Column and the same Discriminator Value. An error message appears if the user tries to define such a duplicate subtype.

- The *Value Definition* field on the screen will be populated by the system if a Discriminator Column is chosen that is a key of a lookup-type reference data table. The reference data table record that corresponds to what is selected in Discriminator Value is examined to see if it has a column that contains a definition in addition to the code and description. Again, this is a benefit of the way the Repository deals with reference data, as will be explained in the next chapter.

Conclusion

This chapter has introduced the basic Business Rules Repository design for relationships, pathways, and subtypes. Relationship metadata can be extracted from a data modeling tool, but subtype metadata typically cannot. Pathway metadata must be derived from relationship metadata. Even though some relationship metadata can be extracted from a data modeling tool, it may be insufficient for the needs of the

Repository. Thus, additional functionality has been built for the Repository to manage relationship, pathway, and subtype metadata.

A difficult issue in this area is that some of the concepts are not commonly discussed, even by data modelers. Also, it can be difficult to distinguish between what is metadata and what is business data. In particular, when dealing with reference data there is no clean break. It is precisely these issues that are largely responsible for the complexity that keeps business rule definition as something that is implemented by human programmers writing code. However, with a little effort, the concepts can be understood and applied to create the functionality needed as a basis for building a business rules engine.

11

POPULATING REFERENCE DATA IN THE REPOSITORY

Reference data is a class of data that means different things to different people. Some take it to mean any data that a system uses but does not update. Others consider it to be data that is contained in *lookup tables*. These are tables that have structures usually consisting of only a code column and a description column. The reality is that there is no agreed-upon definition of reference data, and that this form of data consists of several categories.

Some data that is considered to be reference data describes parties to transactions, such as customer and product. This kind of reference data does not play a special role in business rules, though it is important in any application. Other reference data can include data that describes the structure of an enterprise, such as the organizational units it consists of, or the chart of accounts it uses. This, too, is important, but not of special interest for business rules.

Lookup tables, though simple in structure, actually encompass several different kinds of reference data. One kind is data that is external to an enterprise and describes things the enterprise does not control, such as country and currency. This type of reference data may play a role in business rules. Another kind of lookup table is used to categorize or classify data, such as industry classifications or credit ratings. This may be used only for reporting purposes, but is also often involved in business rules. A third kind of lookup table specifies different states or types of entities, such as status codes, role codes, and type codes. These are always very important for business rules. Type codes like Customer Type or Product Type are used to identify different sub-types. Status Codes describe the life history of a transaction. For instance, a product may be "Ordered," "Paid for," "Shipped," and "Delivered." Role codes are used to constrain the way a party interacts with an organization. For instance, the same person may be an employee of an enterprise and a customer of the enterprise, and as such special rules may apply to that person. In general, lookup tables may be defined as a special class of reference data as follows:

> Any kind of data that is used solely to categorize other data found in a database, or solely for relating data in a database to information beyond the boundaries of the enterprise.

Not all lookup tables are physically implemented as tables with one code column and one description column. Very often they have additional columns, some of which contain additional descriptive data, and some of which are foreign keys from related lookup tables. Sometimes a lookup table has more than a single code column as its primary key—though this is comparatively rare.

Lookup-type reference data is the type of reference data that must be managed in order to build an effective business rules engine. From now on, it will be referred to simply as *reference data*. The first step to dealing with it is to try to standardize it, and this is discussed in the next section.

Standards for Reference Data

To a data modeling tool one entity is just the same as any other entity. No data modeling tool has any special mechanism for distinguishing reference data from any other entity an analyst cares to define in the tool. Yet, this has to be done for the Business Rules Repository. A relatively easy way is to use naming conventions in the modeling tool, and that approach is used here. The naming convention for table names described in Chapter 8 dictates that the physical name of a reference data table should always end in "_R". If this convention is followed in building a data model, then it is quite easy to parse the metadata imported from the data modeling tool to determine which tables are reference tables and which are not.

As noted earlier, reference tables often have a single column as a primary key. It is much easier to work with reference data if a standard is adopted that all reference tables have a single column as a primary key. Because this column is often a code, it should always be of character datatype. A further standard is that the code cannot exceed 10 characters in length. All of this is quite easy to adopt when creating a data model and should not cause any difficult design issues.

Reference tables nearly always have a description column—a translation of the code. Occasionally, reference tables can be found that have no description. In these tables the code serves as the description. However, a standard is again needed to make it possible for the business rules engine to work with all reference data tables, and the standard adopted here is that a reference table must always have a column that is a description.

Reference tables very rarely have a column to define the meaning of the code and description. Most IT staff rely on the contents of the description column for this purpose. Yet this is often inadequate. For instance, a **Country** table may have a record with a code of "CPR" and a description of "China." However, the organization that has created this record may want "China" to exclude Hong Kong and Taiwan, but to include Macao and Tibet. This definition, or explanation, must be captured, and the best way to do it is to have an additional column for a definition in every reference table. The column must be of unlimited length, that is, a memo-type datatype. This is another standard adopted here.

Extending the **Table** Entity

Now that standards for reference data have been presented, the Business Rules Repository must be enhanced to manage it. Reference tables must be clearly identified. This is achieved by adding the attribute *Table Reference Data Indicator* to the **Table** entity (**TAB_TABLE_M**). It is implemented as the column TAB_REFTAB_I and is Character (1). It is set to a value of "Y" if the record in **TAB_TABLE_M** is for a reference table. These changes were described in detail in Chapter 8.

Extending the **Column** Entity

A major objective for the Business Rules Repository is that when a user selects a column that is associated with a reference table, it must be easy to present the user with a list of the contents (codes, descriptions, and definitions) in the reference table. To do this the **Column** entity must be extended.

For any reference table it is necessary to know which column represents the code, which represents the description, and which represents the definition. This means that the following attributes must be added to the **Column** entity:

- *Column Description Indicator.* This indicates whether the current column is a description column. The standard adopted here is that there is one such column per reference table. In fact, other kinds of table may also have description columns, so it is not confined only to reference tables. Thus, *Column Description Indicator* may be useful to the rules engine designer in areas beyond reference data.

- *Reference Data Definition Column Indicator.* This indicates that a column is a definition column in a reference data table.

The attribute *Column Primary Key Indicator* already exists in the **Column** entity and indicates whether a column is a primary key. For a reference table this will be the code column.

ATTRIBUTE LOGICAL NAME	COLUMN PHYSICAL NAME	COLUMN DATATYPE
Column Description Indicator	COL_DESC_I	Character (1)
Reference Data Definition Column Indicator	COL_REFTABDEFN_I	Character (1)
Column Reference Table FK Indicator	COL_REFTABFK_I	Character (1)

TABLE 11.1 Additional Columns in **COL_COLUMN_M (Column)** Table

Tables that are not reference tables may be related to reference tables. If so, the primary key of the reference table will be migrated into the table. The previous chapter described ways in which foreign keys can be recognized, including how to identify the parent table and the parent column for such migrated columns. However, it is also necessary to know whether a foreign key belongs to a reference table. To achieve this level of detail it is necessary to add another attribute to the Column entity:

- *Column Reference Table FK Indicator.* This indicates whether a foreign key in a table that is not a reference table is a migrated key from a table that is a reference table.

These new additions to the **Column** entity are physically implemented in **COL_COLUMN_M** as shown in Table 11.1.

Populating the Reference Data Metadata

The metadata already imported into the Business Rules Repository is used to populate the metadata columns introduced for reference data. This is done as follows:

- *Table Reference Data Indicator* (TAB_REFTAB_I) in **TAB_TABLE_M** is set to "Y" for each table whose physical name ends in "_R".

- *Column Description Indicator* (COL_DESC_I) in **COL_COLUMN_M** is set to "Y" for the longest character column belonging to each reference table. In other words, for each table the longest character column is assumed to be a description.

- *Reference Data Definition Column Indicator* (COL_REFTABDEFN_I) in **COL_COLUMN_M** is set to "Y" for each memo datatype column belonging to a reference table. It is assumed there is no more than one memo column per reference table and that this contains the definition of the code value.

- *Column Reference Table FK Indicator* (COL_REFTABFK_I) in **COL_COLUMN_M** is set to "Y" if its parent column is the primary key of a reference table.

Listing 11.1 shows the function to perform these updates.

LISTING 11.1
Function to Update Reference Table Metadata

```
Private Function PopRefData() As String
'********************************************************************
' Populates relevant data in COL_COLUMN_M and TAB_TABLE_M with
' metadata about reference data
'
' Parameters: None
'
' Returns: "Y" indicates successful completion
'********************************************************************

Dim rstRel As ADODB.Recordset, cmd As ADODB.Command, strSQL As
String
Dim strLast As String, lngAffected As Long

    PopRefData = "Y"
    Set rstRel = New ADODB.Recordset
    Set cmd = New ADODB.Command
    cmd.ActiveConnection = CurrentProject.Connection
    cmd.CommandType = adCmdText

    strSQL = "UPDATE TAB_TABLE_M SET TAB_REFTAB_I = 'N' "
    cmd.CommandText = strSQL
    cmd.Execute lngAffected
    strSQL = "UPDATE COL_COLUMN_M SET COL_DESC_I = 'N', " _
          & "COL_REFTABDEFN_I = 'N', " _
          & "COL_REFTABFK_I = 'N' "
    cmd.CommandText = strSQL
    cmd.Execute lngAffected

    strSQL = "SELECT * FROM TAB_TABLE_M"
    rstRel.Open strSQL, CurrentProject.Connection, _
```

```
            adOpenKeyset, adLockOptimistic, adCmdText
    Do While Not rstRel.EOF
      If Right(rstRel("TAB_PHYSNAME_T"), 2) = "_R" Then
        rstRel("TAB_REFTAB_I") = "Y"
        rstRel.Update
      End If
      rstRel.MoveNext
    Loop
    rstRel.Close

    strSQL = "SELECT A.TAB_REFTAB_I, B.* FROM TAB_TABLE_M A,
COL_COLUMN_M B "  _
          & " WHERE A.TAB_PHYSNAME_T = B.TAB_PHYSNAME_T AND
A.TAB_REFTAB_I = 'Y'"  _
          & " ORDER BY B.TAB_PHYSNAME_T, COL_DTPLEN_N DESC         "
    rstRel.Open strSQL, CurrentProject.Connection,  _
          adOpenKeyset, adLockOptimistic, adCmdText
    strLast = "!"
    Do While Not rstRel.EOF
      If strLast <> rstRel("TAB_PHYSNAME_T") And rstRel("DTTP_C") =
"CHAR" Then
        rstRel("COL_DESC_I") = "Y"
        rstRel.Update
      End If
      If rstRel("DTTP_C") = "MEMO" Then
        rstRel("COL_REFTABDEFN_I") = "Y"
        rstRel.Update
      End If
      strLast = rstRel("TAB_PHYSNAME_T")
      rstRel.MoveNext
    Loop
    rstRel.Close

    strSQL = "SELECT A.TAB_REFTAB_I, C.* FROM TAB_TABLE_M A,
COL_COLUMN_M B, "  _
          & " RKEY_RELKEYATT_M C "  _
          & " WHERE A.TAB_PHYSNAME_T = B.TAB_PHYSNAME_T AND
A.TAB_REFTAB_I = 'Y'"  _
          & " AND B.COL_C = C.COL_PARENT_C "  _
          & " AND B.COL_PK_I = 'Y' "
    rstRel.Open strSQL, CurrentProject.Connection,  _
```

```
                adOpenKeyset, adLockOptimistic, adCmdText
    Do While Not rstRel.EOF
      strSQL = "UPDATE COL_COLUMN_M SET COL_REFTABFK_I = 'Y' " _
            & " WHERE COL_C = '" & rstRel("COL_CHILD_C") & "'"
      cmd.CommandText = strSQL
      cmd.Execute lngAffected
      rstRel.MoveNext
    Loop
    rstRel.Close

    Set rstRel = Nothing
    Set cmd = Nothing

End Function
```

Reference Data Default Values

Reference data is usually regarded as business data, and nearly all systems have screens that manage it. Thus, there is no point building the functionality to manage reference data in the business rules engine. However, there is one other aspect of reference data that does need to be captured. As discussed previously, reference data is used to identify subtypes. In the design presented here, each subtype is associated with a single business rule that is used to identify the subtype. Once identified, a subtype is "labeled" by using an indicator or reference data code value. If a reference data code value is used, there should be one rule to set each value of the codes found in the parent reference table (since each one corresponds to a different subtype).

These business rules typically consist of a set of conditions. If the conditions are true, then the reference data value associated with the rule is populated into the target column. However, if the conditions evaluate to false, should the rule do nothing? In fact, it is not wise for a rules engine to simply do nothing. An example can illustrate the problem.

Suppose that there is a requirement for the sample application to determine if an individual investment is high risk, medium risk, or low risk. To meet this requirement a new reference data table is implemented called **Investment Risk Type**. The new table has three columns: *Investment Risk Type Code, Investment Risk Type Description*, and *Investment Risk Type Definition*. It is populated with three records, as shown in Table 11.2. A column for *Investment Risk Type Code* is also added to the **Investment** table. The design is summarized in Figure 11.1.

INVESTMENT RISK TYPE CODE	INVESTMENT RISK TYPE DESCRIPTION
HIGH	High Risk Investment
MEDIUM	Medium Risk Investment
LOW	Low Risk Investment

TABLE 11.2 Data Contents of **Investment Risk Type** Table

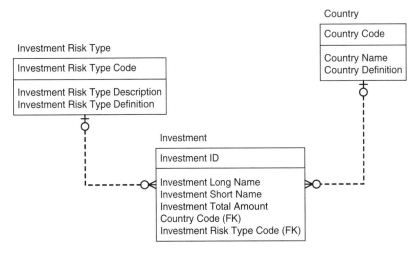

FIGURE 11.1
Investment Risk Type

Now let us suppose that the business rules for determining whether an investment is high, medium, or low risk are those shown in Table 11.3. For each rule, if the condition that makes up the rule evaluates as true, then the corresponding value of *Investment Risk Type Code* is used to populate the *Investment Risk Type Code* column in the **Investment** table.

Now that the rules have been defined, they can be applied to some investment data, as shown in Table 11.4.

Table 11.4 shows right away that the rules have failed to populate Investment Risk Type Code for two records: "NJ Tex-Mex Restaurants" and "On-Line Dogfood." This has left *Investment Risk Type Code* with null values for these records. The reason for this is that the person who created the rules has not created a set of rules that covers all possibilities, but perhaps they were not aware of this.

While it is not possible for a rules engine to determine if a user is entering rules that make business sense, leaving reference data code values null as in Table 11.4 is

RULE NUMBER	INVESTMENT RISK TYPE CODE	RULE DESCRIPTION
R1	HIGH	If the investment is located outside of the United States or Canada and has a value of $20,000,000 or greater
R2	MEDIUM	If the investment is located outside of the United States or Canada and has a value of $10,000,000 or greater, but less than $20,000,000
R3	LOW	If the investment is located within the United States or Canada and has a value of $5,000,000 or less

TABLE 11.3 Business Rules for Determining Investment Risk Type

INVESTMENT NAME	COUNTRY OF LOCATION	INVESTMENT AMOUNT	RULE THAT APPLIES	INVESTMENT RISK TYPE CODE
Bulk Catfood Corp	USA	$4,500,000	R3	LOW
Industrial Falafal	Bulgaria	$35,000,000	R1	HIGH
NJ Tex-Mex Restaurants	USA	$15,000,000		
Oil Refinery	Trinidad	$17,000,000	R2	MEDIUM
On-Line Dogfood	Canada	$12,000,000		

TABLE 11.4 Execution of Rules to Determine Investment Risk Type

dangerous. A better approach is to add one additional record to Table 11.2 with *Investment Risk Type Code* equal to "UNKNOWN" and *Investment Risk Type Description* equal to "Unknown Investment Risk Type." Then the rules need to be changed so that if they encounter an Investment Risk Type Code that is null, each rule can set it to "UNKNOWN" before executing its conditional logic. If the conditional logic evaluates to true, then the value of "UNKNOWN" will be overwritten; otherwise it will persist.

It also happens that even in well-formed sets of rules that do not have the kinds of logical gaps seen in Table 11.3, there is a value like "UNKNOWN" or some other default value. Thus, reference data management ultimately requires that there should be one default value for each reference data table. This is then used in the rules that execute to set values from the reference data table. The rules engine can also pre-

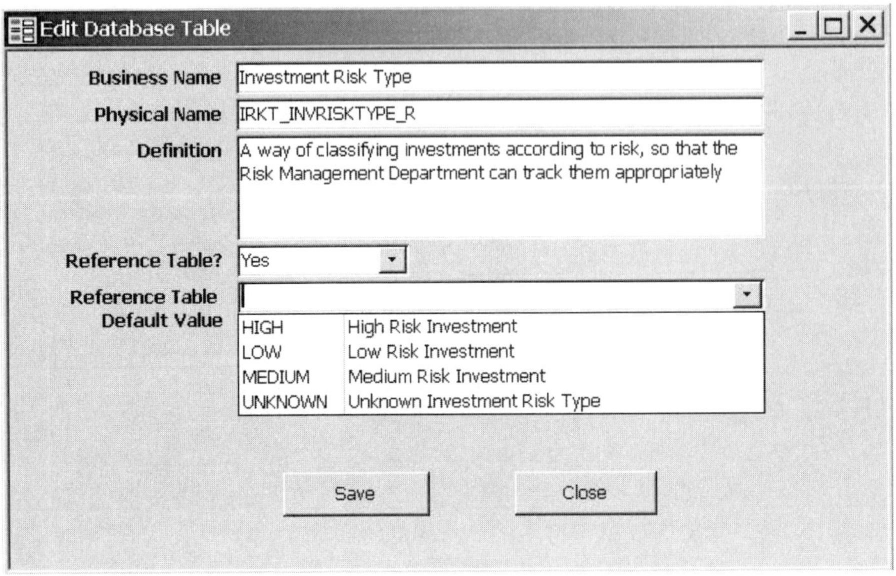

FIGURE 11.2
Edit Database Table

populate foreign keys of the reference data table with the default value prior to running any rules. Thus, in the example above, *Investment Risk Type Code* in the Investment table could be set to "UNKNOWN" before any of the rules were executed.

In order to implement this design, there needs to be a way of selecting the default value for each reference table. Fortunately, this is very easy to implement. An additional column needs to be added to the **Table** table (**TAB_TABLE_M**) called *Table Reference Table Default Value*. This is physically implemented as TAB_REFDFT-VAL_T with a datatype of Character (10). It will be recalled that a design standard was adopted that all reference data tables would have a single primary key column that must be of Character datatype with a length no greater than 10.

The screen where table data can be updated needs to be changed to enable the user to populate *Table Reference Table Default Value*. This screen can be accessed in the sample application by selecting **Database Maintenance** from the main menu, and then **Edit Database Tables** from the popup that appears. The user is next asked to select a business process, and then a business process step. Next, a list of all the database tables involved in the business process step appears. If the user selects a table that is a reference data table, the screen shown in Figure 11.2 is displayed.

This screen was discussed in more detail in Chapter 8. What is important for reference data is that if the selected table is a reference data table, then a combo box appears at the bottom of the screen containing codes and descriptions. These codes and descriptions are taken directly from the reference data table. The user can select the default value, which can be accessed later by the rules engine when rules associated with the reference data table are being defined.

Conclusion

Reference data is a complex area. It is business data, but is deeply entwined in the metadata that is required to define business rules. A business rules engine must have a strategy for managing reference data, in particular because reference data is so often used to identify subtypes. The design described here has a number of advantages that will become apparent when rules definition interfaces and code generation routines are discussed.

12 DEFINING BUSINESS PROCESSES AND RELATED INFORMATION

Creating a business rules engine that permits users to define business rules can be overwhelming. In a short time it is easy for users to define dozens or perhaps hundreds of rules. If there is no intuitive logical structure within which the users can organize and keep track of these rules, there may be a limit to how useful the rules engine is.

Users tend to categorize the rules into sets, and they often think about the sets rather than the individual rules. This is not surprising, since it is not possible to accurately remember the details of more than just a few rules at a time. The rules sets nearly always correspond to the business processes that exist for the business domain covered by the application that runs the rules engine. If the application truly mirrors the business domain, then the application's processes will correspond to the underlying business processes. Associating business rules with the application's processes permits sets of rules to be defined that are easy and natural to work with from the user's perspective. It is therefore important that the application be designed in a way that reflects the business processes, though how to create such a design is a topic in itself that cannot be dealt with in this book.

A related issue is that the business engine will fire rules not individually, but rather in sets. Under normal circumstances, a user invokes an application process and will expect that the appropriate rules for this process will then be fired in the correct sequence. Users do not want to be in the position of being responsible for selecting each rule in a process and then firing it individually, until all rules for a given process have been executed. Therefore, even solely from the perspective of rule execution, rules have to be grouped into sets. As was described in Chapter 7, these sets tend to correspond to business process steps, that is, the individual steps that make up business processes.

If an application is built such that its processes mirror the business process steps that the users are familiar with, how can business rules be associated with these process steps? This chapter deals with extensions to the repository design and rules engine functionality that are required to organize the business rules into these sets. The functionality provides not only a means of organizing business rules, but also the basis for invoking rules sets. It also enables us to build the first part of the rules engine interface needed for the definition of business rules.

Extensions to Business Rules Repository

Figure 12.1 shows the extensions to the Business Rules Repository to accommodate the metadata needed to define business processes and related entities.

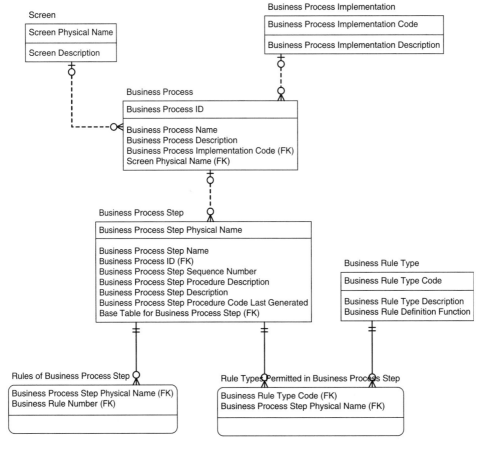

FIGURE 12.1
Extensions to Business Rules Repository for Metadata Related to Business Processes

The new entities added to the Repository are the following:

- **Business Process**: A general process that the business performs. A **Business Process** may be related to a screen (but not always). A **Business Process** is always implemented using a particular **Business Process Implementation**.

- **Business Process Implementation**: The software environments in which business processes can be implemented. This will dictate the kind of program code that is generated for any rule that runs within a business process. The environments used in the sample application are screens and batch processes. Stored procedures are another environment in which business rules code frequently needs to be generated.

- **Screen**: A screen that has been constructed for data entry in the system. It is often important for users to know which business processes (and hence which rules) are tied to particular screens in an application. Auditors may also ask for this kind of information.

- **Business Process Step**: A specific step within a **Business Process**. It has a sequence number that dictates the sequence in which the step runs, although some steps in a **Business Process** may not need to be run sequentially. An important item to note here is that one **Business Process Step** is based on one database table, called *Base Table for Business Process Step*. Only columns from this table and all of its parent tables are available for the definition of rules for a given **Business Process Step**. This serves to ensure that the rules associated with a **Business Process Step** are a truly coherent set of rules. It also helps to avoid circular references as discussed in Chapter 7.

- **Business Rule Type**: This describes all the different types of business rules that can be handled by the rules engine. Each **Business Rule Type** has one routine that is used to define rules of this type, and this is also captured in **Business Rule Type**. In the sample application, all such rule type definition routines are screens.

- **Rule Types Permitted in Business Process Step**: Only certain types of business rules make sense for a given **Business Process Step**. This book recommends that rule types be as specific to the business at hand as possible. Therefore, it can be expected that some rule types will apply only to a particular **Business Process Step**, and that many will apply to just a few **Business Process Steps**. The rules engine designer, perhaps in collaboration with business analysts, will have to populate this table. It will serve to restrict the types of business rules that can be defined for any **Business Process Step**. This is another way in which order is enforced on the rules definition process.

- **Rules of Business Process Step**: In business rules engines there is always the danger that business rules will be defined within **Business Process Steps**. If this

ENTITY	TABLE
Screen	SCR_SCREEN_M
Business Process Implementation	BPTP_BIZPROCTYPE_M
Business Process	BPROC_BIZPROCESS_M
Rule Types Permitted in Business Process Step	RTBS_RULTYPBIZSTEP_M
Business Rule Type	BRTP_BIZRULETYPE_M
Business Process Step	BPSP_BIZSTEPPROC_M
Rule Types Permitted in Business Process Step	RBSP_RULESOFSTEP_M

TABLE 12.1 Physical Implementation of Entities for Metadata Related to Business Processes

design approach is adopted, then there can be problems if the same rule has to be used by more than one **Business Process Step**. The user will be forced to define the rule separately in each **Business Process Step** that needs to run it. Such a design is bad. A business rule should be defined only once, even if it has to be used by many **Business Process Steps**, and even if these are implemented in different software environments.

The entity **Rules of Business Process Step** contains all the rules that are associated with one **Business Process Step**. It is an association entity between **Business Process Step** and **Business Rule**, and it permits one business rule to be associated with many **Business Process Steps**. In this way a business rule only has to be defined once.

Tables 12.1 and 12.2 show the physical implementations of the entities in Figure 12.1 in the sample application.

This completes the extension to the Business Rules Repository needed to handle metadata related to business processes. We will now consider these tables in more detail, as well as the functionality needed for this part of the business rules engine.

Business Processes

Business processes are rather high-level entities. However, there is some information that needs to be captured for them. Figure 12.2 shows the screen to select an existing business process, or to begin the creation of a new one. In the sample application this screen can be accessed by selecting **Repository Functions** on the main menu, and then **Business Processes** on the popup that appears.

The screen in Figure 12.2 leads to the screen shown in Figure 12.3 if the **Select** or **Add New** buttons are pressed.

TABLE	COLUMN	ATTRIBUTE	DATATYPE
SCR_SCREEN_M	SCR_PHYSNAME_T	Screen Physical Name	Character (20)
SCR_SCREEN_M	SCR_DESC_T	Screen Description	Character (80)
BPTP_BIZPROCTYPE_M	BPTP_C	Business Process Implementation Code	Character (10)
BPTP_BIZPROCTYPE_M	BPTP_DESC_T	Business Process Implementation Description	Character (10)
BPROC_BIZPROCESS_M	BPROC_C	Business Process ID	Character (10)
BPROC_BIZPROCESS_M	BPTP_C	Business Process Implementation Code	Character (10)
BPROC_BIZPROCESS_M	SCR_PHYSNAME_T	Screen Physical Name	Character (10)
BPROC_BIZPROCESS_M	BPROC_NAME_T	Business Process Name	Character (20)
BPROC_BIZPROCESS_M	BPROC_DESC_M	Business Process Description	Character (120)
RTBS_RULTYPBIZSTEP_M	BPSP_PHYSNAME_T	Business Process Step Procedure Physical Name	Memo
RTBS_RULTYPBIZSTEP_M	BRTP_C	Business Rule Type Code	Character (40)
BRTP_BIZRULETYPE_M	BRTP_C	Business Rule Type Code	Character (10)
BRTP_BIZRULETYPE_M	BRTP_DESC_T	Business Rule Type Description	Character (10)
BRTP_BIZRULETYPE_M	BRTP_FUNCTION_T	Business Rule Definition Function	Character (80)
BPSP_BIZSTEPPROC_M	BPSP_PHYSNAME_T	Business Process Step Procedure Physical Name	Character (80)
BPSP_BIZSTEPPROC_M	TAB_PHYSNAME_T	Base Table for Business Process Step	Character (40)
BPSP_BIZSTEPPROC_M	BPROC_C	Business Process ID	Character (50)
BPSP_BIZSTEPPROC_M	BPSP_SEQ_N	Business Process Step Sequence Number	Character (10)
BPSP_BIZSTEPPROC_M	BPSP_PROCDESC_M	Business Process Step Procedure Description	Integer
BPSP_BIZSTEPPROC_M	BPSP_LASTCODEGEN_D	Business Process Step Procedure Code Last Generated	Memo
BPSP_BIZSTEPPROC_M	BPSP_NAME_T	Business Process Step Name	Date/Time
BPSP_BIZSTEPPROC_M	BPSP_STEPDESC_M	Business Process Step Description	Character (120)
RBSP_RULESOFSTEP_M	BPSP_PHYSNAME_T	Business Process Step Procedure Physical Name	Memo
RBSP_RULESOFSTEP_M	BRULE_NUMBER_C	Business Rule Number	Character (40)
			Character (5)

TABLE 12.2 Physical Implementation of Attributes for Metadata Related to Business Processes

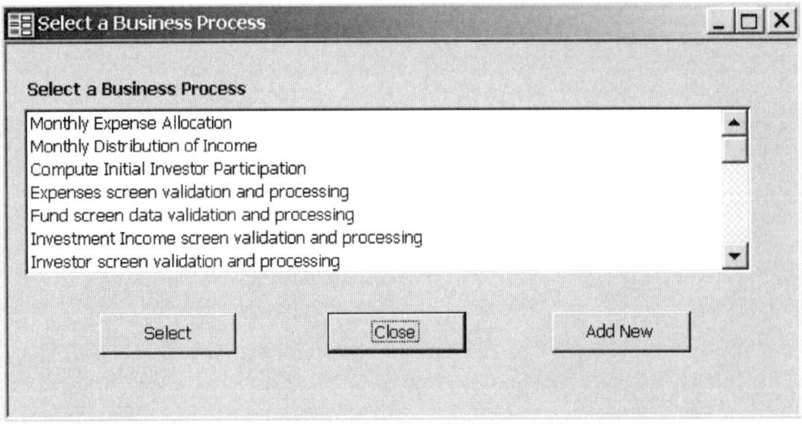

FIGURE 12.2
Select a Business Process

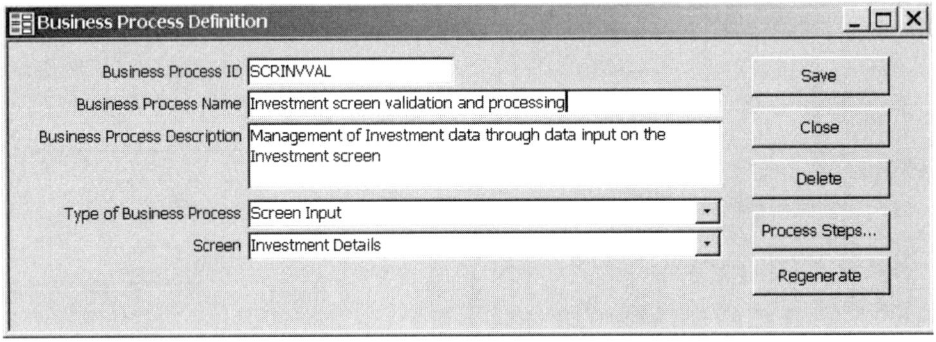

FIGURE 12.3
Business Process Definition Screen

The Business Process Definition Screen shown in Figure 12.3 allows for some basic information to be input about the business process, as follows:

- *Business Process ID*: This is an acronym created by the user to refer to a Business Process. No two Business Processes can use the same acronym.

- *Business Process Name*: A descriptive name for the Business Process.

- *Business Process Description*: A description of the Business Process.

- *Type of Business Process*: This is the **Business Process Implementation** for the currently selected Business Process and is equivalent to *Business Process Implementation Code* in Figure 12.1. Once this has been chosen and rules have been defined within the Business Process, it cannot be changed. It determines the kind of program code that will be generated.

- *Screen*: This is only displayed if the *Type of Business Process* (i.e., *Business Process Implementation Code*) chosen is "Screen." It is the screen (if any) with which this Business Process is associated.

Other important additional functionality in this screen is represented by the following buttons:

- **Delete**: This deletes a Business Process, but only if no Business Process Steps have been defined for it.
- **Process Steps**: This allows the user to drill down to the Business Process Steps for this Business Process.
- **Regenerate**: This will regenerate all the executable code, containing all the business rules, for this Business Process. It is important to be able to do this in case the user has doubts about whether the executable code for a Business Process is synchronized with the corresponding rule definitions.

This screen will be updated by the rules engine designer, perhaps with the help of a business analyst.

Of course, the rules engine designer does not even need to build screens to input this information. Some designers prefer not to have screens, but rather to directly update the required information in the tables of the database. This is usually driven by the fear that other staff could gain access to these screens and interfere with the rules engine designer's work. However, it is not necessarily always the task of a rules engine designer to update this information. In some circumstances business analysts may need to play a role. Furthermore, even rules engine designers can lose track of all the business processes and business process steps input into the rules engine. These screens help to manage this information. Therefore, it is a good idea to use screens for updating this area of the rules engine, although it may be necessary to implement a high level of security.

Business Process Implementation

Business Process Implementation definitions are required for the **Business Process** definition screen (where they are called *Type of Business Process*). There are only a very few kinds of **Business Process Implementation** that occur in any business rules engine. This table can probably can be populated directly by the rules engine designer, without the need for any data entry interface to be built.

Screen

Screen information is also needed for the **Business Process** definition screen. **Screens** can be built over a long period during application development, and their physical names need to be coordinated with the programmers building them. Thus, it is better

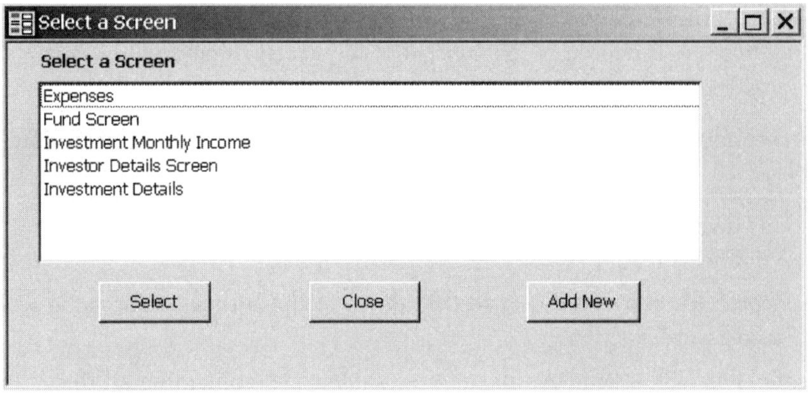

FIGURE 12.4
Select a Screen

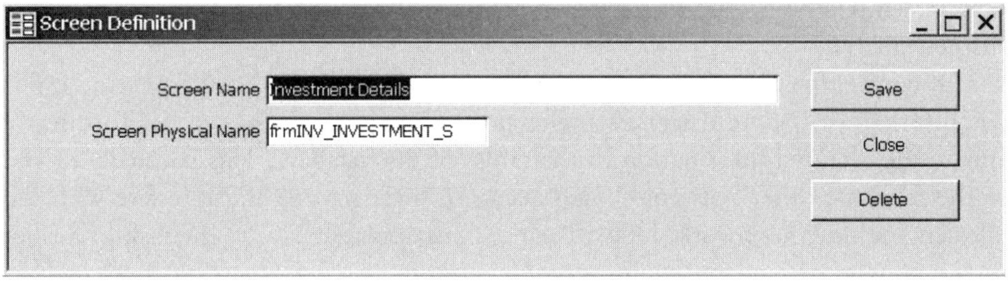

FIGURE 12.5
Edit Screen Information

to have a data entry interface to define **Screen** metadata. Figures 12.4 and 12.5 show this interface.

In the sample application this functionality can be accessed by selecting **Repository Functions** on the main menu, and then **Screen Definitions** on the popup that appears.

Business Process Step

If the **Process Steps . . .** button is clicked on the Business Process screen shown in Figure 12.3, the screen shown in Figure 12.6 appears. This lists all the Business Process Steps in the Business Process, and the sequence in which they should be run.

Selecting a Business Process Step in this screen leads to the screen shown in Figure 12.7.

The Business Process Step Definition screen allows the following information to be defined:

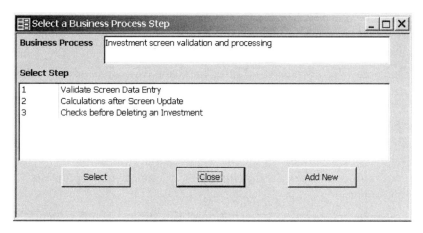

FIGURE 12.6
Select a Business Process Step

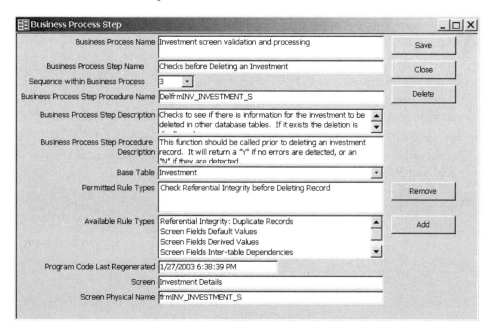

FIGURE 12.7
Business Process Step Definition

- *Business Process Step Name:* A descriptive name for the Business Process Step.
- *Sequence Within Business Process:* The sequence within the overall Business Process where this Business Process Step runs. No two steps in a Business Process can have the same sequence number. This concept does not apply to

all Business Process Steps. There are some Business Processes, particularly screens, where the sequence is dictated in advance rather than being assigned by an analyst.

- *Business Process Step Procedure Name:* This is the name that will be given to the routine that will be generated by the business rules engine to contain the processing for the Business Process Step. A business rules engine not only generates program code for business rules; it must also generate code for Business Process Steps. It is important that the names used here be coordinated with the programmers working on the main application, because the programmers must insert the calls that invoke the routine at the appropriate points in the application.

- *Business Process Step Description:* A description of this Business Process Step from the viewpoint of the business.

- *Business Process Step Procedure Description:* A description of the Business Process Step from the technical perspective. This will enable the programmers to understand how the rules engine runs the routine generated for the Business Process Step.

- *Base Table:* A table of the application database that is a point of reference for this Business Process Step. Only columns belonging to this table and its parents are available for rule definition purposes. For some rule types, such as those for screen validations, only the columns of this table are available.

- *Permitted Rule Types / Available Rule Types:* These two list boxes define the types of business rules that can be used in this Business Process Step. The **Add** and **Remove** buttons allow these types to be added to or removed from the Business Process Step. However, no rule type can be removed if there are rules defined for it that are associated with the current Business Process Step.

    When this functionality is invoked records are added to or removed from the table **Rule Types Permitted in Business Process Step (RTBS_RULTYPBIZSTEP_M)**.

The remaining information displayed on this screen is taken from earlier screens that were accessed prior to arriving at the Business Process Step definition screen.

The rules engine designer, perhaps working with business analysts, will enter the data on the Business Process Step definition screen.

Business Rule Types

Information about Business Rule Types is required for the Business Process Step definition screen. Rather than design and build an interface for data entry of this

OBJECT	DESCRIPTION
Menu to Define Screens	Repository Functions > Screen Definitions
Menu to Define Business Processes	Repository Functions > Business Processes
Business Process Selection Screen	frmSelBP
Business Process Definition Screen	frmBP. Accessed from frmSelBP
Business Process Step Selection Screen	frmSelBPStep. Accessed from frmBP
Business Process Step Definition Screen	frmBPSP. Accessed from frmSelBPStep

TABLE 12.3 Objects in the Sample Application for Managing Metadata Related to Business Processes

information, it is probably simpler if the rules engine designer directly updates the table where it resides (**BRTP_BIZRULETYPE_M**).

Conclusion

At this point, the Business Rules Repository has been extended to include metadata related to business processes, and functionality has been built in the rules engine to permit this metadata to be defined. Table 12.3 shows the relevant objects in the sample application.

The reader can examine the program code of the sample application to see how this functionality is implemented.

The new tables and functionality provide a large part of the rules engine infrastructure that enables the definition of business rules. As will be discussed in subsequent chapters, the user can define rules from the perspective of Business Processes and Business Process Steps. Rules for any Business Process Step will be confined to the rule types allowed for that step and will operate on the base table defined for that step and, if applicable, its parent tables. This framework places order on how users can think about and manage business rules, by ensuring as much as possible that the rules are grouped into logically related sets.

13 EXTENDING THE DATABASE

In a traditional systems development project, a database is built and rarely changed after it is implemented. The database typically originates from a data model that is designed over the course of the analysis and design phases of the project. At first, this data model is designed at the conceptual level, showing major entities and relationships in the business domain that is being modeled. Gradually, it is evolved into a logical data model, which should have all entities present in third normal form, complete primary keys for these entities, and all the relationships between the entities. Sometimes there is an attempt to produce a "fully attributed" logical data model. If this is done, it is expected that all entities in the logical data model have all the attributes needed to meet the information requirements of the system. After the logical data model is built, a physical data model is derived from it. This may be selectively denormalized for performance reasons, for example, and it must have all the attributes required for each entity, because it will be the model from which the physical database is generated.

Once the physical database is implemented, it is typically controlled by database administrators (DBAs). The tasks of a DBA include placing the database on servers or mainframes, setting up access rights, implementing backup and recovery procedures, and attempting to tune the database to increase performance. If a change needs to be made to the database structure (e.g., adding a new column to a table), it usually involves development staff making changes in a development version, testing it, and then asking the DBAs to implement the change in the production environment. Depending on the organization, this can involve a large number of "bureaucratic" tasks.

The business rules approach, with its promise of flexibility and increasing organizational agility, does not quite fit with the traditional approach to database implementation and maintenance for the following reasons.

- A successful business rules approach really does require working with a normalized logical data model of the business domain covered by the application. For every denormalization in the data model, additional processing has to be built into the business rules engine.

- If a business rule updates an attribute in the database (as it frequently does), and the rule is not known until after implementation (as is the case for many rules), then the database must be changed to add a new attribute (i.e., column or field) to store the results of the rule. It is very unlikely that the target attribute will have been thought about prior to implementation. Involving DBAs in the implementation of the new column can be time-consuming and difficult.

- More rarely, business rules may need to operate on new instances of a class of existing entities. For instance, data may be imported into the system from a variable number of interface files. For each new file, a new set of tables may need to be defined to receive the data, check it for accuracy, and then merge it into a final table where the data is combined. Again, involving DBAs in the implementation of the new tables can be time-consuming and difficult. This aspect of rules engines is not dealt with further in this book, but it can happen, and designers should be aware of it.

- Sometimes users need to categorize data for reporting purposes. This means that new reference tables have to be introduced for the categorization and linked to the data being categorized. Business rules are then defined to actually do the categorization. These categorizations may not be known before the system is built—for example, if they arise as the result of new government regulations. Again, this is a rare requirement and is not dealt with further in this book, but it can sometimes happen.

- Organizationally speaking, DBAs are often rather remote from users. A DBA's area of expertise is usually the database software he or she works with, rather than the general business processes of the organization the DBA works for. Similarly, non-IT staff often find it difficult to understand the detail of the tasks that DBAs perform. Having business users directly interact with DBAs without the mediation of business or systems analysts may provoke problems.

Thus, there is a strong chance of encountering organizational difficulties when extending a database to accommodate user-defined business rules. Even if these difficulties can be overcome, there is the technical challenge of building functionality in the rules engine so that users can add columns. However, unless this can be done, users will be confined to defining rules for database columns implemented prior to the application going into production—an unacceptable limitation for a business rules approach. These challenges will be examined in the remainder of this chapter.

Limits of Database Extension

It is important to place boundaries on how a database can be extended when building a business rules engine. The approach followed in this book is that it makes sense to build a business rules engine to extend and add flexibility to the core capabilities of a system. Given this, one of the requirements for the business rules engine is a good logical data model that is directly implemented as a physical database. Users should be permitted to construct business rules within the context of this model. However, they cannot change the fundamental structure of the model. The elements that comprise the fundamental structure of the model are the following:

- Entities
- The primary key attributes of entities
- Relationships
- The semantic definitions of each of the entities and attributes in the model

In short, this means that users can only extend the database by adding new non-primary-key columns to existing tables. Users cannot be allowed to add foreign keys in the nonkey areas of tables, that is, create additional relationships between existing entities in the data model.

Users should not be allowed to make changes to a database that affect the structure of the model on which it is built because users generally are not database designers. They usually do not understand the rules of data modeling and database design, such as how to ensure that a database table is in third normal form. Without this knowledge they would almost certainly introduce design problems into a database if they were allowed to alter its fundamental structure.

Sometimes, systems developers try to provide users with general fields in database tables, as shown in Figure 13.1. These fields are predefined but are not initially used for anything. Occasionally, they are termed "filler," which derives from a feature of the COBOL language that allows for unused data definitions. The idea is that if a user needs an extra field, then there is a set of them ready for use. This approach also means that there is no need to actually change the structure of the database—the new fields are defined when the database is first implemented and then just sit there waiting to be used.

The problem with this approach is that the semantic definitions of the entities and attributes in a database are part of its structure and we do not want users to change them after implementation. Suppose a database table has a column with a

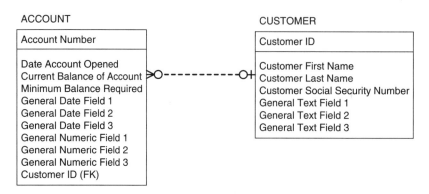

FIGURE 13.1
Predefining General-Purpose Columns in Database Tables

business name of "General Date Column 1" at implementation and a business definition of "A general date column to be used at a later time for whatever the requirement the user specifies." There could be many such columns in many tables across a
database. It is very easy to lose control of which have been used and which have not.
Furthermore, it may be difficult to enforce the updating of the business definitions,
which only adds to the confusion about what, if anything, these columns are used
for. Beyond this, it encourages users, and indeed developers, to think of columns in
a database as just a set of "buckets" that can be used to hold whatever data they feel
like at any particular time. This mindset can slowly lead to a breakdown of the semantic integrity of a database, which means that nobody can confidently understand the
meaning of the data, and so they cannot trust it.

Unfortunately, the practice of defining database columns that are general-purpose
"buckets" is fairly common, and many system developers even hold this out as an
advantageous design feature. Even worse is the case of the use (or reuse) of columns
intended from the start to hold a specific piece of business information. This tends
to happen when users feel that a database column has never really been used, or is
no longer used. For example, a credit card issuer may have a database table with a
column called *Finance Charges on Unpaid Annual Fees.* The issuer may have stopped
charging annual fees, but may want to charge for unpaid overlimit fees (an overlimit
fee is a fee charged for exceeding the credit limit on the card). The users may decide
to use *Finance Charges on Unpaid Annual Fees* for this purpose (e.g., to avoid dealing
with the DBAs). From now on, all users have to understand that the column *Finance
Charges on Unpaid Annual Fees* really means *Finance Charges on Unpaid Overlimit
Fees.* This is typically never documented and again leads to the gradual breakdown
in semantic integrity of the database.

It is very important that building a business rules engine not make it easier to create these problems. If a new business rule calculates some information that needs to be stored in a new database column, then a new column should be created for this data. Admittedly, this will not prevent users from trying to use existing columns to store something different. However, as we shall see, it is possible to a large extent to design a rules engine that can detect the reuse of columns for different business rules and prevent it from happening. Perhaps more important is implementing a design that encourages the development of a mindset among users of the application that database columns are specific items of information. Everything should be done to discourage users from thinking that database columns are just "buckets" that can contain anything.

In general, therefore, users should be limited in the way they can extend the database to adding new nonforeign key columns to the nonkey areas of database tables.

It was noted in the previous section that there may be a need to introduce new tables for categorizing data in ways not anticipated before the system was implemented, or to clone a set of a few tables to run a new instance of a business process, such as importing data from a new interface file. These are more challenging requirements for building a business rules engine, although they are seen much less frequently than the need to add new database columns. Since they are complex and extensive topics, they are not dealt with further in this book, although the design of the Business Rules Repository can be extended to accommodate them.

Sometimes there is a requirement to add new tables to deal with the underlying business processes for which the database has been built. This kind of large-scale change originates from significant changes in the underlying business and should be dealt with by the systems development team responsible. It means that the team will have to add to, or change, the data model that was originally developed for the application. Such requirements are really beyond the kind of change that can be accommodated by implementing new business rules. Indeed, it is very difficult to conceive of how a business rules engine could be designed to handle this situation. Traditional system development approaches may be the only viable alternative for such fundamental restructuring.

In summary, there will always be a need to allow users to add specific nonkey columns when they define new business rules. The functionality that must be built to enable this is discussed in the next section.

Adding New Columns to Existing Tables

Many business rules will require a new column to be added to an existing database table. As discussed previously, these columns will be nonforeign key columns of the nonkey areas of tables. That is, they will not be primary keys, and they will not be foreign keys. This section discusses how to implement such new columns.

Identifying the Target Table

If a user needs to implement a new database column associated with a new business rule, the user must have an idea of where the column fits in the system in terms of data. In other words, the user must to be able to identify the database table to which the new column will be added. Sometimes the user may be so familiar with the system that he or she knows immediately. This may be the case with consultants who tailor packages for implementation at a particular client. At other times, users may not be so confident, and there must be a good way for users to find out which table they need to work with. The search can be narrowed by first asking the user to identify the business process, or business process step, in which the rule will be executed. In general, users are good at understanding processes. They think in these terms, and the user interfaces of most applications are typically organized by business processes. Therefore, a good approach is to first ask the user to identify the business process and business process step where they want to execute the new rule, and then to present the tables that participate in the process step.

The Business Rule Repository is designed to hold information about business processes and business process steps, as discussed in Chapter 12. This chapter also introduced the standard that a business process step is associated with one base table. The assumption is that all business rules that execute in a business process step will operate on this table or any of its parents. Business rules will not operate on tables that are child tables of the base table or that are unrelated to the base table. This is an important simplifying assumption for the design of the Business Rules Repository and the operation of the rules engine. However, it is a highly justifiable assumption: business process steps really do operate on just a small cluster of related database tables.

In the sample application, the main menu item **Database Maintenance** has an option **Edit Database Columns**. If this is selected, the screen to select a business process appears, as shown in Figure 13.2.

After the user selects a business process, the screen to select a business process step within the selected business process appears, as shown in Figure 13.3.

After the user selects a business process step, the system displays the screen shown in Figure 13.4.

The screen in Figure 13.4 shows the base table associated with the currently selected business process step and all the parent tables for this base table.

A *parent* table in this case means not only immediate parents, but also grandparents, great-grandparents, and so on, all the way up the hierarchy to tables that have no parents of any kind. In the screen shown in Figure 13.4, the selected business process step "Compute Initial Investor Participation" has **Investor Position** as its base table. The location of **Investor Position** in the overall data model is shown in Figure 13.5.

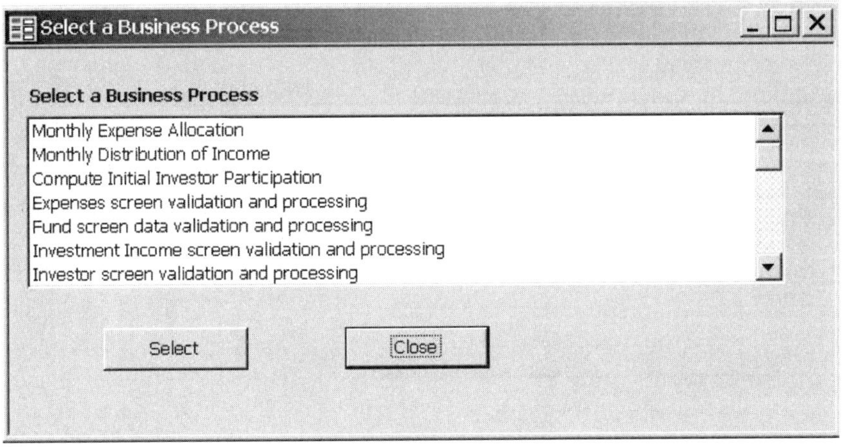

FIGURE 13.2
Screen to Select Business Process

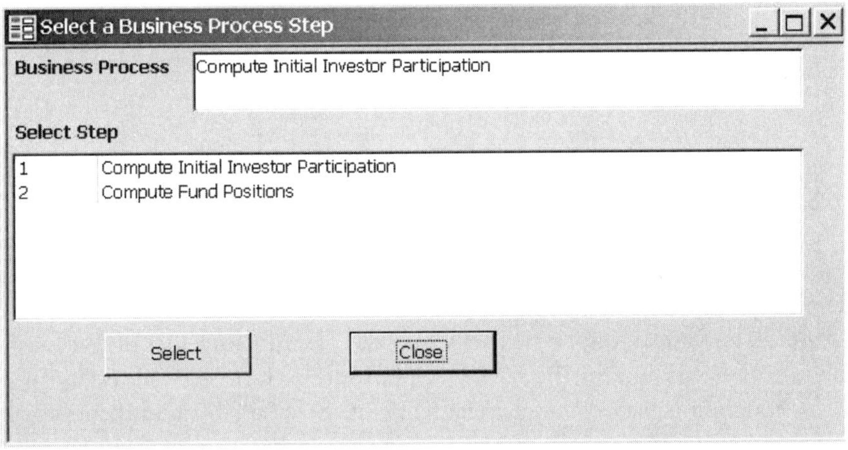

FIGURE 13.3
Screen to Select a Business Process Step

Figure 13.4 lists all the parent tables of **Investor Position**. The table with the highest level relative to **Investor Position** is **Region**, which is a great-grandparent.

How is it possible to build a list like that shown in Figure 13.4 for a selected database table? The answer lies in the **Relationship (REL_RELATIONSHIP_M)** table in the Business Rules Repository, which was discussed in Chapter 10. This table contains one record for every relationship in the data model of the business area. Each

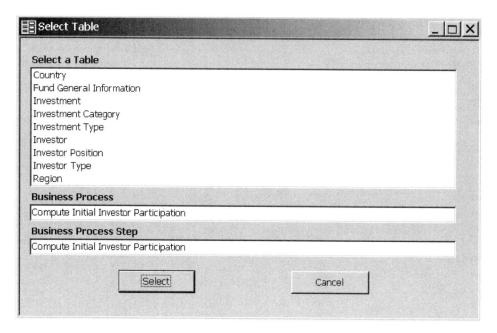

FIGURE 13.4
List of Tables Related to a Business Process Step

Relationship record contains the parent table and child table for the relationship described by that record. It is a simple matter to find all relationships where the child table is the base table associated with the currently selected business step. The parent tables in these relationships are then used to find other relationships where the parent tables are themselves child tables. This recursive process continues until no further relationships can be found. It is a little tricky to code. The function IdentifyParTabs() in the module GeneralFuncs in the sample application performs the necessary processing. This function is passed the physical name of the base table and identifies all parent tables.

There is one important point about the design of IdentifyParTabs() and the screen shown in Figure 13.4. IdentifyParTabs() uses a special column in the **Table** table (**TAB_TABLE_M**) to identify the currently selected table and its parents. This column is the *Table Currently Selected Indicator* (TAB_CURRSEL_I). It is set to "Y" for the currently selected table and its parents, and the screen shown in Figure 13.4 uses it to build its list of tables. Figure 13.7 below shows the new column in Table. However, this design effectively makes this part of the rules engine functionality single-user and means that no two persons add new columns at the same time. It is unlikely that two or more users would want to simultaneously define new columns, but not impossible. The rules engine designer will have to determine whether this is

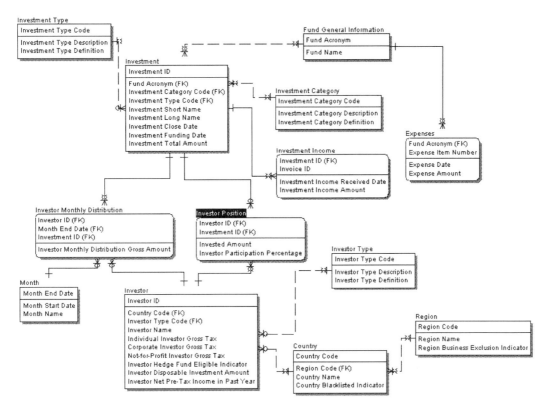

FIGURE 13.5
Table **Investor Position** in the Overall Data Model

a requirement. If it is, the design needed will be different from that presented here. If it is not, the design presented here can be used, but should have some added functionality so that if one user is adding columns, another user cannot also add columns. The topic of whether one or more users can simultaneously work with rules engine functionality is also discussed in different contexts in subsequent chapters. It is something that needs to be considered, but must be driven by known, quantified requirements, rather than simply the prejudices or past experience of the rules engine designer. Building a fully multiuser rules engine takes a great deal of additional work; such a rules engine may not be needed, or may be needed so rarely that the additional development cost and effort is not justified.

One other design point is that the rules engine designer may not wish to allow users to add new columns to all tables. This requirement can be implemented by adding a column called *Table User Extendable Indicator* to the **Table** entity, physically implemented as TAB_USEREXTERND_I in the table **TAB_TABLE_M**. Only if this

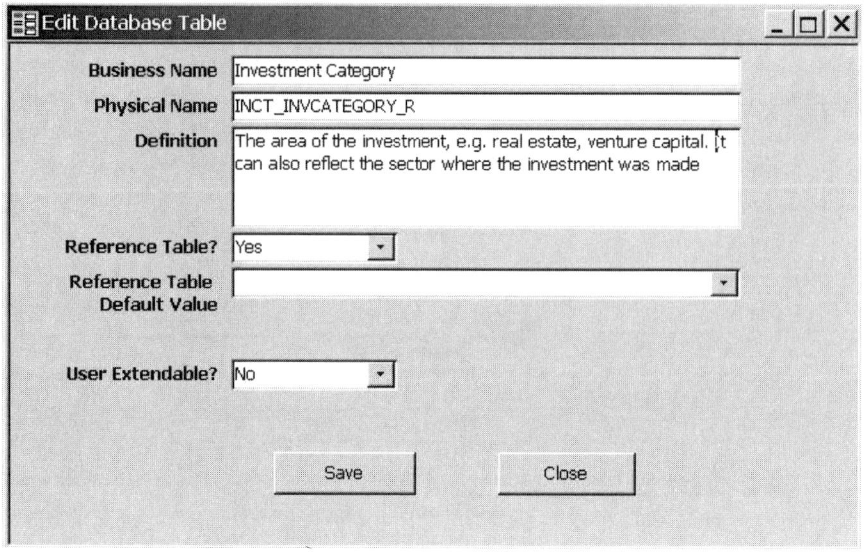

FIGURE 13.6
Implementing User Extendable Tables

is set to "Y" can the table be extended by users. Figure 13.7 below shows the new column in **Table**. The system development team will have to populate this indicator before the system goes live. One easy way to achieve this is to include it on the screen where **Table** information is updated. In the sample application, this screen is accessed by selecting **Database Maintenance** on the main menu and then **Edit Database Tables** on the popup that appears. After a table is selected, the screen shown in Figure 13.6 is displayed.

The combo box at the bottom of the screen switches on and off the capability for users to add more columns to the selected table.

Displaying the Structure of the Target Table

Let us return to the sequence of screens that lead the user to the point where he or she can edit information about columns. Once the user has found the needed table in the screen shown in Figure 13.4, information about it must be displayed. This information must come from the Business Rules Repository. The two main tables of the Repository that are required for this are **Table** and **Column**, as shown in Figure 13.7.

The information in these three tables is used in the screen shown in Figure 13.8, which allows the user to add new columns and edit certain metadata for existing columns.

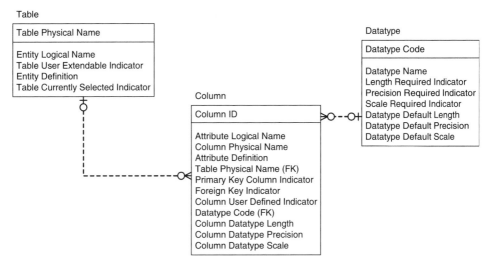

FIGURE 13.7
Fragment of Business Rules Repository for Displaying Column Information

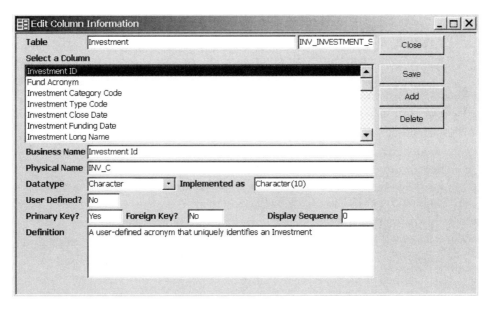

FIGURE 13.8
Screen to Edit Column Information

The screen shown in Figure 13.8 consists of the following items:

- **Table Name:** This enables users to recall the table they are working with. The business name is certainly required. The rules engine designer may also wish to include the physical name of the table, as has been done here. This information cannot be edited. The table name is taken from the column *Entity Name* (TAB_ENTLOGNAME_T) in the **Table (TAB_TABLE_M)** table. The physical name of the table comes from *Table Physical Name* (TAB_PHYSNAME_T) in the **Column (COL_COLUMN_M)** table.

- **Column List:** A list of all columns in the table, arranged in order with primary key columns first, followed by foreign key columns, followed by all other columns. Within this order, columns are listed alphabetically by business name. Business names come from the column *Attribute Logical Name* (COL_ATTLOGNAME_T) in the **Column** table.

- **Business Name:** The business name of the column. It is taken from the column *Attribute Logical Name* (COL_ATTLOGNAME_T) in the **Column** table. The user can change this information. It is important to ensure that users with a good knowledge of the business review these names. They are one of the most important items of metadata used by the rules engine and must be unambiguous and easily understood by users. Business names can change from organization to organization, and there is no guarantee that something called by one name in one organization will have the same name in another organization.

- **Physical Name:** Often users are familiar with, or want to know, the physical names of columns. This information can only be changed when the user adds a new column. After a column has been added, the physical name cannot be changed. This screen field is populated using the column *Column Physical Name* (COL_ATTLOGNAME_T) in the **Column** table.

- **Datatype:** This is the basic list of datatypes that users can use to implement columns. The user cannot edit it for an existing column, but must enter it for a new column. This screen field is populated using the column *Datatype Type Code* (DTTP_C) in the **Column** table. This column is a foreign key from the **Datatype Type (DTTP_DTPTYPE_R)** table.

- **Implemented As:** Shows the details of how the column datatype is implemented in the database. This screen field is populated using the column *Datatype Code* (DTP_C) in the **Column** table.

- **User Defined:** This is set to "Yes" if the column has been defined by a user (as opposed to being defined in the original data model for the business area covered by the application). It is assigned automatically by the system and cannot be edited. This screen field is populated using the column *Column User Defined Indicator* (COL_USERDEFINED_I) in the **Column** table.

- **Attribute Definition:** Users need to see this for many reasons, such as to understand that they will not be adding a column that already exists. The user can edit this information. The screen field is populated using the column *Column Definition* (COL_ATTDEFN_M) in the **Column** table.

For existing columns only the Business Name and Definition fields can be edited on this screen. The user simply enters the new values and presses the **Save** button. The metadata is then saved in the **Column** table (**COL_COLUMN_M**). If the user wishes to add a new column or delete an existing column, the process is a little more complex.

Adding a New Column

When the user wishes to add a new column, the following fields have to be updated on the Edit Column Information screen:

- **Business Name:** Unfortunately, there is no guarantee that good business names will be entered. Users should be encouraged to give a descriptive unambiguous name to any new column they create. It should be pointed out that this name will be used on screens to identify the column. This also means that any name should not be too long. It may be wise to impose a size limit or give a warning message if the size exceeds, say, 80 characters.

  There should be an edit check to ensure that this business name is not already used for an existing column. The edit check is implemented by searching the **Column** (**COL_COLUMN_M**) table for an identical value in the column *Attribute Logical Name* (COL_ATTLOGNAME_T).

- **Physical Name:** There should definitely be a size limit on this field. It is necessary to ensure that the physical name of the column will not exceed what is allowed by common database software. Currently, 30 characters is a reasonable limit.

  Furthermore, it may not be wise to let users construct the entire physical name of the column. For instance, each column could be prefixed with an identifier of, say, up to five characters that identifies the table, and each should be suffixed with a two-character indicator that indicates the usage of the column (e.g., "DT" for date, "PC" for percentage, "AM" for monetary amount). The user would then enter only a central node for the name, and the prefix and suffix would be automatically appended by the system, with underscores separating them. This approach ensures that columns are easily recognized within a general scheme of naming conventions that applies throughout the rest of the database. It is the approach used in the sample application.

  There should be an edit check to ensure that this physical name is not already in use in the selected table. The edit check is implemented by

ITEMS PRESENTED TO USER	UNDERLYING SQL SERVER DATATYPE
Short Text	Char (30)
Long Text	Varchar (250)
Count	Decimal (12)
Percentage	Decimal (5,2)
Monetary Amount	Decimal (15,2)
Ratio	Decimal (5,8)
Indicator	Character (1)
Date	Datetime

TABLE 13.1 Sample Set of Datatypes for Presentation to User in an Application with SQL Server as the Underlying Database

searching the **Column (COL_COLUMN_M)** table for an identical value in the column *Column Physical Name* (COL_PHYSNAME_T). Physical Name should only contain letters, numbers, and underscores, and there should be edit checks to enforce this. The letters should be converted to uppercase. This protects against creating column names that are invalid for the underlying database, and it helps to prevent users from trying to introduce duplicate columns. It is also wise to remove any leading and trailing spaces introduced by the user.

- **Definition:** This is absolutely necessary and should be created with care. The user who creates a new column may not be the same person who has to use it. Also, users rotate jobs and leave the organization, so it is necessary that the definition be accessible to other persons in case the user who created the column is not available to provide an explanation in person. It is difficult to build an edit check for a good definition, and not even professional database designers always provide definitions for attributes in the data models they create. However, everything should be done to encourage this practice.

- **Datatype:** Datatypes are rather technical and may be a little confusing for users to deal with. A reasonable approach is to give the user a set of limited choices as shown in Table 13.1. In this example the user is presented with a preset list of choices for datatype, each of which has a corresponding "real" datatype for the underlying database software. If such an approach is desired, the table **Datatype** in Figure 13.3 can be altered to accommodate it.

Note that "memo" columns can sometimes be a problem. These are datatypes that let a column contain a very large (perhaps unlimited) amount of text. Some database servers have restrictions on their use. Furthermore, it is difficult to see why a user should define such a column to receive the results of the execution of a business rule. For this reason they are not dealt with here.

The sample application uses this design approach, though with the more restricted set of datatypes found in the **Datatype Type (DTTP_DTPTYPE_M)** table. This may not be an adequate approach for many rules engines.

Besides data entry on the Edit Column Information screen, there are a couple of other considerations needed to complete the design for adding columns to database tables:

- **NULL versus NOT NULL**: Having user-defined columns as NULL makes the application more robust. In particular, SQL commands cannot fail because no value was provided for the user-defined column. This does not mean that the designer gives up the capacity to specify a column as being required to have a value. This can be stored as a separate item of metadata if it is needed. However, a "required column" only makes sense for the definition of a column that stores something that the user enters on a screen. This can be implemented as a type of business rule, as we shall see in later chapters.

- **Default Value**: Columns can have default values, but the only case where this is usually considered is for numeric datatypes. This is because if a NULL value is used in calculations, the program will crash in most environments. It is safer to use zero as a default value for numeric datatypes. Again, the designer may have particular needs, such as a default value for dates. In these cases the Business Rules Repository can easily be extended to accommodate them.

- **Excluded Tables**: As discussed earlier in this chapter there may be a need to allow users to add columns only to certain tables. These tables will have the column *Table User Extendable Indicator* (TAB_USEREXTEND_I) in the **Table (TAB_TABLE_M)** entity set to a value of "Y". If the user selects a table for which new columns are not allowed and presses the **Add** button on the Edit Column Information screen, an error message is displayed that prevents the user from adding a new column.

- **User Confirmation**: Users should be given an opportunity to confirm that they wish to add a new column, before the database is updated. This is especially important where the user enters only a fragment of the physical name for the new column. The confirmation message should reflect the complete name of the new column, as shown in Figure 13.9.

The information discussed above is sufficient to create the new column. Listing 13.1 shows the basic code to add the new column. Note that default values may require an explicit update statement to set the value in existing records. For example, in Microsoft Access, even if a new column is added with default value, it will have a value of NULL in existing records. Only in records inserted after the column has been added will the default value be set.

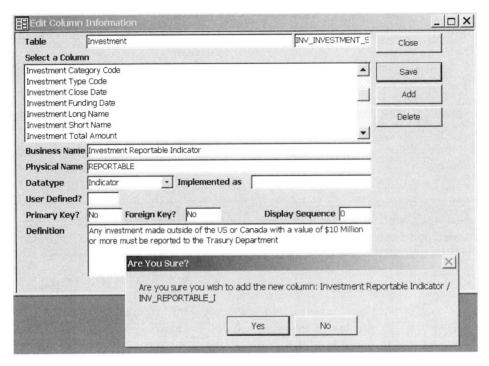

FIGURE 13.9
Confirmation Message for Addition of a New Column

LISTING 13.1
Program Code to Add a New Column

```
Public Function AddColumn(strTable As String, strColumn As String, _
                    strDatatype As String, strNumInd) As
String
'******************************************************************
' This function adds a new column to a database table
' Parameters:
' strTable = Physical Name of Table
' strColumn = Name of Column
' strDataType = Name of DataType
' strNumInd = Indicator "Y" if Numeric column
'
' Returns: "Y" upon completion
```

```
'******************************************************************
Dim cmd As ADODB.Command, strSQL As String, lngAffected As Long

  AddColumn = "N"

  'Set up Access Command Object
  Set cmd = New ADODB.Command
  cmd.ActiveConnection = CurrentProject.Connection
  cmd.CommandType = adCmdText

  ' Format SQL command text
  strSQL = " ALTER TABLE " & strTable _
         & " ADD COLUMN " & strColumn & " " & strDatatype _
         & " NULL "

  ' If this is a numeric column, give it a DEFAULT value of zero
  If strNumInd = "Y" Then
    strSQL = strSQL & " DEFAULT 0 "
  End If

  cmd.CommandText = strSQL
  cmd.Execute lngAffected

  ' If this is a numeric column, make sure the column is set to
  ' zero in existing records (not all databases do this)
  If strNumInd = "Y" Then
    strSQL = "UPDATE " & strTable & " SET " & strColumn & " = 0"
    cmd.CommandText = strSQL
    cmd.Execute lngAffected
  End If

  AddColumn = "Y"
  Set cmd = Nothing

End Function
```

Updating the Repository for the New Column

It is a good design approach to add the new column before attempting to update the Business Rules Repository. This is because if something goes wrong with the addition of the new column, and the program crashes, the Repository will not be updated. Of course, there is always a chance that the new column will be added and something will go wrong with the update of the Repository. Maintaining the synchronization of the Repository and database is dealt with in the next chapter.

When the Repository is updated, the new column should be clearly identified as being user defined. A *Column User Defined Indicator* in the **Column** table is used for this purpose, as shown in Figure 13.7. This is useful in future actions, particularly for permitting users to delete columns.

The designer may wish to store other metadata at the time of update, such as the user id of the user who created the column, and the date and time when this occurred.

Modifying an Existing Column

Once a column is created, it is really not practical to change any of its specifications in the physical database. Its physical name and datatype cannot be changed at all in some databases. Even in the ones that allow such changes, there may be problems with datatype conversions. The cleanest way to deal with this requirement is to delete the column and create it again. Deleting the column is discussed in the next section.

However, it is valuable for users to be able to change the *Attribute Logical Name* (taken from the screen field "Business Name") and *Attribute Definition* (taken from the screen field "Definition") for any database column. This functionality is present in the screen shown in Figure 13.9. However, some care is needed for such changes, especially in the case of *Attribute Logical Name*. For instance, if an *Attribute Logical Name* has been used for many years in screens and reports, it may be confusing to change it.

Deleting Columns

If users are allowed to add new columns to database tables, should they be allowed to delete them? One approach to business rules engine design is not to let users delete columns at all. This simplifies life for the developers of the rule engine, and in some cases may not really matter to the users too much if, for example, they are only going to define a few additional columns during the lifespan of an application. On the other hand, it is unwise to allow the buildup of unwanted user-defined columns in a database. If this happens, not only does it look messy, but users have to wonder whether or not each user-defined column is actually used. This introduces uncertainty that counteracts the benefits of the business rules approach.

The design shown in Figure 13.7 does permit users to delete ("drop") user-defined columns. The user must first select the column, and it must be a column that was previously defined by a user (not one that was imported from the original data model of the business area). The designer may wish to add additional security features, such as restricting this functionality to a higher user level, or restricting columns in particular tables to particular users.

Once a user has selected a column to delete, then three edit checks have to be performed:

- Is there any data in this column? If so, the user should at a minimum be given a warning message. Users may still be permitted to delete the column, but they will understand that they are losing data. Some rules engine designers may choose to prohibit deletion of any columns containing data.

- Is the column populated as the result of a business rule? If so, users should not be allowed to delete the column until they have deleted the business rule.

- If the column is not populated as the result of a business rule, is it referred to in any way by any business rule? If so, users should not be allowed to delete the column until these rules have been changed so the column is no longer used in them, or the rules have been deleted altogether.

The code for these edit checks is shown in Listing 13.2.

LISTING 13.2
Edit Checks Prior to Dropping a User-Defined Column

```
Public Function ChkColumnUse(strTable As String, strColumn As
String, _
                           strNumInd) As Long
'********************************************************************
' This function checks if a column is used (contains real values)
' in a database table
' Parameters:
' strTable = Physical Name of Table
' strColumn = Name of Column
' strNumInd = Indicator "Y" if Numeric column
'
' Returns: Number of records where column has a true value
'********************************************************************
Dim rstChk As ADODB.Recordset, strSQL As String
```

```
   ChkColumnUse = 0

   Set rstChk = New ADODB.Recordset

   strSQL = "SELECT COUNT(*) AS MYCOUNT " _
          & " FROM " & strTable _
          & " WHERE " & strColumn & " IS NOT NULL "
   If strNumInd = "Y" Then
     strSQL = strSQL & " AND " & strColumn & " <> 0"
   End If

   ' It is assumed that numeric columns have 0 as a default value.
   ' We assume that for numeric columns zero and null values mean
   ' that the column is not used
   rstChk.Open strSQL, CurrentProject.Connection, _
         adOpenKeyset, adLockOptimistic, adCmdText
   If rstChk("MYCOUNT") <> 0 And Not IsNull(rstChk("MYCOUNT")) Then
     ChkColumnUse = rstChk("MYCOUNT")
   End If

End Function

Public Function ChkColAsRuleTgt(strTable As String, strColumn As
String) As Long
'*******************************************************************
' This function checks if a column is used as a target of a rule
'-i.e. it stores the result of a rule
' Parameters:
' strTable = Physical Name of Table
' strColumn = Name of Column
'
' Returns: 0 if the column is not used as a rule target; 1 if it
' is        ( a column should only be the target of 1 rule)
'*******************************************************************
Dim rstChk As ADODB.Recordset, strSQL As String

   ChkColAsRuleTgt = 0

   Set rstChk = New ADODB.Recordset
```

```
        strSQL = "SELECT COUNT(*) AS MYCOUNT " _
                & " FROM BRULE_BIZRULE_M A, " _
                & "      COL_COLUMN_M B " _
                & " WHERE A.COL_C = B.COL_C " _
                & "   AND B.TAB_PHYSNAME_T = '" & Trim(strTable) & "' " _
                & "   AND B.COL_PHYSNAME_T = '" & Trim(strColumn)
    & "'"

    rstChk.Open strSQL, CurrentProject.Connection, _
            adOpenKeyset, adLockOptimistic, adCmdText
    If rstChk("MYCOUNT") <> 0 And Not IsNull(rstChk("MYCOUNT")) Then
        ChkColAsRuleTgt = rstChk("MYCOUNT")
    End If

End Function

Public Function ChkColAsRuleSrc(strTable As String, strColumn As
String) As Long
'*******************************************************************
' This function checks if a column is used as a source column for
' a rule
'
' Parameters:
' strTable = Physical Name of Table
' strColumn = Name of Column
'
' Returns: 0 if the column is not used as a rule target;
'          otherwise the number of times it is used in Business
'          Rule Versions
'*******************************************************************
Dim rstChk As ADODB.Recordset, strSQL As String

    ChkColAsRuleSrc = 0

    Set rstChk = New ADODB.Recordset

    strSQL = "SELECT COUNT(*) AS MYCOUNT " _
            & " FROM BSC_BIZRULESRC_M A, " _
            & "      COL_COLUMN_M B " _
            & " WHERE A.COL_C = B.COL_C " _
```

```
             & "    AND B.TAB_PHYSNAME_T = '" & Trim(strTable) & "' " _
             & "    AND B.COL_PHYSNAME_T = '" & Trim(strColumn) & "'"


   rstChk.Open strSQL, CurrentProject.Connection, _
           adOpenKeyset, adLockOptimistic, adCmdText
   If rstChk("MYCOUNT") <> 0 And Not IsNull(rstChk("MYCOUNT")) Then
      ChkColAsRuleSrc = rstChk("MYCOUNT")
   End If


End Function
```

Even if the edit checks are passed, users should be asked a couple of times if they really want to delete the column, so they have ample chance to reconsider their choice.

The programming needed to drop a column varies from database to database. Listing 13.3 shows how it can be done for Microsoft Access. SQL Server similarly can use ALTER TABLE . . . DROP COLUMN syntax.

Updating the Repository after Dropping the Column

It is a good design approach to drop the column before attempting to update the Business Rules Repository. This is because if something goes wrong and the program crashes, the column will probably still be there and the Repository will not have been updated. Maintaining the synchronization of the Repository and database is dealt with in the next chapter.

When the Repository is updated. the dropped column should be deleted from the **Column** table.

The designer may have reasons why they do not want to permit users to drop columns, or the database software may not permit this to be done programmatically. In such cases, a design alternative is to add a *Column Unused Indicator* to the **Column** table. A control could be added to the screen shown in Figure 13.8 in order to update *Column Unused Indicator*. If *Column Unused Indicator* is populated with a "Y", the system can prevent the column involved from ever again participating in a business rule. The edit checks described in the previous section should still be run. Also, it would be wise to set the column's values to NULL after updating *Column Unused Indicator*. After all, if this column is not used, why should any values remain in it?

LISTING 13.3
Dropping a Column from a Database Table

```
Public Function DropColumn(strTable As String, strColumn As
String) As String
'******************************************************************
' This function drops a column from a database table
' Parameters:
' strTable = Physical Name of Table
' strColumn = Name of Column
'
' Returns: "Y" upon completion
'******************************************************************
Dim cmd As ADODB.Command, strSQL As String, lngAffected As Long

    DropColumn = "N"

    'Set up Access Command Object
    Set cmd = New ADODB.Command
    cmd.ActiveConnection = CurrentProject.Connection
    cmd.CommandType = adCmdText

    ' Format SQL command text
    strSQL = " ALTER TABLE " & strTable _
           & " DROP COLUMN " & strColumn & " "
    cmd.CommandText = strSQL
    cmd.Execute lngAffected

    DropColumn = "Y"
    Set cmd = Nothing

End Function
```

The system can reduce the visibility of the column in the screens displayed to the user. Unfortunately, separate report writing packages will still "see" the column, and it will thus still be available for reports.

One problem with dropping columns and deleting the metadata from the repository is that there is no information left to show that they ever existed. This can create a problem for auditors. One way to capture what happened is to have a Repository table that is a **Column Delete Log**. This can be a simple copy of the **Column** table. The metadata for deleted columns can be added to the log just before being deleted from the **Column** table. The log can have extra columns for the date and time of deletion, the user who performed the deletion, and perhaps even a reason for the deletion.

Dealing with Database Administrators

Generally speaking, database administrators do not like modifications to database structures that do not follow predefined change control procedures. Such change control procedures vary from organization to organization and frequently include steps that appear to add no value to the management and integrity of the databases concerned. Overall, they do serve to limit systems development teams from making frequent changes to production databases and acquiring sloppy habits because they can easily "fix things in production." The change control procedures also usually have backout steps. These are actions to be taken if the new functionality fails to work correctly.

This traditional change control does not work very well with a business rules approach. It works quite well for traditional systems, where large chunks of functionality are typically implemented at one time. However, this is far larger than what is involved in introducing a single column for a new business rule. It should also be noted that a somewhat different approach is used when implementing new versions of purchased software packages. Here the DBAs are often not so closely involved in the management of the database. Rather, new versions are tested in separate environments and moved to production when they are approved by business users.

Since a business rules approach does not fit with the normal ways in which DBAs work, there can be problems. DBAs may object to users being able to define columns in a production database. These objections can be dealt with in a number of ways, depending on the organization and application involved.

- **Total autonomy:** In this scenario, the users are completely responsible for the application and maintenance of their database. This is not a worthwhile use of users' time if it involves much in the way of database maintenance. It is an option for personal or small departmental systems, such as those using Microsoft Access.

- **Semi-autonomy:** In this scenario DBAs provide usual support services (e.g., backups, restores, application of database operating software upgrades) but do not object to users defining columns. DBAs can sometimes be persuaded to go along with this if the database involved resides on a different server (or other physical environment) from other databases. Thus, if the database in question crashes, no other databases or systems will be affected. It is also worth pointing out that adding a nonkey column is unlikely to affect the database and is a much smaller change than DBAs normally process through their change control procedures. DBAs may have fewer objections if the application is departmental in scope, rather than an enterprise-level database.

- **Low Postproduction Activity:** Some business rules applications really only require business rules to be defined prior to production use. Usually the application is in a nonproduction environment when this is done. Even if the application is in a production environment, it may not be used for production purposes until after the rules are built. In this situation DBAs may agree to relax their change control procedures, or at least not enforce them until the application is officially in production.

- **Specific Timing:** DBAs may agree to permit users to define new columns at certain times—usually when there is low activity in terms of changes. This could be over a weekend that is between the 10th and 20th of a month. The reason is that at these times there will be more DBA support if anything goes wrong.

- **Copying from Preproduction:** This situation involves copying the production database into another environment, usually called a preproduction environment, and making the changes there. The changes are then tested and if the test is successful, the database is copied back to production. Obviously, care has to be taken not to lose or modify the production data in this cycle, and it all needs to be done in a timely fashion.

- **Traditional Change Control:** In this scenario, the user adds a column to a nonproduction environment and then tests the change. If everything tests out correctly, the change in the database table (and corresponding metadata in the Business Rules Repository) are moved over into the production environment. This may or may not require quite a lot of additional functionality to be built, depending on the environment. Some databases allow table replication, so the tables of the Business Rules Repository can easily be copied via a replication feature. Then the structural change to the table to which the user added a column needs to be applied. A reasonable way to do this is to write a program to compare the structure of the production table with the nonproduction version. The differences detected can be expressed in terms of SQL statements to bring the production table into the same state as the nonproduction one. These SQL statements can then be handed over to the DBA, who implements them in production.

Perhaps in the future, the functions of DBAs and the capabilities of relational database management software may become more attuned to working with business rules approaches. Until that happens, there is the potential for conflict with business rules approaches, and ways will have to be found to mitigate these problems.

Conclusion

In this chapter we have reviewed the need to allow users to extend the database, and we have seen programming constructs that can implement this requirement. However, if users are to be as self-reliant as possible, they need to view the database and be provided with some utilities to manage it and column information in the Business Rules Repository. We will discuss these needs in the next chapter.

14 MANAGING THE DATABASE

In the previous chapter we saw how users can extend the database by adding new columns to tables. These columns are often needed to support new business rules that the users define. If users are to work with the database in this way, they must be provided with the means to manage their work, especially to investigate and resolve possible problems. A business rules engine cannot create an application that is a black box from the user's perspective. What is more, in many business rules engine projects there is simply not a team of IT staff available to support users in the same way that there may be for a traditional systems development project. Even if there were IT staff available, they would not be able to undertake support activities until they had a good idea of what the users had done within the rules engine in terms of defining new columns and rules. This is because problems that users encounter often revolve around business issues, rather than the functionality of the rules engine itself. Business-related issues are much more common than instances of a rules engine breaking or crashing. If the latter happens the team that built the rules engine must be called in to help. However, business-related issues that have arisen because users are able to add more columns to the database need a different approach. A good response is to create rules engine functionality that can help users manage their extensions to the database, so that the users can be as self-sufficient as possible.

A primary need for managing both new columns and business rules is to make all data in the database visible to users. This can be used to physically see the new columns and to see the values with which business rules are populating them. Another need is to ensure that the database structure and Business Rules Repository are always synchronized. The Repository is the part of the rules engine that makes it possible to define business rules and create executable versions of them. There must be a way of assuring users that the Repository has correctly captured the metadata belonging to the database tables that hold business-related data.

It is also important for users to understand what they have done in terms of defining new columns, and to understand how these columns are being used. Functionality needs to be introduced into the rules engine to track these columns. In particular, users need to be able to view the contents of the columns they add, and indeed of all columns in all database tables.

Viewing the Database Tables

In the previous chapter we discussed how users can identify a database table to which they are interested in adding columns. The design alternatives presented there for identifying database tables also apply to a user who wants to view data in a particular table. The alternatives were:

- Present the user with a simple list of all the database tables that hold business-related data, and ask the user to select one.
- Ask the user to identify the business process and business process step in which he or she is interested, and then display the set of tables that applies to the selected business process step. The user makes a selection from this list.

It seems that as the complexity of an application grows, the second alternative makes it easier for users to work with the application. However, the rules engine designer must ensure that users can quickly view any table, something that is better achieved with the first alternative. It is the first alternative that is implemented in the sample application where the contents of database tables are viewed (see below for details of the menu options to select). The reader can contrast it with the second alternative, which is used, for example, in defining new columns as described in the previous chapter.

When a user has identified a table it seems rather simple to select all records from it and display them. However, there are a number of design questions to be answered. These are dealt with next.

Displaying Logical or Physical Names

It is a good idea to display the data retrieved from a database table in a grid format, with one record per row. This is a very common format, which permits users to quickly scan a large number of records. The columns of the grid display represent database columns. The headers of these columns identify what they are. Should the column headers be attribute logical names or column physical names? Most database software packages (or programming languages that work with databases) have utilities for displaying grids that have the *Column Physical Name* as the column header. It is somewhat more difficult to replace these with *Attribute Logical Name*, but to users it is often more helpful to see *Attribute Logical Name* in column headers. Fortunately, with the Business Rules Repository it is possible to do this.

For a display with *Column Physical Name* we only need to issue a basic SQL SELECT statement such as:

```
SELECT *
FROM [Table Selected by User]
```

To use *Attribute Logical Name* requires a little more programming. A good approach is to use *Attribute Logical Names* as alias names for *Column Physical Names*. This is the technique used by the function SetTabLogical() shown in Listing 14.1. SetTabLogical() is passed the physical name of a database table and builds a SQL SELECT statement for the table.

LISTING 14.1
Function to Create a SQL SELECT Statement for a Table Display with Attribute Logical Names as Column Headers

```
Public Function SelTabLogical(strTable as string) As String
'*******************************************************************
' Returns a SQL command string that permits Access to display
' a results set with logical (business) names for columns
'
' Parameters:
' strTable = Physical Name of Table
'
' Returns: A SQL SELECT command string with Logical Column Names
'*******************************************************************
Dim rstCols As ADODB.Recordset, strSQL As String, strCol As String

    SelTabLogical = ""

    Set rstCols = New ADODB.Recordset

    strSQL = "SELECT * " _
            & " FROM COL_COLUMN_M   " _
            & " WHERE TAB_PHYSNAME_T = '" & Trim(strTable) & "' " _

            & " ORDER BY COL_DISPLAYSEQ_N "
```

```
        rstCols.Open strSQL, CurrentProject.Connection, _
            adOpenKeyset, adLockOptimistic, adCmdText
    If Not rstCols.EOF Then
      SelTabLogical = "SELECT "
      Do While Not rstCols.EOF
        ' Put in comma if not the first column
        If SelTabLogical <> "SELECT " Then
          SelTabLogical = SelTabLogical & ", "
        End If
        strCol = rstCols("COL_ATTLOGNAME_T")
        ' Use Physical Name if Logical Name is too long
        If Len(rstCols("COL_ATTLOGNAME_T")) > 32 Then
          strCol = rstCols("COL_PHYSNAME_T")
        End If
        SelTabLogical = SelTabLogical & rstCols("COL_PHYSNAME_T") &
  " AS [" _
            & strCol & "]"
        rstCols.MoveNext
      Loop
      SelTabLogical = SelTabLogical & " FROM " & strTable
    End If
    rstCols.Close
    Set rstCols = Nothing

    ' Display error message if the table is not in the repository
    If SelTabLogical = "" Then
      MsgBox "Error in Function SelTabLogical: No records in
  COL_COLUMN_M " _
            & "for Table " & strTable
    End If

End Function
```

This function uses logical rather than physical names as aliases for the names of the columns it selects.

Once the SQL statement has been created, it needs to be executed and the results displayed to the user. In Microsoft Access, one way to do this is to create a query, and then either let users open it by themselves, or open a screen based on the query. Listing 14.2 shows how to use the function defined in Listing 14.1 to build such a query.

LISTING 14.2

Function to Build a Microsoft Access Query That Displays a Database Table Using Attribute Logical Names

```
Public Function CreTabDisp(strTable As String) As String
'********************************************************************
' This function creates a Microsoft Access query that displays the
' contents of a table. The query is named "qry" followed by the
' name of the table
'
' Parameters:
' strTable = Physical Name of Table
'
' Returns: "Y" if completes successfully
'********************************************************************
Dim dbMy As Database, qdfMy As QueryDef, strQryName As String,
strSQL

CreTabDisp = "N"
Set dbMy = CurrentDb()

strQryName = "qry" & Trim(strTable)

' Delete the query if it already exists.  Note this is DAO code.
For Each qdfMy In dbMy.QueryDefs
  If qdfMy.Name = strQryName Then
    dbMy.QueryDefs.Delete qdfMy.Name
  End If
Next
dbMy.QueryDefs.Refresh

strSQL = SelTabLogical(strTable)

Set qdfMy = dbMy.CreateQueryDef(strQryName, strSQL)
CreTabDisp = "Y"

End Function
```

Regrettably, in other software environments, this is a little more difficult. The programmer must build the column headers separately and then display the results. This requires making sure that the columns match the order of the data displayed below them. Listing 14.3 shows how to do this within Macromedia's Cold Fusion language.

Listing 14.3 illustrates the flexibility provided by languages that are interpretive rather than compiled. The Cold Fusion EVALUATE command is necessary to easily meet the requirement. EVALUATE is akin to the Eval() function in Access and macro substitution in other programming languages. It executes the contents of the variable that is passed to it, as if it were program code, and returns any value that results from the execution. This kind of flexibility greatly aids business rule approaches and metadata engineering in general and is more difficult to provide in compiled languages.

The examples in Listings 14.1 and 14.3 can be combined in a grid display that contains other metadata from the repository. There can easily be a toggle for the user to switch between *Column Physical Name* and *Attribute Logical Name*. This is useful, for example, when reports are built using a third-party reporting tool that displays only physical names. The user can then easily see the equivalent.

There can be a couple of design issues in the general approach presented here. For instance, users may create *Attribute Logical Names* that are quite long. Long texts are sometimes unhelpful as column headers in a grid display, especially if they widen the columns too much. A maximum length of about 30 seems to be the best. These issues can be overcome by adding and storing another metadata item *Attribute Short Name* in the **Column** table of the Business Rules Repository. *Attribute Short Name* can be defaulted to the value of *Attribute Logical Name* and the user can change it to contain a shorter or abbreviated version of *Attribute Logical Name* for use where space is an issue. The code in Listings 14.1 and 14.3 could then be changed to use *Attribute Short Name* instead of *Attribute Logical Name*.

The database server may also cause problems in this regard. If the user creates an *Attribute Logical Name* that is longer than the maximum column name length allowed by the database server being used, the code in Listing 14.1 would crash without the test that substitutes *Column Physical Name* for *Attribute Logical Name*. Using the leftmost number of characters of the *Attribute Logical Name* up to the maximum allowed by the database is not good, because it can result in duplicate *Attribute Logical Name* aliases being assigned, which will also cause the code to crash.

Another issue is that some fields contain amounts of data that are excessive for grid-like displays. Memo columns that contain potentially unlimited amounts of text fall into this category, as do long character columns. If desired these can easily be eliminated from the grid display. The datatype for each column is carried in the **Column** table (COL_COLUMN_M) in the field *Datatype Code* (DTP_C). The **Column** table also contains *Column Datatype Length* (COL_DTPLEN_N). Thus the SQL SELECT statement in Listing 14.1 that retrieves information from the **Column**

LISTING 14.3
Cold Fusion Code to Display a Database Table Using Attribute Logical Names

```
<!--- strTable has already been defined and contains the name
      of the table to be displayed   --->

<CFQUERY NAME="GetCols">
 SELECT * FROM COL_COLUMN_M
 WHERE TAB_PHYSNAME_T =  '#strTable#'
 ORDER BY COL_DISPLAYSEQ_N
</CFQUERY>

<table>
<!--- First display the column headers --->
<tr>
<CFLOOP QUERY="GetCols">
  <td><CFOUTPUT>#GetCols.COL_ATTLOGNAME_T#</CFOUTPUT></td>
</CFLOOP>
</tr>

<!--- Get the data to be displayed --->
<CFQUERY NAME="GetData">
 SELECT * FROM #strTable#
</CFQUERY>

<!--- Loop through the data one record at a time --->
<CFLOOP QUERY="GetData">
  <tr>
  <!--- For each record get the order of physical names from the
        GetCols query—so they match the column headers--->
  <CFLOOP QUERY="GetCols">
    <CFSET strColumn = "GetData." & COL_PHYSNAME_T>
    <!--- The EVALUATE command returns the contents of the Cold
Fusion statement contained in the variable strColumn --->
    <CFSET MyValue = Evaluate(strColumn)>
    <td><CFOUTPUT>#MyValue#</CFOUTPUT></td>
  </CFLOOP>
  </tr>
</CFLOOP>

</table>
```

table could be modified as follows to eliminate memo columns and character columns over 150 characters long:

```
strSQL = "SELECT * " _
       & " FROM COL_COLUMN_M    " _
       & " WHERE TAB_PHYSNAME_T = '" & Trim(strTable) & "' "
       & "    AND DTP_C <> 'MEMO' "
       & "    AND NOT(DTP_C = 'CHAR' AND COL_DTPLEN_N > 150) "
```

If this is done, the programmer should be aware that the SQL SELECT command that selects data from the desired database table may need to be changed to have an explicit field list rather than using SELECT * as in Listing 14.3 above. In the approach used in Listing 14.3 this is not necessary, but the author has seen implementations where it was needed.

Order of Columns

When presenting a grid-like display to the user, it is important to have a meaningful order to the columns displayed, going from left to right. Table 14.1 shows the order used in the sample application.

Each of the categories in Table 14.1 may actually contain several columns. It is a good idea to order them by *Attribute Logical Name* within each category. An exception is foreign key (FK) columns. Sometimes a parent entity has more than one primary key column, and thus these columns migrate together into the child table. It is confusing to separate these columns in the display.

Although the order in Table 14.1 makes sense in a lot of cases and can be generated programmatically, it is by no means certain that it will apply universally. In any database there may be tables where some different kind of order makes more sense to the user, and there may be no logic that can be implemented via metadata engineering that can generate this order. In these cases the display sequence must be set manually.

To accommodate these requirements, a reasonable design is to add a new column to the **Column** table, which holds the display order sequence number for each column within the table concerned. This column can also be used to hold the display sequence if the sequence is set either manually or programmatically. The latter use is important since it may be quite complex to recalculate the column sequence every time a display is required, and having the information in the database means that a SQL SELECT command can immediately return the list of columns in the desired sequence. Additionally, a column can be added to the **Table** table that indicates whether the display order will be set manually or programmatically for the table concerned.

Figure 14.1 shows the columns *Table Manual Display Order Indicator* added to the **Table** table and *Column Display Sequence Number* added to the **Column** table. If

DISPLAY ORDER	PRIMARY KEY (PK) COLUMN?	FOREIGN KEY (FK) COLUMN?	DESCRIPTION
1	Yes	N/A	Any date columns that are part of the primary key, irrespective of whether they are foreign key columns. When a table has a date column as part of the primary key, the date is nearly always the most important column for users.
2	Yes	Yes	Foreign key (FK) columns that are part of the primary key. FK columns are inherited from parent entities and are thus usually more important than Primary Key (PK) columns that are not FKs. FK columns from the same parent should be kept together in the display.
3	Yes	No	Primary key column(s) that are not foreign keys or dates. These are any columns remaining in the PK. All PK columns should be displayed before any non-PK columns.
4	No	Yes	FK columns that are not part of the PK and are not from lookup-type reference tables. FK columns are always more important than non-FK columns. Parent tables that are not reference data tables are usually parties to transactions and are thus more important than reference data tables. FK columns from the same parent should be kept together in the display.
5	No	Yes	FK columns from lookup-type reference tables that are not part of the PK. FK columns are always more important than non-FK columns. Parent tables that are reference data tables are usually used to categorize data and are thus usually less important than parent tables that are not reference data tables. FK columns from the same parent should be kept together in the display.
6	No	No	Text columns that are not part of the primary key. Texts usually have descriptions that are important to understand the whole record (row) being displayed.
7	No	No	Date columns that are not part of the primary key. If dates exist, they usually describe activities that are important for understanding the entire row.
8	No	No	Numeric columns that are not part of the primary key.
9	No	No	Any other columns.

TABLE 14.1 Recommended Order for Columns in Grid-like Display

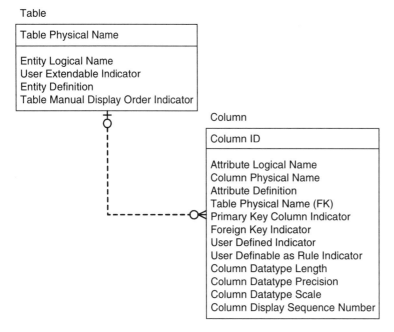

Table

| Table Physical Name |
| Entity Logical Name
User Extendable Indicator
Entity Definition
Table Manual Display Order Indicator |

Column

| Column ID |
| Attribute Logical Name
Column Physical Name
Attribute Definition
Table Physical Name (FK)
Primary Key Column Indicator
Foreign Key Indicator
User Defined Indicator
User Definable as Rule Indicator
Column Datatype Length
Column Datatype Precision
Column Datatype Scale
Column Display Sequence Number |

FIGURE 14.1
Columns for Display Sort Order

the order is set programmatically, then Listing 14.4 provides a function that will do this in accordance with the recommendations in Table 14.1.

Having done all this work, it is now an easy matter to change the code in Listing 14.1 so that when columns are displayed in the correct order. All that needs to be done is to add the clause "ORDER BY COL_DISPLAYSEQ_N" to the SQL SELECT command that retrieves data from **COL_COLUMN_M**. A similar change needs to be implemented in Listing 14.3.

Figure 14.2 shows a grid display of the **Investment** tables in the sample application created using the design techniques described above.

Sort Order of Data

The order in which columns should be displayed has been discussed. The order in which data (rows) returned from the target database table should be displayed is a different consideration. The sample application uses Microsoft Access, which contains functionality that permits the sort order of data to be changed. If the rules engine designer is working in a software environment that does not have this kind of functionality, then it can become a problem because sort order of data is usually impor-

LISTING 14.4

Automatically Setting the Display Order of Columns of a Table

```
Public Function SetDispSeq(strTable As String) As String
'*******************************************************************
' This function populates the column Column Display Sequence
' Number (COL_DISPLAYSEQ_N) in the Column table.  This is used
' when data from The underlying table is displayed in a grid-
' format to the user
'
' Parameters:
' strTable = Physical Name of Table
'
' Returns: Y if completes successfully
'*******************************************************************
Dim cmd As ADODB.Command, strSQL As String, rstCols As
ADODB.Recordset
Dim lngAffected As Long, intCount As Integer

  SetDispSeq = "N"

  Set rstCols = New ADODB.Recordset
  strSQL = "SELECT TAB_MANUALDISPORDER_I " _
          & " FROM TAB_TABLE_M   " _
          & " WHERE TAB_PHYSNAME_T = '" & Trim(strTable) & "'"
  rstCols.Open strSQL, CurrentProject.Connection, _
          adOpenKeyset, adLockOptimistic, adCmdText
  If rstCols("TAB_MANUALDISPORDER_I") = "Y" Then
    MsgBox "Function SetDispSeq: Table " & strTable _
          & " has its column display order set manually, not
programatically"
    rstCols.Close
    Set rstCols = Nothing
    Exit Function
  End If

  rstCols.Close

  'Set up Access Command Object
  Set cmd = New ADODB.Command
```

```
cmd.ActiveConnection = CurrentProject.Connection
cmd.CommandType = adCmdText

' Set all columns for this table to have an initial display
' sequence of 0
strSQL = " UPDATE COL_COLUMN_M SET COL_DISPLAYSEQ_N = 0"
cmd.CommandText = strSQL
cmd.Execute lngAffected

' Set Display Sequence to 1 for PK Columns that are Data
' datatype
strSQL = " UPDATE COL_COLUMN_M SET COL_DISPLAYSEQ_N = 1 " _
       & " WHERE TAB_PHYSNAME_T = '" & Trim(strTable) & "' " _
       & " AND COL_PK_I = 'Y' AND DTP_C = 'DATETIME' "
cmd.CommandText = strSQL
cmd.Execute lngAffected

' Set Display Sequence to 2 for PK Columns that are FK columns
strSQL = " UPDATE COL_COLUMN_M SET COL_DISPLAYSEQ_N = 2 " _
       & " WHERE TAB_PHYSNAME_T = '" & Trim(strTable) & "' " _
       & " AND COL_PK_I = 'Y' AND COL_FK_I = 'Y' " _
       & " AND COL_DISPLAYSEQ_N = 0 "
cmd.CommandText = strSQL
cmd.Execute lngAffected

' Set Display Sequence to 3 for PK Columns that are FK columns
strSQL = " UPDATE COL_COLUMN_M SET COL_DISPLAYSEQ_N = 3 " _
       & " WHERE TAB_PHYSNAME_T = '" & Trim(strTable) & "' " _
       & " AND COL_PK_I = 'Y' AND (COL_FK_I <> 'Y' OR COL_FK_I
IS NULL) " _
       & " AND COL_DISPLAYSEQ_N = 0 "
cmd.CommandText = strSQL
cmd.Execute lngAffected

' Set Display Sequence to 4 for FK Columns that are not PK columns
' and whose parents are NOT lookup-type reference tables
' See function SetRefTabDescCol for how COL_FKREFTABDESCCOL_C is
' populated When this column is null, the parent is not a
' lookup-type reference table
strSQL = " UPDATE COL_COLUMN_M SET COL_DISPLAYSEQ_N = 4 " _
```

```
               & " WHERE TAB_PHYSNAME_T = '" & Trim(strTable) & "' " _
               & " AND COL_FK_I = 'Y' AND (COL_PK_I <> 'Y' OR COL_PK_I
    IS NULL) " _
               & " AND COL_FKREFTABDESCCOL_C IS NULL " _
               & " AND COL_DISPLAYSEQ_N = 0 "
       cmd.CommandText = strSQL
       cmd.Execute lngAffected


       ' Set Display Sequence to 5 for FK Columns that are not PK
       ' columns and whose parents ARE lookup-type reference tables
       ' See function SetRefTabDescCol for how COL_FKREFTABDESCCOL_C is
       ' populated When this column is not null, the parent is a
       ' lookup-type reference table
       strSQL = " UPDATE COL_COLUMN_M SET COL_DISPLAYSEQ_N = 4 " _
               & " WHERE TAB_PHYSNAME_T = '" & Trim(strTable) & "' " _
               & " AND COL_FK_I = 'Y' AND (COL_PK_I <> 'Y' OR COL_PK_I
    IS NULL) " _
               & " AND COL_FKREFTABDESCCOL_C IS NOT NULL " _
               & " AND COL_DISPLAYSEQ_N = 0 "
       cmd.CommandText = strSQL
       cmd.Execute lngAffected


       ' Set Display Sequence to 6 for non-PK columns that are text
       ' columns
       strSQL = " UPDATE COL_COLUMN_M SET COL_DISPLAYSEQ_N = 6 " _
               & " WHERE TAB_PHYSNAME_T = '" & Trim(strTable) & "' " _
               & " AND (COL_PK_I <> 'Y' OR COL_PK_I IS NULL) " _
               & " AND (DTP_C = 'CHAR' OR DTP_C = 'VARCHAR' OR DTP_C =
    'TEXT') " _
               & " AND COL_DISPLAYSEQ_N = 0 "
       cmd.CmmandText = strSQL
       cmd.Execute lngAffected


       ' Set Display Sequence to 7 for non-PK columns that are date
       ' columns
       strSQL = " UPDATE COL_COLUMN_M SET COL_DISPLAYSEQ_N = 7 " _
               & " WHERE TAB_PHYSNAME_T = '" & Trim(strTable) & "' " _
               & " AND (COL_PK_I <> 'Y' OR COL_PK_I IS NULL) " _
               & " AND DTP_C = 'DATETIME' " _
               & " AND COL_DISPLAYSEQ_N = 0 "
```

```
   cmd.CommandText = strSQL
   cmd.Execute lngAffected


   ' Set Display Sequence to 8 for non-PK columns that are numeric
   ' columns
   strSQL = " UPDATE COL_COLUMN_M SET COL_DISPLAYSEQ_N = 8 " _
        & " WHERE TAB_PHYSNAME_T = '" & Trim(strTable) & "' " _
        & " AND (COL_PK_I <> 'Y' OR COL_PK_I IS NULL) " _
        & " AND (DTP_C = 'DECIMAL' OR DTP_C = 'NUMERIC' " _
        & " OR DTP_C = 'INT' OR DTP_C = 'LONG') " _
        & " AND COL_DISPLAYSEQ_N = 0 "
   cmd.CommandText = strSQL
   cmd.Execute lngAffected


   ' Set Display Sequence to 9 for other columns
   strSQL = " UPDATE COL_COLUMN_M SET COL_DISPLAYSEQ_N = 9 " _
        & " WHERE TAB_PHYSNAME_T = '" & Trim(strTable) & "' " _
        & " AND COL_DISPLAYSEQ_N = 0 "
   cmd.CommandText = strSQL
   cmd.Execute lngAffected


   ' Now we have the general sequence set.  Next, set it properly.
   ' Get the columns in order of the current Display Sequence,
   ' then the parent table (so columns from the same parent sort
   ' together), then the logical name.  Update COL_DISPLAYSEQ_N with
   ' the ordinal position in this sequence.
   strSQL = "SELECT * " _
         & " FROM COL_COLUMN_M " _
         & " WHERE TAB_PHYSNAME_T = '" & Trim(strTable) & "' " _
         & " ORDER BY COL_DISPLAYSEQ_N, TAB_FKPARENT_T,
COL_ATTLOGNAME_T "
   rstCols.Open strSQL, CurrentProject.Connection, _
        adOpenKeyset, adLockOptimistic, adCmdText
   intCount = 0
   Do While Not rstCols.EOF
     intCount = intCount + 1
     strSQL = " UPDATE COL_COLUMN_M SET COL_DISPLAYSEQ_N = " &
CStr(intCount) _
         & " WHERE COL_C = '" & rstCols("COL_C") & "' "
     cmd.CommandText = strSQL
     cmd.Execute lngAffected
```

```
        rstCols.MoveNext
    Loop
    rstCols.Close

    Set rstCols = Nothing
    Set cmd = Nothing

End Function
```

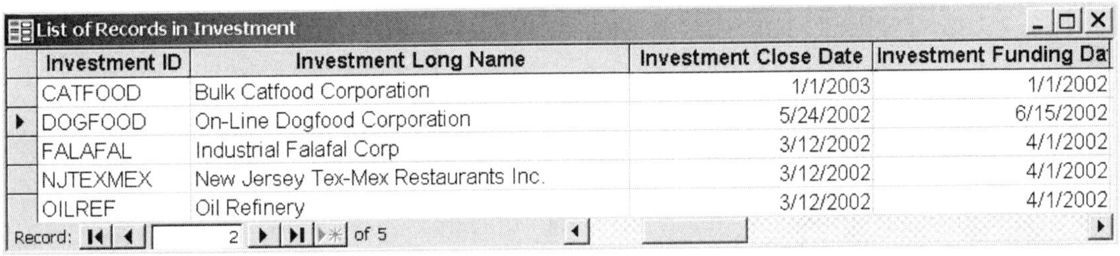
List of Records in Investment

Investment ID	Investment Long Name	Investment Close Date	Investment Funding Da
CATFOOD	Bulk Catfood Corporation	1/1/2003	1/1/2002
DOGFOOD	On-Line Dogfood Corporation	5/24/2002	6/15/2002
FALAFAL	Industrial Falafal Corp	3/12/2002	4/1/2002
NJTEXMEX	New Jersey Tex-Mex Restaurants Inc.	3/12/2002	4/1/2002
OILREF	Oil Refinery	3/12/2002	4/1/2002

Record: 2 of 5

FIGURE 14.2
Grid Display of **Investment** (INV_INVESTMENT_S) Table

tant to users. A good approach is to enhance the SQL SELECT statement produced by the function SetTabLogical() (see Listing 14.1). The statement should order the data by the first three or four columns in the display order sequence. If any of these columns are dates, then it is probably best to use descending sequence instead of ascending. The changes to SetTabLogical() required to do this are very easy to implement.

Dealing with Large Numbers of Records

Sometimes database tables can contain thousands or even millions of rows. This is typical of tables that contain periodic activity, such as daily account activity in financial applications, but it can be found across a wide spectrum of computerized systems. Displaying the entire contents of a table may be impractical, or even impossible. The best approach is usually to filter the contents of the target table to produce some manageable subset. There is functionality to filter data in Microsoft Access, in which the sample application is written. If such functionality is not available in the software environment used by the rules designer, then something will have to be implemented.

Search functionality that can filter records is not too difficult to create. Where dates are part of the primary key, it is possible to ask the user to input a date range. Otherwise, the description column for any table is identified in the **Column** table by the attribute *Column Description Indicator* (COL_DESC_I). The user can be asked to input a search string that can then be used to search the corresponding column in the table containing the business data using SQL "like" syntax.

Many rules engines are designed to work in applications that are logic intensive rather than being data intensive. Such applications work with comparatively small amounts of data, but relatively large amounts of business logic. In these situations it makes little sense to build additional functionality to search database tables. Rules designers should consider whether their application really requires this functionality before attempting to implement it.

Detailed Record Display

The grid display in Figure 14.2 is often not sufficient for users' needs when it comes to viewing one record (one row in the grid display). Most of the time, not all columns can be seen because the display is wider than the screen. Any reference table data is shown as codes rather than descriptions. Furthermore, if there are foreign keys from parent entities, it is often necessary to view more information from the parent table. In addition, there is no data about what child records, if any, the current record has.

The best way to meet the demand for detailed information is to provide an additional display for one record at a time. A good design approach to providing a means for users to reach such a display is to simply let them select individual records in the screen shown on Figure 14.2.

Record Numbers and Problems with Record Selection

At this point there can be a problem with certain software environments. In Microsoft Access, if a record is selected from a form control such as a list box or combo box, then only one column associated with the data displayed in the list box or combo box is returned to the program logic to identify which record was chosen. Yet the data displayed may come from a table that has many primary key columns. Simply choosing *one* of these columns will never identify a specific record.

A good design alternative to overcome this limitation of many software environments is to add a column to each table in the database that contains a Record Number. A *Record Number* is a column that contains a value (usually a number) that uniquely identifies a record in a database table. This design approach is often a bone of contention between programmers and data modelers and needs some further consideration. From the programmer's perspective it is very desirable for each database table to have a single primary key (PK) column that is essentially a record number. Here are some of the reasons:

- It is more difficult to program for a PK that has multiple columns rather than a single column.

- The programmer's tools often do not adequately support having more than one column in a PK for certain functions (such as selecting a record from a list box).

- Programmers often have a limited understanding of the business problem domain compared to the programming tools they work with and do not understand the semantics that lie behind the designs of PKs. Therefore, they do not appreciate why these data constructs are necessary.

- The software tools may encourage this way of thinking. For example, Microsoft Access has an autonumber datatype that is essentially a record number. In building a new table, if the programmer does not specify any key columns, Access will offer to add a new autonumber column as the key.

Data modelers know that the truth contained in a logical data model requires that PKs consist of multiple attributes. This is especially true for identifying relationships between entities. In such relationships, the child entity must have more PK columns than the parent, and so is guaranteed to have a PK consisting of multiple attributes. These attributes are transformed into multiple PK columns when the database is physically implemented. However, many programmers cannot see the point of this and will never be convinced. Disputes thus arise in many projects. Often neither side can articulate its requirements—both just feel they are right. Users cannot appreciate such disputes, and to them the parties resemble the Lilliputians in Gulliver's Travels who were divided into two political parties that argued endlessly about which end to start eating a boiled egg from.

Data modelers should take the limitations of programming languages seriously, but without compromising good modeling practices. A reasonable design is to add a column that is a record number, but use it only to identify a selected record and not for other purposes. It cannot be part of the primary key and should not be used where the PK columns can be used without difficulty. Furthermore, a *Record Number* column should be regarded as metadata, not data. It really is metadata and has nothing to do with the business domain underlying the data model. It has no business meaning; it is simply a system-assigned code that uniquely identifies a record. A record is a construct of a database, not something that exists for a business (an instance of an entity is what exists for the business).

If we regard a *Record Number* column as metadata, then we are justified in giving it the same column name in every table in the database, such as RECORD_ID_C. This design is similar to the way update datetime stamps and user ids are put on records to indicate who created and last updated a record, and when this was done. The design also helps to break the programmer's logic in thinking of *Record Number* as the primary key. The datatype can be whatever suits the underlying database and can be a sequential number or a randomly assigned string. If a sequential number is chosen, programmers must not be allowed to infer sequence from it in program code (e.g., that a record with a higher number was added at a later time). It is to be used purely as a unique identifier of a record and must not have more intelligence attributed to it. However, there can be restrictions depending on the underlying database. For instance, Microsoft Access only allows one Autonumber datatype column per table; Oracle 8 requires a trigger to be set up so the database populates the new field. Such restrictions take some extra work to overcome.

Listing 14.5 shows a function that adds a column RECORD_ID_C to each table that lacks it, and also updates the Business Rules Repository.

Record Number certainly makes building rules engine functionality very much easier than would be possible without it. As we shall see in subsequent chapters it is used in many different areas within the sample application.

LISTING 14.5
Adding a Record Number to Each Table

```
    Public Function AddRecordID() As Long
'****************************************************************
' Adds the column RECORD_ID_C to each table that lacks it.  Also
' updates the Column table to add the metadata for the new column.
' Makes a list of what happened in the NotePad table
' Parameters: None
'
' Returns: Number of tables to which the RECORD_ID_C was added
'****************************************************************
Dim rstCols As ADODB.Recordset, strSQL As String, cmd As
ADODB.Command
Dim lngAffected As Long, strCol As String, strUser As String,
rstChk As ADODB.Recordset
Dim strText As String, tblMy As ADOX.Table, colMy As ADOX.Column
Dim catMy As ADOX.Catalog, strGo As String, strText2 As String
```

```
AddRecordID = 0

Set rstCols = New ADODB.Recordset
Set rstChk = New ADODB.Recordset
Set cmd = New ADODB.Command
Set catMy = New ADOX.Catalog
catMy.ActiveConnection = CurrentProject.Connection

cmd.ActiveConnection = CurrentProject.Connection
cmd.CommandType = adCmdText

' Delete all records for this user from the Notepad table
lngAffected = CleanOutNotePad()

' Get all tables that do not have a RECORD_ID_C column
strSQL = "SELECT * FROM TAB_TABLE_M " _
      & " WHERE RIGHT(TAB_PHYSNAME_T,2) <> '_M' AND NOT EXISTS
" _
      & " (SELECT * FROM COL_COLUMN_M WHERE " _
      & "   COL_ATTLOGNAME_T = 'RECORD_ID_C' AND " _
      & "   TAB_PHYSNAME_T = TAB_TABLE_M.TAB_PHYSNAME_T) "
rstCols.Open strSQL, CurrentProject.Connection, _
      adOpenKeyset, adLockOptimistic, adCmdText
Do While Not rstCols.EOF
   ' Access only allows one Autonumber field per table, so
   ' check if the table already has one
   strSQL = "SELECT * FROM COL_COLUMN_M " _
         & " WHERE TAB_PHYSNAME_T = '" &
rstCols("TAB_PHYSNAME_T") & "' " _
         & " AND DTP_C = 'AUTONUMBER'"
   rstChk.Open strSQL, CurrentProject.Connection, _
      adOpenKeyset, adLockOptimistic, adCmdText

   strGo = "Y"
   strText2 = rstCols("TAB_PHYSNAME_T")
   Set tblMy = catMy.Tables(strText2)
   For Each colMy In tblMy.Columns
      If colMy.Name = "RECORD_ID_C" Then
         strGo = "N"
```

```
        End If
    Next

    If Not rstChk.EOF Then
      ' Write a message to the notepad if we cannot add Record
      ' ID
      strText = "Table: " & rstCols("TAB_PHYSNAME_T") _
            & " Already has one Autonumber field (" &
Trim(rstChk("COL_PHYSNAME_T")) _
              & ")-cannot add RECORD_ID_C "
      strText = AddNotePadLine(strText)
    Else
      ' It is OK to add Record ID
      AddRecordID = AddRecordID + 1
      ' Add Record ID to the table
      If strGo = "Y" Then
        strSQL = " ALTER TABLE " & rstCols("TAB_PHYSNAME_T") _
          & " ADD COLUMN RECORD_ID_C COUNTER " _
          & " NOT NULL "
        cmd.CommandText = strSQL
        cmd.Execute lngAffected
      End If
      ' Add a new record to the Column table
      strCol = GetNextColID()
      strSQL = "INSERT INTO COL_COLUMN_M " _
            & " (COL_C, TAB_PHYSNAME_T, COL_PHYSNAME_T,
COL_ATTLOGNAME_T, " _
            & "  DTP_C, COL_PK_I, COL_FK_I, COL_ATTDEFN_M, DTTP_C)" _
            & " VALUES ('" & strCol & "','" &
rstCols("TAB_PHYSNAME_T") _
            & "','RECORD_ID_C', 'Record Number', 'AUTONUMBER',
'N','N', " _
            & " 'A unique number for this record','NUMERIC')"
      cmd.CommandText = strSQL
      cmd.Execute lngAffected
      '  Add a line to the Notepad
      strText = "Table: " & Trim(rstCols("TAB_PHYSNAME_T")) _
            & " Added field RECORD_ID_C"
      strText = AddNotePadLine(strText)
    End If
    rstChk.Close
```

```
        rstCols.MoveNext
    Loop

    rstCols.Close
    Set rstChk = Nothing
    Set rstCols = Nothing
    Set cmd = Nothing

End Function
```

Displaying the Detailed Record

When it comes to displaying the record information, the Internet environment is frankly better than Windows-based tools. Much more complex record displays can be built, and hyperlinks with the **Back** button provide a greater variety of navigation options. For Access, perhaps the simplest way to display the information is to gather it from the database and place it in a special table that is then displayed as a control in a form.

In order to do this in Access the rules engine actually has to build a *form*, the Access system object that is a screen. The form can display what is shown in Figure 14.2 and can trap a double-click event on any row that can then be used to display the detailed screen. Listing 14.6 shows two functions used by the sample application for these purposes. The first, RunViewData(), opens a form to display the contents of a selected database table. If no form exists for the selected table, the function BldForm() is called to create it. BldForm() uses some techniques specific to Microsoft Access to build the display shown in Figure 14.2 rather than the general techniques described above. The rules designer should take advantage of functionality offered by the software used to build the rules engine in this way, but should also be aware that if such functionality is not available, it may be necessary to use more general designs, such as the code in Listing 14.1.

BldForm() essentially mimics what Listing 14.1 does, building Access controls instead of a SQL SELECT statement. The function builds a screen that will display what is shown in Figure 14.2, and which will also respond to a double-click on any row in the display by invoking the function RunDispRec().

In the sample application this functionality can be accessed by selecting **Database Maintenance** on the main menu, and then **View Data** on the popup that appears. The screen shown in Figure 14.3 is displayed and allows the user to select a database table.

LISTING 14.6
Functions to Build and Display Forms Showing Table Data

```
    Public Function RunViewData(strTable As String) As String
'********************************************************************
' Manages the viewing of screens that display table information.
' The function searches to find if a display form exists for the
' specified table.  If none exists, BldForm() is called to build
' the form. The form is then opened
'
' Parameters:
' strTable = Physical name of selected table
'
' Returns: "Y" if form had to be built.  Otherwise "N"
'********************************************************************

Dim strGo As String, aob As AccessObject, strFrmCaption As String

   RunViewData = "N"
' Does the form already exist?  If not, create it.
   strFrmCaption = "frmList" & strTable
   strGo = "N"
   For Each aob In CurrentProject.AllForms
     If aob.Name = strFrmCaption Then
        strGo = "Y"
     End If
   Next
   If strGo = "N" Then
     strGo = BldForm(strTable)
     RunViewData = "Y"
   End If

   DoCmd.OpenForm strFrmCaption, acFormDS

End Function


Public Function BldForm(strTable As String) As String
'********************************************************************
' Builds a form to display the contents of a database table
```

```
'
' Parameters:
' strTable = Physical name of selected table
'
' Returns: "Y" if form is built successfully
'********************************************************************

Dim frm As Form, strText As String, strSQL As String, rstCols As
ADODB.Recordset
Dim strName As String, ctl As Control, rstTable As ADODB.Recordset
Dim strFrmCaption As String, aob As AccessObject, strGo As String,
frm2 As Form
Dim ctl2 As TextBox

  BldForm = "N"
  Set rstCols = New ADODB.Recordset
  Set rstTable = New ADODB.Recordset

  strSQL = "SELECT * FROM TAB_TABLE_M " _
          & " WHERE TAB_PHYSNAME_T = '" & strTable & "' "
  rstTable.Open strSQL, CurrentProject.Connection, _
        adOpenKeyset, adLockOptimistic, adCmdText

  strText = "List of Records in " & rstTable("TAB_ENTLOGNAME_T")
  strFrmCaption = "frmList" & strTable

  ' Does the form already exist?  If so, delete it.
  strGo = "N"
  For Each aob In CurrentProject.AllForms
    If aob.Name = strFrmCaption Then
      strGo = "Y"
    End If
  Next
  If strGo = "Y" Then
    DoCmd.DeleteObject acForm, strFrmCaption
  End If

  ' Create the new form
  Set frm = CreateForm(, "Normal")
```

```
  frm.Caption = strText
  strName = frm.Name
  strText = strTable
  frm.RecordSource = strText
  frm.DefaultView = 2
  frm.AllowAdditions = False
  frm.AllowDeletions = False
  frm.AllowEdits = False
  frm.AutoCenter = True
  frm.HasModule = True


  ' Add the columns
  strSQL = "SELECT * FROM COL_COLUMN_M " _
           & " WHERE TAB_PHYSNAME_T = '" & strTable & "' " _
           & " ORDER BY COL_DISPLAYSEQ_N "
  rstCols.Open strSQL, CurrentProject.Connection, _
          adOpenKeyset, adLockOptimistic, adCmdText
  Do While Not rstCols.EOF
     strText = rstCols("COL_PHYSNAME_T")
     Set ctl2 = CreateControl(strName, acTextBox, acDetail, "",
strText)
     ' Set the column header to the the Attribute Logical Name
     ctl2.Name = rstCols("COL_ATTLOGNAME_T")
     ' When the user double-clicks on a row this gets executed
     ctl2.OnDblClick = "=RunDispRec('" & strTable &
"',RECORD_ID_C)"
     rstCols.MoveNext
  Loop

  DoCmd.Close acForm, strName, acSaveYes
  DoCmd.Rename strFrmCaption, acForm, strName
  BldForm = "Y"


End Function
```

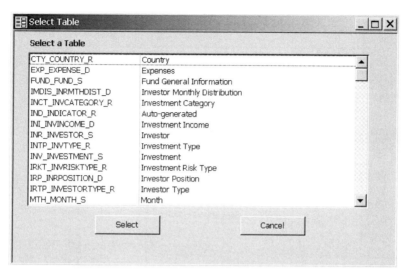

FIGURE 14.3
Select a Database Table

If the user selects a database table, such as **Investment,** in the screen shown in Figure 14.3, the screen shown in Figure 14.2 appears. If the user double-clicks on a row in this screen, then the screen shown in Figure 14.4 appears.

This screen shows both data and metadata for the selected record. As mentioned above, it is based on a table into which data is copied especially for the screen. This table is called **Record Display,** and its structure is shown in Figure 14.5.

The rules engine populates this table with one record per column in the database selected by the user. **Record Display** contains both data and metadata. The data comes from the actual record that the user selected. The metadata comes from the Business Rules Repository. All parent tables of the selected table are also found, and the rules engine is able to determine what the parent records are in these tables. After all, one record can only have one parent record per relationship. Each of these parent table records also has its data and metadata put into **Record Display.** Thus, as the user scrolls down the display in Figure 14.4, details of all parent records are displayed. This can be seen in Figure 14.6 and is the equivalent of a SQL JOIN between the selected records and all parent records. The user does not have to worry about how any of this is done because the rules engine takes care of all the navigation involved using the Business Rules Repository.

Figure 14.4 also illustrates the way in which reference data can be dealt with. If the user clicks on a column that is a code value in a parent reference data table, then the description as well as the code is displayed. Furthermore, at the bottom of the

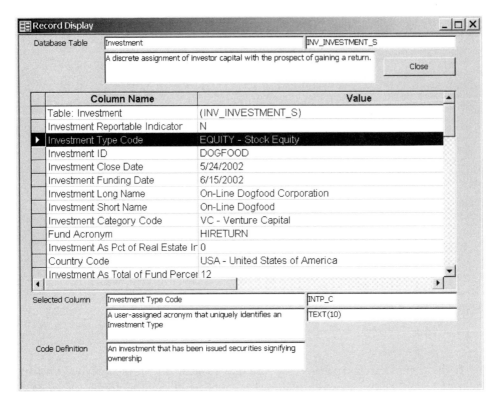

FIGURE 14.4
View Individual Record

Record Display

| User ID (FK) |
Record Display ID
Column ID (FK)
Table Physical Name (FK)
Attribute Logical Name
Column Physical Name
Display Field Name
Display Field Value
Record ID

FIGURE 14.5
Record Display (RDISP_RECDISPLAY_M) Table

screen, a definition is displayed for the selected reference data table code. This is achieved by means of the metadata stored in the Repository for reference data, which was discussed in Chapter 11.

One other design point is that the **Record Display** table has *User ID* as part of its primary key. This permits the functionality to work within a multiuser environ-

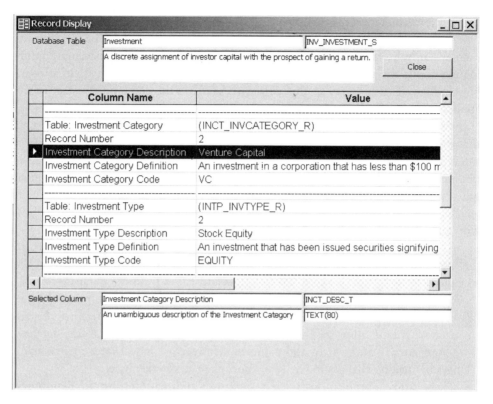

FIGURE 14.6
Parent Record Details for Selected Record

ment. Each user sees only the information he or she is working with. It is quite likely that different users will want to view data simultaneously.

The functionality required to produce this display is fairly complex, and if the reader wishes to examine it in more detail, it can be found in the form frmRDISP in the sample application, and the function RunDispRec() in the module DBMaint.

At this point the functionality to permit users to view data in a dynamic fashion has been created. If users add new columns, they can see them immediately. If users define new business rules that populate column values, then these values can also be seen immediately. Having such functionality is very important for the success of a business rules engine. There is also one other area of database management that needs to be handled, and that is ensuring that the database is synchronized with the Repository. This requirement is discussed in the next section.

Synchronizing the Database and Business Rules Repository

Having a Business Rules Repository is the basis for the user-defined business rules approach, but what happens if the Repository and the underlying database become unsynchronized? Tables and columns may exist in the Repository, but not in the database, or vice versa. The designer must face the possibility that this can happen. Events such as hardware failure can cause the Repository to end up with inaccurate information about the underlying database. There is also the possibility that software bugs in the rules engine can do this, too, particularly in the development stage of the application.

The best solution is to build a Repository synchronization function that ensures that the Repository accurately describes the structure of the database. This function can report on errors it finds, and automatically repair certain error conditions. It is not the only function we will have to build to ensure the integrity of the rules engine, but it is a very important one.

The basic discrepancies that the Repository synchronization checker must deal with and the automatic corrections it should make are shown in Table 14.2.

All discrepancies detected and automatic correction actions must be reported to the user. The automatic correction actions described in Table 14.2 are based on the fact that it is really not safe to delete columns and tables from the database because business information can be lost. The database may not even allow columns and tables to be dropped. Similarly, information may be lost if datatypes are changed, and again the database may disallow it. The only safe change that can be made to the database if a discrepancy is found is to add columns. However, it is still safer to resolve all changes by making changes to the Repository than to the database.

There can be a problem with deleting column information from the Repository, which must be done to correct certain discrepancies. If the columns that need to be

DISCREPANCY	AUTOMATIC CORRECTIVE ACTION
A table exists in the Repository but not in the underlying database	Delete the table information (and associated columns) from the Repository
A table exists in the underlying database but not in the Repository	Add the table information to the Repository
A column exists in the Repository but not in the underlying database	Delete the column information from the Repository
A column exists in the underlying database but not in the Repository	Add the column information to the Repository
A column exists in both the Repository and database, but there is conflicting physical metadata about it. In particular, the datatype information may be different	Change the column information in the Repository

TABLE 14.2 Discrepancies Between the Repository and Database, and Automatic Corrective Actions

deleted have been used in business rules, the columns should not be deleted until the rules have been changed. It is therefore necessary that the Repository synchronization checker determine whether any columns that need to be deleted have been used in business rules.

How can the Repository synchronization checker find out what is happening in the underlying database? There are a number of ways to do this. Each database server generally has a *system catalog*—a set of master tables that contain information about the structure of the database. This can be read, but it is nearly always different for each database server. There is also the possibility that SQL commands can be used to obtain the structural information required. Usually, directly reading the system catalog is the fastest and easiest way to proceed.

Another problem that faces the designer is where the Business Rules Repository is "self-aware." The Repository is "self-aware" if the metadata of the tables of the Repository is itself stored in the tables of the Repository. In general, it is not a good idea to let users see this information, and it is not clear what advantages there can be to storing this information in the Repository. The greatest need for the Repository Synchronization Checker is to fix any problems that arise when users extend the database tables holding business data. The users are never going to extend the Repository tables that hold metadata. Also, the Repository is quite complex, and the users should not be put in the position of having to figure out whether the metadata they are viewing pertains to the Repository tables or the tables that hold business-related data. It is recommended, therefore, that the information about the tables of the Repository not be included in the Repository itself, and that these tables be excluded from the Repository Synchronization Checker. The latter can be achieved by naming conventions. In this book, all Repository tables have physical names that end with "_M". No other kind of table is named in this way.

One other issue that can come up is that there can be database "system" tables in the system catalog. These are tables that the database creates automatically so that it can manage itself. They should be excluded from the Repository Synchronization Checker. Sometimes this can be done via naming conventions. For instance, in Microsoft Access, the system tables all have names that begin with "MSYS". In other cases there is a "type" column or property that indicates whether the "object" in the system catalog is a database table or something else. In Microsoft Access, the **Tables** collection of the **Catalog** includes system tables (and queries and other objects). Each **Table** in this collection has a property called **Type**. When **Type** = "TABLE" the object is a database table; if it has another value it is not a database table.

Listing 14.7 shows a Repository Synchronization Checker for Microsoft Access. This function performs the checks and corrective actions described above, and when it completes it displays a report of its activities to the user. This is very important because the user may have to take further action depending on what errors were found. It should also be remembered that the Repository Synchronization Checker

LISTING 14.7
The Repository Synchronization Checker

```
Public Function SynchReposDB() As String
'*********************************************************************
' The Repository Synchronization Checker.
' The first section looks at each table in the System Catalog
' (except for system tables and tables of the Repository itself).
' These tables, and their columns, are checked to see if they
' exist in the Repository.  If they do not, they are added to the
' Repository.  If they are found, but there are differences in the
' datatypes, these are also updated in the repository.
'
' The second section reads the repository to see if tables and
' columns in it exist in the database.  If they do not, they are
' removed.  The only exception is if they are used in business
' rules—in which case they are left alone.
'
' At the end the user is shown all errors detected and actions
' taken.
'
' Parameters: None
'
' Returns: The Repository's code for the datatype
'*********************************************************************


Dim cnn As ADODB.Connection, cat As ADOX.Catalog, tbl As
ADOX.Table
Dim col As ADOX.Column, strFound As String, rstChk As
ADODB.Recordset
Dim strSQL As String, strTab As String, cmd As ADODB.Command,
lngAffected As Long
Dim rstMeta As ADODB.Recordset, intTable As Integer, intColumn As
Integer
Dim strTable As String, strField As String, strCol As String,
strTabOK As String
Dim rstCols As ADODB.Recordset, strColOK As String, lngCount1 As
Long
Dim lngCount2 As Long, intDelCol As Integer, intDelTab As Integer
Dim intErr As Integer, strText As String, strDTPOK As String,
intUpd As Integer
```

```
Dim strDTTP As String, intScale As Integer, intPrecision As
Integer, intLen As Integer
Dim strOldDTP As String, intOldLen As Integer, intOldScale As
Integer
Dim intOldPrecision As Integer

  SynchReposDB = "N"

  Set cnn = CurrentProject.Connection
  Set cat = New ADOX.Catalog
  cat.ActiveConnection = CurrentProject.Connection
  Set cmd = New ADODB.Command
  cmd.ActiveConnection = CurrentProject.Connection
  cmd.CommandType = adCmdText
  Set rstMeta = New ADODB.Recordset
  Set rstChk = New ADODB.Recordset
  Set rstCols = New ADODB.Recordset
  intTable = 0
  intColumn = 0
  intDelTab = 0
  intDelCol = 0
  intErr = 0
  intUpd = 0

  ' Delete all records for this user from the Notepad table
  lngAffected = CleanOutNotePad()

  ' SECTION 1: Each table and column in the System Catalog must
  ' be present in the Business Rules Repository
  ' Look at each table in the system catalog
  For Each tbl In cat.Tables
    ' Ignore System Tables and tables of the Repository itself
    If tbl.Type = "TABLE" And Right(tbl.Name, 2) <> "_M" Then
      ' Is the table defined in the Business Rules Repository?
      strTable = tbl.Name
      strSQL = "SELECT * FROM TAB_TABLE_M " _
          & " WHERE TAB_PHYSNAME_T = '" & strTable & "'"
      rstMeta.Open strSQL, CurrentProject.Connection, _
        adOpenKeyset, adLockOptimistic, adCmdText
      If rstMeta.EOF Then
```

```
        ' If not defined, add table to Business Rules Repository
        strSQL = "INSERT INTO TAB_TABLE_M " _
            & "(TAB_PHYSNAME_T, TAB_ENTLOGNAME_T) VALUES " _
            & "('" & strTable & "', 'Auto-generated') "
        cmd.CommandText = strSQL
        cmd.Execute lngAffected
        intTable = intTable + 1
        ' Write a message to the notepad for the added table
        strText = "Table: " & strTable _
            & " was in the database, but not in the Repository. " _
            & "It has now been added to the Repository."
        strText = AddNotePadLine(strText)
    End If
    rstMeta.Close

    ' Look at each column of the table in the system catalog
    For Each col In tbl.Columns
        strField = col.Name

        ' Is the column defined in the Business Rules Repository?
        strSQL = "SELECT * FROM COL_COLUMN_M " _
            & " WHERE TAB_PHYSNAME_T = '" & strTable & "' " _
            & " AND COL_PHYSNAME_T = '" & strField & "'"
        rstMeta.Open strSQL, CurrentProject.Connection, _
            adOpenKeyset, adLockOptimistic, adCmdText
        If rstMeta.EOF Then
            ' If the column is not defined, add it to the Business
            ' Rules Repository
            strCol = GetNextColID()
            strText = TransDBType(col)
            strDTTP = GetDataTypeType(strText)
            ' For Access, we only user length in the repository
            ' for Text datatype and scale and precision are always
            ' 0 in our repository
            ' For other databases, e.g. SQL Server, Oracle, these
            ' must have values
            If strText <> "TEXT" Then
                intLen = 0
            End If
            intScale = 0          ' Put in real value if SQL Server,
Oracle, etc.
```

```
            intPrecision = 0    ' Put in real value if SQL Server,
Oracle, etc.
            strSQL = "INSERT INTO COL_COLUMN_M " _
                & "(COL_C, TAB_PHYSNAME_T, COL_ATTLOGNAME_T, DTP_C,
COL_PHYSNAME_T," _
                & " COL_DTPLEN_N, COL_DTPSCALE_N,
COL_DTPPRECISION_N, DTTP_C) VALUES " _
                & "('" & strCol & "', '" & strTable & "', 'Auto-
generated'," _
                & "'" & strText & "'," _
                & "'" & strField & "'," _
                & CStr(intLen) & "," _
                & CStr(intScale) & "," & CStr(intPrecision) _
                & ",'" & strDTTP & "')"
            cmd.CommandText = strSQL
            cmd.Execute lngAffected
            intColumn = intColumn + 1
            ' Write a message to the notepad for the added column
            strText = "Table: " & strTable _
              & " / Column: " & strField _
              & " was in the database, but not in the Repository.
" _
              & "It has now been added to the Repository."
            strText = AddNotePadLine(strText)
        Else
            ' If the column is defined, is the datatype correct?
            ' If not, update the Repsoitory
            strDTPOK = "Y"
            strOldDTP = rstMeta("DTP_C")
            intOldLen = Nz(rstMeta("COL_DTPLEN_N"))
            intOldScale = Nz(rstMeta("COL_DTPSCALE_N"))
            intOldPrecision = Nz(rstMeta("COL_DTPPRECISION_N"))
            strText = TransDBType(col)
            strDTTP = GetDataTypeType(strText)
            ' Check datatype
            If strText <> rstMeta("DTP_C") Then
                strSQL = "UPDATE COL_COLUMN_M SET DTP_C = '" &
strText & "', " _
                    & " DTTP_C = '" & strDTTP & "' " _
                    & " WHERE COL_PHYSNAME_T = '" & strField & "'
```

```
"  _
                              & " AND TAB_PHYSNAME_T = '" & strTable & "'"
                cmd.CommandText = strSQL
                cmd.Execute lngAffected
                strDTPOK = "N"
             End If
             ' Check Length
             intLen = col.DefinedSize
             If strText <> "TEXT" Then
                intLen = 0
             End If
             If intLen <> rstMeta("COL_DTPLEN_N") Then
                strSQL = "UPDATE COL_COLUMN_M SET COL_DTPLEN_N = " &
CStr(intLen) _
                      & " WHERE COL_PHYSNAME_T = '" & strField & "'
"  _
                      & " AND TAB_PHYSNAME_T = '" & strTable & "'"
                cmd.CommandText = strSQL
                cmd.Execute lngAffected
                strDTPOK = "N"
             End If
             ' Check Scale—for Access this is always 0 in our
             ' repository—but in e.g. SQL Server, Oracle it will
             ' have a value that must be checked
             intScale = col.NumericScale
             If 1 = 1 Then
                intScale = 0
             End If
             If intScale <> rstMeta("COL_DTPSCALE_N") Then
                strSQL = "UPDATE COL_COLUMN_M SET COL_DTPSCALE_N = "
& CStr(intScale) _
                      & " WHERE COL_PHYSNAME_T = '" & strField & "'
"  _
                      & " AND TAB_PHYSNAME_T = '" & strTable & "'"
                cmd.CommandText = strSQL
                cmd.Execute lngAffected
                strDTPOK = "N"
             End If
             ' Check Precision—for Access this is always 0 in our
             ' repository—but in e.g. SQL Server, Oracle it will
             ' have a value that must be checked
```

```
                intPrecision = col.Precision
                If 1 = 1 Then
                   intPrecision = 0
                End If
                If intPrecision <> rstMeta("COL_DTPPRECISION_N") Then
                   strSQL = "UPDATE COL_COLUMN_M SET COL_DTPPRECISION_N
= " _
                            & CStr(intPrecision) _
                            & " WHERE COL_PHYSNAME_T = '" & strField & "'
" _
                            & " AND TAB_PHYSNAME_T = '" & strTable & "'"
                   cmd.CommandText = strSQL
                   cmd.Execute lngAffected
                   strDTPOK = "N"
                End If
                ' If there were changes, write to Notepad
                If strDTPOK = "N" Then
                   strText = "Table " & strTable & " Column " &
strField _
                            & "Datatype changed in Repository.
Datatype/Length/Scale/Precision was " _
                            & strOldDTP & "/" & CStr(intOldLen) & "/" _
                            & CStr(intOldScale) & "/" & CStr(intOldPrecision) _
                            & "-Updated to: " & strText & "/" & CStr(intLen) &
"/" _
                            & CStr(intScale) & "/" & CStr(intPrecision)
                   strText = AddNotePadLine(strText)
                   intUpd = intUpd + 1
                End If
             End If
             rstMeta.Close
          Next
       End If
    Next

    ' SECTION 2: Each table and column in the Business Rules
    ' Repository must be present
    ' in the database (i.e. in the System Catalog)
    strSQL = "SELECT * FROM TAB_TABLE_M"
    rstMeta.Open strSQL, CurrentProject.Connection, _
             adOpenKeyset, adLockOptimistic, adCmdText
```

```
   strTabOK = "N"
   Do While Not rstMeta.EOF
     For Each tbl In cat.Tables
       If tbl.Name = rstMeta("TAB_PHYSNAME_T") Then
         strTabOK = "Y"
         strSQL = "SELECT * FROM COL_COLUMN_M " _
                & " WHERE TAB_PHYSNAME_T = '" & _
rstMeta("TAB_PHYSNAME_T") & "'"
         rstCols.Open strSQL, CurrentProject.Connection, _
            adOpenKeyset, adLockOptimistic, adCmdText
         Do While Not rstCols.EOF
           strField = rstCols("COL_PHYSNAME_T")
           strColOK = "N"
           For Each col In tbl.Columns
             If col.Name = strField Then
               strColOK = "Y"
             End If
           Next
           If strColOK = "N" Then
               ' Is this column used in any business rules as a
               ' source? It should not be
               lngCount1 = _
ChkColAsRuleSrc(rstMeta("TAB_PHYSNAME_T"), strField)
               If lngCount1 <> 0 Then
                 ' Write a message to the notepad
                 strText = " Error: Table: " & _
rstMeta("TAB_PHYSNAME_T") _
                 & " / Column: " & strField _
                 & " is in Repository, but not in database. " _
                 & "CANNOT DELETE IT BECAUSE IT IS USED IN RULES
AS SOURCE."
                 strText = AddNotePadLine(strText)
                 intErr = intErr + 1
               End If
               ' Is this column used in any business rules as a
               ' target? It should not be
               lngCount2 = _
ChkColAsRuleTgt(rstMeta("TAB_PHYSNAME_T"), strField)
               If lngCount2 <> 0 Then
                 ' Write a message to the notepad
```

```
                        strText = " Error: Table: " &
rstMeta("TAB_PHYSNAME_T") _
                        & " / Column: " & strField _
                        & " is in Repository, but not in database. " _
                        & "CANNOT DELETE IT BECAUSE IT IS USED IN RULES
AS TARGET."
                        strText = AddNotePadLine(strText)
                        intErr = intErr + 1
                    End If
                    ' If OK, delete
                    If lngCount1 = 0 And lngCount2 = 0 Then
                        strSQL = "DELETE FROM COL_COLUMN_M " _
                        & " WHERE TAB_PHYSNAME_T = '" &
rstMeta("TAB_PHYSNAME_T") & "' " _
                        & " AND COL_PHYSNAME_T = '" & strField & "' "
                        cmd.CommandText = strSQL
                        cmd.Execute lngAffected
                        intDelCol = intDelCol + 1
                        ' Write a message to the notepad
                        strText = "Table: " & rstMeta("TAB_PHYSNAME_T")
_
                        & " / Column: " & strField _
                        & " is in Repository, but not in database. " _
                        & "Deleted from Repository."
                        strText = AddNotePadLine(strText)
                    End If
                End If
                rstCols.MoveNext
            Loop
            rstCols.Close
        End If
    Next

    ' If we did not find the table in the database, we should
    ' remove it from the Business Rules Repository
    If strTabOK = "N" Then
        strTabOK = "Y"
        strSQL = "SELECT * FROM COL_COLUMN_M " _
                & " WHERE TAB_TABLE_M = '" &
rstMeta("TAB_PHYSNAME_T") & "'"
```

```
        rstCols.Open strSQL, CurrentProject.Connection, _
            adOpenKeyset, adLockOptimistic, adCmdText
      Do While Not rstCols.EOF
          strField = rstCols("COL_PHYSNAME_T")
          ' Is this column used in any business rules as a source?
          ' It should not be
          lngCount1 = ChkColAsRuleSrc(rstMeta("TAB_PHYSNAME_T"),
strField)
          If lngCount1 <> 0 Then
            strTabOK = "N"
            ' Write a message to the notepad
            strText = " Error: Table: " & rstMeta("TAB_PHYSNAME_T")
_
                    & " / Column: " & strField _
                    & " is in Repository, but not in database. " _
                    & "CANNOT DELETE IT BECAUSE IT IS USED IN
RULES."
            strText = AddNotePadLine(strText)
            intErr = intErr + 1
          End If
          ' Is this column used in any business rules as a target?
          ' It should not be
          lngCount2 = ChkColAsRuleTgt(rstMeta("TAB_PHYSNAME_T"),
strField)
          If lngCount2 <> 0 Then
            strTabOK = "N"
            ' Write a message to the notepad
            strText = " Error: Table: " & rstMeta("TAB_PHYSNAME_T")
_
                    & " / Column: " & strField _
                    & " is in Repository, but not in database. " _
                    & "CANNOT DELETE IT BECAUSE IT IS USED IN
RULES."
            strText = AddNotePadLine(strText)
            intErr = intErr + 1
          End If
          ' If OK, delete
          If lngCount1 = 0 And lngCount2 = 0 Then
            strSQL = "DELETE FROM COL_COLUMN_M " _
              & " WHERE TAB_PHYSNAME_T = '" &
rstMeta("TAB_PHYSNAME_T") & "' " _
```

```
                        & " COL_PHYSNAME_T = '" & strField & "' "
                cmd.CommandText = strSQL
                cmd.Execute lngAffected
                intDelCol = intDelCol + 1
                ' Write a message to the notepad
                strText = "Table: " & rstMeta("TAB_PHYSNAME_T") _
                        & " / Column: " & strField _
                        & " is in Repsoitory, but not in database. " _
                        & "Deleted from Repository."
                strText = AddNotePadLine(strText)
            End If
            rstCols.MoveNext
        Loop
        rstCols.Close
        ' If no column of the table was used in business rules,
        ' remove the table from the Business Rules Repository
        If strTabOK = "Y" Then
            strSQL = "DELETE FROM TAB_TABLE_M " _
                & " WHERE TAB_PHYSNAME_T = '" &
rstMeta("TAB_PHYSNAME_T") & "' "
            cmd.CommandText = strSQL
            cmd.Execute lngAffected
            intDelTab = intDelTab + 1
            ' Write a message to the notepad
            strText = "Table: " & rstMeta("TAB_PHYSNAME_T") _
                    & " is in Repsoitory, but not in database. " _
                    & "Deleted from Repository."
            strText = AddNotePadLine(strText)
        Else
            strText = " Error: Table: " & rstMeta("TAB_PHYSNAME_T") _
                    & " is in Repsoitory, but not in database. " _
                    & "CANNOT DELETE IT BECAUSE ITS COLUMNS ARE
USED IN RULES."
            strText = AddNotePadLine(strText)
            intErr = intErr + 1
        End If
    End If
    rstMeta.MoveNext
  Loop
```

```
    rstMeta.Close
    Set rstMeta = Nothing
    Set rstChk = Nothing

    ' Write Final messages to the notepad
    strText = RepeatStr("-", 100)
    strText = AddNotePadLine(strText)
    strText = AddNotePadLine("SUMMARY:")
    strText = CStr(intTable) & " Tables added to Repository "
    strText = AddNotePadLine(strText)
    strText = CStr(intColumn) & " Columns added to Repository "
    strText = AddNotePadLine(strText)
    strText = CStr(intDelTab) & " Tables removed from Repository "
    strText = AddNotePadLine(strText)
    strText = CStr(intDelCol) & " Columns removed from Repository "
    strText = AddNotePadLine(strText)
    strText = CStr(intUpd) & " Column datatypes updated in
  Repository "
    strText = AddNotePadLine(strText)
    If intErr <> 0 Then
       strText = CStr(intErr) & " Problems found when trying to
  delete Repository Tables/Columns "
       strText = AddNotePadLine(strText)
       strText = "- Remove the business rules associated with these
  columns "
       strText = AddNotePadLine(strText)
       strText = "- Then rerun the Repository Synchronization "
       strText = AddNotePadLine(strText)
    End If

    DoCmd.OpenForm "frmNotePad"
    SynchReposDB = "N"

  End Function
```

is really looking for errors that occurred with user-defined columns. Thus, if errors are detected, the user should be somewhat familiar with the columns concerned because it will have been the user, or a colleague, who attempted to define the column that is in error. The Repository Synchronization Checker should never detect an error with a column that is not user-defined, but there is always a possibility that this can

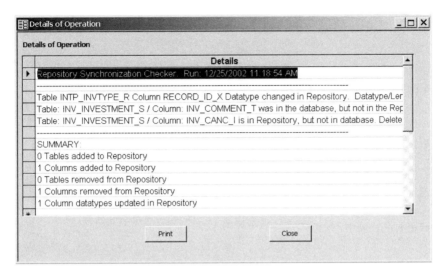

FIGURE 14.7
Results Display from the Repository Synchronization Checker

happen. The designer may wish to have the Repository Synchronization Checker display an additional message to the user to escalate this kind of error to the application support team.

After the Repository Synchronization Checker shown in Listing 14.7 is executed, details of its operation are displayed in the screen shown in Figure 14.7. The list in this screen can be printed.

Conclusion

This chapter has introduced a number of items of rules engine functionality that are needed to manage the database on which the rules engine operates. These functions are primarily required to support users as they add new columns to extend the database tables that contain business-related data. At this point the basic Business Rules Repository has been built, and the minimum required management capabilities have been created for it. The Repository can now be used for defining business rules and creating executable versions of them. This topic is introduced in the next chapter and continues for several subsequent chapters.

15

IMPLEMENTING A SIMPLE BUSINESS RULE

In the previous chapters the rules engine infrastructure was created to manage business processes and related metadata. This provides the basis on which the components to define rules can be created. In this chapter we will see how to build everything that is needed to manage a rule type. The rule type selected is a rather simple one: it validates that data has been entered for required fields on a screen. All the components required to deal with this rule type will be built: the interface to define the rules; the routines to store the metadata; the routines to generate the code; and the interface to execute the generated code.

Rules Definition Interface

If users are to define business rules, how should they access them? One design alternative is to have rule definition functionality available at many points in an application, such as the screens that invoke particular processes. This may be a good design for applications that only have a little rules engine functionality. However, in situations where many business processes can have business rules defined for them, it is better to have a single place in the application from which rule definitions can be accessed. This is the design adopted in the sample application, and the screen that is the starting point for defining business rules is shown in Figure 15.1.

The Business Rules Summary Screen summarizes the business rules that have been defined for any Business Process Step. When a rule is selected its definition and rule type are displayed. So far, we have not defined any rules, so this part of the screen does not contain any information. The information used in the screen comes from the Repository tables and functionality discussed in previous chapters. The fields displayed on the screen are as follows:

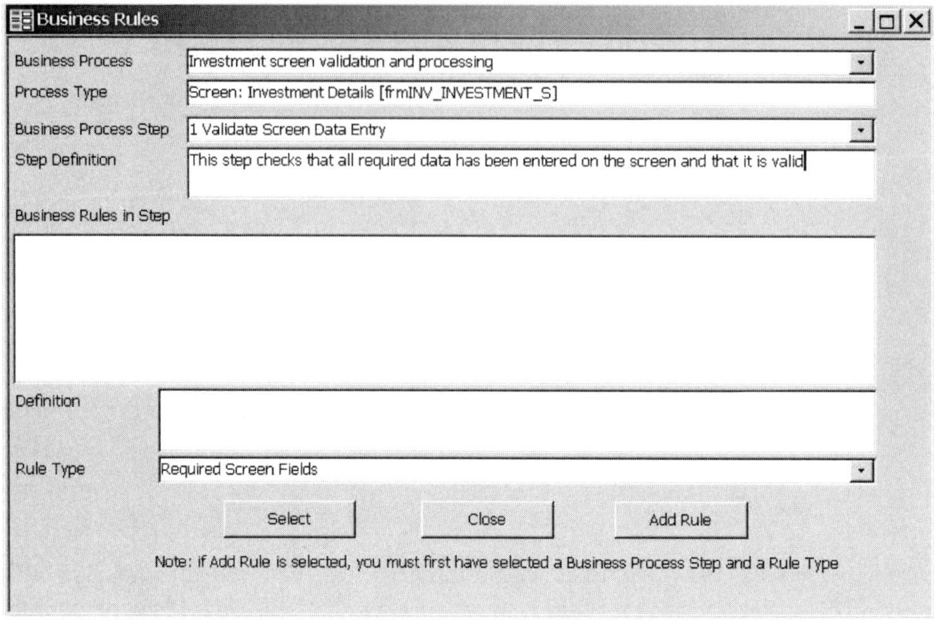

FIGURE 15.1
Business Rules Summary Screen

- *Business Process*: This combo box contains a list of the business processes defined for the application. When a new business process is selected, the combo box *Business Process Step* is rebuilt to include only business process steps for the selected business process.

- *Process Type*: This is the environment within which the business process is executed. In the sample application there are two kinds of environment: screens and batch processes. If the business process is for a screen, additional information for the screen is shown.

- *Business Process Step*: This combo box contains all the business process steps for the selected *Business Process*. It is rebuilt when a different *Business Process* is selected. When a different *Business Process Step* is selected, the list box containing the rules that have been associated with the *Business Process Step* is rebuilt, as is the combo box containing the rule types permitted for the *Business Process Step*. *Business Process Steps* are shown in the sequence in which they run, prefixed by their sequence number.

- *Business Rules in Step*: This list box shows all the *Business Rules* associated with the *Business Process Step*. The user's business rule number and rule name are displayed. When the user clicks on a *Business Rule*, the *Rule Type* combo box is set the to the rule type of this rule.

- *Rule Type*: This combo box contains all the permitted *Rule Types* for the currently selected *Business Process Step*. If a *Business Rule* is clicked on, it shows the rule type of this rule.

To define a new rule, the appropriate business process step and rule type must be selected. In the example discussed in this chapter, rules will be defined for the Investment Definition Screen. This is a screen where information about investments can be entered. There is one business process for this screen. The relevant business process step is "Validate Screen Data Entry" and the rule type is "Screen Required Fields."

Defining Rules for the Investment Screen

Before proceeding any further, let us consider the application screen in the sample application where investment details are added. This is the screen we will use as an example for building a number of business rule types and defining business rules. In the sample application it is accessed by selecting **Application Functions** on the main menu, and then **Enter Investment Details** on the popup that appears. It is shown in Figure 15.2.

This screen is designed to capture information when the organization for which the application has been created (Big Bubble Brokers, or "BBB") makes an investment

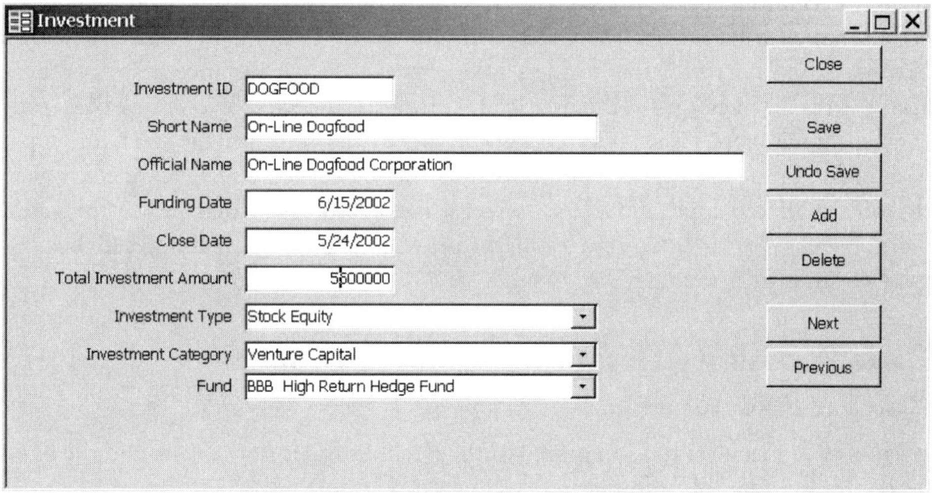

FIGURE 15.2
Investment Details Screen

in a business of some kind. The physical name of the screen is frmINV_INVEST
MENT_S, and it updates data in the database table **INV_INVESTMENT_S**.

There are actually several types of rule that can be involved in edit checks for any
screen. These are listed in Table 15.1. What is interesting about these rule types is
that they must be executed in the sequence shown in Table 15.1. This sequence will
make sense to any IT professional and is not something that a rules engine could ever
infer. Rather than have the rules engine deal with the sequence, a sequence number
is stored in the Repository in the **Business Rule Type** table.

Thus, for edit validation rules, there is a general prescribed sequence for rule
types. The sequence in which these rule types must be run is shown in Table 15.1.
A number of these rule types are discussed in more detail in this and the next few
chapters. The Business Rules Repository table **Business Rule Type**
(**BRTP_BIZRULETYPE_M**) must be updated with the codes and names representing these business rule types, along with the names of the rule definition functions for each rule type and their sequence numbers. The rule definition functions,
as we shall see, are the interfaces where rules are defined. There is one and only one
rule definition function per rule type.

In the business process step to validate inputs on the investment screen (or indeed
any screen), the business rules for these rule types must be executed sequentially in
the order shown in Table 15.1. Only if all the rules of one type are passed successfully should the rules of the rule type that is next in sequence be run. For example,
if not all required fields are entered, then there is no point in running the rules for
valid datatypes.

What this means for the rules engine is that any business process step that concerns a screen must generate code that has the rules in this sequence. The generated
code for such a business process step will also have to have some additional code
beyond that required for the business rules themselves. For instance, it will be necessary to display messages to the user, and if errors are detected by one rule type, processing should stop, rather than continuing on to the rules for the next rule type.
This code cannot be inferred from individual rule types, but is really connected with
the objects of the application (e.g., screens, batch processes) that utilize the rules.
Thus, there is more to building a business rules engine than the capabilities for dealing
with business rules themselves.

Basic Repository Design for Holding Business Rules Metadata

Business rule metadata must be stored in the Business Rules Repository, and the basic
design for holding this information is shown in Figure 15.3.

Each business rule has its basic metadata stored in the entity **Business Rule**. The
entity **Business Rule Type** contains a list of all the rule types, and each business rule

SEQUENCE (BRTP_SCREENSEQ_N)	BUSINESS RULE TYPE DESCRIPTION (BRTP_DESC_T)	DEFINITION (BRTP_DEFN_M)	BUSINESS RULE TYPE CODE (BRTP_C)
1	Required Screen Fields	Check all fields that must have a value.	SCRREQ
2	Valid Datatypes for Screen Fields	If a field has a value, is the value of the expected datatype? For example, a numeric field cannot contain alphabetic characters.	SCRVDTYPE
3	Screen Fields Valid Ranges	Certain fields can have values only within specific ranges. For example, a date field may not have a value prior to 1/1/2000.	SCRVRANGE
4	Check for Duplicate Records	If a record is to be added or updated, duplicates cannot be allowed.	REFINTDUP
5	Referential Integrity for Dependent Records	If a record is deleted or has its primary key changed, are child records affected?	REFINTDEL
6	Cross Checks for Screen Fields	Some edit checks involve checking the value entered in one field against values entered in other fields.	SCRXCHK

TABLE 15.1 Rule Types for Screen Edit Checks

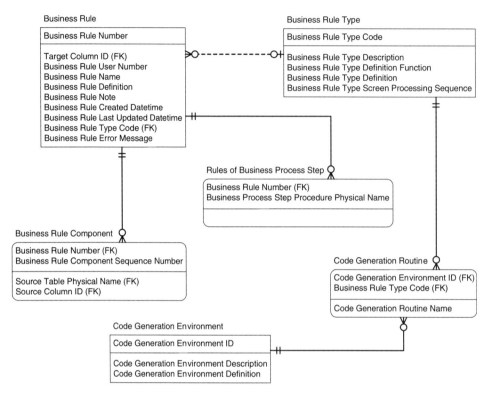

FIGURE 15.3
Basic Design for Business Rules Metadata

must be identified with a rule type. A business rule may be composed of a number of components. These are primarily any tables, columns, or other system objects that are needed by the rule. For instance, a rule may perform a calculation such as A = B + C + D. "B," "C," and "D" are considered to be components of the rule, and their metadata is stored in **Business Rule Component**. **Business Rule Component** is not required for the simple rule type discussed in this chapter and is not dealt with further for the moment. It is explored more in Chapter 16.

The detailed structure of **Business Rule** is as follows:

- *Business Rule Number*: A system-assigned number that uniquely identifies each business rule. All business rules should have a number. The format used in this book is RNNNN. Each *Business Rule Number* begins with "R" and is followed by four digits—for example, "R0001".

- *Target Column ID*: The great majority of business rules operate on a single column in the database—for example, to calculate a value for it, or to validate the values it contains. *Target Column ID* represents this column and is taken from *Column ID* in the **Column** entity.

- *Business Rule Type Code*: This identifies the type of business rule and is taken from the entity **Business Rule Type**.

- *Business Rule User Number*: *Business Rule Number* is used by the system, but often users have their own particular scheme identifying business rules. *Business Rule User Number* permits this. When a new business rule is created it defaults to the value of *Business Rule Number*. Thereafter, the user can change it.

- *Business Rule Name*: A business rule must have a descriptive name. This is particularly necessary when working with lists of business rules.

- *Business Rule Definition*: A business rule must have a definition. The definition should be written in specific terms that have meaning for the business.

- *Business Rule Note*: Any additional information about the business rule can be captured in *Business Rule Note*.

- *Business Rule Error Message*: Certain business rules validate data. These can have a *Business Rule Error Message* to display to the user when an error is detected. Some people feel that this purpose is served by the *Business Rule Definition*. However, many users request error messages that are different from the *Business Rule Definition*.

- *Business Rule Created Datetime*: The date and time when the business rule was first created.

- *Business Rule Last Updated Datetime*: The date and time when the business rule was last updated.

It should be clearly understood that the design of the **Business Rule** table presented here is oriented to what is needed for business rules engines. As pointed out in Chapter 7, there are other dimensions to business rules management that have little to do with rules engines, such as obtaining clear statements of rules from users and determining which organizational units apply them. These other aspects of rules management also require a Repository and the capacity to store rule metadata. They are not dealt with in this book, but the rules engine designer should be aware that they exist.

Business rules can be associated with a particular **Business Process Step** by including them in the entity **Rules of Business Process Step**. This entity is an association between **Business Process Step** and **Business Rule**. It means that business rules can be defined independently of any particular **Business Process Step**, and that one **Business Rule** can be associated with several **Business Process Steps**.

The detailed structure of **Rules of Business Process Step** is as follows:

- *Business Rule Number*: The primary key of **Business Rules**.

- *Business Process Step Procedure Physical Name*: The primary key of **Business Process Step**.

The design approach in this book is that the business rules definition functionality is actually driven from a business process step perspective. Figure 15.1 shows that the user must select a business process step and business rule type in order to define a new business rule. This design is more natural for a user and immediately organizes rules into sets of related rules in the mind of the user. A design whereby rules are defined without reference to business process steps and are associated with business process steps at a later stage is less easy for users to work with. However, the design approach used in this book does require more functionality to be created during business rule definitions, as will be seen.

Another issue, which will become apparent as the functionality for the individual rule types is built, is that each rule type has a somewhat distinct set of metadata required to define it. The design shown in Figure 15.3 meets the goal of having all business rules easily accessible in one place. However, many rule types require these entities to be extended with one or two additional attributes that are needed for some special aspect of the rule type concerned. This is why it is not possible to start with an exact design for **Business Rule** and **Business Rule Component**—they need to evolve as the number of implemented rule types grows. The alternative design would be to have two such tables for every rule type. This would quickly spawn many tables and create an administrative nightmare that would make the programming for the rules engine components more difficult. Therefore, as new rule types are introduced in this and subsequent chapters, required modifications to **Business Rule** and **Business Rule Component** will also be discussed.

The entity **Business Rule Type** in Figure 15.3 has the following structure:

- *Business Rule Type Code*: A user-defined acronym that uniquely identifies a business rule type.

- *Business Rule Type Description*: The name of the rule type.

- *Business Rule Type Definition Function*: The physical name of the rules engine object that is the rule definition interface for this rule type. In the sample application all rule definition interfaces are Microsoft Access forms.

- *Business Rule Type Definition*: A full description and definition of the rule type.

- *Business Rule Type Screen Processing Sequence*: This implements the sequence shown in Table 15.1. It is the sequence in which rules of this rule type fire when a screen data entry occurs.

The entity **Code Generation Environment** in Figure 15.3 identifies the various kinds of programming environments for which code will have to be generated. The rules engine, as we shall see, must generate code not only for individual rules, but also for business process steps. Each programming language in which the rules have to be implemented represents one code generation environment. However, even within a single programming language, or its equivalent, there can be different code generation environments. This is the case with Microsoft Access, where the system objects available when screens are being dealt with are different from those for batch processes. This is dealt with in more detail later in this chapter. The structure of the **Code Generation Environment** entity is as follows:

- *Code Generation Environment ID*: A user-defined acronym that uniquely identifies a code generation environment.

- *Code Generation Environment Description*: The name of the code generation environment.

- *Code Generation Environment Definition*: A full description and definition of the code generation environment.

The remaining entity in Figure 15.3 is **Code Generation Routine**. This is the association between **Business Rule Type** and **Code Generation Environment**. It defines the rules engine function that generates code for a given rule type in a given code generation environment. After even a few rule types have been created, it is difficult to keep track of all the code generation routines that have been implemented. The **Code Generation Routine** helps in this regard. It also helps to reduce the need to update central rules engine functionality every time a new rule type is implemented. The part of the rules engine that generates code looks at this table to find the functions that are used to generate code. Thus, all that needs to be done for a new rule type is to create the definition interface and update **Business Rule Type** with this information. The next step is to create the code generation routines, and then update the **Code Generation Routine** table to reflect the new code generation routines. The rules engine code generation functionality can then easily find the code generation routines whenever it encounters a rule for the new rule type. The structure of the **Code Generation Routine** entity is as follows:

- *Code Generation Environment ID*: A user-defined acronym that uniquely identifies a code generation environment.

- *Business Rule Type Code*: A user-defined acronym that uniquely identifies a business rule type.

- *Code Generation Routine Name*: The physical name of the rules engine object that is the code generation routine for the current rule type in the current code generation environment. In the sample application all code generation routines are VBA functions in Microsoft Access.

Tables 15.2 and 15.3 show the physical implementation of the tables just discussed.

Let us now begin to build the functionality for the first rule type: **Required Screen Fields**.

ENTITY	TABLE
Business Rule	BRULE_BIZRULE_M
Business Rule Component	BRC_BIZRULECOMP_M
Rules of Business Process Step	RBSP_RULESOFSTEP_M
Business Rule Type	BRTP_BIZRULETYPE_M
Code Generation Environment	CGE_CODEGENENV_M
Code Generation Routine	CGR_CODEGENROUTINE_M

TABLE 15.2 Physical Implementation of Entities That Store Business Rule Metadata

Accessing the Rules Definition Interface for Rule Type Required Screen Fields

The starting point for the definition of rules for **Required Screen Fields** is the screen shown in Figure 15.1. To create a new rule of this type for the Investment screen, the user selects the business process for the Investment screen, the business process step for validating data entry on this screen, and the rule type **Required Screen Fields**. The user presses the **Add Rule** button. The business rules engine must now present the user with the definition interface for this rule type.

The rules engine does this by retrieving the record for **Required Screen Fields** from the table **BRTP_BIZRULETYPE_M** (**Business Rule Type**). This record contains the name of the definition function for this rule type. In the case of the sample application all definition functions are Microsoft Access forms. The business rule type **Required Screen Fields** is represented by *Business Rule Type Code* (BRTP_C) of "SCRREQ" in this table. The corresponding *Business Rule Type Definition Function* (BRTP_FUNCTION_T) is "frmRULE_SCRREQ". This is the name of the Microsoft Access form for defining the **Required Screen Fields** rule type. The system simply has to invoke it.

The user has made a number of choices on the Business Rule Summary screen shown in Figure 15.1. These need to be remembered by the rules engine for processing later on. This information comes from the part of the Business Rules Repository discussed in Chapter 12. The rules engine must remember the following:

- The business process selected on the Business Rule Summary screen.

- The implementation environment for the business process selected on the Business Rule Summary screen. This is found by looking up the selected business process in the **BPROC_BIZPROCESS_M** (**Business Process**) table. In the current example the business process "Investment screen validation and processing" was chosen. It is represented by a *Business Process ID* (BPROC_C) with a value of "SCRINVVAL". The record in BPROC_BIZPROCESS_M has

TABLE	ATTRIBUTE	COLUMN	DATATYPE
BRULE_BIZRULE_M	Business Rule Number	BRULE_NUMBER_C	Character (5)
BRULE_BIZRULE_M	Target Column ID	COL_C	Character (4)
BRULE_BIZRULE_M	Business Rule User Number	BRULE_USER_C	Character (20)
BRULE_BIZRULE_M	Business Rule Name	BRULE_NAME_T	Character (120)
BRULE_BIZRULE_M	Business Rule Definition	BRULE_DEFN_M	Memo
BRULE_BIZRULE_M	Business Rule Note	BRULE_NOTE_M	Memo
BRULE_BIZRULE_M	Business Rule Created Datetime	BRULE_CREATE_D	Date/Time
BRULE_BIZRULE_M	Business Rule Last Updated Datetime	BRULE_UPD_D	Date/Time
BRULE_BIZRULE_M	Business Rule Type Code	BRTP_C	Character (10)
BRULE_BIZRULE_M	Business Rule Error Message	BRULE_ERR_T	Character (250)
BRULE_BIZRULE_M	Business Rule Number	BRTP_C	Character (10)
BRC_BIZRULECOMP_M	Business Rule Component Sequence Number	BRC_SEQUENCE_N	Integer
BRC_BIZRULECOMP_M	Source Table Physical Name	TAB_PHYSNAME_T	Character (50)
BRC_BIZRULECOMP_M	Source Column ID	COL_C	Character (4)
BRTP_BIZRULETYPE_M	Business Rule Type Code	BRTP_C	Character (10)
BRTP_BIZRULETYPE_M	Business Rule Type Description	BRTP_DESC_T	Character (80)
BRTP_BIZRULETYPE_M	Business Rule Type Function Definition	BRTP_FUNCTION_T	Character (80)
BRTP_BIZRULETYPE_M	Business Rule Type Definition	BRTP_DEFN_M	Memo
BRTP_BIZRULETYPE_M	Business Rule Type Screen Processing Sequence	BRTP_SCREENSEQ_N	Integer
RBSP_RULESOFSTEP_M	Business Process Step Procedure Physical Name	BPSP_PHYSNAME_T	Character (40)
RBSP_RULESOFSTEP_M	Business Rule Number	BRULE_NUMBER_C	Character (5)
CGE_CODEGENENV_M	Code Generation Environment ID	CGE_C	Character (10)
CGE_CODEGENENV_M	Code Generation Environment Description	CGE_DESC_T	Character (80)
CGE_CODEGENENV_M	Code Generation Environment Definition	CGE_DEFN_M	Memo
CGR_CODEGENROUTINE_M	Code Generation Environment ID	CGE_C	Character (10)
CGR_CODEGENROUTINE_M	Business Rule Type Code	BRTP_C	Character (10)
CGR_CODEGENROUTINE_M	Code Generation Routine Name	CGR_NAME_T	Memo

TABLE 15.3 Physical Implementation of Columns that Store Business Rule Metadata

Business Process Implementation Code (BPTP_C) with a value of "SCREEN". This indicates that we are dealing with a screen. The record has *Screen Physical Name* (SCR_PHYSNAME_T) set to "frmINV_INVESTMENT_S". This is the screen on which the business rules that are to be defined will operate. The rules engine must also remember it.

- The business process step selected on the Business Rule Summary screen.

- The base table connected with the business process step. This is found by looking up the selected business process step in the **BPSP_BIZSTEPPROC_M (Business Process Step)** table. In the current example the business process step "Validate Screen Data Entry" was chosen. It is represented by a *Business Process Step Procedure Physical Name* (BPSP_PHYSNAME_T) with a value of "ScrChkfrmINV_INVESTMENT_S". The record in BPSP_BIZSTEPPROC_M has *Base Table for Business Process Step* (TAB_PHYSNAME_T) with a value of "INV_INVESTMENT_S"—which represents the **Investment** table.

- The rule type selected on the Business Rule Summary screen.

The way that this information is "remembered" by the rules engine of the sample application is by storing it in public variables. In other software environments a different technique may be required.

At this point, the interface to define the rules for **Required Screen Fields** can be considered.

Interface to Define Rule Type for Required Screen Fields

The rule type to enforce data entry for a field entered on a screen is conceptually simple. The minimum metadata required is the name of each field that has to have a value entered for it. Of course there is also general metadata needed for business rules, as has been discussed above. A reasonable design for the interface is shown in Figure 15.4.

The fields on this screen are as follows:

- **Screen:** The name of the screen for which rules will be defined. The physical name is shown here also. This data cannot be edited by the user.

- **Required Fields:** These are the screen fields that the user has determined to be required, and they in fact are the rules. The rule number is displayed next to the name of the required field.

    This is not necessarily a list of all the **Required Screen Fields** for the **Investment** table. Rather it is a list of such fields that are associated with the current business process step. It is possible to have a **Required Screen Field**

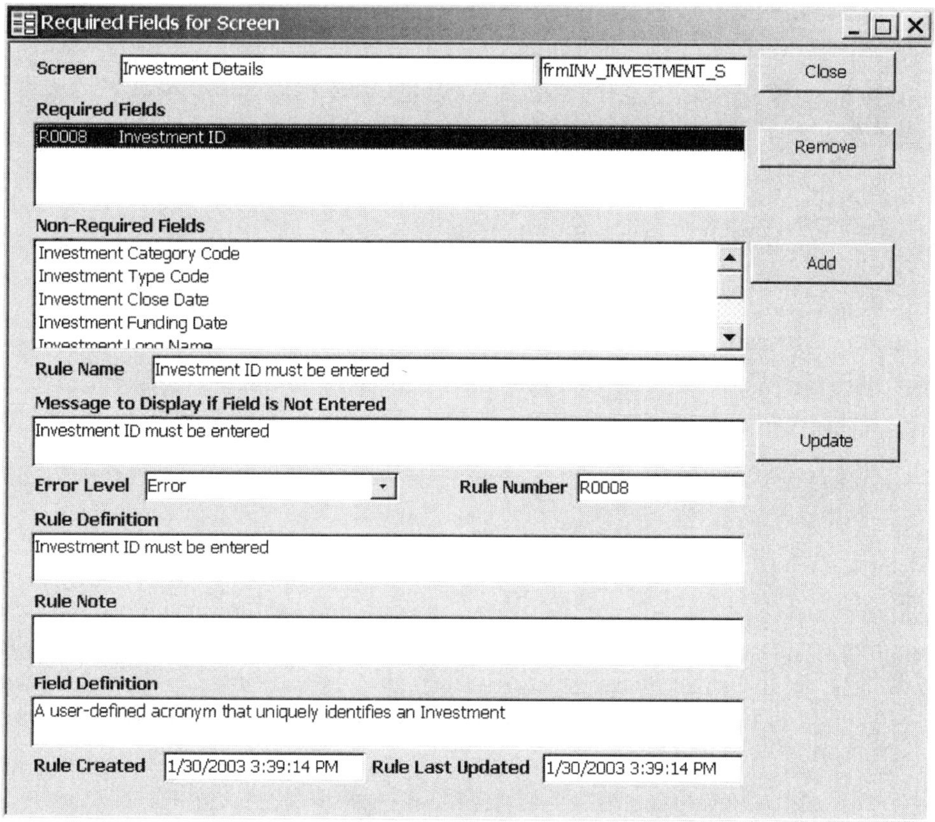

FIGURE 15.4
Screen for Defining Business Rules of Rule Type **Required Screen Fields**

rule for the **Investment** table that is not associated with the current business process step.

- **Non-Required Fields**: The columns from the **Investment** table that have not been defined as **Required Screen Fields**, or have been defined as **Required Screen Fields** but are not associated with the current business process step.

- **Rule Name**: The name of the business rule.

- **Message to Display if Field Is Not Entered**: If the rule is fired and detects an error condition, this is the message that will be displayed to the user.

- **Error Level**: The seriousness with which this error is treated.

- **Rule Number**: The user can define business rule numbers here.

- **Rule Definition**: The definition of the business rule.

- **Rule Note**: Miscellaneous information that needs to be recorded for the business rule.

- **Field Definition**: When the user clicks on an item in the list box of *Required Fields* or *Non-Required Fields*, the attribute definition (COL_ATTLOGNAME_T) for the column is retrieved from the **Column** table (**COL_COLUMN_M**). Attribute names, which are shown in the two lists, may not be sufficient for a user to identify a field. This data cannot be edited by the user.

- **Rule Created**: The date and time when the rule was first created. This data cannot be edited by the user.

- **Rule Last Updated**: The date and time when the rule was last updated. This data cannot be edited by the user.

Now let us look more closely at how the rule definition interface works.

Preliminary Processing

All relational databases enforce the need to have nonnull values in the primary key columns of a database. This has implications for the rule type **Required Screen Fields**. Any field on the screen that is a primary key column must be a **Required Screen Field**. The rule definition interface, therefore, ensures that this is the case by doing the following:

- The rule definition interface finds all the primary key columns for the base table (**Investment**) associated with the currently selected business process step ("Validate Screen Data Entry") for the currently selected business process ("Investment screen validation and processing"). To do this the system must find all primary key columns for the base table that are *Target Column IDs* in any business rules of the type **Required Screen Fields**. The primary key columns are found by selecting records from the **Column** table where the *Column Primary Key Indicator* (COL_PK_I) is set to "Y". These are then compared to records in the **Business Rule** table (**BRULE_BIZRULE_M**) where *Business Rule Type Code* is "Required Screen Fields" (BRTP_C = "SCRREQ").

- For each primary key column of the base table that cannot be found in the **Business Rule** table, a new business rule is created automatically. The *Business Rule Number* is incremented from the previously assigned *Business Rule Number*, and this is also used as the *Business Rule User Number*. A *Business Rule Error Message* is created by taking the *Attribute Logical Name* of the primary key column from the **Column** table and adding text to say that it has not been entered on the screen. This is also used for the *Business*

Rule Name and *Business Rule Definition*. The *Business Rule Type Code* is set to
"SCRREQ".

The ability to perform this kind of automatic generation of rules is a
direct result of the Repository design, which includes a great deal of database
design metadata.

- Next, the **Rules of Business Process Step** table (RBSP_RULESOFSTEP_M)
  is searched to determine whether all business rules of the type **Required Screen
  Fields** for the primary key columns of the currently selected base table are
  included in RBSP_RULESOFSTEP_M for the currently selected business
  process step. If they are not present, they are added to this table. This connects
  all **Required Screen Fields** rules for primary key columns of the currently
  selected base table to the currently selected business process step.

What is interesting to note about this preliminary processing is how specific it is
to the rules of the type **Required Screen Fields**. It will not be found in the definition
interface for any other rule type. Yet it is also very necessary. If the rules engine did not
have this functionality users might sometimes forget to define **Required Screen Field**
rules for primary key columns. This would lead to program crashes if the application
attempted to insert new records in a base table with null primary key columns. A rules
engine design that allows such gaps would probably not be received well by users.

A second lesson is just how important analysis is for each rule type. Different rule
types may share a lot of metadata, but they can behave in radically different ways. It is
vital to work through exactly how a rule type will function within the application as a
whole. It may not be immediately obvious that there is a natural connection between
the enforcement of nonnull primary key columns in databases and the rule type for
Required Screen Fields. However, the rules engine designer must be able to think
across all dimensions of the application, the software environment, and the underlying business.

Details of the Rule Definition Interface

Let us now look a little more closely at how the rule definition interface shown in
Figure 15.4 works. The following are the most important points regarding this
functionality:

- To create a new rule, the user clicks on the desired field in the *Non-Required
  Fields* list. This also has the effect of refreshing the *Field Definition* in the lower
  part of the screen. Next the user presses the **Add** button. The system first
  determines whether a **Required Screen Fields** rule already exists for this
  column. Remember that it is possible that such a rule has been defined already,
  for another screen, and it is simply not associated with the current business
  process step. If the rule does not exist, it is created, and then the rule is

associated with the currently selected business process step. The same default values are created for the new rule as discussed in the previous section.

- When the user clicks on a field in the *Required Fields* list, all of the information in the lower part of the screen is refreshed.

- The user can update information for a rule by changing it and then clicking the **Update** button.

- In the field *Message to Display if Field is Not Entered*, it is a good idea to include a reference to the Rule Number. When users receive error messages they sometimes have questions about them. If there is a rule number associated with the error message, then the possibility exists that the rule can be further researched. With more advanced rules engine approaches, users may even be able to look up the metadata stored for the business rule, and thus answer their own questions.

- *Error level* indicates how serious the error is if the user does not enter data for the specified field. It affects what action is taken if an error is detected when the rule fires. However, the system enforces a level of "Error" for rules that are for primary key columns—the user cannot change it. Error level is also used in a number of other rule types. This information is stored in the **Error Level** table (**ELVL_ERRORLEVEL_M**), the contents of which are shown in Table 15.4.

- *Rule Number* is set to the system's internal rule number when a new rule is added. Thereafter the user can override it with his or her own rule number. However, the system always checks to determine whether a rule number specified by the user has been used for another rule.

- When the user clicks the **Remove** button, the record that associates the currently selected rule with the currently selected business process step is removed from the **Rules of Business Process Step** (**RBSP_RULESOFSTEP_M**) table. If the rule is no longer associated with any business process steps then it is completely deleted.

ERROR LEVEL CODE	ERROR LEVEL DESCRIPTION
00	Normal
04	Informatory
08	Warning
12	Error
16	Severe Error

TABLE 15.4 Error Level Values and Meanings

There is no other rule checking in this instance. The column concerned may be used in other rules, but we do not need to restrict the removal of the **Required Screen Fields** validation rule if this happens. All we are doing is validating the data that goes into the field in question (i.e., ensuring that a value is populated and that it is an acceptable value).

There is more to deleting rules in more complex rule types, and this is a topic we shall return to.

This functionality is implemented in the sample application. It does not require very advanced design or programming skills. Perhaps the only complex item is the SQL statement that determines which columns of the base table have not yet been placed in **Required Screen Fields** rules, or exist in **Required Screen Fields** rules that are not yet associated with the currently selected business process step. Listing 15.1 shows the SQL statement used for this purpose. Table 15.5 explains the items that occur in Listing 15.1.

Integrating the Business Rules into the Application Screen

At this point we have captured all the metadata we need to define business rules that check whether a field on a screen must be entered, but this is only half the battle.

LISTING 15.1
SQL Statement to Select Columns Not Included in Business Rules of Type **Required Screen Fields** for the Currently Selected Business Process Step

```
SELECT COL_C, COL_PHYSNAME_T, COL_ATTLOGNAME_T
FROM COL_COLUMN_M
WHERE TAB_PHYSNAME_T = GetSelTab() AND
 (((Exists (SELECT COL_C FROM BRULE_BIZRULE_M  WHERE
TAB_PHYSNAME_T = GetSelTab()  AND BRTP_C = "SCRREQ" AND COL_C =
COL_COLUMN_M.COL_C))=False))

UNION

SELECT A.COL_C, A.COL_PHYSNAME_T, A.COL_ATTLOGNAME_T
FROM COL_COLUMN_M A, BRULE_BIZRULE_M B
WHERE A.COL_C = B.COL_C
    AND B.BRTP_C = "SCRREQ"
AND B.BRULE_NUMBER_C NOT IN
(SELECT BRULE_NUMBER_C FROM RTBS_RULTYPBIZSTEP_M WHERE
BPSP_PHYSNAME_T = GetSelBizStep())

ORDER BY COL_ATTLOGNAME_T;
```

ITEM	DESCRIPTION
COL_COLUMN_M	The **Column** table
COL_C	Column ID
COL_PHYSNAME_T	Column Physical Name
COL_ATTNAME_T	Attribute Logical Name
TAB_PHYSNAME_T	Table Physical Name
GetSelTab()	A function that returns the currently selected table, such as "INV_INVESTMENT_S"
BRULE_BIZRULE_M	The **Business Rule** table
BRTP_C	Business Rule Type Code
BRULE_NUMBER_C	Business Rule Number
RTBS_RULTYPBIZSTEP_M	The **Rule Types Permitted in Business Process Step** table
GetSelBizStep()	A function that returns the currently selected business process step, such as "ScrChkfrmINV_INVESTMENT_S"

TABLE 15.5 Explanation of Items In Listing 15.1

We now need to generate the code to actually implement these rules in our application. However, before we do that we need to design how the generated code will interact with the Investment Definition screen. It is to validate data entry on this screen that the business rules have been defined.

The elements of the design need to consider the following:

- The generated code should be invoked before the tables associated with the screen are updated.

- The programmer who builds the screen will have to write the line(s) of code that invoke the generated code. The programmer must know how to do this. A good technique is to have a naming convention for the generated code. For example, in Microsoft Access the generated code can be placed in a function that has a name of "ScrChk" followed by the physical name of the screen.

- The generated code should indicate whether any error-level conditions have been encountered. If they have been, the update must not proceed. For Microsoft Access, the generated code can be placed in a function that returns a "Y" if all edit checks are passed. Only if this happens can the update be allowed. A programmer can easily implement this design.

- The business rule metadata we built in the previous sections refers to column names in tables. Program variables used to hold data entered on screens may be different. The variable names need to be matched up with the column names in the generated code. In Microsoft Access this is easy because screen variables in bound forms have the same names as the column names. In other environments there may need to be a global naming convention that instructs programmers who build screens to give screen variables the same names as the columns they update. Naming conventions are perhaps the easiest design approach to implement to meet this requirement, and in any case they are good practice.

- Somehow the variables of the screen, and the values they contain, must be visible to the generated code. This will vary depending on the programming environment, and the designer will need to think carefully about the best approach. In Microsoft Access there is a Form object that can be passed to a function containing the generated code. An example of another environment is Macromedia's Cold Fusion. Using the FuseBox methodology in Cold Fusion would dictate that the generated code be placed in a template that is then "included" via a <CFINCLUDE> statement directly in the program code.

In summary, a reasonable design for our Microsoft Access sample application is to place the generated code in a function called "ScrChk" followed by the screen physical name. This function will have one parameter passed to it—the Form object for the screen being updated. The function will return a "Y" if no errors are encountered, or an "N" if errors were detected.

Once such a design has been worked out it should be applied globally for every screen where updates occur. The work required by the programmer should be just a few lines of simple code in every screen. Programmers may object that when they build a screen they do not want to wait until the business rule logic is generated—they want to test the screen immediately. The answer to this is that the programmer should invoke the rules engine to do this, without building any specific rules. The primary key columns will automatically have rules built for them, but that is all. The generated code will be present and the screen will work.

The required code is easily placed in the Investment screen as shown in Figure 15.2. It is placed in the On Click event of the **Save** button on this screen. When the **Save** button is pressed the On Click event is executed, and the code that runs is shown in Listing 15.2. As can be seen, only a few lines of program code need to be inserted here to invoke the generated code.

The name "Command18_Click()" is the name that Microsoft Access has given to the procedure that is called when the **Save** button is pressed. The declaration of "clsModule" as a new instance of the module "BizRuleCode" is necessary in Access to get a reference to the generated code, which is all housed in the Class Module "BizRuleCode". Other programming environments will have their own specific coding requirements. The programmer has inserted the three lines of code that follow.

LISTING 15.2
Code to Invoke Generated Code to Validate Screen Data Entry

```
Private Sub Command18_Click()
Dim clsModule As New BizRuleCode

    If clsModule.ScrChkfrmINV_INVESTMENT_S(Me) = "Y" Then
        DoCmd.DoMenuItem acFormBar, acRecordsMenu, acSaveRecord, ,
acMenuVer70
    End If


    End Sub
```

The first calls the function containing the generated code, passing the Form object. If the function returns a "Y" (meaning all edit checks were passed successfully) the next line is executed, which updates the underlying database table.

Generating the Code

With this design in hand we can now move to generating the code. Once again we need to think about the general design required. In the sample application, each business process step is considered to be a logical set of rules and has program code generated for it in its entirety. A reasonable approach for the **Required Screen Fields** rule type and the business process steps in which it is found is as follows:

- If the generated code already exists, delete it and rebuild the function (or equivalent programming construct). This means all the code for the business process step must be regenerated.

- If parameters are passed to the generated code, ensure they are received correctly.

- Generate any code needed to initialize the environment. This is important because code has to be generated for business process steps, not just business rules.

- Generate code that is appropriate to the software environment in which the business process runs, such as screens, batch processes, or stored procedures.

- Read all business rules that apply to the current business process step from the Business Rules Repository.

- Build the code for each business rule.

- Generate code needed to close the business process step.

- Ensure that the generated code correctly signals back to the calling environment whether any errors were encountered.

Within this general design framework, when code is generated for each business rule it is important to consider the design at a more detailed level. Elements of a good approach for **Required Screen Fields** are as follows:

- If an error is detected, the user should be provided with one error message listing all the required fields that have not been entered on the Investment Definition screen.

- Only if a rule detects a missing field value, and that rule is associated with an *Error Level Number* of 12 or greater, should the screen update be prevented. If the associated *Error Level Number* is less than 12, then it is considered to be a warning or informatory condition, and the screen update should be allowed to proceed.

Given this, let us now generate the code. This is achieved via a two-step process. The first step is to generate the lines of code in the table **Generated Code (GCDE_GENCODE_M)**. The second step is to take these lines of code and use them to create the function we need in the Microsoft Access Class Module "BizRule-Code". A Class Module is a module that can contain many functions and subroutines.

The first step consists of several substeps, shown in Listings 15.3, 15.4, and 15.5. Listing 15.3 shows the function BldScrRules(), which generates all the code to run an entire business process involving a screen. It invokes all the individual functions needed to generate code in the screen environment. That is, it builds one function for each business process step that exists within the selected business function. Thus, when one business rule is changed, code for every business process in which that rule participates is regenerated.

LISTING 15.3
Function to Control Code Generation for Rules in the Screen Environment

```
Public Function BldScrRules() As String
' This function controls code generation for screens.  It detects
' the type of business process step based on the name of the
' business process step, and calls the routines to process the
' type of step.
Dim strSQL As String, rstBP As ADODB.Recordset, rstBPSP As
ADODB.Recordset
Dim strMy As String, cmd As ADODB.Command, lngAffected As Long

    Set rstBP = New ADODB.Recordset
    Set rstBPSP = New ADODB.Recordset
```

```
' Get the currently selected Business Process
strSQL = "SELECT * FROM BPROC_BIZPROCESS_M WHERE   " _
      & " BPROC_C = '" & kstrSelBP & "'"
rstBP.Open strSQL, CurrentProject.Connection, _
      adOpenKeyset, adLockOptimistic, adCmdText
Do While Not rstBP.EOF
   ' Get all the Business Process Steps for the currently
   ' selected Business Process in sequence
   strSQL = "SELECT * FROM BPSP_BIZSTEPPROC_M WHERE   " _
         & " BPROC_C = '" & rstBP("BPROC_C") & "' " _
         & " ORDER BY BPSP_SEQ_N "
   rstBPSP.Open strSQL, CurrentProject.Connection, _
         adOpenKeyset, adLockOptimistic, adCmdText
   Do While Not rstBPSP.EOF
      ' Select the kind of Business Process Code Generation Step
      ' Routine to call based on the Code Generation Environment
      ' ID for this step
      kstrSelBPSP = rstBPSP("BPSP_PHYSNAME_T")
      If rstBPSP("CGE_C") = "SCRDE" Then
        strMy = BldScrEditChks()
      End If
      If rstBPSP("CGE_C") = "SCRDEL" Then
        strMy = BldScrEditChks()
      End If
      If rstBPSP("CGE_C") = "BATCH" Then
        strMy = BldBatchRules()
      End If
      ' Generate the module code
      strMy = WriteFunction()
      rstBPSP.MoveNext
   Loop
   rstBPSP.Close
   rstBP.MoveNext
Loop
rstBP.Close

Set rstBP = Nothing
Set rstBPSP = Nothing

End Function
```

The main point of interest in Listing 15.3 is that the function calls different functions to build rules for different kinds of code generation environments. Every business process step is associated with a single code generation environment (represented by the column CGE_C in Listing 15.3). Code generation environments usually represent different programming languages in which business rules need to be implemented. However, a single programming interface such as Microsoft Access (the equivalent of one programming language) may require different kinds of code generation when different programming objects are used—such as forms (screens) or batch functions. This is simply due to what Access provides the programmer to work with. Even within forms, there may be different code generation environments—for example, when a screen updates data versus when a screen deletes a record. Again this is due to the functionality that Access provides to the programmer. In the sample application there are code generation environments for screen data entry, record deletion in screens, and batch processes. The business process step "Validate Screen Data Entry" is associated with a code generation environment of "Screen Data Entry" (CGE_C = "SCRDE"). Thus, in Listing 15.3 the function BldScrEditChks() is called to generate code for this business process step.

The code for BldScrEditChks() is shown in Listing 15.4.

LISTING 15.4
Function to Create a Routine to Validate Screen Inputs

```
Public Function BldScrEditChks() As String
' This function generates code for Screen Edit Check type business
' process steps
Dim cmd As ADODB.Command, strSQL As String, strLine As String,
rstChk As ADODB.Recordset
Dim strFunction As String, lngAffected As Long, strScreen As
String, intCt As Integer
Dim strFunc As String

  Set cmd = New ADODB.Command
  cmd.ActiveConnection = CurrentProject.Connection
  cmd.CommandType = adCmdText
  Set rstChk = New ADODB.Recordset

  ' Derive the Business Process Step name.
  ' This will be the name of the generated function
  strFunction = GetSelBizStep()

  ' Get screen information
```

```
    strSQL = "SELECT C.* FROM BPROC_BIZPROCESS_M A,
BPSP_BIZSTEPPROC_M B, " _
        & " SCR_SCREEN_M C    " _
        & " WHERE A.BPROC_C = B.BPROC_C " _
        & " AND A.SCR_PHYSNAME_T = C.SCR_PHYSNAME_T " _
        & " AND B.BPSP_PHYSNAME_T = '" & strFunction & "' "
    rstChk.Open strSQL, CurrentProject.Connection, _
        adOpenKeyset, adLockOptimistic, adCmdText
    strScreen = rstChk("SCR_PHYSNAME_T")
    rstChk.Close

    ' Delete all generated code that already exists for this
    ' Business Process Step
    strSQL = "DELETE FROM GCDE_GENCODE_M " _
            & " WHERE BPSP_PHYSNAME_T = '" & strFunction & "'"
    cmd.CommandText = strSQL
    cmd.Execute lngAffected
    ' Write out the Function name and declare variables
    strLine = "Public Function " & strFunction & "(frmMe as form)
As String "
    strLine = WriteGenCode(strFunction, strLine)
    strLine = "Dim intErr as Integer, strErr as string, rstSource as
ADODB.Recordset "
    strLine = WriteGenCode(strFunction, strLine)
    strLine = "Dim strSQL as String, strGo as string, rstRI as
ADODB.Recordset "
    strLine = WriteGenCode(strFunction, strLine)
    ' Write out comments about this code
    strSQL = "SELECT * FROM SCR_SCREEN_M " _
            & " WHERE SCR_PHYSNAME_T = '" & strScreen & "'"
    rstChk.Open strSQL, CurrentProject.Connection, _
        adOpenKeyset, adLockOptimistic, adCmdText
    strLine = "'' This Function validates data entry on the screen
" & strScreen
    strLine = WriteGenCode(strFunction, strLine)
    strLine = "''-" & rstChk("SCR_DESC_T")
    strLine = WriteGenCode(strFunction, strLine)
    strLine = "'' Last Generated: " & CStr(Now())
    strLine = WriteGenCode(strFunction, strLine)
    rstChk.Close
    strLine = "'' Tables updated by this screen: "
```

```
  strLine = WriteGenCode(strFunction, strLine)
  strSQL = "SELECT * FROM BPSP_BIZSTEPPROC_M A" _
          & " WHERE BPSP_PHYSNAME_T = '" & strFunction & "' "
  rstChk.Open strSQL, CurrentProject.Connection, _
        adOpenKeyset, adLockOptimistic, adCmdText
  strLine = "'     " & rstChk("TAB_PHYSNAME_T") & "    " _
            & LookTableCol(rstChk("TAB_PHYSNAME_T"),
"TAB_ENTLOGNAME_T")
  strLine = WriteGenCode(strFunction, strLine)
  rstChk.Close

  ' Initialize variables
  strLine = " "
  strLine = WriteGenCode(strFunction, strLine)
  strLine = "Set rstSource = New ADODB.Recordset "
  strLine = WriteGenCode(strFunction, strLine)
  strLine = "Set rstRI = New ADODB.Recordset "
  strLine = WriteGenCode(strFunction, strLine)
  strLine = "intErr = 0 "
  strLine = WriteGenCode(strFunction, strLine)
  strLine = "strErr = """" "
  strLine = WriteGenCode(strFunction, strLine)

  ' Find all business rule types associated with the currently
  ' selected business process step.  They should be in the order
  ' in which they run for a screen (use BRTP_SCREENSEQ_N for
  ' this)
  strSQL = "SELECT A.*, B.* FROM BRTP_BIZRULETYPE_M A,
CGR_CODEGENROUTINE_M B, " _
        & " BPSP_BIZSTEPPROC_M C " _
        & " WHERE A.BRTP_C = B.BRTP_C " _
        & " AND C.CGE_C = B.CGE_C " _
        & " AND C.BPSP_PHYSNAME_T = '" & strFunction & "' " _
        & " ORDER BY A.BRTP_SCREENSEQ_N "
  rstChk.Open strSQL, CurrentProject.Connection, _
        adOpenKeyset, adLockOptimistic, adCmdText
  intCt = 0
  Do While Not rstChk.EOF
    intCt = intCt + 1
    strLine = " "
    strLine = WriteGenCode(strFunction, strLine)
```

```
        strLine = "'' Section " & CStr(intCt) & ": " &
    rstChk("BRTP_DESC_T")
        strLine = WriteGenCode(strFunction, strLine)
        ' This is the name of the code generation function for the
        ' current rule type in the code generation environment of the
        ' currently selected business process step
        strFunc = rstChk("CGR_NAME_T")
        ' Execute the code generation function for the rule type
        strLine = Eval(strFunc)
        rstChk.MoveNext
    Loop

    ' Finish up
    strLine = " "
    strLine = WriteGenCode(strFunction, strLine)
    strLine = "Set rstSource = Nothing "
    strLine = WriteGenCode(strFunction, strLine)
    strLine = strFunction & " = ""Y"" "
    strLine = WriteGenCode(strFunction, strLine)
    strLine = "End Function"
    strLine = WriteGenCode(strFunction, strLine)

    Set cmd = Nothing
    Set rstChk = Nothing
End Function
```

What the code in BldScrEditChks() does is to create a routine for an entire business process step. It does not generate the code to execute the rules defined for the selected business process step. Rather, it created a programming "shell" within which the rule code is executed. There are several points of interest concerning Listing 15.4:

1. The function GetSelBizStep() is used to find the physical name of the currently selected business process step. The name of the generated function will be this name. This makes sense since the rules engine creates one function per business process step into which all the rules associated with that business step are packaged.

2. The generated code is written out in records in the **Generated Code** table (**GCDE_GENCODE_M**). The function WriteGenCode() is used for this purpose. The first parameter passed to this function is the name of the currently selected business process step. The second parameter is the line of

code to be written out. There is an optional third parameter, which is *Business Rule Number*. It is only used when WriteGenCode() is called from functions that generate code for business rules. In BldScrEditChks() only code for the business process step is being generated, so this parameter is not used here.

3. BldScrEditChks() gathers data about the screen so it can create comments in the code that it generates.

4. BldScrEditChks() deletes all code that exists for the function for which it is generating code in the **Generated Code** table (**GCDE_GENCODE_M**).

5. The next step is to create lines of code for declaring the function and the parameter passed to it. Also, the variables to be used in the function are declared.

6. At this point, BldScrEditChks() outputs lines of code that are comments. These indicate the name of the screen whose validation function is being written, and the date and time when this was done. The designer can choose to add other comments.

    This illustrates the comparative ease with which comments can be put into generated code by a business rules engine. In a traditional hand-coded systems development project, the programmers may not have access to (or may not trust) the metadata for the system. This reduces the quantity and reliability of comments that appear in the code. Another problem is that some programmers are too lazy or sloppy to put in good comments. The business rules engine can overcome these issues with little additional effort.

7. Next, lines of code are generated to initialize variables.

8. Next, information is obtained from the **Business Process Step** (**BPSP_BIZSTEPPROC_M**), **Code Generation Routine** (**CGR_CODEGENROUTINE_M**), and **Business Rule Type** (**BRTP_BIZRULETYPE_M**) tables. This is a list of the business rule types that are permitted for the currently selected business process step, and the names of the code generation routines for each business rules step in the code generation environment of the currently selected business process step. Each business rule type can have a different code generation function for each code generation environment. The business rule types are listed in an order that makes sense for screen processing and is summarized in Table 15.1. Each code generation function is executed in turn.

9. Finally, BldScrEditChks() writes code to determine whether the generated function should show the user any error message, and whether it should return a value of "Y" or "N" to signify that the edit validation checks were passed or failed. Code is also generated to end the function.

For business rules of the type **Required Screen Fields**, the code generation function BldSCRREQ() is called. This function is shown in Listing 15.5.

The function in Listing 15.5 works as follows:

LISTING 15.5
Function to Generate Code for **Required Screen Fields** Business Rules

```
Public Function BldSCRREQ()
' Generates code for business rules of the type Screen Required
' Fields
Dim strSQL As String, rstRule As ADODB.Recordset, cmd As
ADODB.Command
Dim lngAffected As Long, strLine As String, strFunction As String

   BldSCRREQ = "Y"
   Set rstRule = New ADODB.Recordset
   strFunction = GetSelBizStep()

   ' Get all relevant business rules
   strSQL = "SELECT A.*, B.*, A.COL_C AS COL_C FROM BRULE_BIZRULE_M
A, COL_COLUMN_M B, " _
           & " RBSP_RULESOFSTEP_M C      " _
           & " WHERE A.BRTP_C = 'SCRREQ' " _
           & " AND A.COL_C = B.COL_C " _
           & " AND A.BRULE_NUMBER_C = C.BRULE_NUMBER_C " _
           & " AND C.BPSP_PHYSNAME_T = '" & GetSelBizStep() & "'"
   rstRule.Open strSQL, CurrentProject.Connection, _
           adOpenKeyset, adLockOptimistic, adCmdText
   Do While Not rstRule.EOF
      strLine = BldRuleComms(strFunction, rstRule("BRULE_NUMBER_C"))
      strLine = "'' " & rstRule("COL_ATTLOGNAME_T") & " (" &
rstRule("COL_PHYSNAME_T") & ")"
      strLine = WriteGenCode(strFunction, strLine,
rstRule("BRULE_NUMBER_C"))
      If rstRule("ELVL_C") >= "12" Then
         strLine = "'' This field is required "
      Else
         strLine = "'' If this field is not entered the user is
given a warning "
      End If
      strLine = WriteGenCode(strFunction, strLine,
rstRule("BRULE_NUMBER_C"))
```

```
    strLine = "If isnull(frmMe." & rstRule("COL_PHYSNAME_T") & ")
Then "
    strLine = WriteGenCode(strFunction, strLine,
rstRule("BRULE_NUMBER_C"))
    If rstRule("ELVL_C") >= "12" Then
      strLine = "  intErr = intErr + 1"
      strLine = WriteGenCode(strFunction, strLine,
rstRule("BRULE_NUMBER_C"))
    End If
    strLine = "  strErr = strErr & """ & rstRule("BRULE_ERR_T") &
""" & Chr(10) & Chr(13) "
    strLine = WriteGenCode(strFunction, strLine,
rstRule("BRULE_NUMBER_C"))
    strLine = "End If"
    strLine = WriteGenCode(strFunction, strLine,
rstRule("BRULE_NUMBER_C"))

    rstRule.MoveNext
  Loop
  rstRule.Close

  strLine = "If intErr > 0 then"
  strLine = WriteGenCode(strFunction, strLine)
  strLine = "  MsgBox strErr"
  strLine = WriteGenCode(strFunction, strLine)
  strLine = "  " & strFunction & " = ""N"" "
  strLine = WriteGenCode(strFunction, strLine)
  strLine = "  Exit Function"
  strLine = WriteGenCode(strFunction, strLine)
  strLine = "End if"
  strLine = WriteGenCode(strFunction, strLine)

  Set rstRule = Nothing
  Set cmd = Nothing

End Function
```

1. It first finds all the business rules for the currently selected business process step that are of the type **Required Screen Fields**. It does not process them in any particular order. If the designer wishes to introduce a sequence to this process, the Business Rules Repository will have to be extended to let the user specify a sequence number for each field to be checked. This is not difficult to do.

2. For each rule retrieved (i.e., for each required field) the function first generates comments in the code providing the logical and physical name of the field, and whether the lack of an entered value will generate an error or a warning.

   Again we see the relative ease with which a business rules engine can add comments to generated code.

3. Next, the actual rule code is generated. The entered field is tested for a null value. If nulls are found, the error message defined for the business rule is displayed to the user. If errors that have an *Error Level Number* of "12" or higher are found, the function is stopped.

On the whole the functions in Listings 15.3, 15.4, and 15.5 are not very difficult program code to write. However, one problem area in all is the treatment of single and double quotes.

If a single quote is placed in a string that then gets processed by a SQL INSERT or UPDATE command, it will in general cause the execution to crash. This is because the SQL engine thinks that the single quote represents the termination of a string field value. The standard way to get around this is to have double single quotes. This "escapes" the single quote problem. If your programming environment does not support this, then you must find another way. One method is to substitute another character for the single quote in the generated code. A good candidate is the caret symbol ^, since it is almost never used by users. Thus, in the generated lines of code in **GCDE_GENCODE_M** the single quotes are replaced by carets. When the process to write the generated code to the Class Module BizRuleCode runs, it can replace the carets with single quotes in the records it reads from **GCDE_GENCODE_M**.

The issue with double quotes is a little different. The code we generate will inevitably contain double quotes in Access VBA. The code we use to generate this code will itself contain double quotes. Unless the double quotes being written in the generated code are "escaped," you will get syntax errors because Access thinks that the line of code that generates code has terminated incorrectly. To "escape" double quotes in the generated code, simply write pairs of them. These will translate into one double quote character in the generated code. If your programming environment does not permit this, you should consider substituting a different character for the double quote, in the way that substituting a caret for the single quote was described above.

Working with double quotes and the concatenation operator "&" makes writing code to generate code very tricky. It is sometimes difficult to recognize which code is doing the generating and which code is generated. This is true in all programming environments, and care is needed.

The Generated Code

The code that was written was placed in the **Generated Code** table (**GCDE_GENCODE_M**). The structure of this table is shown in Figure 15.5.

The **Generated Code** table has relationships with the **Business Rule** table and **Business Process Step** table. These relationships mean that the code for any business rule can easily be deleted from the table, and that the functions that correspond to entire business process steps can easily be created, as will be discussed later. Apart from these uses, the **Generated Code** table is not really useful for metadata management and should not be used for this purpose, such as for reporting on business rules. Its only real use is as a temporary staging area for code prior to writing this code out in system objects such as functions or subroutines. Trying to use it for metadata management is dangerous, because so much of the relevant metadata is hidden in the *Generated Code Line* column at this point and can only be extracted by parsing it. Code parsing must be avoided at all costs in a business rules engine design, because it is difficult to do and yields unreliable results. A great deal of effort has already been put into the design of the Business Rules Repository. If more metadata needs to be managed, this core design should be extended. Constructs that contain actual code, such as the **Generated Code** table, should not be used for this purpose.

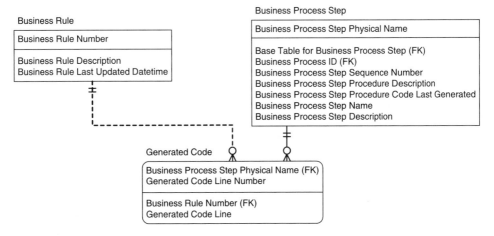

FIGURE 15.5
Generated Code Table

Having populated the **Generated Code** table, the next step is to create the actual executable code in the sample application. The design considerations for this are as follows:

- All generated code is written out as functions in the Class Module BizRuleCode.

- A Class Module in Microsoft Access resembles a program in other languages. The functions it contains can be called from other parts of the application.

- An entire function is generated for each business process step. The name of the function is the same as the *Business Process Step Physical Name*. This makes it easy to match up the generated code in the application with the metadata. It is highly advisable to use such naming conventions across as much of the chain of business rule generation as possible.

- The entire function is generated, even if it contains many business rules but only one of them has changed. As we shall see later, rule dependency can change across a set of rules even if only one rule changes. Regenerating the entire function each time, as opposed to just regenerating the piece of it that corresponds to the changed rule, avoids the risk of creating rule dependency problems.

- Functions rather than subroutines are created because in many circumstances a return code is required to be passed back to the part of the application that invokes the generated code. Functions explicitly permit return values.

The function WriteFunction() creates the function in the Class Module BizRule-Code. Listing 15.6 shows how Writefunction() works.

LISTING 15.6
The Function WriteFunction()

```
Public Function WriteFunction() As String
' Writes out generated code as entire functions
Dim mdlFunction As Module, lngSLine As Long, lngSCol As Long,
lngELine As Long
Dim lngECol As Long, lngSLine2 As Long, lngSCol2 As Long,
lngELine2 As Long, lngECol2 As Long
Dim lngLines As Long, intCt As Integer, rstPrg As ADODB.Recordset,
strSQL As String
Dim cmd As ADODB.Command, lngAffected As Long, strFunction As
String

    WriteFunction = "Y"
```

```
strFunction = GetSelBizStep()
Set rstPrg = New ADODB.Recordset
strSQL = "SELECT * FROM GCDE_GENCODE_M " _
        & " WHERE BPSP_PHYSNAME_T = '" & strFunction & "' " _
        & "ORDER BY GCDE_LINE_C"
rstPrg.Open strSQL, CurrentProject.Connection, _
        adOpenKeyset, adLockOptimistic, adCmdText

DoCmd.OpenModule "BizRuleCode"

Set mdlFunction = Modules("BizRuleCode")

If mdlFunction.Find("'" & strFunction & "----Start", lngSLine,
lngSCol, lngELine, lngECol) = True Then
    If mdlFunction.Find("'" & strFunction & "----End", lngSLine2,
lngSCol2, lngELine2, lngECol2) = True Then
        mdlFunction.DeleteLines lngSLine, (lngSLine2-lngSLine + 1)
    End If
End If

lngLines = mdlFunction.CountOfLines
intCt = lngLines + 1

mdlFunction.InsertLines intCt, "'" & strFunction & "----Start"
intCt = intCt + 1

Do While Not rstPrg.EOF
  mdlFunction.InsertLines intCt, rstPrg("GCDE_LINE_T")
  intCt = intCt + 1
  rstPrg.MoveNext
Loop
rstPrg.Close

mdlFunction.InsertLines intCt, "'" & strFunction & "----End"
intCt = intCt + 1

DoCmd.Close acModule, "BizRuleCode", acSaveYes

' Update the Business Process Step table with the datetime of
' the code generation
Set cmd = New ADODB.Command
```

```
cmd.ActiveConnection = CurrentProject.Connection
cmd.CommandType = adCmdText
strSQL = "SELECT * FROM BPSP_BIZSTEPPROC_M " _
        & " WHERE BPSP_PHYSNAME_T = '" & strFunction & "'"
rstPrg.Open strSQL, CurrentProject.Connection, _
        adOpenKeyset, adLockOptimistic, adCmdText
' If the Business Process Step is not in the table, add it
If rstPrg.EOF Then
   strSQL = "INSERT INTO BPSP_BIZSTEPPROC_M " _
         & "(BPSP_PHYSNAME_T, BPSP_NAME_T, BPSP_LASTCODEGEN_D) " _
         & " VALUES ('" & strFunction & "', 'Business Process
Step: " & strFunction _
         & "',Now() )"
   Else
   strSQL = "UPDATE BPSP_BIZSTEPPROC_M SET " _
         & "BPSP_LASTCODEGEN_D = Now() " _
         & " WHERE BPSP_PHYSNAME_T = '" & strFunction & "'"
End If
cmd.CommandText = strSQL
cmd.Execute lngAffected

Set cmd = Nothing
Set rstPrg = Nothing
Set mdlFunction = Nothing

End Function
```

WriteFunction() uses specific Microsoft Access functionality to perform its task. It scans the BizRuleCode module to find where the function to be generated starts and ends. This is achieved by placing comments at the start and end of each generated function so that WriteFunction() can recognize it. At the start of each function the comment contains the function name followed by "----Start", and at the end of each function the comment contains the function name followed by "----End". This delimits the code for each function in a way that makes it easy to manipulate. Other approaches will need to be found in other programming language environments, but it does seem that there are usable approaches in most of these environments.

When Should Code Be Generated?

All of the basic components to generate code are now in place. It remains to link the generation of the code to the updating of the of the rule definitions in the screen for the rule type Required Screen Fields shown in Figure 15.4.

Code generation actually does not have to happen every time this screen is viewed. It only needs to be done if the definition of a business rule has changed since the code for the corresponding business process step was last generated. There needs to be some metadata to do this, and Figure 15.5 shows a reasonable design approach. In Figure 15.5, the **Business Rule** table has a column *Business Rule Last Updated Datetime* (BRULE_UPD_D) that is updated every time the user updates the definition of the business rule. The **Business Process Step** table has a column *Business Process Step Procedure Code Last Generated* (BPSP_LASTCODEGEN_D) which is updated by the WriteFunction() function, every time the code for the business process step is recreated. The rules engine needs to check whether any business rule associated with a business process step has a value of *Business Rule Last Updated Datetime* that is greater than the value of *Business Process Step Procedure Code Last Generated* for the business process step. If one or more business rules meet this condition, then the code is regenerated.

A function called IsGenCodeUpToDate() uses this approach to determine whether a given generated business process step's code is up-to-date with respect to the metadata for the business rules that are incorporated in it. Listing 15.7 shows the code for the function, which returns a "Y" if the business process step's code was generated after the last business rule for the business process step was updated, or an "N" if any of the rules associated with the business process step have been updated since the code was last generated.

LISTING 15.7
Function IsGenCodeUpToDate()

```
Public Function IsGenCodeUpToDate() As String
'*********************************************************************
' Determines if a Business Process Step Procedure needs to have
' its code regenerated. Finds the last time the Business
' Process Step Procedure was generated and compares it to the
' last time a business rule of this Business Process Step
' Procedure was updated. It uses the function GetSelBizStep() to
' determine the name of the currently selected Business
' Process Step Procedure
```

```
'
' Parameters: None
' Returns: "Y" if the function code was generated after the last
' business rule was updated; "N" if any business rule was updated
' after the function code was last regenerated.
'*******************************************************************
Dim cmd As ADODB.Command, strSQL As String, lngAffected As Long
Dim rstFunc As ADODB.Recordset, rstRule As ADODB.Recordset
Dim dFunc As Date, dRule As Date, strFunction As String
Dim strMin As String, strMax As String

  dFunc = CDate("1/1/1980")
  dRule = CDate("1/1/1980")


  strFunction = GetSelBizStep()

  Set rstFunc = New ADODB.Recordset
  Set rstRule = New ADODB.Recordset
  strSQL = "SELECT * FROM BPSP_BIZSTEPPROC_M " _
        & " WHERE BPSP_PHYSNAME_T = '" & GetSelBizStep() & "'"
  rstFunc.Open strSQL, CurrentProject.Connection, _
        adOpenKeyset, adLockOptimistic, adCmdText

  strSQL = "SELECT B.BRULE_UPD_D FROM RBSP_RULESOFSTEP_M A,
BRULE_BIZRULE_M B " _
        & " WHERE A.BRULE_NUMBER_C = B.BRULE_NUMBER_C " _
        & " AND A.BPSP_PHYSNAME_T = '" & GetSelBizStep() & "' "
_
        & " ORDER BY B.BRULE_UPD_D DESC "
  rstRule.Open strSQL, CurrentProject.Connection, _
        adOpenKeyset, adLockOptimistic, adCmdText

  If Not rstFunc.EOF Then
    If Not IsNull(rstFunc("BPSP_LASTCODEGEN_D")) Then
      dFunc = rstFunc("BPSP_LASTCODEGEN_D")
    End If
  End If
  If Not rstRule.EOF Then
    If Not IsNull(rstRule("BRULE_UPD_D")) Then
      dRule = rstRule("BRULE_UPD_D")
```

```
        End If
    End If

    IsGenCodeUpToDate = "Y"
    If dRule > dFunc Then
        IsGenCodeUpToDate = "N"
    End If

    rstRule.Close
    rstFunc.Close

    Set rstRule = Nothing
    Set rstFunc = Nothing

End Function
```

LISTING 15.8
Conditional Code Generation in Required Screen Fields Rule Definition Screen

```
Private Sub Command25_Click()
Dim strText As String
    DoCmd.Close

    If IsGenCodeUpToDate() = "N" Then
        strText = RegenBizProc()
        MsgBox "Rule Code has been regenerated"
    End If
End Sub
```

The last step is to link the entire code generation functionality to the definition of business rule metadata. There are many ways to do this. The option chosen in the sample application is to use the **Close** button on the rule definition screens. For instance, when the **Close** button is pressed on the Required Screen Fields rule definition screen, the code in Listing 15.8 is executed.

The code in Listing 15.8 closes the screen, and then tests whether any rules associated with the currently selected business process step have been changed. If rules have changed then the RegenBizProc() function is called to regenerate the code for the business process step. RegenBizProc() actually finds all business processes which have rules that have been updated since the code for the business process was last updated. It then regenerates the code for them. In this way, the code will be regenerated not only for the current business process step, but also for all business process steps affected by the changed rules. After all, the rules engine design permits one rule to be associated with any number of business process steps. Listing 15.9 shows the code for RegenBizProc().

This is the final component of the code generation functionality. We now have the capacity to define business rules of the **Required Screen Fields** type and immediately execute them in the application environment.

Examples of Business Rules

Using the rules engine functionality built in this chapter, a number of **Required Screen Fields** have been created. Listing 15.10 shows the code that has been generated.

LISTING 15.9
Function RegenBizProc()

```
Public Function RegenBizProc() As String
'******************************************************************
' This process finds all business processes associated with changed
' rules so that they can be regenerated
' Parameters: None
'
' Returns: "Y"
'******************************************************************
Dim strSQL As String, rstRule As ADODB.Recordset, strSaveBP As
String
Dim strSaveBPSP As String, strSaveFrm As String, strSaveTab As
String
Dim strLast As String, strMy As String

   RegenBizProc = "Y"
   ' Save public variables for the current environment
   If Not IsNull(kstrSelBP) Then
     strSaveBP = kstrSelBP
   End If
   If Not IsNull(kstrSelBPSP) Then
     strSaveBPSP = kstrSelBPSP
   End If
```

```
   If Not IsNull(kstrSelFrm) Then
     strSaveFrm = kstrSelFrm
   End If
   If Not IsNull(kstrSelTab) Then
     strSaveTab = kstrSelTab
   End If

   ' Find what business processes have steps with code that was
   ' generated prior to changes in the rules used in these steps
   Set rstRule = New ADODB.Recordset
   strSQL = "SELECT D.* AS BIZPROC FROM BPSP_BIZSTEPPROC_M A, " _
          & "RBSP_RULESOFSTEP_M B, BRULE_BIZRULE_M C,
BPROC_BIZPROCESS_M D" _
          & " WHERE A.BPSP_PHYSNAME_T = B.BPSP_PHYSNAME_T " _
          & " AND B.BRULE_NUMBER_C = C.BRULE_NUMBER_C " _
          & " AND A.BPROC_C = D.BPROC_C " _
          & " AND A.BPSP_LASTCODEGEN_D < C.BRULE_UPD_D " _
          & " ORDER BY D.BPROC_C"
   rstRule.Open strSQL, CurrentProject.Connection, _
          adOpenKeyset, adLockOptimistic, adCmdText
   strLast = "!"
   Do While Not rstRule.EOF
     kstrSelBP = rstRule("BPROC_C")
     ' Regenerate the Business Process
     If strLast <> rstRule("BPROC_C") Then
       If rstRule("BPTP_C") = "SCREEN" Then
         strMy = BldScrRules()
       End If
       If rstRule("BPTP_C") = "BATCH" Then
         strMy = BldBatchRules()
       End If
     End If
     strLast = rstRule("BPROC_C")
     rstRule.MoveNext
   Loop
   rstRule.Close
   Set rstRule = Nothing

   'Restore the environment
   If Not IsNull(strSaveBP) Then
     kstrSelBP = strSaveBP
```

```
      End If
    If Not IsNull(strSaveBPSP) Then
      kstrSelBPSP = strSaveBPSP
    End If
    If Not IsNull(strSaveFrm) Then
      kstrSelFrm = strSaveFrm
    End If
    If Not IsNull(strSaveTab) Then
      kstrSelTab = strSaveTab
    End If
  End Function
```

LISTING 15.10
The Code Generated to Validate Inputs on Screen frmINV_INVESTMENT_M

```
'ScrChkfrmINV_INVESTMENT_S----Start
Public Function ScrChkfrmINV_INVESTMENT_S(frmMe As Form) As String
Dim intErr As Integer, strErr As String, rstSource As
ADODB.Recordset
Dim strSQL As String, strGo As String, rstRI As ADODB.Recordset
' This Function validates data entry on the screen
' frmINV_INVESTMENT_S—Investment Details
' Last Generated: 2/7/2003 4:42:38 PM
' Tables updated by this screen:
'    INV_INVESTMENT_S   Investment

Set rstSource = New ADODB.Recordset
Set rstRI = New ADODB.Recordset
intErr = 0
strErr = ""

' Section 1: Required Screen Fields
 ' Rule: R0008 / User Rule: R0008
 ' Rule Name: Investment ID must be entered
' Investment ID (INV_C)
' This field is required
If IsNull(frmMe.INV_C) Then
  intErr = intErr + 1
  strErr = strErr & "Investment ID must be entered (Error Code:
```

```
R0008)" & Chr(10) & Chr(13)
End If
  ' Rule: R0011 / User Rule: R0011
  ' Rule Name: Fund Acronym must be entered
' Fund Acronym (FUND_C)
' This field is required
If IsNull(frmMe.FUND_C) Then
  intErr = intErr + 1
  strErr = strErr & "Fund Acronym must be entered (Error Code:
R0011)" & Chr(10) & Chr(13)
End If
  ' Rule: R0012 / User Rule: R0012
  ' Rule Name: Investment Category Code must be entered
' Investment Category Code (INCT_C)
' This field is required
If IsNull(frmMe.INCT_C) Then
  intErr = intErr + 1
  strErr = strErr & "Investment Category Code must be entered
(Error Code: R0012)" & Chr(10) & Chr(13)
End If
  ' Rule: R0013 / User Rule: R0013
  ' Rule Name: Investment Close Date must be entered
' Investment Close Date (INV_CLOSE_D)
' This field is required
If IsNull(frmMe.INV_CLOSE_D) Then
  intErr = intErr + 1
  strErr = strErr & "Investment Close Date must be entered (Error
Code: R0013)" & Chr(10) & Chr(13)
End If
  ' Rule: R0014 / User Rule: R0014
  ' Rule Name: Investment Funding Date must be entered
' Investment Funding Date (INV_FUNDING_D)
' This field is required
If IsNull(frmMe.INV_FUNDING_D) Then
  intErr = intErr + 1
  strErr = strErr & "Investment Funding Date must be entered
(Error Code: R0014)" & Chr(10) & Chr(13)
End If
  ' Rule: R0015 / User Rule: R0015
  ' Rule Name: Investment Short Name must be entered
' Investment Short Name (INV_SHORTNAME_T)
```

```
' This field is required
If IsNull(frmMe.INV_SHORTNAME_T) Then
   intErr = intErr + 1
   strErr = strErr & "Investment Short Name must be entered (Error
Code: R0015)" & Chr(10) & Chr(13)
End If
 ' Rule: R0016 / User Rule: R0016
 ' Rule Name: Investment Type Code must be entered
 ' Investment Type Code (INTP_C)
 ' This field is required
If IsNull(frmMe.INTP_C) Then
   intErr = intErr + 1
   strErr = strErr & "Investment Type Code must be entered (Error
Code: R0016)" & Chr(10) & Chr(13)
End If
 ' Rule: R0017 / User Rule: R0017
 ' Rule Name: Investment Long Name should be entered
 ' Investment Long Name (INV_LONGNAME_T)
 ' If this field is not entered the user is given a warning
If IsNull(frmMe.INV_LONGNAME_T) Then
   strErr = strErr & "Investment Long Name should be entered (Error
Code: R0017)" & Chr(10) & Chr(13)
End If
 ' Rule: R0018 / User Rule: R0018
 ' Rule Name: Investment Total Amount should be entered
 ' Investment Total Amount (INV_TOTAL_A)
 ' If this field is not entered the user is given a warning
If IsNull(frmMe.INV_TOTAL_A) Then
   strErr = strErr & "Investment Total Amount should be entered
(Error Code: R0018)" & Chr(10) & Chr(13)
End If
If intErr > 0 Then
   MsgBox strErr
   ScrChkfrmINV_INVESTMENT_S = "N"
   Exit Function
End If
Set rstSource = Nothing
ScrChkfrmINV_INVESTMENT_S = "Y"
End Function
'ScrChkfrmINV_INVESTMENT_S----End
```

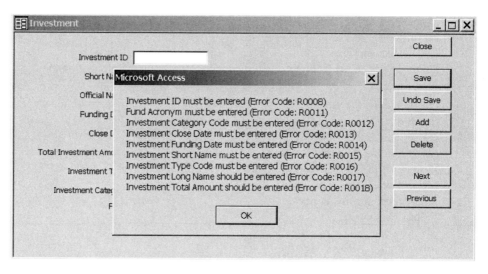

FIGURE 15.6
Test of Required Screen Field Validation Checks

This code is relatively simple, reasonably easy to read, and well commented. These are all advantages that the designer should strive for.

Figure 15.2 illustrated the Investment screen, with which the defined rules are associated in this example. If the user goes to that screen and adds a new record, and then presses the **Save** button without entering any data, all the defined business rules will detect errors. Figure 15.6 shows what happens.

With the design approach described here it only takes a couple of minutes to define and implement the business rules needed to create the checks shown in Figure 15.6.

Design Review

This chapter has covered some fundamental constructs of the business rules engine. It is worth reviewing the design that has been introduced, and the corresponding elements of the sample application. Table 15.6 summarizes what happens when the user defines **Required Screen Fields** rules for the Investment screen, in terms of what the user sees and what the rules engine in the sample application does.

Conclusion

This chapter has described how a simple business rule type is implemented. A screen has been designed and built where the rules can be defined. Functions that generate

STEP	DESCRIPTION	FUNCTIONALITY IN SAMPLE APPLICATION
1	User invokes Business Rule Summary Screen (see Figure 15.1).	Select **Business Rules > Define Business Rules** in the menu. The Business Rules Summary Screen (form frmSelBRULE) appears.
2	On this screen the user selects the Business Process "Investment screen validation and processing" and the Business Process Step "Validate Screen Data Entry". The list of rules defined for this business process step appears. The user clicks on one and presses the **Select** button. Alternatively, the user selects a Rule Type of **Required Screen Fields** and presses the **Add Rule** button	Functionality in the Business Rules Summary Screen (form frmSelBRULE) enables the user to do this.
3	The **Required Screen Fields** rule definition screen appears (see Figure 15.4).	Form frmRULE_SCRREQ is invoked.
4	The user clicks on one of the fields in the Non-Required Fields list box and then presses the **Add** button.	Code within frmRULE_SCRREQ checks whether the selected field is already defined in a business rule for the rule type **Required Screen Fields**. If it is not, the business rule is created automatically. The rule is then associated with the currently selected business process step.
5	The user clicks on the **Close** button of the **Required Screen Fields** rule definition screen.	The function IsGenCodeUpToDate() (in module GeneralFuncs) is invoked. It determines whether any business rules associated with the currently selected business process step have been updated since the code for the business process step was last generated.
6	Function to find business processes whose rules have changed is invoked.	If IsGenCodeUpToDate() determines that the code must be regenerated, the function RegenBizProc() is invoked. This function calls other functions that build code for each business process for which rules have changes. For the currently selected business process, the function BldScrRules() is invoked.
7	Function to generate code for business process is invoked.	If RegenBizProc() determines that the code must be regenerated, the function BldScrRules() is

TABLE 15.6 Summary of Design for Rule Definition and Code Generation for Required Screen Fields Associated with Investment Screen

STEP	DESCRIPTION	FUNCTIONALITY IN SAMPLE APPLICATION
		invoked. This function calls other functions that build code for each business process step associated with the currently selected business process. For the currently selected business process step, the function BldScrEditChks() is invoked.
8	Function to generate code for business process step is invoked.	BldScrEditChks() is the function associated with the currently selected business process step "Validate Screen Data Entry". This generates code for the business process step in general, and then calls functions to generate code for each business rule type associated with the business process step, in the code generation environment associated with the business process step. The function that generates code for the business rule type **Required Screen Fields** in the "Screen Data Entry" code generation environment is BldSCRREQ().
9	Function to generate code for **Required Screen Fields** business rules associated with currently selected business process step is invoked.	BldSCRREQ() finds each **Required Screen Fields** business rule associated with the currently selected business process step. It generates the code necessary to execute each rule. The code is stored in the **Generated Code** table.
10	After all code has been generated for a business process step, it is written out as a function.	BldScrRules() invokes the function WriteFunction(). This deletes and then recreates the function corresponding to the currently selected business process step in the Class Module BizRuleCode. For the currently selected business process step this is the function "ScrChkfrmINV_INVESTMENT_S". The code stored in the **Generated Code** table is used to create the function.
11	Code generation is complete. A message is displayed to the user to confirm this.	Control returns to the Business Rules Summary Screen (form frmSelBRULE). The code associated with the **Close** button displays the confirmation message.
12	The user goes to the Investment screen (see Figure 15.2). If the user does not enter a value for any field which has a **Required Screen Fields** business rule associated with it, an error message appears.	Select **Application Functions > Enter Investment Details** in the menu. The Investment screen (form frmINV_INVESTMENT_S) appears. The code associated with the **Save** button of this screen calls the function "ScrChkfrmINV_INVESTMENT_S".

TABLE 15.6 *Continued*

code from the rule metadata have also been designed and built. Everything has been tied into the operational system.

This general design, and much of the program logic, can be reused or adapted for use with other business rule types. However, all rule types tend to have their own unique characteristics, which need to be reflected in the design for the interface to capture them, and the functionality to generate code for them. In the next few chapters, the basic design approach will be extended to cover other rule types needed to fully validate the inputs on the Investment screen. Additional functionality needed for more complex business rules will also be introduced.

16

MORE EDIT VALIDATION RULES, RULE COMPONENTS, AND RULE VERSIONS

The previous chapter dealt with the **Required Screen Fields** rule type, which enables users to specify screen fields for which data must be entered. There are a number of other rule types that are needed to completely validate screen inputs, and in this chapter, two of these additional rule types will be considered:

- Valid Datatypes for Screen Fields
- Screen Fields Valid Ranges

The first rule type is similar in complexity to the **Required Screen Fields** rule type considered in the previous chapter. However, the second rule type is somewhat more complex than the **Required Screen**. In particular, it requires the business rules engine to deal with business rule components and business rule versions. In order to do this, it is necessary to extend the Business Rules Repository and the general functionality needed to manage business rules.

Valid Datatypes for Screen Fields

If a field is entered on a screen in order to update a column in a database table, then the data entered into the field must match the datatype of the column. What is entered on the screen does not necessarily have to be the same datatype as the column, but it must be directly translatable into a valid value for the column's datatype. For example, a screen field may capture a date in character format that can be translated into a date datatype when the database is updated.

In Microsoft Access a screen field that is tied to a database column gets validated automatically by Access, to ensure the data entered into it is consistent with the column's datatype. This is not true for many other programming environments, and it is also not true for Access screen fields that are not directly "bound" to a database column. In these situations the user can enter any characters into the field. The screen field essentially has a character datatype, and it is necessary to validate that what the user types into it can be translated to a valid value in the destination column's datatype. For example, it should not be permitted to type letters into a field that will be used to update a numeric column. The rule type to enforce this requirement is **Valid Datatypes for Screen Fields**.

In theory, there is no need to get users to define validation rules to check the datatype of entered data. All the metadata required is already in the Business Rules Directory, since it contains the datatypes for the columns that are to be populated. The rules engine itself could automatically create rules to check the entry of valid datatypes. However, we should remember that one of our design goals is not to create "black box" components for the rules engine. The users should have access to all rules. Indeed, it is a good idea to allow users to edit the error messages that appear when invalid datatypes are detected. Users may well be able to construct more meaningful error messages than the rules engine can create automatically. For these reasons, the rules to validate datatypes are fully exposed to the user in the sample application.

There is also the matter of metadata columns in database tables. These are columns such as last date and time of update, or *Record ID* in the sample application. They do not store meaningful business data, but rather contain metadata required for internal application functionality. These columns are typically populated automatically by the system, not by any data entered by a user. The designer may wish to restrict such columns from being presented to the user in the screen to define valid datatype rules (or other rule definitions screen). This could be achieved by adding an extra column to the **Column** table to identify such columns. In the sample application presented here this has not been done to simplify the functionality that has to be built.

Other design decisions include:

- All errors detected for this type of rule are considered to be errors, so users are not asked whether they want to consider them as warnings, or any less severe kind of error.

- These rules fire after the rules that determine if data has been entered for required fields. This is enforced by having the code generation routine for the business process step (function BldScrEditChks() in module BuildCode in the sample application) create the code for these rules after the rules that check for entry of required fields.

- If the rules that check for data entry of required fields find errors, the user is advised of these errors and the rules to check valid datatypes are not invoked. This is done in the generated code by presenting the user with a list of the errors detected, and then exiting the generated function for the business process step.

- It is likely that some of the fields that will be checked will not be required fields, so they may contain valid null values. There is no point in checking datatypes if a null value is present. Thus, the rules only check the data in a field if its contents are not null.

- The very first time that the user selects a screen to enter valid datatype checks, the rules to check all numeric and date fields are automatically generated. This is not done for character fields. Character fields, after all, can have any characters entered into them, and so nothing special usually has to be done for them in terms of datatype validation.

  This is as far as the sample application goes along the path of "automatically" generating rules, even though all the rules to detect invalid datatypes could in theory be generated without user intervention.

Rule Definition Interface for *Valid Datatypes for Screen Fields*

The point in the rules engine where the user starts to define rules to enforce valid datatypes in screen fields is the Business Rules Summary Screen shown in Figure 16.1.

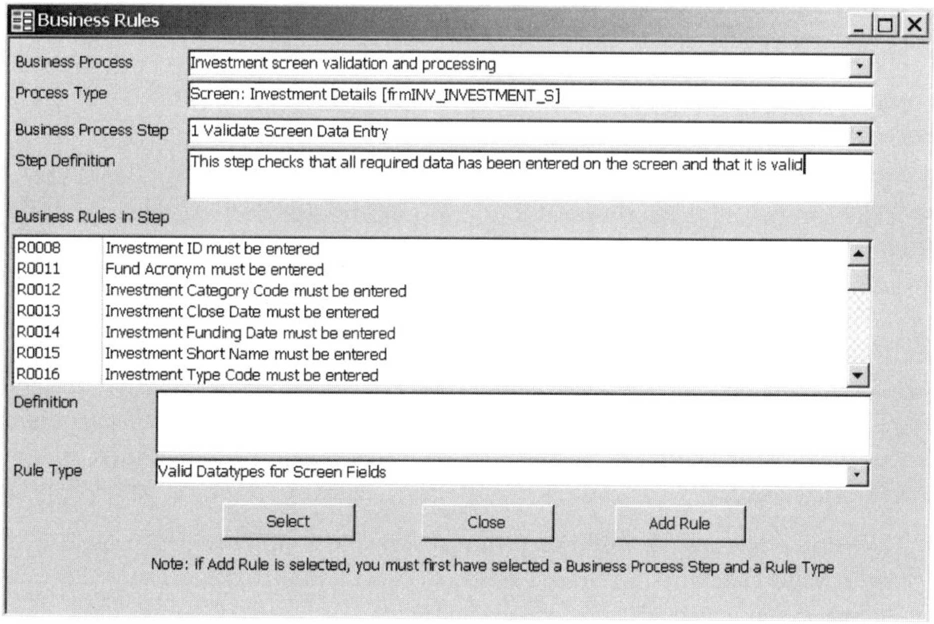

FIGURE 16.1
Business Rules Summary Screen

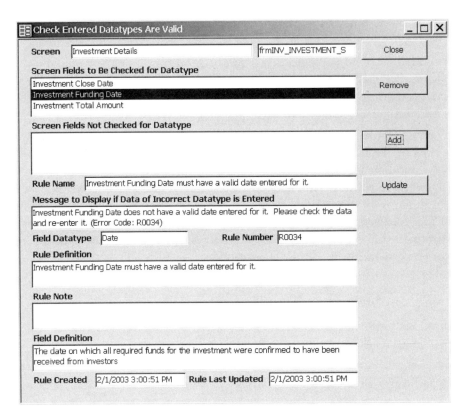

FIGURE 16.2
Screen to Define Rules for **Valid Datatypes for Screen Fields**

The user selects the appropriate business process step, and the rule type **Valid Datatypes for Screen Fields** and presses the **Add Rule** button.

The screen for defining **Valid Datatypes for Screen Fields** rules now appears. It is similar to the screen for specifying required fields discussed in the previous chapter and is shown in Figure 16.2.

The programming constructs within this rule definition screen, and for the corresponding code generation function, are very similar to those for the **Required Screen Fields** rule definition screen and its associated code generation function. The major differences are:

- When the rule type definition screen is first invoked for a business process step, **Valid Datatypes for Screen Fields** rules are automatically generated for numeric and date fields, as discussed above.

- If the generated rule detects an error, the error level is always considered to be "error" rather than "warning" or "informatory." The user cannot change this in the rule definition interface.

- The user can remove any rule from the business process step. In the case of **Required Screen Fields** rules, the user was not allowed to remove rules for primary key values.

- The code generation function generates an entirely different piece of code for each business rule. A fragment of the generated code is shown in Listing 16.1.

LISTING 16.1
Generated Code Implementing **Valid Datatypes for Screen Fields** Rules

```
' Section 2: Validate Datatypes of Entered Data
' Investment Close Date (INV_CLOSE_D)
' This field must have a datatype of date
If Not IsNull(frmMe.INV_CLOSE_D) Then
   If Not IsDate(frmMe.INV_CLOSE_D) Then
      intErr = intErr + 1
      strErr = strErr & "Investment Close Date does not have a
valid date entered for it.  Please check the data and re-enter it.
(Error Code: R0031)" & Chr(10) & Chr(13)
   End If
End If
' Investment Total Amount (INV_TOTAL_A)
' This field must have a datatype of numeric
If Not IsNull(frmMe.INV_TOTAL_A) Then
   If Not IsNumeric(frmMe.INV_TOTAL_A) Then
      intErr = intErr + 1
      strErr = strErr & "Investment Total Amount does not have a
valid number entered for it.  Please check the data and re-enter
it. (Error Code: R0033)" & Chr(10) & Chr(13)
   End If
End If
' Investment Funding Date (INV_FUNDING_D)
' This field must have a datatype of date
If Not IsNull(frmMe.INV_FUNDING_D) Then
   If Not IsDate(frmMe.INV_FUNDING_D) Then
      intErr = intErr + 1
      strErr = strErr & "Investment Funding Date does not have a
valid date entered for it.  Please check the data and re-enter it.
(Error Code: R0034)" & Chr(10) & Chr(13)
   End If
End If
```

```
If intErr > 0 Then
  MsgBox strErr
  ScrChkfrmINV_INVESTMENT_S = "N"
  Exit Function
End If
```

This shows how the rules engine framework built in the previous chapter can easily be adapted for new rule types, and how the interface for one rule type can resemble that for another.

Rather than go through all the program logic associated with the **Valid Datatypes for Screen Fields** rule type, the relevant objects in the sample application are listed in Table 16.1. The reader can use these to examine the details of the implementation.

This new rule type has not required the introduction of any fundamental new components into the rules engine, but has been implemented creating components based on marginal extensions to the rules engine. However, the next rule type will require fundamental new rules engine components and an appreciation of new concepts that underlie these components.

Screen Fields Valid Ranges

The rule types that have been discussed so far have been somewhat simple in structure. These rule types check if something (a column value) is in one state or if it is not. If the rule exists, it performs the check. If the rule does not exist, no check is performed. The next rule type that will be discussed, **Screen Fields Valid Ranges**, is different. This rule type permits the definition of minimum and maximum possible values for data entered in a field on a screen. Any values entered that are outside this range will cause an error message to be displayed to the user.

There are two new concepts that have to be considered if we are to successfully implement the rule type to validate data ranges. These concepts are *rule components* and *rule versions*, and it is necessary to consider how to deal each of them in the Business Rules Repository before discussing the details of how to implement the rule type itself.

Introducing Rule Components

If the rule type is to define the minimum and maximum values that a screen field can accommodate, these must be stored in the Business Rules Repository. This is metadata that is unique to this rule type. All rule types tend to have unique metadata, but most rule types have more metadata than the simple rule types that have

ITEM	APPLICATION OBJECT	DESCRIPTION
Menu access		On the menu, select **Business Rules > Define Business Rules**. The Business Rule Summary Screen appears. Select Business Process "Investment screen validation and processing." Select Business Process Step "Validate Screen Data Entry." Select Rule Type **Valid Datatypes for Screen Fields** and press the **Add Rule** button. The rule definition screen now appears.
Lookup table code for Rule Type	BRTP_BIZRULETYPE_M	This table contains a record with a code value of "SCRVDTYPE", and a rule definition function of "frmRULE_SCRVDTYPE".
Rule Type Definition Screen	frmRULE_SCRVDTYPE	This screen is shown in Figure 16.2 and has a class module containing code.
Currently selected business process	Name of business process is "Investment screen validation and processing," and code is "SCRINVVAL". This information is stored in the **Business Process** table **BPROC_BIZPROCESS_M**.	The business process is selected on the Business Rules Summary Screen.
Currently selected business process step	Name of business process step is "Validate Screen Data Entry," and code is "ScrChkfrmINV_INVESTMENT_S". This information is stored in the **Business Process Step** table BPSP_BIZSTEPPROC_M.	The business process step is selected on the Business Rules Summary Screen.
Currently selected rule type	Name of rule type is "Valid Datatypes for Screen Fields," and code is "SCRVDTYPE". This information is stored in the **Business Rule Type** table **BRTP_BIZRULETYPE_M**.	The business rule type is selected on the Business Rules Summary Screen.

TABLE 16.1 Application Objects for Rule Type **Valid Datatypes for Screen Fields**

ITEM	APPLICATION OBJECT	DESCRIPTION
Business rules table	**BRULE_BIZRULE_M**	This stores the metadata defining the Business rules and is updated from frmRULE_SCRVDTYPE
General routine for generating code for currently selected business process in the screen environment	BldScrRules()	This function is in the module BuildCode. It is called from the screen frmRULE_SCRVDTYPE when the **Close** button is clicked.
General routine for generating code for a business process step within the currently selected business process	BldScrEditChks()	This function is in the module BuildCode. It is called from BldScrRules().
Specific routine to generate code for rules to check valid datatypes	BldSCRVDTYPE()	This function is in the module BuildCode and is called from BldScrEditChks().
Database table containing generated code	GCDE_GENCODE_M	
Routine that places the generated code in a function that is called to run the rules	WriteFunction()	This function is in the module BuildCode. It is called from the screen frmRULE_SCRVDTYPE when the **Close** button is clicked.
The generated function containing the rules	ScrChkfrmINV_ INVESTMENT_S	This function is the code that is generated. It is in the class module BizRuleCode.
Invocation of generated code	frmINV_INVESTMENT_S	This is the application screen where users enter investment data. When the **Save** button is pressed, the generated code is invoked.

TABLE 16.1 *Continued*

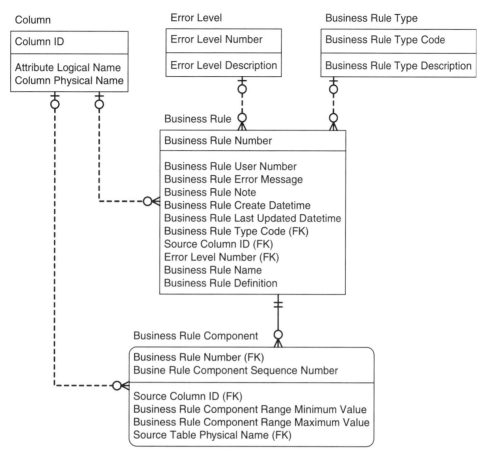

FIGURE 16.3
Business Rule Component

been discussed so far. For instance, derivation rule types frequently populate a column with a value by examining the contents of several other columns. Thus, rules frequently have inherent "one-to-many" relationships where one rule utilizes many other "things" in its operation. These "things" are nearly always columns in the database. Our Business Rules Repository must allow us to deal with these "things" individually, and it is not possible to accommodate their metadata in the **Business Rule** entity (**BRULE_BIZRULE_M**). This is intended for metadata about which there is one value per business rule. Rather, we must create a new entity in our Business Rules Repository model. This is shown in Figure 16.3 and is called **Business Rule Component**. It is intended to accommodate each individual element of logic of which a business rule is composed. In nearly all the rule types we will consider, an element of logic is centered on an individual database column that is used in the rule logic. Thus, **Business Rule Component** has *Source Column ID* in it.

For the rule type to check valid ranges for data entered on screens, we do not actually need to deal with *Source Column ID* in **Business Rule Component**. This is because the rule does not need to consider any column other than the one whose value is being data entered (the target column). What we do need is a place to house the minimum allowed value and maximum allowed value that are part of this rule type. This has been accomplished by adding attributes to **Business Rule Component**: *Business Rule Component Range Minimum Value* and *Business Rule Component Range Maximum Value*. The column *Source Table Physical Name* is also included in **Business Rule Component**. This is not theoretically needed because it can be found by looking up the *Source Column ID* in the *Column* table. However, having *Source Table Physical Name* in the **Business Rules Component** table makes it much easier to program the functionality required for the business rules engine.

An alternative design would be to place these two attributes in the **Business Rule** entity. However, we wish to reserve this entity for metadata concerning the rule itself and the target column (if any), and not for the metadata about the component logic of the rule. *Business Rule Component Range Minimum Value* and *Business Rule Component Range Maximum Value* are really part of the component logic in this rule type.

Business Rule Component is physically implemented as table **BRC_BIZRULE COMP_M**. Table 16.2 shows the physical column names and datatypes in this table.

There will only be one record in BRC_BIZRULECOMP_M for each rule that is defined for the **Screen Fields Valid Ranges** rule type.

The **Business Rule Component** table and the **Business Rule** table will have to be extended for other rule types, and these extensions will be discussed as each rule type is considered.

ATTRIBUTE LOGICAL NAME	COLUMN PHYSICAL NAME	COLUMN DATATYPE
Business Rule Number	BRULE_NUMBER_C	Character (5)
Business Rule Component Sequence Number	BRC_SEQUENCE_N	Integer
Source Column ID	COL_C	Character (4)
Source Table Physical Name	TAB_PHYSNAME_T	Character (50)
Business Rule Component Range Minimum Value	BRC_RANGEMINVAL_T	Character (20)
Business Rule Component Range Maximum Value	BRC_RANGEMAXVAL_T	Character (20)

TABLE 16.2 Basic Structure of Table **BRC_BIZRULECOMP_M**

Introducing Rule Versions

The next major piece of functionality that has to be added to the Business Rules Repository is needed to deal with rule versions.

Design for Rule Versions

What is different about the **Screen Fields Valid Ranges** rule type is that it is possible for it to have different versions across time. The rule types discussed earlier could either be implemented or not. The error messages and metadata about these rules could be changed over time, but not the fundamental logic of each rule itself. The **Screen Fields Valid Ranges** rule type can, in theory, be changed across time so that the ranges are different. For instance, for the first year in which the sample application is implemented, values in *Investment Funding Date* may not be allowed to be prior to 1/1/2000. In later years, it may be decided that the legal partnerships responsible for these investments must be wound up by 1/1/2011, and so no investments can be made after 1/1/2009. Thus, the rule for *Investment Funding Date* must be changed to have a range where the minimum is 1/1/2000 and the maximum is 1/1/2009.

Therefore, the **Screen Fields Valid Ranges** rule used to check the valid range of the data entered for *Investment Funding Date* will have one version at one time and another version at another time. The application's database, in turn, will have some data in it that was validated with one version of the rule, and other data that was validated with the second version of the rule.

The overall design of our application must be sufficient to allow us to match data that is constrained by the rule with the rule version that constrained it when it was populated into the database. This makes it possible to audit any data that is constrained by rules at any point in the life cycle of the application.

Suppose that the second version the **Screen Fields Valid Ranges** rule for *Investment Funding Date* was not implemented until the middle of 2009, and that an auditor finds a value of 2/2/2009 for *Investment Funding Date* in the database. The auditor can see that the current rule states that *Investment Funding Date* cannot have a value greater than 1/1/2009. Clearly something is wrong. The explanation is that this value of *Investment Funding Date* was subject to the first version of the rule, and the second version was implemented only after *Investment Funding Date* was populated with 1/1/2009. The auditor cannot conclude that the business rules are not working, and that the controls of the system are broken. Rather, this is a more localized error caused by users not changing the rule in a timely manner—bad, but perhaps excusable.

Being able to capture business rule versions and being able to understand how they affect data in a database are major benefits of a business rules approach. Indeed, they may be legal or regulatory requirements in some business areas. It also compares favorably with traditional hand-coded logic, where reverse engineering is often needed to even find what logic constrains a given column. Actually trying to determine how this logic led to the population of certain values in the database may be even more difficult with traditional systems. Furthermore, old code may be deleted, so it is often impossible to reconstruct what the old versions of the rule were. Unless programmers are careful to include times and dates of changes, it is difficult to figure out the time periods for which old rule versions were in effect in traditional applications.

One word of caution: if there is no requirement to ever utilize rule versions, it is probably better not to implement them, because they require additional development and maintenance effort.

The design to implement rule versions is relatively simple: it is to replicate the entities **Business Rule** and **Business Rule Component** as **Business Rule Version** and **Business Rule Component Version**, respectively. Each of the two new entities has a new key attribute added to it, *Business Version Number*. This is a sequence number that is incremented for each version of a rule. The first version of any rule has a *Business Version Number* of "1," the next one has a value of "2," and so on. Thus, the oldest version has a number of "1," and the most recent version of the business rule has the highest value of *Business Version Number* for the rule concerned. This is illustrated in Figure 16.4.

The only other new attribute that has been added is *Business Rule Version Created Datetime*. This is the date and time that the version was created. Thus, in the Business Rules Repository, the current version of any business rule is contained in **Business Rule** and **Business Rule Component**. **Business Rule Version** and **Business Rule Component Version** contain now-unused versions of business rules that have been superseded.

It is even possible to have business rule versions for rules that are no longer in effect—that is, rules that have been deleted from **Business Rule** and **Business Rule Component**. This is quite valid because we need to know whether a particular item of data was ever constrained by a business rule. Now, none of this fits well with conventional notions of referential integrity, which basically state that if a parent record is deleted its children must be deleted also, or "orphan" records will be created. Thus, the relationship lines in Figure 16.4 are not quite accurate in this regard—they should indicate that a parent record is optional for the relationship **Business Rule** to **Business Rule Component**, and for the relationship **Business Rule Component** to **Business Rule Component Version**. However, referential integrity, as it is commonly understood, takes no account of time or evolution. The reality is that the conventional understanding of referential integrity must never blind us to the possibility of the need to record valid prior states described by metadata (and indeed also by regular data).

Business Rule Version is implemented as table **BRV_BIZRULEVERSION_M**, and **Business Rule Component Version** as table **BRCV_BIZRULECOMPVER_M**. Tables 16.3 and 16.4 show the physical column names and datatypes in the tables.

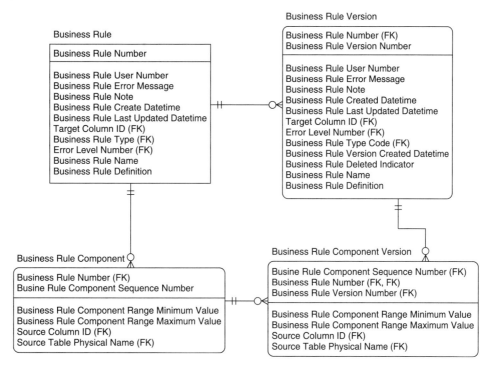

FIGURE 16.4
Entities for Business Rule Versions

ATTRIBUTE LOGICAL NAME	COLUMN PHYSICAL NAME	COLUMN DATATYPE
Business Rule Number	BRULE_NUMBER_C	Character (5)
Business Rule Version Number	BRV_VERSIONNUM_N	Integer
Business Rule User Number	BRULE_USER_C	Character (20)
Business Rule Error Message	BRULE_ERR_T	Character (255)
Business Rule Note	BRULE_NOTE_M	Memo
Business Rule Created Datetime	BRULE_CREATE_D	Date/Time
Business Rule Last Updated Datetime	BRULE_UPD_D	Date/Time
Target Column ID	COL_C	Character (4)
Error Level Number	ELVL_C	Character (2)
Business Rule Type Code	BRTP_C	Character (10)
Business Rule Name	BRULE_NAME_T	Character (120)
Business Rule Definition	BRULE_DEFN_M	Memo
Business Rule Version Created Datetime	BRV_CREATE_D	Date/Time
Business Rule Deleted Indicator	BRULE_DELETED_I	Character (1)

TABLE 16.3 Structure of Table **BRC_BIZRULECOMP_M**

ATTRIBUTE LOGICAL NAME	COLUMN PHYSICAL NAME	COLUMN DATATYPE
Business Rule Number	BRULE_NUMBER_C	Character (5)
Business Rule Version Number	BRV_VERSIONNUM_N	Integer
Business Rule Component Sequence Number	BRC_SEQUENCE_N	Integer
Source Column ID	COL_C	Character (4)
Source Table Physical Name	TAB_PHYSNAME_T	Character (50)
Business Rule Component Range Minimum Value	BRC_RANGEMINVAL_T	Character (20)
Business Rule Component Range Maximum Value	BRC_RANGEMAXVAL_T	Character (20)

TABLE 16.4 Structure of Table **BRCV_BIZRULECOMPVER_M**

Creating New Versions

We need to distinguish between updating a rule and creating a new version of it. Updating a rule merely changes the metadata stored in **Business Rule** and **Business Rule Component** in accordance with what the user has data entered. When a new version is created, the existing records in **Business Rule** and **Business Rule Component** are inserted into **Business Rule Version** and **Business Rule Component Version**, respectively, and given a new value of *Business Rule Version Number.* Then, whatever the user has data entered is used to update the records in **Business Rule** and **Business Rule Component**.

It is possible to create a design that insists that every change to a business rule results in a new version. However, a business rule version is really designed to capture a change in a business rule for a business reason. It is not intended to capture the fact that a user made a typographic error that they corrected a few minutes later. Also, rules may be defined before a system goes live, and they may not be accurately formulated until shortly before production implementation occurs. There is little point in storing rule versions for preproduction phases of an application.

The easiest design to accommodate these requirements is to let users decide whether they want to simply update a rule, or if they want to create a new version of it. This approach is taken in the sample application used in this book. There is indeed a risk that the users will decide to update a rule when they should have created a new version of it. In certain environments such a risk may not be acceptable, and the design will have to be changed to meet these different requirements. Design must follow requirements.

Business rule versions should not be edited or deleted. They represent what was happening in the application at a certain point in time, and they cannot be changed.

When a current business rule is deleted, it is a good design element to create a new version of the rule before the relevant records are deleted from **Business Rule** and **Business Rule Component**. This can be done automatically, without any choice being provided to the user. If the rule ever needs to be recreated, the tables **Business Rule Version** and **Business Rule Component Version** can be searched to find the appropriate rule version. Such a search can be difficult, since the original rule has been deleted. In the design presented here, for some rule types, only one rule is allowed per target column. For these rule types it is possible to search through **Business Rule Version** to find deleted rules. This search can be conducted using *Column ID* and *Business Rule Type Code* in **Business Rule Version**. However, for some other rule types this is simply not possible.

One other requirement that the design should accommodate is to easily identify rule versions for business rules that have been deleted. Accordingly, **Business Rule Version** has the attribute *Business Rule Deleted Indicator* added to it. This is set to "Y" if the version was created when a business rule was deleted.

Implementing the Rule Type for **Screen Fields Valid Ranges**

Now that we have seen the concepts that underlie the elements of the Business Rules Repository that deal with rule components and rule versions, we can implement the **Screen Fields Valid Ranges** rule type. Figure 16.5 shows the screen for the definition of rules of this type.

This screen has a button to revise the rule, as well as a button to update the rule. If users click on the button to update the rule, they are asked if they wish to proceed and reminded that they may wish to consider creating a new version of the rule instead of directly updating it.

There is a screen field that shows the number of versions that exist, and a button that will display prior versions. When the user clicks on this button, a screen like that shown in Figure 16.6 appears. This screen displays what has been recorded for the prior versions of the rule. The most recent version appears first, followed by successively older versions.

Returning to the main screen shown in Figure 16.5, the code to add a new rule has been changed somewhat. When the user clicks on a field in the list "Screen Fields Not Checked for Valid Range", the following happens:

- The system determines if a **Screen Fields Valid Ranges** rule exists for the selected field. The system searches the **Business Rule** table (**BRV_BIZRULE_M**) for a rule with the *Target Column ID* equal to the

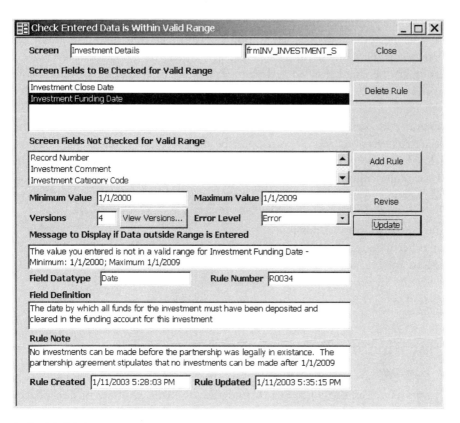

FIGURE 16.5
Screen to Define Rule Type **Screen Fields Valid Ranges**

selected field and a *Business Rule Type Code* equal to "SCRVRANGE". If such a rule exists, it is simply associated with the currently selected business process step by adding a new record to the table **Rules of Business Process Step (RBSP_RULESOFSTEP_M)**.

- If no **Screen Fields Valid Ranges** rule exists for the selected field, then the system determines whether any prior versions exist for it. The system searches the **Business Rule Version** table (**BRV_BIZRULEVERSION_M**) for a rule with the *Target Column ID* equal to the selected field and a *Business Rule Type Code* equal to "SCRVRANGE". If such a prior version exists, the function BringBackVersion() is executed. This creates a new rule using the information stored in the tables containing rule version information.

- If no prior version of the business rule exists, the rule is created using the information on the screen.

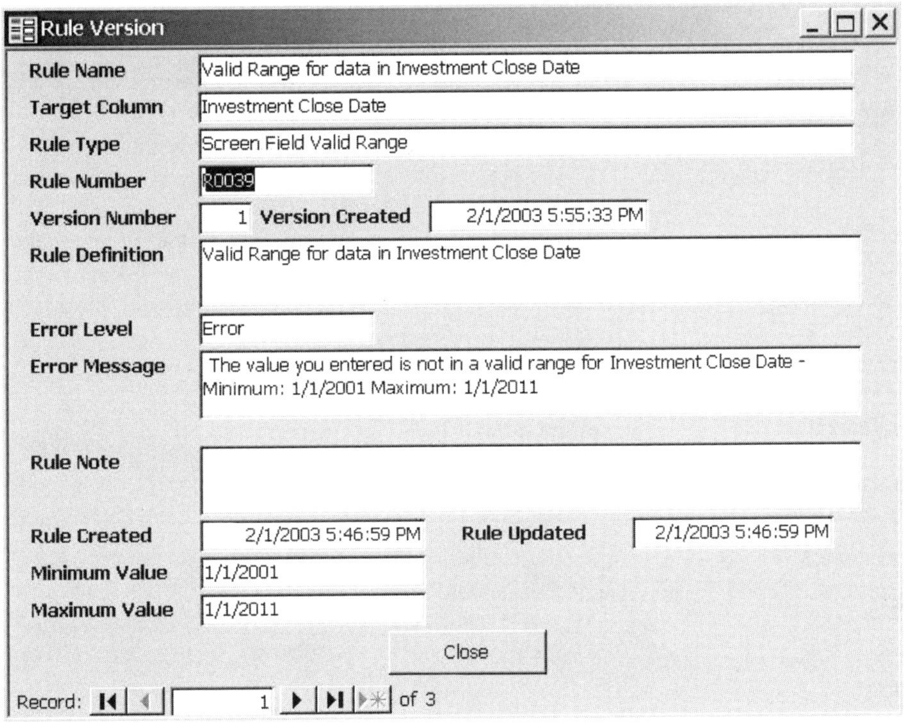

FIGURE 16.6
Rule Versions Display Screen

Some additional routines have to be written in the sample application to take care of the requirements of this screen. They are described in Table 16.5, and the reader can examine the code in the sample application to find out more about them.

On the rule type definition screen shown in Figure 16.5, there is one field to enter the minimum permitted value and another to enter the maximum permitted value. The data entered into these fields gets stored in table **BRC_BIZRULE COMP_M** (**Business Rule Component**) in fields BRC_RANGEMINVAL_T and BRC_RANGEMAXVAL_T. These columns are of character datatype, but the user may need to define rules for date or numeric target columns. This means that what the user enters in character format must be translatable to valid values in these other datatypes. Listing 16.2 shows a function written to check whether the user has entered a valid representation of a date.

Tables **BRULE_BIZRULE_M** (**Business Rule**) and **BRC_BIZRULECOMP_M** (**Business Rule Component**) are only updated if the minimum and maximum allowed values entered by the user are valid representations of the datatype of the target column of the rule. Functions to check whether various datatypes are correctly

ROUTINE	DESCRIPTION
CreateVersion()	Creates a new version of a business rule from the current business rule. It is executed prior to the current business rule being updated or deleted. It is in module BizRuleVersions.
BringBackVersion()	Finds the last version for a deleted rule and makes it the current version of the rule. It is in module BizRuleVersions.
PriorRuleVerNum()	Determines the number of versions that exist for a business rule. It is in module BizRuleVersions.
ChkStrNumber()	Determines whether a character value contains a valid number. It is in module GeneralFuncs.
ChkStrDate()	Determines if a character value contains a valid date. It is in module GeneralFuncs. See also Listing 16.1.
ChkRange()	Validates the values entered for the permitted minimum and maximum values. It is in the class module of the form frmRULE_SCRVRANGE.

TABLE 16.5 Functions in Sample Application to Deal with Rule Components, Rule Versions, and Rule Type **Screen Fields Valid Ranges**

LISTING 16.2
Function to Check Whether a String Value Contains a Valid Representation of a Date

```
Public Function ChkStrDate(strIn as String) As String
'*********************************************************************
' Determines if a string is a valid representation of a date.
'
' Parameters:
' strIn = String containing value to be tested
'
' Returns: "Y" if input string contains a valid date; otherwise
' "N"
'*********************************************************************
Dim dMy As Date
  ChkStrDate = "N"
  If IsDate(strIn) Then
    If Not IsNull(strIn) Then
      dMy = CDate(strIn)
```

```
      If IsDate(dMy) Then
         ChkStrDate = "Y"
      End If
    End If
  End If

End Function
```

LISTING 16.3
Fragment of Code Generated to Implement Rules of Type **Screen Fields Valid Ranges**

```
' Section 3: Validate Ranges of Entered Data
' Investment Close Date (INV_CLOSE_D)
' This field must have a minimum value of: 1/1/2001
' This field must have a maximum value of: 1/1/2011
If Not IsNull(frmMe.INV_CLOSE_D) Then
  If frmMe.INV_CLOSE_D < #1/1/2001# Or _
     frmMe.INV_CLOSE_D > #1/1/2011# Then
    intErr = intErr + 1
    strErr = strErr & "The value you entered is not in a valid
range for Investment Close Date—Minimum: 1/1/2001 Maximum:
1/1/2011" & Chr(10) & Chr(13)
  End If
End If
If intErr > 0 Then
  MsgBox strErr
  ScrChkfrmINV_INVESTMENT_S = "N"
  Exit Function
End If
```

represented by character values are used in many different places in business rules engines.

The construction of the definition screen for the rule type **Screen Fields Valid Ranges** is now complete. The code generation routine for this rule type generates program code to implement the rules. An example is shown in the code fragment in Listing 16.3.

Table 16.6 lists the objects in the sample application that are relevant for the rule type **Screen Fields Valid Ranges**. The reader can use this information to examine the detailed implementation in the sample application.

ITEM	APPLICATION OBJECT	DESCRIPTION
Menu access		On the menu, select **Business Rules > Define Business Rules**. The Business Rule Summary Screen appears. Select Business Process "Investment screen validation and processing." Select Business Process Step "Validate Screen Data Entry." Select Rule Type **Screen Fields Valid Ranges** and press the **Add Rule** button. The rule definition screen now appears.
Lookup table code for Rule Type	BRTP_BIZRULETYPE_M	This table contains a record with a code value of "SCRVRANGE" and a rule definition function of "frmRULE_SCRVRANGE".
Rule Type Definition Screen	frmRULE_SCRVRANGE	This screen is shown in Figure 16.5 and has a class module containing code.
Currently selected business process	Name of business process is "Investment screen validation and processing," and code is "SCRINVVAL". This information is stored in the **Business Process** table **BPROC_BIZPROCESS_M**.	The business process is selected on the Business Rules Summary Screen.
Currently selected business process step	Name of business process step is "Validate Screen Data Entry," and code is "ScrChkfrmINV_ INVESTMENT_S". This information is stored in the **Business Process Step** table **BPSP_BIZSTEPPROC_M**.	The business process step is selected on the Business Rules Summary Screen.
Currently selected rule type	Name of rule type is "Valid Datatypes for Screen Fields," and code is "SCRVRANGE". This information is stored in the **Business Rule Type** table **BRTP_BIZRULETYPE_M**.	The business rule type is selected on the Business Rules Summary Screen.

TABLE 16.6 Application Objects for Rule Type **Screen Fields Valid Ranges**

ITEM	APPLICATION OBJECT	DESCRIPTION
Business rules table	**BRULE_BIZRULE_M**	This stores the metadata defining the business rules and is updated from frmRULE_SCRVRANGE.
General routine for generating code for currently selected business process in the screen environment	BldScrRules()	This function is in the module BuildCode. It is called from the screen frmRULE_SCRVRANGE when the **Close** button is clicked.
General routine for generating code for a business process step within the currently selected business process	BldScrEditChks()	This function is in the module BuildCode. It is called from BldScrRules().
Specific routine to generate code for rules to check valid ranges	BldSCRVRANGE()	This function is in the module BuildCode and is called from BldScrEditChks().
Database table containing generated code	GCDE_GENCODE_M	
Routine that places the generated code in a function that is called to run the rules	WriteFunction()	This function is in the module BuildCode. It is called from the screen frmRULE_SCRVDTYPE when the **Close** button is clicked.
The generated function containing the rules	ScrChkfrmINV_INVESTMENT_S	This function is the code that is generated. It is in the class module BizRuleCode.
Invocation of generated code	frmINV_INVESTMENT_S	This is the application screen where users enter investment data. When the **Save** button is pressed, the generated code is invoked.

TABLE 16.6 *Continued*

Conclusion

In this chapter we have seen another simple rule type, **Valid Datatypes for Screen Fields**. This was similar to the **Required Screen Fields** rule type we covered in the previous chapter, and we were able to reuse much of the design (and programming) from this earlier rule type. We then moved on to a more complex rule type, **Screen Fields Valid Ranges**, which required the use of rule components and rule versions. The result is that we now have a rules engine that can accept definitions and generate code for three rule types, all of which validate inputs on data entry screens. We have also added to the richness of metadata in the business rules repository, which positions us to do additional administrative functions, such as determining what version of a rule was in force when a particular piece of data was populated. In the next chapter we shall move on to additional rule types with even more complexity.

17

RULE TYPES FOR CHECKING REFERENTIAL INTEGRITY

At this point we have dealt with three fairly simple rule types that validate data entered on screens. However, there are a number of other types of rules that are required to fully validate screen data, and some of the most important concern referential integrity. Referential integrity is an essential part of any application that works with a database. Referential integrity represents an additional set of business rules that ensure the following:

- Primary key columns of a database table must contain nonnull values.

- Duplicate records cannot exist in the same database table. A duplicate record is one that has primary key values that are identical to those of some other record in the database table.

- If a database table is a child table of one or more parent tables, then for every record in the child table there must be a corresponding record in each parent table. An exception may be made if the migrated foreign key column in the child contains a null value, in which case there does not have to be a parent record. Another way of looking at this is that there cannot be orphan records in the child table. An orphan record is one where a value in a child table's foreign key column cannot be found in the parent table from which this foreign key originated.

Referential integrity rules are one of the few kinds of business rules that can be completely defined in a data model, although not all data modeling tools do a thorough job, and not all data modelers bother to completely define the referential integrity rules.

Modern databases also contain features that enforce at least some aspects of referential integrity. Quite often the rules are enforced by causing a program crash if they are violated, which is not a very graceful way of dealing with error detection, but may be the only option for the database. Databases usually have to enforce referential integrity in the most general way since they know nothing of the applications that are built on them.

In this chapter we shall look at referential integrity rules as they apply to data entry on screens in the sample application. Although the referential integrity rules can be derived from the metadata in the Business Rules Repository, the design presented here will open them up to users for viewing and updating. This follows the principle of providing maximum user visibility to all business rules, rather than hiding them in black boxes.

It is important to note that referential integrity rules can only be derived without user intervention if the data model on which the application is built is normalized. If the data model is denormalized, the primary key columns of the tables may not be the true key columns. This causes headaches in determining what is truly a duplicate record within any given table. It creates even bigger headaches when the rules engine tries to manipulate child, and especially grandchild, records in any way at all. This is because the "key" columns that are migrated from the parent to the child and grandchild are not the real key columns at all. The result is that many more rules need to be implemented, not only to protect referential integrity between these tables in terms of their actual (albeit fake) primary keys, but also in terms of the columns that should have been the primary keys in the first place. To avoid such problems, only fully normalized database designs should be used for applications that have business rules engines implemented on top of them.

The rules to ensure that values exist in primary key columns (i.e., so that these columns do not contain null values) have already been discussed in Chapter 15. Therefore, only the remaining types of referential integrity rules are discussed in this chapter. These are the rule types that prevent duplicate records and orphan records.

Since the referential integrity rules are more complex than the ones previously dealt with, there are several new concepts and new items of rule engine functionality that have to be considered for them, as follows:

- Rule definition screens that deal with one rule at a time. The previous rule types dealt with sets of rules on a single rule definition screen.

- Prevention of the definition of duplicate rules. How is it possible to make sure the user does not define the same rule twice?

- Business rule status. Complex business rules may need to change status over the life of an application.

- Additional control over rule deletion. Deleting rules has already been discussed, but additional controls are still required.

First, the rule type that prevents the addition of duplicate records will be discussed.

Prevention of Duplicate Records

There are two ways in which a table can end up with duplicate records. The first is when a new record is added to the table. The primary key columns of this record may contain values that are found in another record in the same table. The second way is that after a record is successfully added to a table it may be updated so that the values in its primary key columns change. These values may now duplicate what is found in another record in the same table. For instance, one new record may be added to the **Investment** table with a value of *Investment ID* (the primary key column) equal to "DOGFOOD", and another record may be added with an *Investment ID* of "CATFOOD". If the user tries to add another record with *Investment ID* of "DOGFOOD", this is an error. It is also an error if the user tries to change the "CATFOOD" record to "DOGFOOD".

The risk of duplication may be reduced by disallowing the updating of primary key columns after a record has been added to a table. This works well with records that are updated through screens, but does not eliminate the possibility of an accidental duplicate when a new record is added. A second method is to delete any record in a table that may have the same primary key values as the record being added. This sounds a little strange, but it is frequently used quite legitimately in batch processes that work with periodic data. For instance, a banking system may have a **Daily Account** table with a primary key of *Account Number* and *Processing Date*. Every day, new records are inserted into the **Daily Account** table for all active accounts, but before this is done all records for the current (and future dates) are deleted. This enables the process to be rerun on demand without creating duplicate records.

Let us assume that we cannot use any of these techniques to reduce the risk of record duplication in the sample application. The most difficult design issue is that we need to know whether the current record is a duplicate of another record—but if a duplicate record is found, how can it be told apart from the current record? For instance, suppose a new record is added to the **Investment** table with an *Investment ID* (the single primary key column for this table) that has a value of "DOGFOOD". It is fairly simple to search the **Investment** table to see if any other record has an *Investment ID* of "DOGFOOD" before the new record is actually added to the table. Suppose that we want to change the *Investment ID* of an existing record from "CATFOOD" to "DOGFOOD". Depending on the programming environment it may be difficult to do this, since the current record has to be excluded from the search. In other words, there needs to be a way to identify a record other than by using the values in the primary key. In the design presented here, the column *Record ID* is used to recognize the current record. *Record ID* is a record number column that the application adds to the structure of every table, and which contains a unique "record number." It is used to enable the rules engine to uniquely identify a record—precisely what is needed in the current situation.

Building the Rule Type for *Check for Duplicate Records*

This rule type is going to be somewhat more complex than the previous rule types we dealt with. It differs in the following ways:

- Each of the previous rule types had a target column—one column for which some set of properties were validated. The **Check for Duplicate Records** rule type is not like this. Its target is an entire table, rather than any particular column.

- The previous rule types had a one-to-one correspondence with a target column. Thus, it was easy to build an interface where all the rules for a given business process step were shown on the rule definition screen, since this could be done using the list boxes showing the columns belonging to the base table. This is not possible with the **Check for Duplicate Records** rule type, because these rules do not have a one-to-one correspondence with individual columns in a table.

- Because the previous rule types had a one-to-one correspondence with table columns, it was easy to design an interface that prevented users from creating two versions of the same rule, thus duplicating the rule. There is no such easy way of preventing the definition of duplicate rules for the **Check for Duplicate Records** rule type.

- The previous rule types did not use multiple records in the **Business Rule Component** table. The **Check for Duplicate Records** rule type will sometimes need to use multiple records in this table, as we shall see.

There are thus several new design challenges for the **Check for Duplicate Records** rule type, and the same challenges apply to the more complex rule types that will be discussed in subsequent chapters.

One design issue that will be disposed of immediately is the problem of displaying all the rules of the type **Check for Duplicate Records** that have been defined a single business process step. Rather than build new screens, each of which will list all the rules of a single rule type within a selected business process step, the Business Rules Summary screen can be modified to do this. The reader may still wish to build one screen per rule type to list all the rules of the selected type for the selected business process step, since this can provide the user with more information specific to the selected rule type. However, the design shown in Figure 17.1 is a reasonable approach.

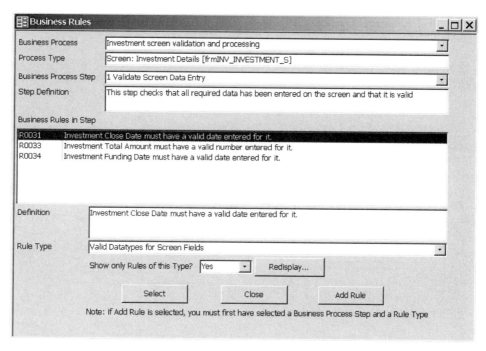

FIGURE 17.1
Enhanced Business Rules Summary Screen

In Figure 17.1, the Business Rules Summary screen has been modified to allow the user to redisplay the list of business rules for the selected business process step, such that only rules for the currently selected rule type are displayed. The combo box and **Redisplay . . .** button under the Rule Type combo box achieve this. Thus, the user simply selects the desired rule type and presses **Redisplay . . .** , and the screen refreshes to show only rules belonging to the selected rule type that have been defined for the selected business process step.

The rule definition interface for the **Check for Duplicate Records** rule type is shown in Figure 17.2.

When the user invokes this screen for the first time, the rules engine needs to automatically create rules for the primary key columns. After all, no two records in a database can contain identical values in their primary key columns. This is fairly simple to do. The rule definition consists of creating one record in the **Business Rules** table for the new rule, and one record in the **Business Rule Component** table for each of the primary key columns in the currently selected base table. The **Column** table has a column called *Column Primary Key Indicator*, which is used to find the primary key columns for the selected table, that is, the table associated with the currently selected business process step.

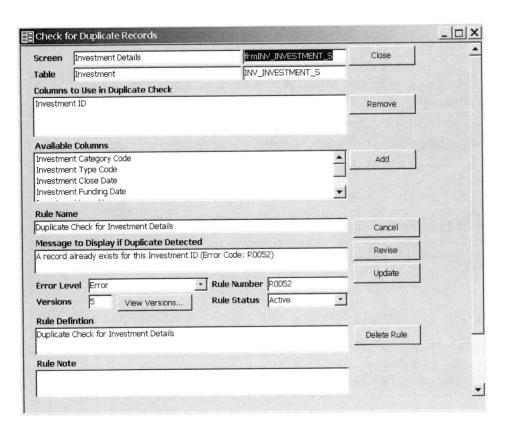

FIGURE 17.2
Rule Definition Interface for Rule Type **Check for Duplicate Records**

The next problem is that the list boxes *Available Columns* and *Columns to Use in Duplicate Check* cannot be directly tied to the **Business Rule** and **Business Rule Component** tables, in the same way that list boxes were in the rule types discussed in previous chapters. The screen shown in Figure 17.2 can display only one rule at a time. The user may need to choose several columns to test for duplicates before updating the rule. In the previous rule definition interfaces, rules were updated when the **Add** and **Remove** buttons were pressed, because each rule dealt with only one column. This also means that users have to be able to leave the screen if they wish to abandon their work. A **Cancel** button has been added for this purpose.

An important lesson from this design is that it is not possible to have a uniform screen design from one rule type definition screen to the next. A great deal can be done to make the look and feel of these screens similar, but rule type definition screens must ultimately have differences. Only by going back to more generalized rule type definition screens can the interface be made more similar from screen to screen.

However, this inevitably makes it more difficult for the user to define rules, because the interface screens are not as specific as they need to be. Specificity of rule type definition screens comes at the price of the user having to learn how to get around each screen. The rules engine designer has to do everything to help users in this regard. For example, documentation on how to use each rule type definition screen is extremely important.

Introducing the Temporary Business Rule Component Table and Multiuser Considerations

The user must be able to select any number of columns for a rule before updating a **Check for Duplicate Records** rule. These are the set of columns for which no two records in a database table can have identical values. The approach used here is to have a temporary table that mirrors the **Business Rule Component** table to hold what the user selects. This temporary table is used only to hold source column information for the currently selected business rule. When the user updates the rule, this information is copied into the **Business Rule Component** table. The **Temporary Business Rule Component** table is identical in structure to the **Business Rule Component** table, with the exception that there is no **Business Rule Number Column**. This is not needed because by the time the **Temporary Business Rule Component** table is used, it is already known what business rule is being updated.

There is an interesting consequence of this design. No more than one user at a time can update any rules in the rules engine if these rules utilize the **Temporary Business Rule Component** table. Some people may immediately react that this is not an acceptable design. They prefer that all systems be fully multiuser. It happens that the sample application is a Microsoft Access file intended for single users, but should real business rule engines be multiuser? The answer is that it depends. Having different users updating business rules at the same time can be extremely dangerous. For instance, if two users are independently updating business rules for the same business process step at the same time, they will almost certainly cause problems for each other.

However, the situation where two users simultaneously update business rules in different business process steps is more likely to be encountered. Can this cause problems? The general design approach presented here separates business rules from business process steps, so that the same rule can be reused in different business process steps. This fits with the design goal of not duplicating business rules. It also means that it is possible that users could come into conflict, even if they are defining business rules in different business process steps. Two users could attempt to change the same business rule. Beyond this, rule dependency is an issue. As we shall see in subsequent chapters, the rules engine sometimes has to determine the sequence in which rules fire. If two users are updating different rules, but there is some overlap in terms of the business processes in which these rules participate, there can be problems. For instance, it is possible to generate circular references, where each rule tries to use the other as an input.

The real answer to the issue of multiuser functionality is that it should be driven by requirements. There is no "best practice" or "right way," although there are clearly limits on how far rule definition functionality can support multiuser requirements. If the rules engine designer finds that there are two general business areas where different sets of users need to work simultaneously, and there is a very high probability the users in each area will not need to reuse rules from the other area, then a multiuser approach to rules definition is justified. It can be implemented in a number of ways. Adding *User ID* to the primary key of the **Temporary Business Rule Component** table would be one. This column could then be used by the rules engine to recognize which records in the **Temporary Business Rule Component** table belong to which user. Alternatively, *Business Process ID* or even *Business Rule Type Code* could be used for this purpose to allow rules for different business processes or business rule types to be defined at the same time.

In regular systems, record locking is used to ensure multiuser environments function correctly. This is not possible in business rules engines because the rule set is so important. Rule dependencies mean that individual rules are not independent of each other. Their definitions affect the sequence in which they run in a business process step. The best advice is therefore to understand the requirements for the independent update of business rules and implement the functionality to support it. For the sample application, the assumption is that only one user will define rules at one time.

Duplicate Rule Detection

The screen shown in Figure 17.2 permits the user to define any number of rules to detect duplicate records. For the Investment Details screen, it is necessary to prevent changes that could lead to records duplicating the primary key column—*Investment ID*. However, it is also legitimate to define a rule that prohibits duplicates in, say, *Investment Short Name* or *Investment Long Name*. There may even be a business rule that no two investments can be closed on the same day, and so the user needs to be able to prohibit duplicates for *Investment Close Date*. In more complex applications, there may be multiple primary key columns on a table. Similarly, the user may wish to prevent duplicates for values across multiple columns that are not primary key columns.

All of this makes it very complicated to detect a duplicate rule definition for the **Check for Duplicate Records** rule type. What essentially has to happen is that if the user selects N columns for duplicate detection, the system needs to find whether any other rule also uses the same N columns for duplicate detection. If such a rule is found, and it is in the current business process step, the user should not be allowed to add the new rule. If the rule is found, but it is not included in the currently selected business process step, the user should be given the opportunity to include it, but again should be prevented from adding a new rule.

Suppose a rule is found that contains the N columns selected for the current rule by the user plus some more columns (say N + 2 columns)? In theory there is no problem. The current rule (using N columns) is going to be more restrictive (disallow more duplicates) than the other rule (with N + 2 columns). What if another rule exists with some, but not all, of the N columns of the current rule (say N − 1 columns)? In this case the other rule will be more restrictive than the current rule. Again, there is no problem in theory. However, there is little point in defining rules for duplicates that will always be prevented anyway by more restrictive rules.

What this shows is that for any rule type, analysis needs to be done to determine what constitutes a duplicate rule definition. The analysis may be quite different from one rule type to the next. There is no uniform way to do it. Even if there is no strict duplication of the rule definition, there may be some potential conflict with other rules of the same type, as we have seen in this example. The rules designer will have to decide how to handle these situations based on requirements. Again, this is a consequence of building interfaces for specific rule types. These issues do not go away if more general rules definition interfaces are used, such as just having a general calculation rule type, or even getting the users to write source code. The issues are simply not recognized or addressed by the rules engine or the rules engine designer in these circumstances. The result is that the users have to put a lot more effort into managing rule definitions manually, and this is a direct contradiction of the reasons for building a business rules engine in the first place.

More Advanced Rule Deletion

The rules interface screens discussed in previous chapters added and removed rules based on manipulating individual columns, since each rule was tied to one and only one column. This was easily done using the **Add** and **Remove** buttons on these screens. However, the screen shown in Figure 17.2 deals with only one rule at a time, and the rule is not tied to one target column. This means that there needs to be an additional button to actually delete the rule.

The functionality built previously to deal with rule deletion had useful design elements. One of these was the option not to delete previous versions of a rule. This permits a deleted rule to be recreated from a prior version. However, recreation in this way is not possible for the **Check for Duplicate Records** rule type, because the algorithm used to search for a prior version of a rule assumes that there can only be one rule for one target column per rule type. The concept of target column does not apply to the **Check for Duplicate Records** rule type because it operates on an entire database table, not on a specific column. Thus, when a **Check for Duplicate Records** rule is deleted, the designer may be tempted to delete all prior versions for it as well, since they cannot be used in the future.

One of the reasons for having prior versions was so that we can know whether a particular rule was used to control database updates in the past. If all prior versions for a rule are deleted, this is no longer possible. This is a problem for the **Check for Duplicate Records** rule, and additional functionality is required to prevent deletions that can cause trouble.

A complementary design approach is to conditionally prevent the deletion of rules. As has been discussed earlier, there are some points in the life cycle of an application where it should be possible to create and delete rules with no controls. For instance, there may be a preproduction phase where rules are defined. In this phase there should be fewer qualms about deleting rules than after the application is in production and updates are being controlled by the rules. A way to implement this requirement is shown in Figure 17.3.

This screen allows system-level restrictions to be set for rule deletion in general. The combo box allows the user to have unrestricted rule deletion, or to restrict rule deletion based on a grace period. This grace period is the number of days from when the rule is created within which the user can delete the rule. For instance, a period of 7 days would allow the user to delete a rule any time from when the rule was first created until 7 days had elapsed. This narrows the window in which the rule can fire and affect the system. This scheme may too restrictive for some situations and not restrictive enough for others. The rules engine designer will have to determine what the requirements are for rule deletion and build the functionality to control it. These requirements may vary widely.

The screen shown in Figure 17.3 has been implemented in the sample application. It can be accessed by selecting **Business Rules** from the main menu and then **Rule Deletion Controls** from the popup that appears.

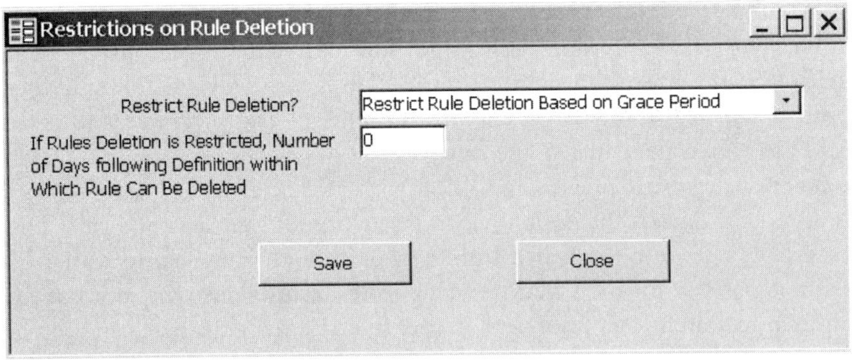

FIGURE 17.3
Rule Deletion Restriction Definition Screen

The sample application has a single function to delete a business rule (function DelBizRule() in module GeneralFuncs). This module compares a business rule's create date (column BRULE_CREATE_D in table **BRULE_BIZRULE_M**) with the current date before attempting to delete it. If the number of days is greater than the grace period, the rule is not deleted.

A further enhancement for rules deletion is required if the rules engine prevents deletion of a rule. If the user does not want to delete the rule, but simply wants to prevent it from firing, what can be done? The answer is to introduce *rule status*. Rule status defines the current status of a business rule. In the sample application there are two statuses, "Active" and "Inactive". The table **Business Rule Status** (**BRST_BRULESTATUS_M**) is implemented to hold these values. It consists of the columns *Business Rule Status Code* and *Business Rule Status Description*. *Business Rule Status Code* is also added to the tables **Business Rule** and **Business Rule Version**. Figure 17.4 summarizes this design.

The status of a business rule is set on the rule definition screen. The screen in Figure 17.2 has a combo box called *Rule Status* for this purpose. If the user tries to change the status of a rule, simple updates are not permitted. Instead, the user is forced to create a new version. In this way the set of prior versions for a rule accurately tracks changes in rule status. The final piece of the design is that if a rule is set to a status of "Inactive," the program logic that generates code ignores it. Thus, inactive rules are never utilized by the business application. However, their metadata remains in the rules engine and can be reactivated or used for audit purposes.

The rules designer can choose to have a much more elaborate set of business rule statuses than is used in the sample application, perhaps something like "Design," "Test," "Quality Assurance," "Production," "Suspended," and "Obsolete." The rules engine could be designed to process these different statuses in different ways, depending on particular requirements. This topic is an important one for the rules engine designer to consider, but space does not permit a more detailed examination of it in this book.

Generating Code to Check for Duplicate Records

The complexities of defining the **Check for Duplicate Records** rule type have now been considered, and several new concepts have been introduced regarding the design of the business rules engine. Code generation for this rule type is also more complex than has been required for the previous rule types. Listing 17.1 shows a fragment of code generated for this rule type.

The code shown in Listing 17.1 has the following important design elements:

- It is intended to implement the rules in the screen data entry environment. It could in theory be implemented in a batch processing environment also, in

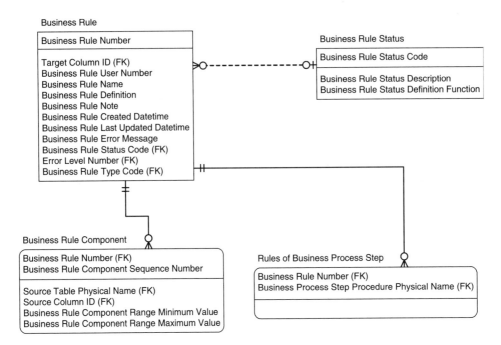

FIGURE 17.4
Introducing Business Rule Status

which case it would need to be modified to pick up the **Investment** record being processed from some other system object such as a recordset.

- Each rule has to search for duplicates in the **Investment** table. This is done by opening a recordset and searching for duplicates. The recordset is based on a SQL SELECT statement that the generated code creates.

- The generated code creates the SQL SELECT statement differently if a record is being added on the **Investment** screen than if a record is being updated on the **Investment** screen. The rules engine uses the column *Record ID* (RECORD_ID_C) to distinguish between these two states. This column is an Access autonumber datatype that is automatically populated by Access after a record is added, so it is null before the record is added. It is important for many rules to understand the difference between a record addition and a record update. This is necessary not for the logical definition of the rule, but rather for its implementation in generated code. The rules engine designer will inevitably have to find some way of telling whether a record is being added or being updated, but this is certainly not something that the user who defines the rules should ever need to specify.

LISTING 17.1

Fragment of Generated Code for Detection of Duplicate Records

```
' Section 4: Check for Duplicate Records
' Check for duplicates in Table Investment
'      —INV_INVESTMENT_S
' Primary Key Column: Investment ID (INV_C)
  strSQL = "SELECT * FROM INV_INVESTMENT_S WHERE INV_C = '" &
frmMe.INV_C & "'"
  If Not IsNull(frmMe.RECORD_ID_C) Then
    strSQL = strSQL & " AND RECORD_ID_C <> " &
CStr(frmMe.RECORD_ID_C)
  End If
  rstSource.Open strSQL, CurrentProject.Connection, _
    adOpenKeyset, adLockOptimistic, adCmdText
  If Not rstSource.EOF Then
    intErr = intErr + 1
    strErr = "A record already exists for this Investment ID
(Error Code: R0052)"
  End If
  rstSource.Close
' Check for duplicates in Table Investment
'      —INV_INVESTMENT_S
' Primary Key Column: Investment Short Name (INV_SHORTNAME_T)
  strSQL = "SELECT * FROM INV_INVESTMENT_S WHERE INV_SHORTNAME_T =
'" & frmMe.INV_SHORTNAME_T & "'"
  If Not IsNull(frmMe.RECORD_ID_C) Then
    strSQL = strSQL & " AND RECORD_ID_C <> " &
CStr(frmMe.RECORD_ID_C)
  End If
  rstSource.Open strSQL, CurrentProject.Connection, _
    adOpenKeyset, adLockOptimistic, adCmdText
  If Not rstSource.EOF Then
    intErr = intErr + 1
    strErr = "Investment Short Name must be unique (Error Code
R0057)"
  End If
  rstSource.Close
  If intErr > 0 Then
    MsgBox strErr
    ScrChkfrmINV_INVESTMENT_S = "N"
    Exit Function
  End If
```

This concludes the examination of the rule type **Check for Duplicate Records**. The next rule type that will be considered is for the kind of referential integrity that controls dependent records in child tables.

Referential Integrity for Dependent Records

Relational databases contain tables that are related to each other. Changes in the primary key of a parent record will affect dependent, or *child*, records in other tables. Figure 17.5 provides an example.

In Figure 17.5 a record in the **Investment** table may contain a record for which child records exist in the **Investor Monthly Distribution**, **Investor Position**, and **Investment Income** tables. For instance, an **Investment** record may have a value of "DOGFOOD" in the *Investment ID* column. Child records in the other three tables will also have "DOGFOOD" as the value in their *Investment ID* columns. If the user changes the value of *Investment ID* from "DOGFOOD" to "CATFOOD" in the **Investment** table, the child records will be left without any corresponding parent

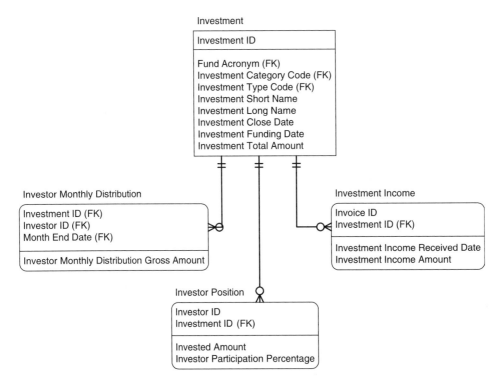

FIGURE 17.5
Dependent Records

record and will become orphans. This loss of referential integrity must be avoided at all costs. There are a number of different options that can be used to control or prevent it:

- **Restrict**. Do not permit any changes to the primary key columns of the parent record if it has any child records in other tables.

- **Cascade**. Cascade the changes to the primary key columns of the parent record to all child records—that is, change the child records synchronously with the parent record.

- **Set Null**. Put a null value in the primary key columns in the child records that are migrated from the parent record. This is not allowed for identifying relationships (where the primary key columns of the parent form part of the primary key of the child).

- **Set Default**. Put a nonnull default value in the primary key columns in the child records that are migrated from the parent record. This is not allowed for identifying relationships.

- **None**. Do nothing. This is not a good option. It will cause loss of referential integrity.

Of all these options, the safest is to restrict changes to the primary key of the parent record if that record has any child records in other tables. This includes not only changes to the primary key values of the parent record, but also any attempts to delete the parent record. This is the option that is followed in the sample application. The other options are more complex to implement and open up the possibility of orphan records. Applications that use business rules engines have chosen to minimize their reliance on IT staff. They do not have teams containing programmers or DBAs standing by to fix referential integrity problems. The safest option is the best for rules engine approaches.

The rule type that implements these checks in the sample application is called **Referential Integrity for Dependent Records**.

Rule Definition Interface for **Referential Integrity for Dependent Records**

The rule definition interface screen for the rule type **Referential Integrity for Dependent Records** is shown in Figure 17.6.

As was noted earlier, referential integrity rules for dependent records can be derived entirely from the original data model of the business area covered by the application. Indeed, users cannot be allowed to define, delete, or inactivate these rules. The rule definition interface shown in Figure 17.6 reflects this: it does not have a **Delete** button; *Rule Status* cannot be changed from "Active"; and the *Error Level*

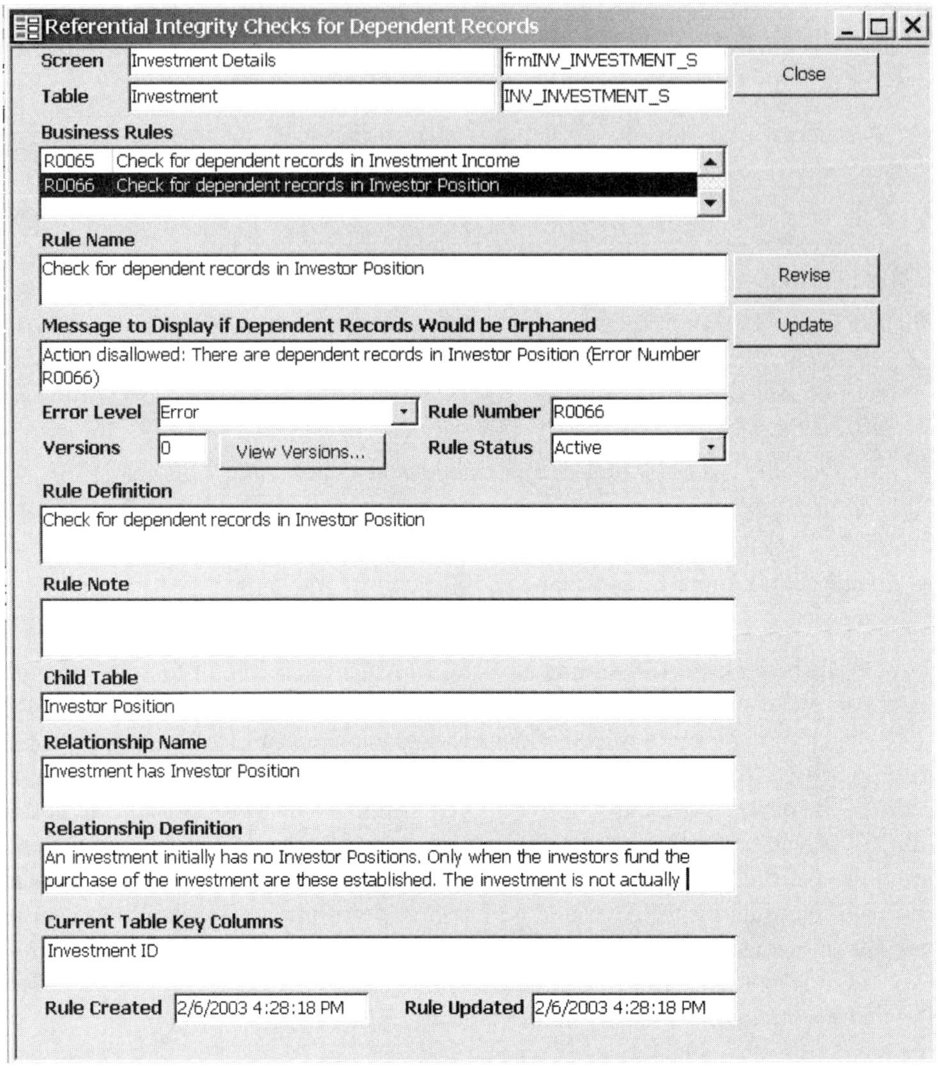

FIGURE 17.6
Rule Definition Interface for Rule Type **Referential Integrity for Dependent Records**

cannot be changed from "Error." Once again we see that every rule type definition interface has unique design elements.

In this definition interface, the design reverts to being able to display all the rules of this rule type for the currently selected business process step. Each rule represents one relationship where the base table of the currently selected business process step is the parent table of the relationship. As can be seen from Figure 17.5 there are three such relationships where the **Investment** table is the parent table. Thus, there are three business rules for the current business process step. These rules are created automatically by the rule definition interface screen when the screen is entered for the first time. Relationship metadata is imported into the Business Rules Repository by the techniques discussed in Chapter 10. It is this metadata that is used to automatically create the rules. Only relationships that were imported from the data model describing the business area are used for this purpose, not additional relationships created in the Repository to limit related records to subtypes within parent and child tables.

There are a number of informational items that appear on the rules definition interface screen. They provide additional information about the selected business rule, but cannot be updated. They consist of *Child Table*, *Relationship Name*, *Relationship Definition*, and *Current Table Key Columns*. This information can greatly help the user in understanding the nature of the business rules, and perhaps also help the user to create more meaningful error messages and rule definitions. It is the design of the Business Rules Repository that permits this metadata to be reused, and again the value of the Repository can be appreciated.

Code Generation for *Referential Integrity for Dependent Records*

The **Referential Integrity for Dependent Records** rule type is the first we have encountered that must be implemented in different business process steps within the sample application. It is needed for the business process steps **Validate Screen Data Entry** and **Checks Before Deleting an Investment** within the business process **Investment Screen Validation and Processing**. The fundamental reason for this is that dependent records can be orphaned either by deleting the parent record or by changing the primary key values of the parent record. Hence, the rule type must be implemented in both business process steps. Prior rule types were confined to the business process step **Validate Screen Data Entry**.

It would be a mistake to create two different rule types, one for when a record is deleted, and another for when a record has its primary key values changed. Even if only one rule type is implemented, there may still be a temptation to define one rule for when a record is deleted and another for when a record has its primary key values changed. Indeed, to a programmer this would seem perfectly natural. After all, the programming needed to check referential integrity in the case of record deletion is somewhat different from the programming required to check referential integrity when primary key values change. If different programming is needed, is it not the case that different rules are needed? The answer is most certainly not. A business rule definition consists of metadata describing conceptual logic. Implementation is something else. It is indeed necessary to implement a **Referential Integrity for Dependent Records** rule differently for record deletion and primary key value changes, but there are not separate rules for each kind of implementation. The rules engine designer must be very careful in rule analysis to capture specific rule types that have business meaning. However, the process cannot go beyond this to spawn additional, unnecessary rule types.

How does the business rules engine cope with the need to implement **Referential Integrity for Dependent Records** rules in different business steps? First of all, the rule type is associated with both the business process steps **Validate Screen Data Entry** and **Checks Before Deleting an Investment** within the business process **Investment Screen Validation and Processing**. This is done using the screens described in Chapter 11. Now, the code generation environment for these two business process steps is different. In Chapter 7 we discussed the possibility that a single business rule definition could be implemented as generated code in a potentially infinite number of software environments, usually represented by different programming languages. The design of the part of the Business Rules Repository that implements this is shown in Figure 17.7.

Each different code generation environment is represented by a record in the **Code Generation Environment** table. A **Business Process Step** is deemed to be implemented in one and only one **Code Generation Environment**. Each **Business Rule Type** has only one definition interface, represented by the column *Business Rule Type Definition Function* in this table. However, a **Business Rule Type** will usually have a different code generation routine for each **Code Generation Environment**. The names of the code generation routines are held in the table **Code Generation Routine**. Thus, when generating the code for a given business process step, the rules

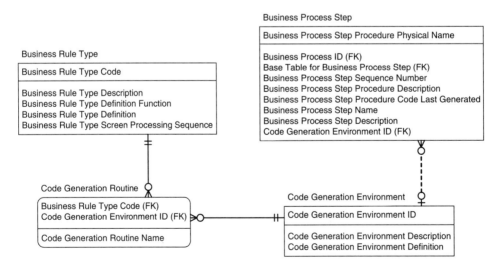

FIGURE 17.7
Business Rules Repository Design for Rule Code Generation Functions

engine uses the *Code Generation Routines* for the **Code Generation Environment** associated with the business process step.

Even within a single programming language it may be necessary to create different implementations of a business rule definition. This is the case with the sample application. The system objects available for rule definition are different for forms (screens) and batch processes in Microsoft Access. Furthermore, the generated code needed for when a record is deleted is simply different compared with that needed when a record has its primary key values changed. This means that for the sample application there are three code generation environments: one for batch processes; one for updating data on screens; and one for deleting records on screens. Table 17.1 summarizes the code generation environments used in the business process steps of the business process for data entry on the Investment screen.

What this means is that the rule type **Referential Integrity for Dependent Records** must have one routine to generate code in the code generation environment "Screen Data Entry" and another for code generation in the environment "Record Deletion on Screen". These routines are represented by two records in the **Code Generation Routine** table. As it happens the differences in the generated code for the two environments are not very great for the rule type **Referential Integrity for Dependent Records**. Thus, a single code generation routine can be given the intelligence to detect which environment it is generating code for. The function BldREFINTDEL() in the module BuildCode in the sample application generates code for the rule type **Referential Integrity for Dependent Records** in the two environments required. When it executes, it looks up the record for the currently selected business process step in the **Business Process Step** table and finds the *Code Generation Environment ID*. This is used to alter the kind of code generated by the function.

It will be recalled that if a rule is changed, then all business processes associated with the changed rule are regenerated. For a business process based on screens, the function BldScrRules() in module BuildCode regenerates the rules. It generates code for each business process step associated with each business process. The rules for **Referential Integrity for Dependent Records** are associated with both **Validate Screen Data Entry** and **Checks before Deleting an Investment** business process steps. Thus,

BUSINESS PROCESS STEP	CODE GENERATION ENVIRONMENT
Validate Screen Data Entry	Screen Data Entry
Checks before Deleting an Investment	Record Deletion on Screen
Calculations after Screen Update	General Batch Process

TABLE 17.1 Code Generation Environments for Business Process Steps of Business Process **Investment Screen Validation and Processing**

changing one of these rules in the context of just one of these business process steps (since the rules engine interface presents rules to the user in the context of business process steps) will result in the regeneration of the code for both business process steps.

The rules designer may or may not follow the detailed design approach for code generation presented here. However, the considerations that have led to this design are probably going to be relevant to any rules engine:

- Is there more than one environment in which code needs to be generated for the rules engine? This may be both for different programming languages, or different settings within a single programming language (or equivalent).

- For a given rule type, what are the environments for which it must generate code? If there is more than one environment, can a single code generation routine cope with the code generation, or does more than one routine have to be created?

- Does the business rules engine correctly regenerate all code when a business rule is updated? This should include code in all code generation environments associated with the rule type of the updated rule.

Conclusion

This chapter has introduced two new rule types, each having design issues that apply to many other rule types. These are the last rule types that we shall consider in the context of validating data entry on screens. In the next chapter we shall see rule types that are implemented within batch processes.

18

WORKING WITH BATCH PROCESSES: SETTING INDICATORS AND REFERENCE DATA CODE VALUES

Thus far, rule types have been considered in the context of data entry on the Investment screen of the sample application. Batch processes are different from screen data entry. They are business process steps where the system updates records in a database, rather than having users do so directly. Users may enter some information on one or more screens that initiate the batch process, but the users are not updating the database a record at a time as they are in screen data entry. An application utilizes these user inputs in order to control the batch process, and perhaps also as default values for some update operations. Batch processes, therefore, rely greatly on business rules. They are generally more complex than business processes associated with screen data entry for the following reasons:

- Most data entry screens only work with one record at a time in one particular table. This base table is usually associated with all the business process steps for the business process defined by the screen. In general, but not always, this means that business rules associated with the screen operate on only this one record and its parent records. Batch processes, by contrast, operate on sets of records within a base table and their parent records. Thus, batch processes must deal with many records at a time. It should be noted that the design approach recommended here is that business rules do not operate on child tables of any base table associated with a business process step.

- When a new record is added via screen data entry, it does not have any child records. These have to be created later. This tends to simplify the business process steps associated with screens, and thus the rule sets that apply to them. Batch processes tend to deal with sets of tables where child records do exists.

Thus, batch processes tend to need business process steps to work with the tables containing these child records. This adds to the business process steps associated with batch processes, and thus increases the number of rules that are needed for batch processes.

In this chapter the ways in which business rules operate within batch processes will be considered. The example used will be a batch business process step associated with the Investment screen. This business process step is called **Calculations after Investment Screen Update** and is run after any record has been updated on the Investment screen. This business process step is not concerned with the record that the user has just updated, but with all records in the **Investment** table.

From now on we shall be looking at batch processes and leaving the realm of business process steps that deal with only one record at a time. However, it should be noted that the examples presented in the previous chapter are only a subset of the business process steps and rule types that may be needed to deal directly with screen data entry. Rules engine designers will encounter the need for additional rule types and other kinds of business process steps than the ones presented in this book in order to comprehensively deal with screen data entry.

In this chapter we shall look at two important rule types: a rule type to populate the value of an indicator; and a rule type to populate the value of a reference table code value. The target columns of these rule types are often used to define subtypes, as discussed in Chapter 10. These subtypes are in turn used to conditionally fire other business rules in batch processes. Thus, the rule types to populate indicator values and code values are very important topics in business rules engine design.

Setting a Value for an Indicator

An indicator is a column that shows some kind of state that either exists or does not exist. In this book, all such columns are considered to have the datatype Character (1); a value of "Y" indicates existence, and any other value indicates nonexistence. An alternative, but somewhat more restrictive, definition of an indicator is that it is a column that indicates whether a condition is true or false. This implies that the name of the column is formulated as a condition, which may not always be easy to do. Indicators may also be physically implemented in a number of ways that are different from the technique used in this book, but the same basic pattern holds.

Indicators must always be distinguished from reference data code values. The latter indicate a variety of valid states, rather than existence. Some reference data codes have only two states (e.g., "Active" and "Inactive") and are often confused with indicators. With an indicator, the condition of existence is usually used to trigger special business rules, and the condition of nonexistence is not used to trigger any special business rules. In the case of reference data code values, each different value can trigger special business rules, even if there are only two such values.

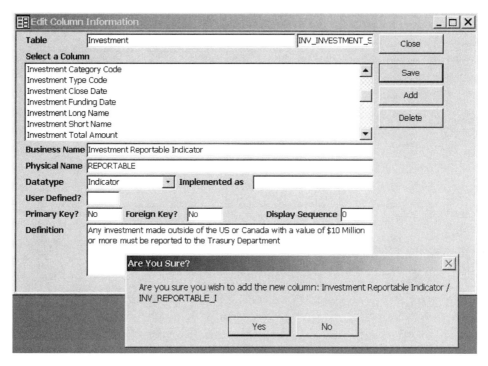

FIGURE 18.1
Adding the Column *Investment Reportable Indicator*

Let us suppose that the U.S. Treasury Department informs Big Bubble Brokers that it must report to the department all investments that are not domiciled in the United States or Canada and that have been funded with $10,000,000 or more of BBB's capital. This new requirement must be complied with immediately. BBB will need a way to track such investments. An indicator is an ideal way to do this. It can be quickly added to the database using the functionality discussed in Chapter 13, as shown in Figure 18.1.

This illustrates the need that often arises to extend the database hand-in-hand with implementing new business rules, and the value of building the functionality that provides this capability.

The new *Investment Reportable Indicator* will have a value of "Y" if the investment is outside of the United States or Canada and BBB has invested $10,000,000 or more in it. Let us now consider the definition interface for the required rule type.

Selecting the Rule Type

As before, the starting point for defining the new rule will be the Business Rules Summary Screen shown in Figure 18.2.

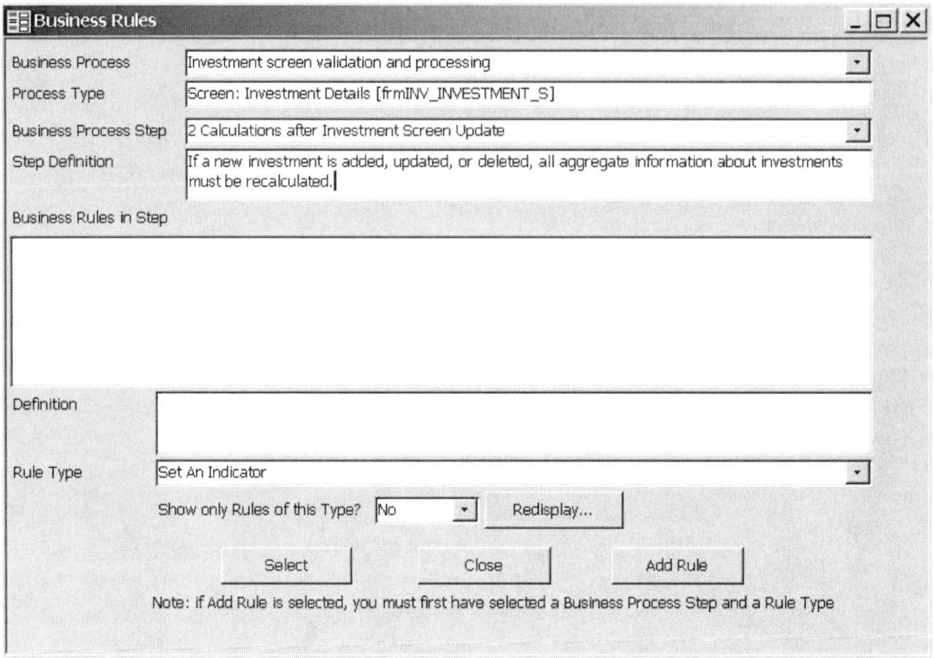

FIGURE 18.2
Business Rules Summary Screen

The rule type **Set An Indicator** is selected for the business process step **Calculations after Investment Screen Update**, and the **Add Rule** button is pressed. At this point the system knows what the base table associated with the business process step is. It also knows how to distinguish indicators from other kinds of columns.

There needs to be a design decision as to whether indicator columns in tables that are parents (or grandparents or great-grandparents) of the base table can be updated by the **Set An Indicator** rule type. The decision made here is that this will not be permitted. One reason is that indicators in parent tables cannot reliably be set based on rules firing for every individual record in the base table (which is how the generated code will implement the executable rules). When one record in the base table is processed the rule may fire and update the indicator in the parent table to "Y." The next record in the base table may cause the indicator to be set to "N." The rules engine designer must decide if a rule type can update columns in the base table, or in the base table and its parent tables. The decision made here regarding indicator columns may not match the requirements in every situation. As discussed before, requirements must drive design. There is no simple "right way."

The screen shown in Figure 18.3 will only display if the user tries to add a new rule. It permits the user to select the appropriate target indicator column for the new

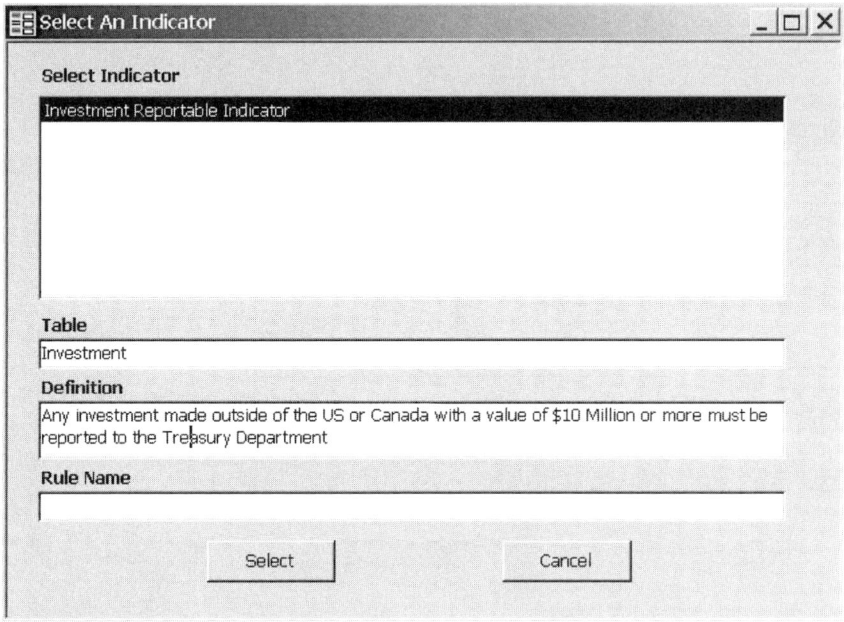

FIGURE 18.3
Choose an Indicator Column

business rule. Only indicator columns from the base table are displayed, although the rules engine has the functionality to display indicator columns from parent tables if this is needed. If the user clicks on a column that already has a **Set An Indicator** rule for it, the *Rule Name* field at the bottom of the screen is populated. After the user selects an indicator column and presses the **Select** button, the rule type definition screen appears.

If the user selects a rule on the business rule definition screen, rather than trying to add the new rule, the screen shown in Figure 18.3 does not appear. Instead the rule type definition screen appears.

The Rule Type Definition Screen

The definition screen for the rule type **Set An Indicator** is shown in Figure 18.4.

This screen permits a user to set a condition that will result in the *Investment Reportable Indicator* being populated with the value "Y." The condition is entered in the four rows of controls that appear under the text "Set the value of this indicator to 'Y' if the following is true". Essentially, each row lets the user select a source column and match it to a value for the source column. If the selected source column is an

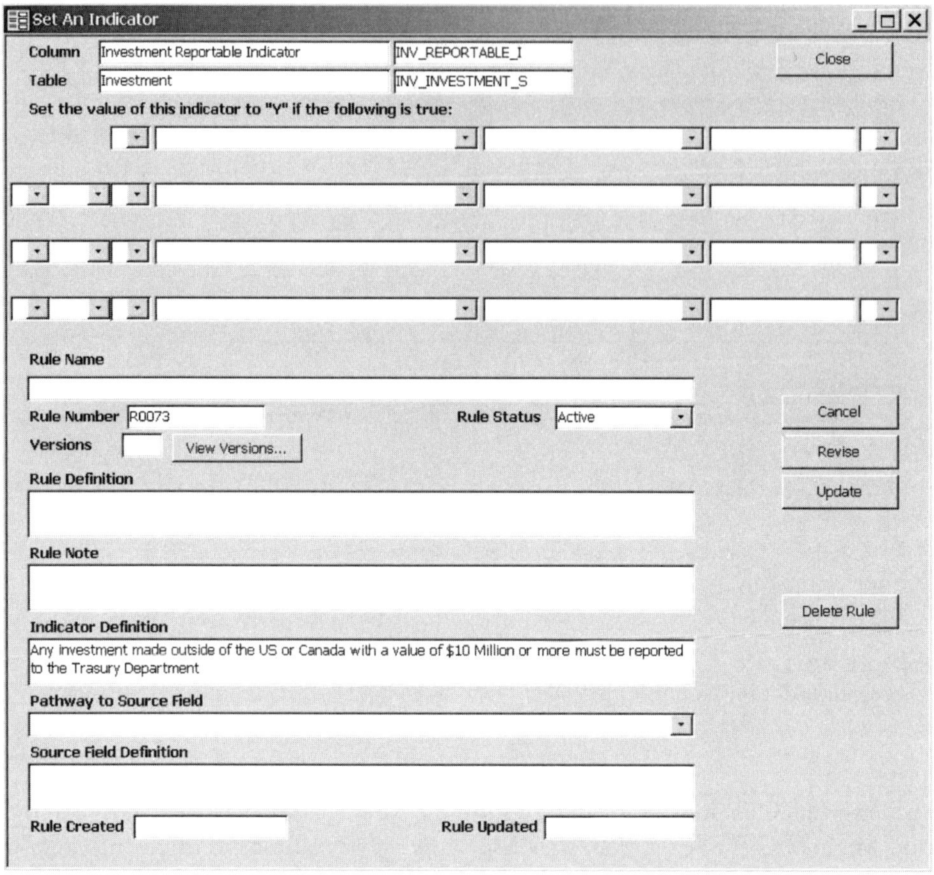

FIGURE 18.4
Set An Indicator Rule Type Definition Screen

indicator or reference data code value, the user is presented with a list of possible values. Otherwise, users must directly enter the value to match to the selected source column. This means that users do not have to know (or guess) the codes that are contained in the many reference data tables in the application. Such a design not only makes the screen easy for the users to work with, but also prevents bad rules definitions due to incorrect codes. Above all, it means that users do not have to type in reference data code values. Rules engines that force users to do this are not only difficult to use and error prone—they also lose the capacity to track what rules individual reference data codes are used in.

The following are the controls on the first row:

1. A combo box containing a parenthesis and blank
2. A combo box containing a list of all columns in the base table and its parent tables
3. A combo box containing comparators (e.g., "equals", "does not equal", "is less than")
4. A text box where a value can be entered
5. A combo box containing a parenthesis and blank

The second, third, and fourth rows each have the following controls:

1. A combo box containing a parenthesis and blank
2. A combo box containing comparators ("and" and "or")
3. A combo box containing a parenthesis and blank
4. A combo box containing a list of all columns in the base table and its parent tables
5. A combo box containing comparators (e.g., "equals", "does not equal", "is less than")
6. A text box where a value can be entered
7. A combo box containing a parenthesis and blank

The way these four rows work is illustrated in Figure 18.5.

- The combo boxes containing parentheses are used to group subconditions.
- When the combo box containing the source columns is used to select a column, the rules engine determines whether the selected column is for an indicator or a reference data code value, or for some other kind of column.

    If the selected column is an indicator or reference data code value, two new combo boxes and a button labeled **Lookup . . .** appear just underneath the first row. The first combo box contains all the data values in the reference table associated with the source column that the user has chosen. If the selected source column is an indicator, this combo box contains a "Yes" and a "No." The subsequent combo box contains a parenthesis and blank. The **Lookup . . .** button is used to see more details of the reference data table.

    If the selected column is an indicator or reference data code value, the controls following the comparator text box are suppressed.

- The comparator combo box is used to select the condition that matches the selected source column to the value.
- If the selected source column is neither an indicator nor a reference data code value, then a text box follows the comparator combo box. The user must enter

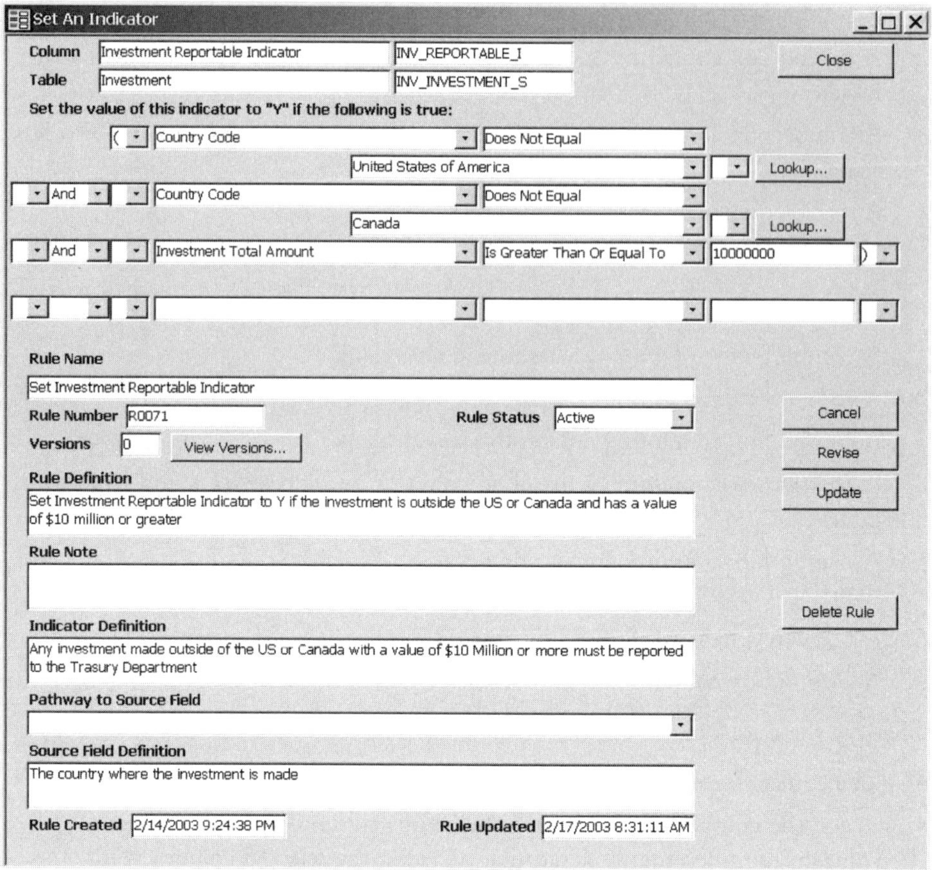

FIGURE 18.5
Rule for Setting *Investment Reportable Indicator*

a value in this combo box consistent with the datatype of the selected source column.

- There are several combo boxes containing just a parenthesis and a blank. There are used to provide logical groupings within the overall condition being defined.

The purpose of this screen design is to enable to user to enter a complex "if" condition that compares between one and four source columns with specific values. A higher-level goal is to avoid rule type definition interfaces that look like query expression builders. All definition interfaces should be independent of any programming languages. This means that users should not be required, or even have the opportunity, to type any kind of programming syntax into the interface. Thus, the only item that users can type into the interface shown in Figure 18.5 is a value to match against a selected source column that is not an indicator or reference data value.

The **Set An Indicator** rule definition interface also utilizes a good deal of metadata to help users understand what they are doing:

- **Indicator Definition:** This shows the attribute definition of the selected indicator (the target of the rule).

- **Source Field Definition:** When the user clicks on a combo box for a source column, the system finds the definition of the selected source column and displays it in this field.

- **Lookup . . . :** When this button is pressed, the screen shown in Figure 18.6 appears. This screen shows information about the reference data table associated with the source column the user has selected. The description column for each record in the reference table is displayed in the list box. When the user clicks on an item in this list box, the code and definition for the selected record are displayed in the lower part of the screen. This gives users full insight into the reference data table, enabling them to use it correctly. It is

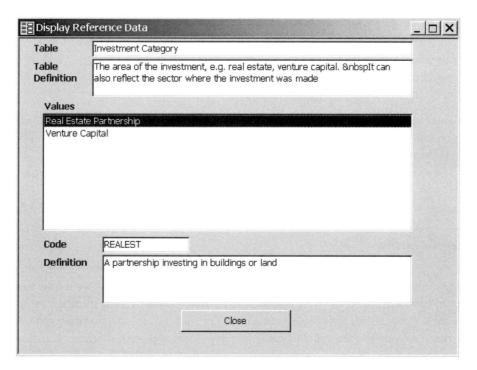

FIGURE 18.6
Display of Reference Data

extremely important to provide this kind of functionality in rules engine design, because reference data tables are important drivers for business rules.

There are a number of edit validations that have to be carried out on the **Set An Indicator** screen:

- If a source column is selected on any row, then a comparator must also be selected and a value must be entered. The value must be either entered directly as data or, if the column is an indicator or reference data code value, selected from the list provided.

- For a source column that is not an indicator or reference data code value, the value that is entered must be a valid representation for the datatype of the selected source column.

- The total number of right parentheses must equal the total number of left parentheses.

- The **Set An Indicator** rule is duplicated if there are two rules governing the population of the same indicator column. The design of the rule type definition interface prevents this, so there is no need to implement an edit check for rule duplication.

- No source column list can contain the column that is the target column of the current rule. This is very important. If it is not implemented, then any rule can contain an internal circular reference. Rather than implement this as an edit check, the combo boxes that list the source columns are built in such a way that the target column is excluded.

There are, of course, other edit checks for general business rule metadata that have been considered in previous chapters—for example, a rule name must be entered. The edit checks that are specific to this rule type are not too difficult to program.

The four rows on the rule type definition screen may not be enough for all rules. If necessary the number of rows can be increased.

Using Pathways

The concept of pathways was introduced in Chapter 10, and it will be recalled that a pathway is a chain of relationships between two tables. Most often there is only one chain of relationships between two tables, but sometimes there can be more than one. This can be a problem for a rule type that takes source columns from any parent of a base table, as the **Set An Indicator** rule type does. Sooner or later a situation will be encountered where a source column is needed from a table that can be reached by more than one pathway from the base table.

Figure 18.7 is the data model for the business area of the sample application.

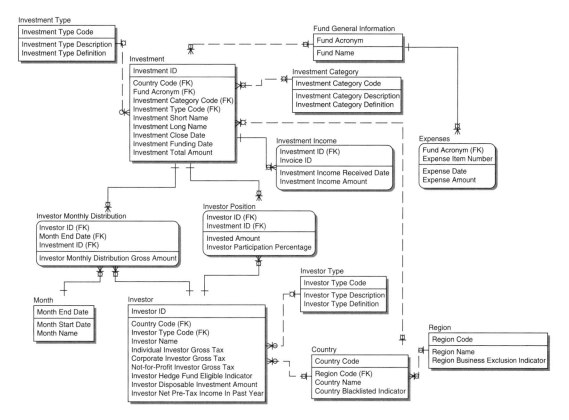

FIGURE 18.7
Data Model of Business Area of Sample Application

Suppose that a user to adds a new column called *Investment Position Alert Indicator* to the table **Investor Position**. The user next defines a rule to populate the new column as shown in Figure 18.8.

The new rule utilizes source columns from the **Country** table. However, as shown in Figure 18.7 there are two pathways to get from **Investor Position** to **Country**. One pathway is via **Investment**, and the other pathway is via **Investor**. The user must specify which pathway to use. This is done using the combo box *Pathway to Source Field*. When the user clicks on a source column combo box, *Pathway to Source Field* is rebuilt to contain all pathways from the base table to the table containing the source field. If the source column is in the **Investor Position** (the same table as the target column) there are no pathways, and the *Pathway to Source Field* combo box is left empty. If the source column is in a table that only has one pathway to the base table (the majority of cases), the *Pathway to Source Field* combo box is populated, and the

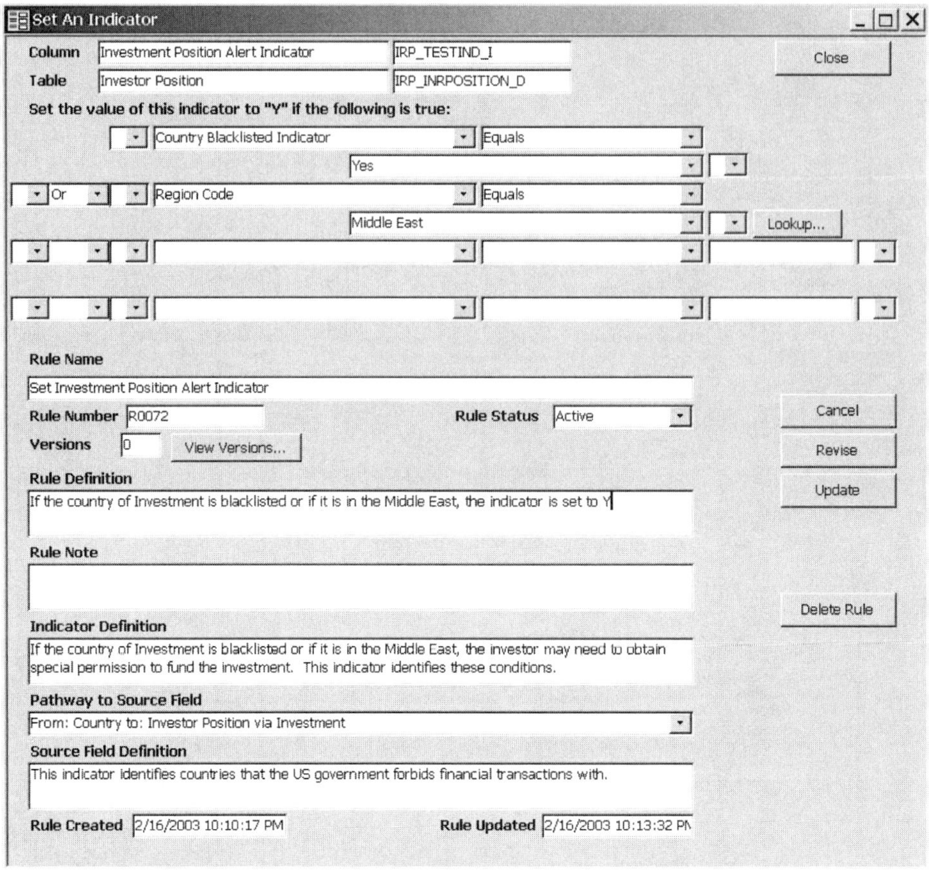

FIGURE 18.8
Set An Indicator Rule Type Definition Where Pathways Are Relevant

system records the single available pathway. If the source column is in a table with more than one pathway to the base table, then the *Pathway to Source Field* table is populated, and if the user has not yet selected a pathway, a warning message is displayed asking the user to select a pathway.

Since it is relatively rare for users to need to select a pathway, there is only one *Pathway to Source Field* combo box, rather than one per source column row. This single combo box applies to the source field that the user is currently working with, rather like the *Source Field Definition* text box.

The *Pathway to Source Field* combo box serves one other purpose. It will be noted that the **Investor** table and **Investment** table each contain a column called *Country*

Code. Thus, in any list of columns from the two tables, *Country Code* will appear twice, which is confusing. One solution would be to rename the columns to *Investment Country Code* and *Investor Country Code*, and indeed this may be the best solution. However, until that is done, the *Pathway to Source Field* combo box can remove potential confusion because it shows the table from which the source column originates. This is a result of the method used to construct pathway names in the sample application. Every pathway name contains the names of the two tables at either end of the pathway.

The rules engine designer may not wish to opt for this particular solution to the problem of duplicate column names in table hierarchies, but the problem is real and can be found in nearly every data model. It needs to be addressed. The issue of defining pathways within rules is even more critical since it directly affects the way in which the rules engine navigates the database to obtain source values. Again, the rules engine designer may not opt for a solution like the one presented here, but the issue must be addressed in such a way that the rules engine can function.

Changes to Repository Tables

There is clearly more metadata for the **Set An Indicator** than has been required for previous rule types. The parentheses, comparators, selected reference data values, and data-entered values on this screen are all new. They need to be stored on the **Business Rule Component (BRC_BIZRULECOMP_M)** table, since they are associated with source columns for the rule. To accommodate them, five new columns have been added to this table:

- *Business Rule Component Pre-Text*. This stores all items that occur before the source column. It includes parentheses and Boolean operators that come before the source column combo box. They are concatenated in this column.

- *Business Rule Component Operator Text*. This stores the comparator value.

- *Business Rule Component Post-Text*. This stores the data-entered value (where a source column is not an indicator or reference data code value) and the parenthesis (if any) that follows it.

- *Business Rule Component Reference Value*. This stores any selected reference data value or indicator value.

- *Pathway Code*. This stores the code that identifies the pathway associated with the source column. If the source column resides in the base table this value is null.

Figure 18.9 shows the new structure of the **Business Rule Component** entity, and Table 18.1 shows its physical implementation.

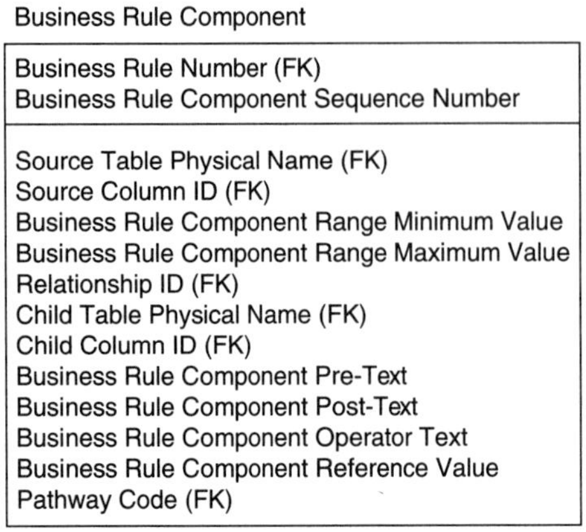

Business Rule Component

| Business Rule Number (FK) |
| Business Rule Component Sequence Number |

| Source Table Physical Name (FK) |
| Source Column ID (FK) |
| Business Rule Component Range Minimum Value |
| Business Rule Component Range Maximum Value |
| Relationship ID (FK) |
| Child Table Physical Name (FK) |
| Child Column ID (FK) |
| Business Rule Component Pre-Text |
| Business Rule Component Post-Text |
| Business Rule Component Operator Text |
| Business Rule Component Reference Value |
| Pathway Code (FK) |

FIGURE 18.9
Enhanced **Business Rule Component** Entity

ATTRIBUTE LOGICAL NAME	COLUMN PHYSICAL NAME	COLUMN DATATYPE
Business Rule Number	BRULE_NUMBER_C	Character (5)
Business Rule Component Sequence Number	BRC_SEQUENCE_N	Integer
Source Table Physical Name	TAB_PHYSNAME_T	Character (50)
Source Column ID	COL_C	Character (4)
Business Rule Component Range Minimum Value	BRC_RANGEMINVAL_T	Character (20)
Business Rule Component Range Maximum Value	BRC_RANGEMAXVAL_T	Character (20)
Relationship ID	REL_C	Character (4)
Child Table Physical Name	TAB_PHYSNAME_T	Character (50)
Child Column ID	COL_C	Character (4)
Business Rule Component Pre-Text	BSC_PRE_T	Character (50)
Business Rule Component Post-Text	BSC_POST_T	Character (50)
Business Rule Component Operator Text	BSC_OPER_T	Character (20)
Business Rule Component Reference Value	BSC_REFVALUE_T	Character (50)
Pathway Code	PWAY_C	Character (4)

TABLE 18.1 Structure of Table **BRC_BIZRULECOMP_M (Business Rule Component)**

The table that contains prior versions of business rule components must also be changed. This is **Business Rule Component Version (BRCV_BIZRULECOM PVER_M)**, and it has the five new columns added to it also.

Updating the *Subtype Table*

In Chapter 10 the need to manage subtypes was discussed. In the design approach recommended in this book, subtypes are identified by an individual indicator or reference data value. The column that is the indicator or reference data value column is called the *Subtype Discriminator Column*. The value in the *Subtype Discriminator Column* that identifies a particular subtype is called the *Subtype Discriminator Value*. Both *Subtype Discriminator Column* and *Subtype Discriminator Value* are located on the **Subtype** table (**STP_SUBTYPE_M**).

If an indicator value or reference data value that is updated by a rule is used to identify a subtype, then it is important to record this fact. Indeed the **Subtype** table does have a *Business Rule Number* column on it that is intended to capture the business rule that is responsible for identifying the subtype. There is little point in defining a subtype and then never creating a business rule to enable the application to identify the records that belong to the subtype. The only exception should be those subtypes that are identified through user data entry.

Thus, when the **Set An Indicator** interface updates the database it must also search the **Subtype** table for the *Discriminator Column* (the *Column ID* of the indicator column). If records in the **Subtype** table are found where the value in *Discriminator Column* is the same as the *Column ID* of the indicator, then *Business Rule Number* (BRULE_NUMBER_C) is populated with the *Business Rule Number* of the current rule.

This ensures that subtypes are correctly managed in the business rules engine.

Deleting a Rule

The **Delete** Button on the **Set An Indicator** rule definition screen removes the association between the current rule and the current business process step. If the currently selected business process step is the only step with which the rule is associated, then the rule can be deleted if the system permits it (see Chapter 17 for a discussion of the controls needed for deleting rules). Otherwise, the rule can only be inactivated. If the rule is deleted or inactivated, then the **Subtype** table is updated to set the *Business Rule Number* in this table to null. If an inactivated rule is made active again, the **Subtype** table is updated yet again to restore the value in *Business Rule Number*.

Code Generation Strategy in Batch Processes

This rule type is the first one we have considered in the context of a business process step that is a batch process. Previously, the rule types were implemented for a screen where only one record was considered at a time. In the context of a batch process, rules must operate on a set of records. That set of records is all the records containing the indicator column for which the **Set An Indicator** rule is being created. In the current example, the indicator column is *Investment Reportable Indicator* in the **Investment** table. Thus, the rule has to process all records in the **Investment** table.

Generally speaking, in batch processes each rule must process all records in the table where the target column is located. However, under some circumstances a rule does not need to process all records in a table. This is not because of anything to do with the rule; rather, it has to do with the business process step. The most common examples are business process steps that deal with periodic data, that is, tables where a date is part of the primary key. For instance, every night a bank may process records in a **Daily Account Activity** database table that has *Account Number* and *Processing Date* as the primary key. Only records for the current day are processed, even though there may be records covering many years. Thus, the business process step controls the set of records with which the business rules within it must work. The rules designer must be aware of the fact that business process steps, particularly those working with periodic data, can restrict the sets of records on which business rules running within such sets work. This requires special code generation techniques. For the moment, however, we shall continue to consider the simpler situation in the current example, where all the records in the **Investment** table are processed.

Another major issue with code generation for batch processes is whether to try to generate a single SQL statement to execute the rule. A single SQL statement can update an entire set of records in a database table in one shot. The alternative is to retrieve all relevant records from the database table and then process them one at a time.

Programmers usually view the single SQL statement more favorably, since it is simpler code and performs much faster. The problem is that business rules with even moderate complexity often cannot be implemented in terms of single SQL statements, and record-at-a-time rather than set-at-time processing is required. Performance may become an issue at this point. However, as discussed earlier, performance issues must be based on facts and requirements, not on aesthetics. If a process takes 2 milliseconds, or 2 minutes, or 2 hours, instead of 1 millisecond, this is not necessarily poor performance. It depends on the time frame within which the enterprise requires the process to run. A process does not have poor performance just because a programmer thinks that it can run faster if it is designed in a completely different way (i.e., by being hand-coded instead of through a business rules approach).

If performance is an issue, it may be necessary to implement as many rules as possible as single SQL statements. Another way to improve performance is to generate stored procedures instead of regular program code. Yet another way is to find a means of not iterating through every record in a table independently for each business rule, but rather to read through all records in a table once and apply relevant business rules within this construct. Thus, code generation techniques may have to be adapted to the context of the business process step. For the current example we shall consider the most flexible and easy-to-implement approach, which is to use record-at-time processing where each business rule operates independently on a set of records.

Rule Dependency and Rule Firing Sequence

In the previous chapters it was possible to arrange in advance the sequence in which rules fired based on rule type. This is because in screen data entry there is a predefined logical sequence for rule types. However, in business process steps that are batch processes, this is simply not possible.

The rules engine must therefore determine the sequence in which the rules will fire. Since the design approach to creating executable rules is to generate program code, the sequence must be determined before the code is generated. The rules will fire in the sequence in which they appear in the code generated for the business process step. In order to do this, the rules engine must determine if the output of one rule is used as an input to another rule. In terms of the design approach used in this book, this means detecting whether the target column of a rule is used as a source column of any other rule that runs in the business process step.

At the same time, the rules engine must detect circular references. These are rules where the target column of one rule is used as the source column of another rule, and the target column of the second rule is used as the source column of the first rule. Actually, circular references more commonly involve a chain of dependent rules, each of which uses the target column of the previous rule as a source column. The final rule in the chain has a target column that is used as a source column in the rule at the start of the chain. Circular references cannot be allowed among the rules in a business process step.

In order to implement rules dependency it is necessary to add one more column to the table **Rules of Business Process Step (RBSP_RULESOFSTEP_M)**. This column is *Rule Sequence Number*, which has a physical name of RBSP_SEQUENCE_N and a datatype of Integer. It shows the sequence in which a rule fires within a given business process step.

The code that determines rule sequence in a business process step and detects circular references is shown in Listing 18.1.

LISTING 18.1
Determining Rule Dependency within a Business Process Step

```
Public Function RuleSequence(strBPSP As String) As String
'*********************************************************************
' Sequences business rules within a business process step.  Also
' detects circular references between business rules.  Updates
' RBSP_SEQUENCE_N in RBSP_RULESOFSTEP_M with sequence number
'
' Parameters: Business Process Step
' Returns: "Y" if no circular references detected; "N" if circular
' references detected.
'*********************************************************************

Dim strText As String, strSQL As String, cmd As ADODB.Command,
lngAffected As Long
Dim rstBPSP As ADODB.Recordset, intCt As Integer, strGo As String,
intLast As Integer
Dim rstLow As ADODB.Recordset

   RuleSequence = "Y"
   Set rstBPSP = New ADODB.Recordset
   Set rstLow = New ADODB.Recordset
   strSQL = "UPDATE RBSP_RULESOFSTEP_M SET RBSP_SEQUENCE_N = 0 " _
          & " WHERE BPSP_PHYSNAME_T = '" & strBPSP & "'"
   Set cmd = New ADODB.Command
   cmd.ActiveConnection = CurrentProject.Connection
   cmd.CommandType = adCmdText
   cmd.CommandText = strSQL
   cmd.Execute lngAffected

   ' Find all rules whose target column is not used as a source
   ' column at all in the current business process step
   strSQL = "SELECT A.* FROM RBSP_RULESOFSTEP_M A, BRULE_BIZRULE_M
B " _
          & " WHERE A.BPSP_PHYSNAME_T = '" & strBPSP & "' " _
          & " AND A.BRULE_NUMBER_C = B.BRULE_NUMBER_C " _
          & " AND B.COL_C NOT IN " _
          & " (SELECT C.COL_C FROM " _
          & " BRC_BIZRULECOMP_M C, RBSP_RULESOFSTEP_M D" _
          & " WHERE C.BRULE_NUMBER_C = D.BRULE_NUMBER_C " _
```

```
                 & " AND D.BPSP_PHYSNAME_T = '" & strBPSP & "') "
        rstBPSP.Open strSQL, CurrentProject.Connection, _
             adOpenKeyset, adLockOptimistic, adCmdText
     Do While Not rstBPSP.EOF
        strSQL = "UPDATE RBSP_RULESOFSTEP_M SET RBSP_SEQUENCE_N = 9999
 "
  _
             & " WHERE BPSP_PHYSNAME_T = '" & strBPSP & "' " _
             & " AND BRULE_NUMBER_C = '" & rstBPSP("BRULE_NUMBER_C")
 & "'"
        cmd.CommandText = strSQL
        cmd.Execute lngAffected
        rstBPSP.MoveNext
     Loop
     rstBPSP.Close

     intCt = 9999
     strGo = "Y"
     intLast = 9999
     Do While strGo = "Y"
        ' Find rules whose target column is used as a source column
        ' in any lower level below the last updated level in the
        ' rule hierarchy
        intCt = intCt-1
        strSQL = "SELECT A.*, B.COL_C FROM RBSP_RULESOFSTEP_M A,
BRULE_BIZRULE_M B " _
             & " WHERE A.BPSP_PHYSNAME_T = '" & strBPSP & "' " _
             & " AND A.BRULE_NUMBER_C = B.BRULE_NUMBER_C " _
             & " AND A.RBSP_SEQUENCE_N <= " & CStr(intCt) _
             & " AND B.COL_C IN " _
             & " (SELECT C.COL_C FROM " _
             & " BRC_BIZRULECOMP_M C, RBSP_RULESOFSTEP_M D" _
             & " WHERE C.BRULE_NUMBER_C = D.BRULE_NUMBER_C " _
             & " AND D.RBSP_SEQUENCE_N = " & CStr(intLast) _
             & " AND D.BPSP_PHYSNAME_T = '" & strBPSP & "') "
        rstBPSP.Open strSQL, CurrentProject.Connection, _
             adOpenKeyset, adLockOptimistic, adCmdText
        If rstBPSP.EOF Then
           strGo = "N"
        Else
           Do While Not rstBPSP.EOF
```

```
            ' Make sure that the target column of the rule is used
            ' ONLY as a source column at the last level processed
            ' in the rule hierarchy
            strSQL = "SELECT COL_C FROM BRC_BIZRULECOMP_M A, " _
                    & " RBSP_RULESOFSTEP_M B " _
                    & " WHERE A.BRULE_NUMBER_C = B.BRULE_NUMBER_C " _
                    & " AND B.RBSP_SEQUENCE_N < " & CStr(intLast) _
                    & " AND B.BPSP_PHYSNAME_T = '" & strBPSP & "'   "
_
                    & " AND A.COL_C = '" & rstBPSP("COL_C") & "'   "
            rstLow.Open strSQL, CurrentProject.Connection, _
                adOpenKeyset, adLockOptimistic, adCmdText
            If rstLow.EOF Then
                strSQL = "UPDATE RBSP_RULESOFSTEP_M SET RBSP_SEQUENCE_N
= " & CStr(intCt) _
                    & " WHERE BPSP_PHYSNAME_T = '" & strBPSP & "' " _
                    & " AND BRULE_NUMBER_C = '" &
rstBPSP("BRULE_NUMBER_C") & "'"
                cmd.CommandText = strSQL
                cmd.Execute lngAffected
            End If
            rstLow.Close
            rstBPSP.MoveNext
        Loop
    End If
    If intCt < 9900 Then
        MsgBox "Too many loops"
        Exit Function
    End If
    intLast = intCt
    rstBPSP.Close
  Loop

  strSQL = "SELECT * FROM RBSP_RULESOFSTEP_M A, BPSP_BIZSTEPPROC_M
B " _
            & " WHERE A.BPSP_PHYSNAME_T = '" & strBPSP & "' " _
            & " AND A.BPSP_PHYSNAME_T = B.BPSP_PHYSNAME_T" _
            & " AND A.RBSP_SEQUENCE_N = 0 "
  rstBPSP.Open strSQL, CurrentProject.Connection, _
        adOpenKeyset, adLockOptimistic, adCmdText
  If Not rstBPSP.EOF Then
```

```
      strText = ""
      RuleSequence = "N"
      MsgBox "Circular references detected in rules in business
process step: " _
            & rstBPSP("BPSP_NAME_T") & ".  Rules concerned will
now be shown. "
    Do While Not rstBPSP.EOF
      strText = strText & rstBPSP("BRULE_NUMBER_C") & "/"
      rstBPSP.MoveNext
    Loop
    rstBPSP.Close
    MsgBox strText
  End If

  Set cmd = Nothing
  Set rstBPSP = Nothing

End Function
```

Generated Code for Simple Set An Indicator Rule

The code generation function for the **Set An Indicator** rule type generates the code shown in Listing 18.2 for the rule example shown in Figure 18.5.

The code loops through every record in the **Investment** (**INV_INVEST-MENT_S**) table and determines whether the conditions are met to update the *Investment Reportable Indicator* with a "Y", or whether it should be updated with an "N."

One particular issue with batch processes that is illustrated here is what to do with source columns that may contain null values. The design approach adopted here is to store each source column value in a variable and then use the variables for the comparisons dictated by the rule. Each variable is initialized with a default value and is only populated with a source column's value if the source column does not contain a null. If this were not done, then the program would crash because Microsoft Access will not permit a null value to be assigned to a variable with a string, numeric, or date datatype. This issue of "null protection" occurs in other code generation environments, too, and is something the rules engine designer must be aware of.

LISTING 18.2
Code Generated for **Set An Indicator** Rule Type

```
Public Function CalcfrmINV_INVESTMENT_S() As String
Dim intErr As Integer, strErr As String, rstSource As
ADODB.Recordset
Dim strSQL As String, strGo As String, strInd As String
Dim strTab As String, strPhysName As String
Dim strSrc1 As String, strSrc2 As String, strSrc3 As String,
strSrc4 As String, strSrc5 As String, strSrc6 As String
Dim dSrc1 As Date, dSrc2 As Date, dSrc3 As Date, dSrc4 As Date,
dSrc5 As Date, dSrc6 As Date
Dim dblSrc1 As Double, dblSrc2 As Double, dblSrc3 As Double,
dblSrc4 As Double, dblSrc5 As Double, dblSrc6 As Double
Dim cmd As ADODB.Command, lngAffected As Long, varMy As Variant
' Last Generated: 2/17/2003 9:46:25 AM

CalcfrmINV_INVESTMENT_S = "Y"
Set rstSource = New ADODB.Recordset
Set cmd = New ADODB.Command
cmd.ActiveConnection = CurrentProject.Connection
cmd.CommandType = adCmdText
  ' Rule: R0073 / User Rule: R0073
  ' Rule Name: Set Investment Reportable Indicator
   ' Target Table:
   '    Investment / INV_INVESTMENT_S
   ' Target Column:
   '    Investment Reportable Indicator / INV_REPORTABLE_I
   ' Source Columns:
   ' Country Code / CTY_C
   ' Country Code / CTY_C
   ' Investment Total Amount / INV_TOTAL_A
   strSQL = "SELECT * FROM INV_INVESTMENT_S "
   rstSource.Open strSQL, CurrentProject.Connection, _
        adOpenKeyset, adLockOptimistic, adCmdText
   Do While Not rstSource.EOF
     strInd = "N"
   ' Set Up Default Values
     strSrc1 = ""
     strSrc2 = ""
     dblSrc3 = 0
     If Not IsNull(rstSource("CTY_C")) Then
```

```
          strSrc1 = rstSource("CTY_C")
        End If
        If Not IsNull(rstSource("CTY_C")) Then
          strSrc2 = rstSource("CTY_C")
        End If
        If Not IsNull(rstSource("INV_TOTAL_A")) Then
          dblSrc3 = rstSource("INV_TOTAL_A")
        End If
         If strSrc1 <> "USA" _
           And strSrc2 <> "CAN" _
           And dblSrc3 >= 10000000 Then
          strInd = "Y"
        End If
        strSQL = "UPDATE INV_INVESTMENT_S SET INV_REPORTABLE_I = '" &
strInd & "'" _
          & " WHERE INV_C = '" & rstSource("INV_C") & "'"
        cmd.CommandText = strSQL
        cmd.Execute lngAffected
        rstSource.MoveNext
     Loop
     rstSource.Close
   Set cmd = Nothing
   Set rstSource = Nothing
   End Function
```

Another problem is that values may have to be surrounded by quotes or other special characters, depending on their implied datatype. Consider the line of generated code

```
If strSrc1 <> "USA" _
```

The value "USA" is being compared to a source column that has a character datatype and thus must be enclosed in quotes. This contrasts with the line of code

```
And dblSrc3 >= 10000000 Then
```

Here the value 10000000 is being compared to a numeric datatype and so must not have any quotes. It is very important to have user-defined values in rules appear in the correct format to match the datatypes of their source columns in the generated code. This is possible because in the **Column** table the column *Datatype Code* can be used to control the format of the generated code to ensure that values respect the datatypes they are supposed to represent.

One other important aspect of this code is that the value of "N" is a default value. Unless the overall condition that makes up the rule is true for a given record, that record will have a value of "N" assigned to its *Investment Reportable Indicator*. A bad design would be not to change the value of *Investment Reportable Indicator* unless the overall condition was found to be true. This would let the value of *Investment Reportable Indicator* that was present when the rule was last run remain unchanged. Yet the rule could have been changed or, more likely, the data for that record could have changed. Suppose a record had a value of "Y" for *Investment Reportable Indicator* the last time the rule was run, and the next time the rule was run the overall condition of the rule was found to be false. If the rule does not update *Investment Reportable Indicator* with an "N" then it is creating an error. The rule in Listing 18.2 does correctly update *Investment Reportable Indicator* with an "N." This issue may seem fairly obvious in the context of the **Set An Indicator** rule type, but it is more difficult to deal with in the rule type **Set A Reference Data Code Value**.

Using Pathways in Generated Code

Figure 18.8 presents an example of a rule that needs to have pathways defined for it. The generated code for this rule is shown in Listing 18.3.

LISTING 18.3
Set An Indicator Rule with Source Columns in Parent Tables

```
Public Function CalcInvPart() As String
Dim intErr As Integer, strErr As String, rstSource As
ADODB.Recordset
Dim strSQL As String, strGo As String, strInd As String
Dim strTab As String, strPhysName As String
Dim strSrc1 As String, strSrc2 As String, strSrc3 As String,
strSrc4 As String, strSrc5 As String, strSrc6 As String
Dim dSrc1 As Date, dSrc2 As Date, dSrc3 As Date, dSrc4 As Date,
dSrc5 As Date, dSrc6 As Date
Dim dblSrc1 As Double, dblSrc2 As Double, dblSrc3 As Double,
dblSrc4 As Double, dblSrc5 As Double, dblSrc6 As Double
Dim cmd As ADODB.Command, lngAffected As Long, varMy As Variant
' Last Generated: 2/17/2003 9:50:19 AM

CalcInvPart = "Y"
```

```
Set rstSource = New ADODB.Recordset
Set cmd = New ADODB.Command
cmd.ActiveConnection = CurrentProject.Connection
cmd.CommandType = adCmdText
 ' Rule: R0072 / User Rule: R0072
 ' Rule Name: Set Investment Position Alert Indicator
  ' Target Table:
  '    Investor Position / IRP_INRPOSITION_D
  ' Target Column:
  '    Investment Position Alert Indicator / IRP_TESTIND_I
  ' Source Columns:
  ' Country Blacklisted Indicator / CTY_BLACKLIST_I
  ' Region Code / RGN_C
  strSQL = "SELECT * FROM IRP_INRPOSITION_D "
  rstSource.Open strSQL, CurrentProject.Connection, _
        adOpenKeyset, adLockOptimistic, adCmdText
  Do While Not rstSource.EOF
    strInd = "N"
  ' Set Up Default Values
    strSrc1 = ""
    strSrc2 = ""
    varMy = GetParentValue(rstSource, "IRP_INRPOSITION_D", _
            "CTY_COUNTRY_R", "0043", 0, "0049")
    If Not IsNull(varMy) Then
      strSrc1 = CStr(varMy)
    End If
    varMy = GetParentValue(rstSource, "IRP_INRPOSITION_D", _
            "CTY_COUNTRY_R", "0044", 0, "0049")
    If Not IsNull(varMy) Then
      strSrc2 = CStr(varMy)
    End If
    If strSrc1 = "Y" _
       Or strSrc2 = "ME" Then
      strInd = "Y"
    End If
    strSQL = "UPDATE IRP_INRPOSITION_D SET IRP_TESTIND_I = '" &
strInd & "'" _
       & " WHERE INR_C = '" & rstSource("INR_C") & "'" _
      & " AND INV_C = '" & rstSource("INV_C") & "'"
    cmd.CommandText = strSQL
    cmd.Execute lngAffected
```

```
        rstSource.MoveNext
    Loop
    rstSource.Close
Set cmd = Nothing
Set rstSource = Nothing
End Function
```

Unlike the rule discussed in the previous section, this rule requires access to source columns that are located in parent tables and not in the base table. The way that this is accomplished is via the function GetParentValue(). This function navigates up the selected pathway to the parent table in which the desired source column resides. It then finds the appropriate row in the parent table based on the current row being processed in the base table. Having found the correct row, it returns the value of the desired source column back to the generated code in Listing 18.3. The program code for GetParentValue() is shown in Listing 18.4.

There are some important design points about GetParentValue().

- GetParentValue() actively uses the Business Rules Repository. It is unlike any of the generated code discussed so far, which could run (but could not be generated) without the Business Rules Repository being part of the overall application.

- GetParentValue() is recursive. It calls itself for every level it has to go through in the chain of relationships that form the pathway. Some programming languages have limits on the number of recursive levels at which a function can be called. The rules designer must ensure that the maximum levels encountered in any pathway cannot exceed the number of recursive levels permitted by the programming language used for the rules engine.

As it happens, there are a multitude of techniques that can be used to implement pathways in business rules engines, and the solution shown here is only one such approach. What is particularly important is that the rules engine designer must decide if the Business Rules Repository will be used in rule definition and code generation, but not in rule execution. There are implications to tying the Business Rules Repository to rule execution—for example, an executable version of the application cannot be distributed without the Business Rules Repository. The rules engine designer must be aware of such implications, which must match the requirements for the rules engine that is being built.

Another issue is that different methods used to implement pathways have different performance characteristics. The rules engine designer may not agree with a method that actively uses the Business Rules Repository because it is slower than is required for their rules engine.

LISTING 18.4
GetParentValue() Function

```
Public Function GetParentValue(rstCurr As ADODB.Recordset, strStTab
As String, _
   strDestTab As String, strCol As String, intLevel As Integer,
strPath As String) As Variant
'*******************************************************************
' Returns a value of a specified column from its table, based on a
' call from a routine that has opened a child table and is
' current on one particular row in that child table
'
' Parameters:
' rstCurr = The currently open recordset.  This is originally the
'              recordset for the child table at the other end of
'              the pathway.
'              However, GetParentValue() opens all intermediate
'              tables as it issues recursive calls as it navigates
'              up the pathway, and these are also contained in this
'              recordset.
' strStTab = The child destination table at one end of the pathway
' strDestTab = The parent destination table at the other end of
' the pathway
' strCol = The Column ID of the column that is being sought
' intLevel = The current level in the pathway in this iteration of
'              GetParentValue()
' strPath = The Pathway ID of the selected pathway between the
'              child table and the parent table
'*******************************************************************

Dim strSQL As String, cmd As ADODB.Command, rstRel As
ADODB.Recordset
Dim intMy As Integer, strKey As String, rstPar As ADODB.Recordset
Dim strGo As String, strText As String, strMy As String, strRel As
String
Dim lngAffected As Long, intCt As Integer, strField As String,
strDTTP As String
Dim rstPK As ADODB.Recordset, strJoin As String, strTab As String
Dim strColName As String, strField2 As String
```

```
Set rstRel = New ADODB.Recordset
Set rstPK = New ADODB.Recordset
Set cmd = New ADODB.Command
cmd.ActiveConnection = CurrentProject.Connection
cmd.CommandType = adCmdText

If intLevel = 0 Then
  strSQL = "SELECT * FROM PWAY_PATHWAY_M    " _
        & " WHERE PWAY_C = '" & strPath & "'"
  rstRel.Open strSQL, CurrentProject.Connection, _
      adOpenKeyset, adLockOptimistic, adCmdText
  intLevel = rstRel("PWAY_TOTLEVEL_N")
  rstRel.Close
End If

strSQL = "SELECT B.* FROM PWAY_PATHWAY_M A, PWL_PWAYLEVEL_M B "
        & " WHERE A.PWAY_C = B.PWAY_C " _
        & " AND A.PWAY_C = '" & strPath & "' " _
        & " AND B.PWL_N <= " & CStr(intLevel) _
        & " ORDER BY B.PWL_N DESC "
rstRel.Open strSQL, CurrentProject.Connection, _
      adOpenKeyset, adLockOptimistic, adCmdText
strTab = rstRel("TAB_PARENT_T")
strRel = rstRel("REL_C")
strSQL = " SELECT * FROM RKEY_RELKEYATT_M WHERE REL_C = '" _
        & strRel & "'"
rstPK.Open strSQL, CurrentProject.Connection, _
      adOpenKeyset, adLockOptimistic, adCmdText
strJoin = ""
Do While Not rstPK.EOF
  If strJoin <> "" Then
    strJoin = strJoin & " AND "
  End If
  strDTTP = LookColumnCol(rstPK("COL_CHILD_C"), "DTTP_C")
  strField2 = rstPK("COL_CHILDPHYSNAME_T")
  If strDTTP = "DATE" Then
    strJoin = strJoin & " " & rstPK("COL_PARPHYSNAME_T") _
          & " = #" & CStr(rstCurr(strField2)) & "# "
  Else
    If strDTTP = "NUMERIC" Then
```

```
            strJoin = strJoin & " " & rstPK("COL_PARPHYSNAME_T") _
                & " = " & CStr(rstCurr(strField2)) & " "
          Else
            strJoin = strJoin & " " & rstPK("COL_PARPHYSNAME_T") _
                & " = '" & CStr(rstCurr(strField2)) & "' "
          End If
        End If
        rstPK.MoveNext
    Loop
    rstPK.Close
    strJoin = "SELECT * FROM " & strTab & " WHERE " & strJoin
    rstPK.Open strJoin, CurrentProject.Connection, _
          adOpenKeyset, adLockOptimistic, adCmdText
    If Not rstPK.EOF Then
      If strTab = strDestTab Then
        strColName = LookColumnCol(strCol, "COL_PHYSNAME_T")
        GetParentValue = rstPK(strColName)
      Else
        GetParentValue = GetParentValue(rstPK, strStTab, _
          strDestTab, strCol, intLevel-1, strPath)
      End If
      rstPK.Close
    End If
    rstRel.Close
    Set rstPK = Nothing
    Set rstRel = Nothing
    Set cmd = Nothing

End Function
```

Setting a Reference Data Table Value

Setting an indicator value (a "Y" or "N") is very similar to the rule type that is needed to set a value for a column that contains reference data codes. However, this new rule type, **Set A Reference Data Code Value**, does have some differences from the **Set An Indicator** rule type.

INVESTMENT TYPE CODE	INVESTMENT TYPE DESCRIPTION
HIGH	High Risk Investment
MEDIUM	Medium Risk Investment
LOW	Low Risk Investment
UNKNOWN	Unknown Investment Risk Type

TABLE 18.2 Investment Risk Type Table

An example of a target column in the sample application that may be populated with **Set A Reference Data Code Value** rules is **Investment Risk Type Code** (IRKT_C) in the **Investment** table (**INV_INVESTMENT_S**). Like all indicators and reference data code values, this could be populated through user data entry, or via a business rule. Let us for the moment suppose it is to be populated by rules. **Investment Risk Type Code** must be populated with one of the codes in Table 18.2.

The records shown in Table 18.2 are contained in the reference data table **Investment Risk Type** (IRKT_INVRISKTYPE_R), and there is, of course, a relationship between the **Investment Risk Type** table and the **Investment** table. The value "UNKNOWN" is the default value. Default values for reference data were discussed in Chapter 11.

The general design approach to the **Set A Reference Data Code Value** rule type, using **Investment Risk Type Code** as an example, is as follows:

- There must be one rule per target column per value of **Investment Risk Type Code**. This contrasts with the **Set An Indicator** rule type where there can only be one rule per target column. Thus, for a given target column, there must be one rule for every value shown in Table 18.2, with the exception of "UNKNOWN," which is the default reference data code value. If any of these required rules are not defined, there will be some code values in Table 18.2 that can never appear in the target column. Such a state will probably lead to application logic problems.

- In the **Set A Reference Data Code Value** rule type, the rule definition interface must ensure that the user selects a value of **Investment Risk Type Code** for each rule. This is not necessary for the **Set An Indicator** rule type where the target column is populated with a value of "Y" if the condition entered by the user is true.

- The value of **Investment Risk Type Code** that is selected for the business rule must be stored in the business rule. This will require adding a new column to the **Business Rule** table.

- If the conditions entered by the user evaluate to true, the target column should be populated with the value of **Investment Risk Type Code** associated with this rule. Otherwise the column should not be updated.

- This approach will mean that there is a set of rules for populating **Investment Risk Type Co**de. It is assumed that all the rules belonging to this set run in the same business process step. The first of these rules that is executed must set the value of the target column to the default value ("UNKNOWN" in this example) on all records before it executes. This is important if the business process step will be run multiple times. After the business process step has run once there will be no null values left in the target column. However, there could be changes in the data that the rules use to evaluate their conditions, or even to the rules themselves. Perhaps these conditions on one particular record would not be met by any rule, and so none of the rules would update the column. In this case, the value in the target column on this record that was set when the business process step was run previously will remain unchanged, unless it is reset to the default value prior to rerunning the business process step. Incorrect values cannot be allowed to persist from previous rule executions. The best way to avoid this problem is to set all the values in the target column to the default value every time the business process step is rerun, at the point where the first rule to set the target column's value is executed. The default value is stored on the **Table (TAB_TABLE_M)** table as discussed in Chapter 11.

There are, of course, other design approaches to implementing this rule type. However, all designs must contend with the specific issues discussed above that are inherent in this rule type. Now let us look in a little more detail at how the design is implemented.

Additions to the Repository

This rule type requires more metadata to be managed. For each rule it is necessary to know not only what the target column is, but also what the selected reference data code value is, and which reference data table it is associated with. Thus, two other columns need to be added to the **Business Rule (BRULE_BIZRULE_M)** table:

- *Reference Data Table:* The reference data table with which the target column is associated. This is a foreign key from the **Table** table and is the physical name of the reference data table. The physical name of the new column is TAB_REFDATA_T, and it has a datatype of Character (30).

- *Reference Data Value:* The reference data code value that is associated with the rule. A standard in the rules engine is that all code values must be of Character

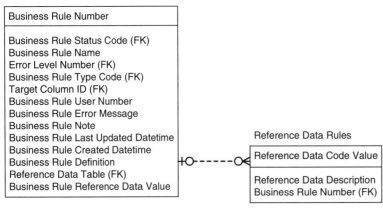

FIGURE 18.10
Reference Data Rules

datatype and have a maximum length of 10. The physical name of the new column is BRULE_REFDATA_T, and it has a datatype of Character (10).

The **Business Rule Version** table also has these new columns added to it.

Since reference data values are found in a great number of small tables in any application database, it is difficult to work with any one of these tables in the context of business rules. Therefore, a table has been added to the Repository for this purpose. The new table is called **Reference Data Rules**, and it is intended as a temporary table to support the rule definition interface for the rule type **Set A Reference Data Code Value**. It simply lists the code values and descriptions of the reference data table with which the rule type is working, together with any rules that have been defined for these code values. This design approach is necessary because reference data is defined in a database as business data (in many different tables), but in a rules engine it sometimes has to be treated as metadata (as if it should be in one table). The design for **Reference Data Rules** is shown in Figure 18.10.

The physical structure of **Reference Data Rules** is shown in Table 18.3.

Selecting a Rule

Once again, the user will begin the rule definition process on the Business Rule Summary Screen shown in Figure 18.2. If the user decides to add a new rule of the type **Set A Reference Data Code Value**, then the screen shown in Figure 18.11 appears.

The screen shown in Figure 18.11 permits the user to select the appropriate target column and reference data code value for the new business rule. The important design elements are as follows:

ATTRIBUTE LOGICAL NAME	COLUMN PHYSICAL NAME	COLUMN DATATYPE
Reference Data Code Value	RDR_C	Character (10)
Reference Data Description	RDR_DESC_N	Character (120)
Business Rule Number	BRULE_NUMBER_C	Character (5)

TABLE 18.3 Structure of Table **RDR_REFDATARULES_M** (Reference Data Rules)

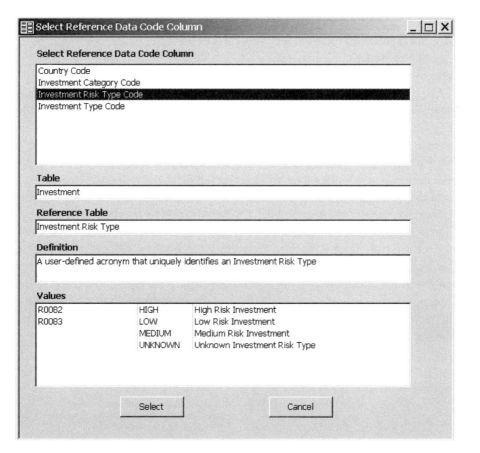

FIGURE 18.11
Select a Reference Data Code Column and Value

- Only columns that are foreign keys from reference data tables are shown. These are identified by a value of "Y" in the column *Column Reference Table PK Indicator* (COL_REFTABPK_I) of the **Column** table. They are shown in the list box Select Reference Data Code Column.

- The screen displays columns only from the base table associated with the currently selected business process step. The rules engine has the functionality to also display columns from parent tables if the designer wants to do this.

- When the user clicks on a column, the other fields on the screen are populated. *Table* shows the name of the table to which the selected column belongs. *Reference Table* shows the name of the reference data table from which the selected table gets its code values. *Definition* is the definition of the selected column.

- The list box Values at the bottom of the screen is also populated when the user clicks on a column in the list box Select Reference Data Code Column. The rules engine determines the reference data table associated with the selected column. This is the value in the **Foreign Key Parent Table (TAB_FKPARENT_T)** of record for the selected column in the **Column** table. Now that the rules engine knows what the associated reference table is, it finds the column that is the primary key of this table, and the column that contains description for each record. These columns are indicated by *Column Primary Key Indicator* (COL_PK_I) and *Column Description Indicator* (COL_DESC_I), respectively, in the **Column** table. The rules engine then selects all records from the reference data table and uses them to populate the **Reference Data Rules** table. Finally, the rules engine determines if there are already business rules defined for any of these values by searching the **Business Rule** table for rules of the type **Set A Reference Data Code Value** where the target column is the column the user has selected on this screen. The reader can explore this series of steps further by looking at the code behind the Select Reference Data Code screen shown in Figure 18.11. This is the form frmSelRefCodeValue in the sample application. If a value does have an associated rule, then the rule number also appears in the Values list box.

- The user must select a value as well as a column before clicking on the **Select** button. When this is done the rule definition screen appears.

The Rule Definition Interface Screen

The rule definition interface screen for the rule type **Set A Reference Data Code Value** is shown in Figure 18.12.

This screen is fairly similar to the rule definition screen for **Set An Indicator**. The major difference is that the selected reference data code value, its description, and its definition are shown at the top of the screen. The conditions that are entered lead to the target column being populated with the selected reference data code value if the conditions evaluate to true when the rule is executed. The rule updates the **Business Rule** table with the selected reference data code value and the reference data table

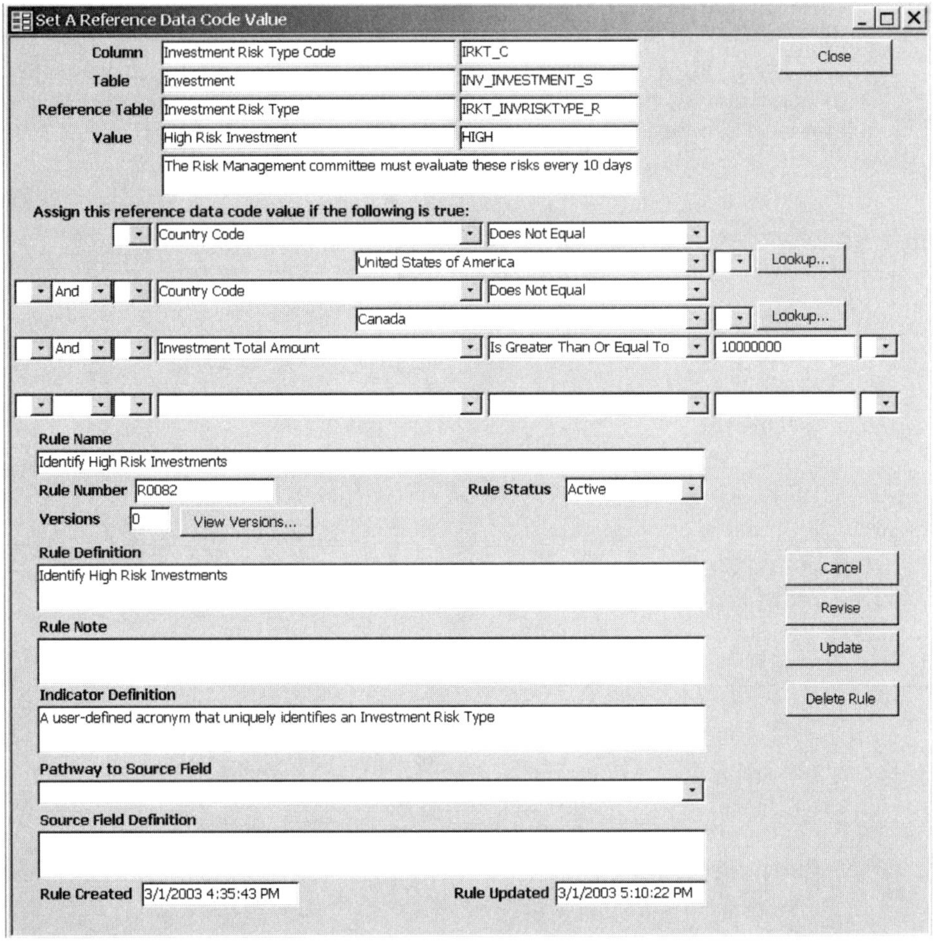

FIGURE 18.12
Definition Screen for Rule Type **Set A Reference Data Code Value**

from which it originated. Other than this the basic functionality is the same as for **Set An Indicator**.

Code Generation

Code generation for the rule type **Set A Reference Data Code Value** is very similar to that for **Set An Indicator**. The main design differences are:

- The target column is updated with a reference data code value, rather than a "Y" or "N."

- The first **Set A Reference Data Code Value** rule for a given target column that runs in a given business process step sets the value of the target column on every record to the default value for the associated reference data table.

These differences can be seen in the generated code in Listing 18.5.

LISTING 18.5
Generated Code for Rule Type **Set A Reference Data Code Value**

```
'CalcfrmINV_INVESTMENT_S----Start
Public Function CalcfrmINV_INVESTMENT_S() As String
Dim intErr As Integer, strErr As String, rstSource As
ADODB.Recordset
Dim strSQL As String, strGo As String, strInd As String
Dim strTab As String, strPhysName As String
Dim strSrc1 As String, strSrc2 As String, strSrc3 As String,
strSrc4 As String, strSrc5 As String, strSrc6 As String
Dim dSrc1 As Date, dSrc2 As Date, dSrc3 As Date, dSrc4 As Date,
dSrc5 As Date, dSrc6 As Date
Dim dblSrc1 As Double, dblSrc2 As Double, dblSrc3 As Double,
dblSrc4 As Double, dblSrc5 As Double, dblSrc6 As Double
Dim cmd As ADODB.Command, lngAffected As Long, varMy As Variant,
strMy As String
' Last Generated: 3/1/2003 5:11:31 PM

CalcfrmINV_INVESTMENT_S = "Y"
Set rstSource = New ADODB.Recordset
Set cmd = New ADODB.Command
cmd.ActiveConnection = CurrentProject.Connection
cmd.CommandType = adCmdText
strMy = LogExecution("CalcfrmINV_INVESTMENT_S", "", 0, "", "SS")
 ' Rule: R0083 / User Rule: R0083
 ' Rule Name: Identify Low Risk Investments
  ' Target Table:
  '    Investment / INV_INVESTMENT_S
  ' Target Column:
  '    Investor Risk Type Code / IRKT_C
  ' Source Columns:
  ' Country Code / CTY_C
  ' Investment Total Amount / INV_TOTAL_A
  strSQL = "UPDATE INV_INVESTMENT_S SET IRKT_C = 'UNKNOWN' "
```

```
   cmd.CommandText = strSQL
   cmd.Execute lngAffected
strSQL = "SELECT * FROM INV_INVESTMENT_S "
rstSource.Open strSQL, CurrentProject.Connection, _
      adOpenKeyset, adLockOptimistic, adCmdText
Do While Not rstSource.EOF
   strInd = "N"
   strSrc1 = ""
   dblSrc2 = 0
   If Not IsNull(rstSource("CTY_C")) Then
     strSrc1 = rstSource("CTY_C")
   End If
   If Not IsNull(rstSource("INV_TOTAL_A")) Then
     dblSrc2 = rstSource("INV_TOTAL_A")
   End If
    If strSrc1 = "USA" _
      And dblSrc2 < 5000000 Then
      strInd = "Y"
   End If
   If strInd = "Y" Then
     strSQL = "UPDATE INV_INVESTMENT_S SET IRKT_C = 'LOW'" _
     & " WHERE INV_C = '" & rstSource("INV_C") & "'"
     cmd.CommandText = strSQL
     cmd.Execute lngAffected
   End If
   rstSource.MoveNext
Loop
rstSource.Close
' Rule: R0082 / User Rule: R0082
' Rule Name: Identify High Risk Investments
 ' Target Table:
 '    Investment / INV_INVESTMENT_S
 ' Target Column:
 '    Investor Risk Type Code / IRKT_C
 ' Source Columns:
 ' Country Code / CTY_C
 ' Country Code / CTY_C
 ' Investment Total Amount / INV_TOTAL_A
strSQL = "SELECT * FROM INV_INVESTMENT_S "
rstSource.Open strSQL, CurrentProject.Connection, _
      adOpenKeyset, adLockOptimistic, adCmdText
```

```
Do While Not rstSource.EOF
  strInd = "N"
  strSrc1 = ""
  strSrc2 = ""
  dblSrc3 = 0
  If Not IsNull(rstSource("CTY_C")) Then
    strSrc1 = rstSource("CTY_C")
  End If
  If Not IsNull(rstSource("CTY_C")) Then
    strSrc2 = rstSource("CTY_C")
  End If
  If Not IsNull(rstSource("INV_TOTAL_A")) Then
    dblSrc3 = rstSource("INV_TOTAL_A")
  End If
   If strSrc1 <> "USA" _
     And strSrc2 <> "CAN" _
     And dblSrc3 >= 10000000 Then
     strInd = "Y"
  End If
  If strInd = "Y" Then
    strSQL = "UPDATE INV_INVESTMENT_S SET IRKT_C = 'HIGH'" _
    & " WHERE INV_C = '" & rstSource("INV_C") & "'"
    cmd.CommandText = strSQL
    cmd.Execute lngAffected
  End If
  rstSource.MoveNext
Loop
rstSource.Close
```

Conclusion

The two rule types discussed in this chapter operate in a batch processing code generation environment and have added to the functionality of the rules engine design. The rule types are somewhat more complex than the rule types discussed in previous sections, particularly with respect to the code generation routines.

Code generation routines tend to be "self-testing" just as a business rules engine in general is "self-documenting." For instance, the **Set An Indicator** rule generation function is fairly complex to develop. However, once it has been coded it can be used to generate many rules. Any problems in the generated rules will be spotted very quickly, leading to corrections in the code generation routine. Generated code is very sensitive, and a slight error will typically lead to a program crash. This high degree of leverage between the code generation routines and the generated code means that once a code generation routine is working correctly it will probably continue to do so. This contrasts with traditional "hand-crafted" code, where not all the logical pathways may be tested, and even those that are tested are only subject to one or a very few individual tests.

With more complex rules, it is also an advantage to have many business rules produced by very similar generated program code. If this program code is examined the similarities stand out. In traditional hand-crafted programs, complex rules tend to be implemented differently every time. Both the design approach and the programming style usually differ with each instance of the rule. This makes the code hard to understand and debug. A code generation routine overcomes these issues with no additional effort on the part of the rules engine designer.

Setting values of indicators and reference data code values are key elements in business rules engines because they permit the identification of subtypes within tables, something that will be taken advantage of in subsequent chapters.

19

IMPLEMENTING RULE TYPES USING RELATIONSHIPS AND SUBTYPES

Thus far the rule types that have been discussed have not used subtypes to restrict update operations. Subtypes are groups of related records that exist within a database table. A subtype nearly always has special business rules that operate on the records that belong to it, but not on the other records in the table. This is why subtypes are so important in any consideration of business rules.

In the design approach followed here a subtype is identified by a single indicator column in the table, or a single value of a reference data code value in a column of the table. There may be complex conditions, expressed in business rules, which lead to the population of the indicator column or the reference data code value that identifies the subtype. Alternatively, the population may come about as the result of direct data entry by users. In any event, having a single data value in one column that identifies a subtype in advance makes it easy to execute the special business rules that apply only to the subtype concerned. If this is not done, the rules engine designer faces the problem of trying to incorporate the logic to identify the subtype within the special rules that operate only on the subtype. Inevitably, this greatly complicates the design of the rule type definition screens, and indeed has a tendency to push their design toward the direct entry of program code. Unfortunately this seems natural for many programmers, who are used to constructs such as the following:

```
If <condition> then
  ...do this
Else
  ...do something different
End if
```

These constructs usually contain more than one business rule, and by their nature it is difficult to create a declarative rule definition interface for them. They also present problems for the separation of rule metadata from executable code. It is to avoid these difficulties that so much of the design of the Business Rules Repository has been geared toward managing subtypes.

In this chapter we shall examine a rule type called **Pay Pro-Rata from Fund to Investment**. This is a rule type that is highly specific to the business of our sample application. In hedge funds and other partnerships it is often necessary to share out profits, expenses, and other monetary amounts among the investors who belong to the fund. Similarly, these monetary amounts also need to be shared out among the things that the fund manages, such as investments. For instance, it may be useful to know what portion of the general operating costs of the fund should be attributed to each investment. This can be compared to the income received from each investment to see if investments are failing to generate enough income to even support the operation of the fund.

This sharing out of a monetary amount from a higher level to a group of participants at a lower level has to be based on some methodology. Most often, the participants have some kind of quantifiable share in the activity at the higher level. Where the participants are investments, and the higher level is the fund, this quantifiable share may be the amount of money placed in each investment as a percentage of all the money placed in all the investments of the fund. This is expressed as a percentage, and by definition all these percentages must add up to 100% at the fund level. In hedge funds and investment partnerships, such percentages are often known as *participation percentages*.

Pay Pro-Rata rules take a monetary amount at a high level (e.g., the fund) and use the participation percentage of each participant (e.g., investment) to allocate a portion of the monetary amount to the participant. The **Pay Pro-Rata from Fund to Investment** rule type adds more specificity by stating that the higher level is represented by the **Fund** table (**FUND_FUND_S**), and the participants are represented by the **Investment** table (**INV_INVESTMENT_S**). The tables involved in the rule type are shown in Figure 19.1.

The rule type works as follows:

- The user identifies a "proceeds" column in the **Fund** table containing the money to be allocated.

- The user identifies a column in the **Investment** table that is a "participation percentage." This tells the rule what percentage of the money in the "proceeds" column in the **Fund** table belongs to each **Investment**.

- Another column in the **Investment** table is identified to hold the result.

Basically the rule computes the result as follows:

Result = Fund Proceeds * Investment Participation Percentage * 0.01

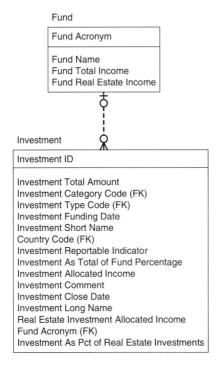

Fund

Fund Acronym
Fund Name Fund Total Income Fund Real Estate Income

Investment

Investment ID
Investment Total Amount Investment Category Code (FK) Investment Type Code (FK) Investment Funding Date Investment Short Name Country Code (FK) Investment Reportable Indicator Investment As Total of Fund Percentage Investment Allocated Income Investment Comment Investment Close Date Investment Long Name Real Estate Investment Allocated Income Fund Acronym (FK) Investment As Pct of Real Estate Investments

FIGURE 19.1

Tables Involved in Rule Type **Pay Pro Rata from Fund to Investment**

The 0.01 is needed to convert the *Investment Participation Percentage* to a ratio, since it is stored as a percentage.

To many people this explanation of **Pay Pro-Rata** rule types in general and the type **Pay-Pro Rata from Fund to Investment** may seem awfully long-winded for such a simple mathematical formula. Yet this is the language that the users utilize, and genuine business concepts lie behind the rule type.

Still, many IT professionals will ask why a general rule type for calculating numbers should not be used instead of the highly specific rule type **Pay Pro-Rata from Fund to Investment**. One answer is that the users would have to enter the full arithmetic expression, and they could get it wrong. In a general calculation rule type, users would be forced to enter syntax, even if it were only mathematical operators. The users could enter incorrect syntax, which is usually very difficult for a rules engine to detect. Yet even a general expression that is syntactically correct may still result in run-time crashes due to user data entry errors. Beyond this, a general expression that runs with no problems may still not be correct from a business perspective—it may generate misleading data. The best way for a rules engine designer to protect against these problems is for the rule types to be as close to declaring the rule as possible rather than entering the mechanics of how it works. This means that the rule type has to be as close to the business as is feasible.

Another advantage of highly specific rules types is that it is possible to reuse the metadata of the rules. For instance, if there is a requirement to list all the participation percentages used in the application, then having specific rule types makes meeting this requirement much easier. If general expressions are used, it is much more difficult to do something like produce a list of participation percentages. In fact, the only recourse may be to undertake reverse engineering. The capacity to utilize metadata specific to rule types is a little understood, but potentially very significant, advantage of the business rules approach.

A natural advantage of having highly specific rule types is that it makes it much easier for a user to work with them to define rules, and it supports the business concepts that users understand. A rules engine should not be designed to turn users into programmers.

Definition Interface for Pay Pro-Rata from Fund to Investment

The starting point for defining a new rule is the Business Rule Selection Screen, as shown in Figure 19.2.

The rule type has previously been associated with the business process step **Calculations after Investment Screen Update** within the business process **Investment screen validation and processing**. After selecting this business process and business process step, the user can select the rule type and press the **Add Rule** button. The rule type definition interface screen then appears, as shown in Figure 19.3.

This screen has the following components:

- *Fund Proceeds to Be Allocated*: This is a list of all numeric columns in the **Fund** table. These are the only columns that can possibly hold a monetary amount. When a column is selected its definition appears in a text box further down the screen.

- *Investment Allocation Percentage*: A list of all numeric columns in the **Investment** table. Only these columns can hold percentages. When a column is selected its definition appears in a text box further down the screen.

- *Investment Field Updated with Result*: A list of all numeric columns in the **Investment** table. When a column is selected its definition appears in a text box further down the screen.

- *Limit by Relationship*: All the relationships between the **Fund** and **Investment** tables are listed in this combo box. This includes relationships from the original data model plus any others that the user may have defined in the rules

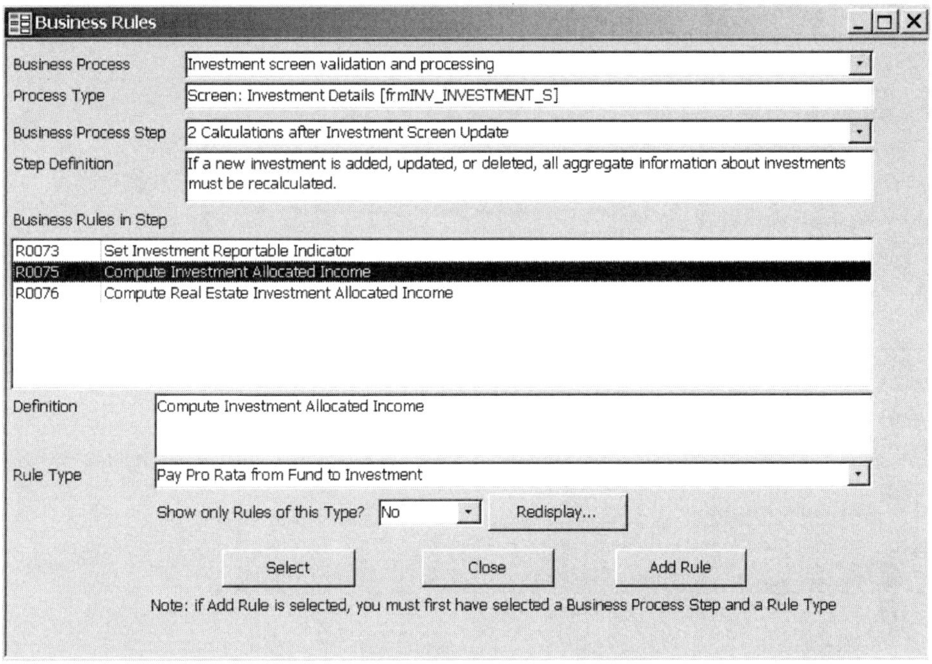

FIGURE 19.2
Define a New **Pay Pro-Rata from Fund to Investment** Rule

engine. As discussed in Chapter 10, these additional relationships can include subtypes in the parent and child tables of the relationship that effectively limit the number of records from either table that participates in the relationship. When a relationship is chosen, its definition appears in a text box further down the screen. If the relationship uses subtypes, the names and definitions of the subtypes appear, also in text boxes further down the screen.

- *Rule Metadata*: A number of screen controls where the user inputs or selects standard rule metadata also appear on the screen.

Other than the standard rule metadata, the only data entry that the user can do is to select the items in the first four combo boxes on the screen: *Fund Proceeds to Be Allocated*, *Investment Allocation Percentage*, *Investment Field Updated with Result*, and *Limit by Relationship*. The user does not have to define any mathematical operation or enter any programming language syntax.

Figure 19.4 shows a completed rule definition.

In the screen shown in Figure 19.4 the basic relationship between **Fund** and **Investment** has been chosen, which, of course, has no subtypes. The three fields chosen in the first three combo boxes of the screen have been added to the **Fund** and

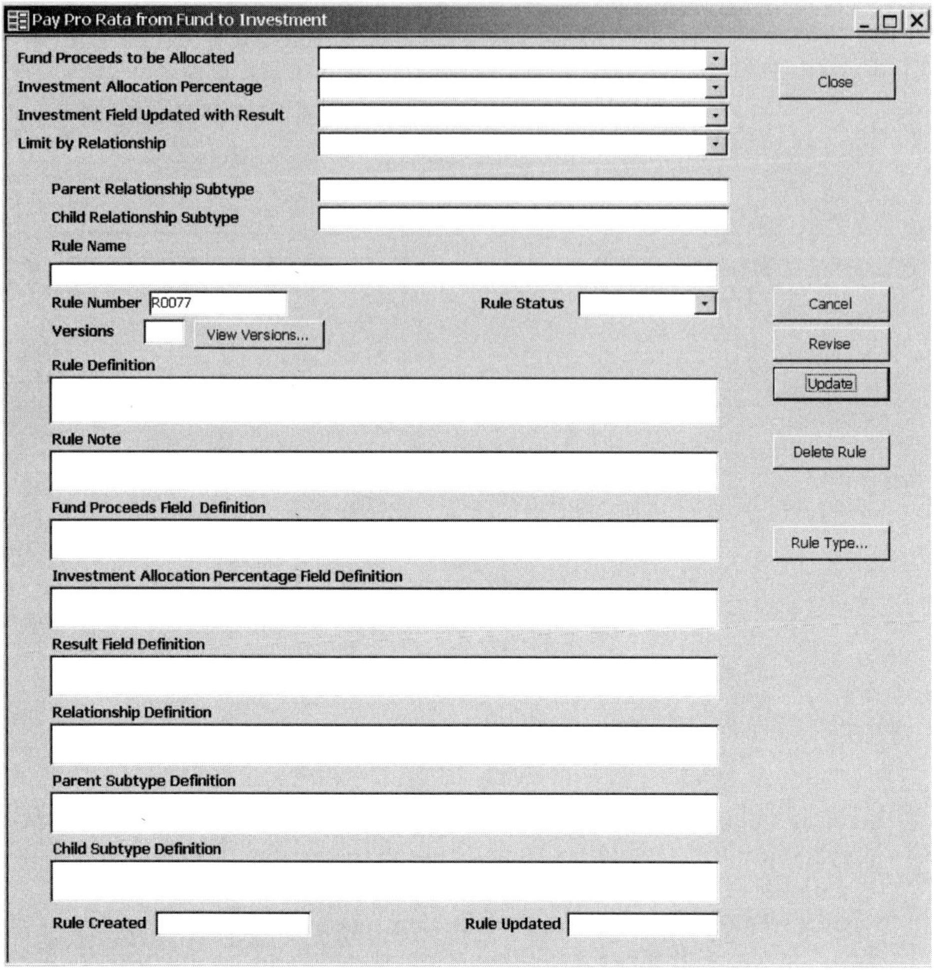

FIGURE 19.3
Definition Interface for Rule Type **Pay Pro-Rata from Fund to Investment**

Investment tables via the column definition interface discussed in Chapter 9—they were not present in the original data model.

Understanding Rule Types

The rule shown in Figure 19.4 states that for each record in the **Investment** table, the column *Investment Allocated Income* will contain an amount pro-rated from the column *Fund Total Income*, taken from the **Fund** record that is the parent of the

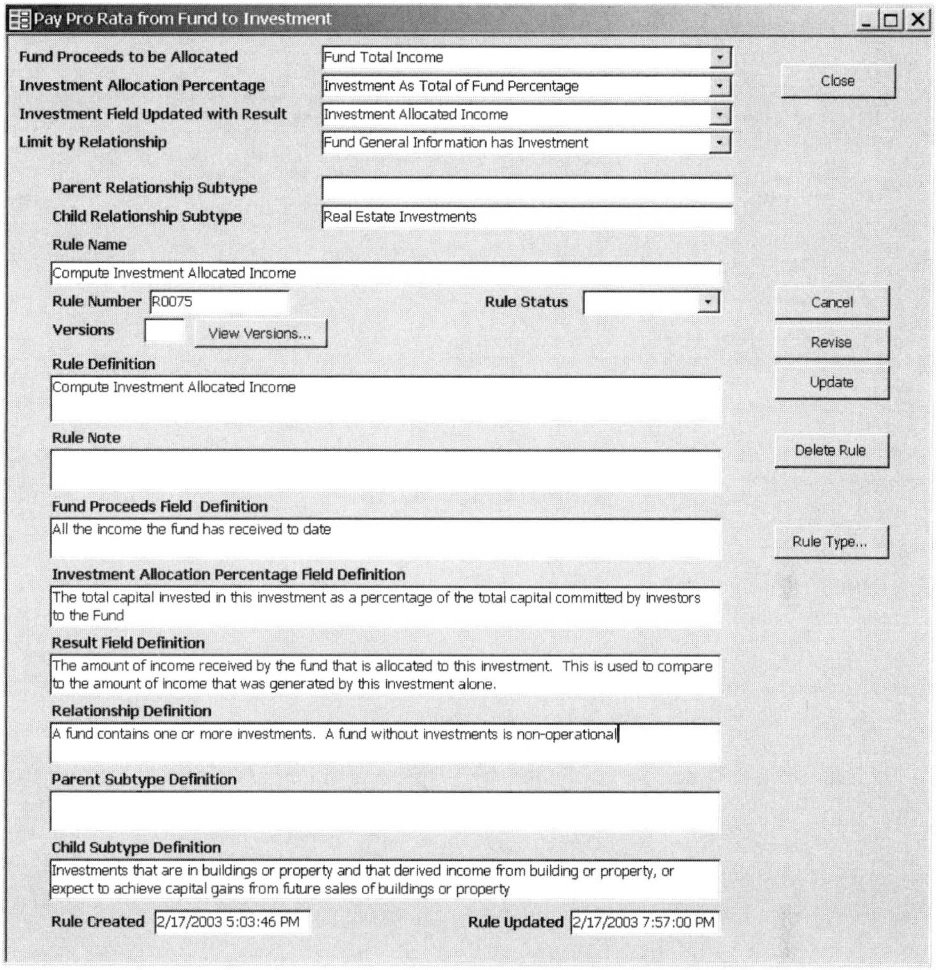

FIGURE 19.4
Rule Defined for **Pay Pro-Rata from Fund to Investment**

Investment record. The column *Investment as Total of Fund Percentage* in the **Investment** table will be the basis for this allocation. The mathematical operation involved is not stated explicitly in the rule definition. It is assumed that it is understood by the user, just as it is assumed that the user understands the business concepts behind this rule type. However, with rule types that are very specific to the business, these are not good assumptions to make. New staff cannot be expected to understand every rule type, and even experienced staff may not deal with all rule types frequently enough to remember all the details about them.

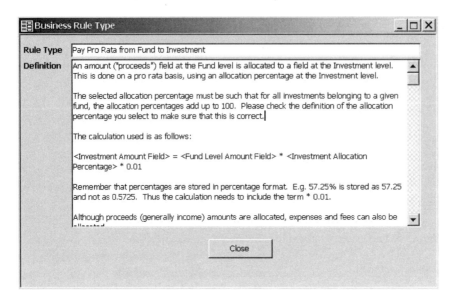

FIGURE 19.5
Definition of Rule Type

These problems can be mitigated by displaying metadata about the rule type. The **Rule Type . . .** button in Figure 19.4 leads to the screen shown in Figure 19.5 when it is pressed.

As the rules engine designer implements rule types that are more and more specific to the business, it becomes increasingly necessary to ensure that users understand how to use these rule types. The information shown in Figure 19.5 may not always be sufficient to achieve this. Therefore, the rules engine designer may find it desirable or even necessary to include additional metadata items in the **Business Rule Type** table (**BRTP_BIZRULETYPE_M**) and to display them on the screen shown in Figure 19.5.

At this point the rule definition interface for this rule type is good enough for users to begin to define rules. The next step is to generate executable code for the rule type.

Code Generation for Pay Pro-Rata from Fund to Investment

The code generated for the rule defined in Figure 19.4 is shown in Listing 19.1.

This code contains some interesting design elements that should be considered:

LISTING 19.1
Generated Code for Rule Type **Pay Pro-Rata from Fund to Investment**

```
Public Function CalcfrmINV_INVESTMENT_S() As String
Dim intErr As Integer, strErr As String, rstSource As
ADODB.Recordset
Dim strSQL As String, strGo As String, strInd As String
Dim strTab As String, strPhysName As String
Dim strSrc1 As String, strSrc2 As String, strSrc3 As String,
strSrc4 As String, strSrc5 As String, strSrc6 As String
Dim dSrc1 As Date, dSrc2 As Date, dSrc3 As Date, dSrc4 As Date,
dSrc5 As Date, dSrc6 As Date
Dim dblSrc1 As Double, dblSrc2 As Double, dblSrc3 As Double,
dblSrc4 As Double, dblSrc5 As Double, dblSrc6 As Double
Dim cmd As ADODB.Command, lngAffected As Long, varMy As Variant
' Last Generated: 2/17/2003 7:58:07 PM

CalcfrmINV_INVESTMENT_S = "Y"
Set rstSource = New ADODB.Recordset
Set cmd = New ADODB.Command
cmd.ActiveConnection = CurrentProject.Connection
cmd.CommandType = adCmdText

  ' Rule: R0075 / User Rule: R0075
  ' Rule Name: Compute Investment Allocated Income
   ' Target Table:
   '    Investment / INV_INVESTMENT_S
   ' Target Column:
   '    Investment Allocated Income / INV_ALLOCINC_A
   ' Source Columns:
   ' Fund Total Income / FUND_TOTINCOME_A
   ' Investment As Total of Fund Percentage / INV_FUNDPCT_A
  strSQL = "SELECT C.*, P.* FROM INV_INVESTMENT_S C, FUND_FUND_S P
"_
        & " WHERE C.FUND_C = P.FUND_C "
  rstSource.Open strSQL, CurrentProject.Connection, _
       adOpenKeyset, adLockOptimistic, adCmdText
  Do While Not rstSource.EOF
  ' Set Up Default Values
    dblSrc1 = 0
    dblSrc2 = 0
    If Not IsNull(rstSource("FUND_TOTINCOME_A")) Then
```

```
            dblSrc1 = rstSource("FUND_TOTINCOME_A")
        End If
        If Not IsNull(rstSource("INV_FUNDPCT_A")) Then
            dblSrc2 = rstSource("INV_FUNDPCT_A")
        End If
        dblSrc4 = 0
        If dblSrc1 <> 0 And dblSrc2 <> 0 Then
          dblSrc4 = dblSrc1 * dblSrc2 * 0.01
        End If
        strSQL = "UPDATE INV_INVESTMENT_S SET INV_ALLOCINC_A = '" &
CStr(dblSrc4) & "'" _
          & " WHERE INV_C = '" & rstSource("INV_C") & "'"
        cmd.CommandText = strSQL
        cmd.Execute lngAffected
        rstSource.MoveNext
    Loop
    rstSource.Close

Set cmd = Nothing
Set rstSource = Nothing
End Function
```

- Since only one relationship is involved in going from the parent table to the child table, and since all columns that the user can select belong only to these tables, pathways are irrelevant to this rule type. Pathways are only relevant where grandparents or parent tables at even higher levels may be involved in the rule.

- The parent and child tables are known in advance, and in this particular example no subtypes occur in the relationship that the user selected. Thus, it is possible to generate a SQL SELECT statement that joins the two tables without any reference to metadata defined by the user. This contrasts with the approach used in the previous chapter where the function GetParentValue() was used to retrieve data values from a parent table. The **Pay Pro-Rata from Fund to Investment** rule type shows how there can be different design approaches for obtaining data from related tables.

- The central mathematical operation is protected from zeroes in any of its terms. This is not really necessary here, but it is necessary when division operations are performed. In division, the rules engine designer must decide what to do if either the numerator or denominator is zero. The relevant code in the above listing is

```
dblSrc4 = 0
  If dblSrc1 <> 0 And dblSrc2 <> 0 Then
    dblSrc4 = dblSrc1 * dblSrc2 * 0.01
  End If
```

The generated code is part of the business process step **Calculations after Investment Screen Update**. This is run when the user accesses the Investment Definition screen and presses either the **Save** button or the **Delete** button. In the sample application this screen is reached by selecting **Application Functions** from the main menu and **Enter Investment Details** from the popup that then appears. The results of the rule firing can be checked by looking at the contents of the **Investment** table using the capabilities to view data discussed in Chapter 14.

Using Subtypes in the Rule Type

Let us suppose that a user wishes to create another rule using the **Pay Pro-Rata from Fund to Investment** rule type. This time, the user just wants to deal with real estate investments. The new rule must allocate all the income the fund receives from real estate investments among the real estate investments in the fund. Figure 19.6 shows the rule that the user creates.

The user has chosen to use the relationship **Fund General Information Has Real Estate Investment**, which limits the **Investment** records appearing in the relationship to those that belong to the subtype **Real Estate Investments**.

The three main advantages of this design are:

- There is no need to have complex conditions to define what a **Real Estate Investment** is as part of this rule definition screen. This is done in a separate rule, or via data entry. Thus, the rule definition interface for **Pay Pro-Rata from Fund to Investment** is kept reasonably straightforward.

- There may be many rules that use the **Real Estate Investment** subtype. There is no need to repeat the conditions identifying the **Real Estate Investment** subtype in all of these rule definitions. If such repetition were necessary, there would be a good chance of variations in the conditions leading to errors in rule execution.

- The rules engine can report on which rules use the **Real Estate Investment** subtype, which may be a considerable advantage for overall management of the application.

The code generated for the rule shown in Figure 19.6 is shown in Listing 19.2.

The way the code generation routine for the rule type deals with subtypes is to amend the SQL SELECT statement generated to read **Fund** and **Investment** records so that the subtype(s) are included. As discussed in Chapter 10, the design approach

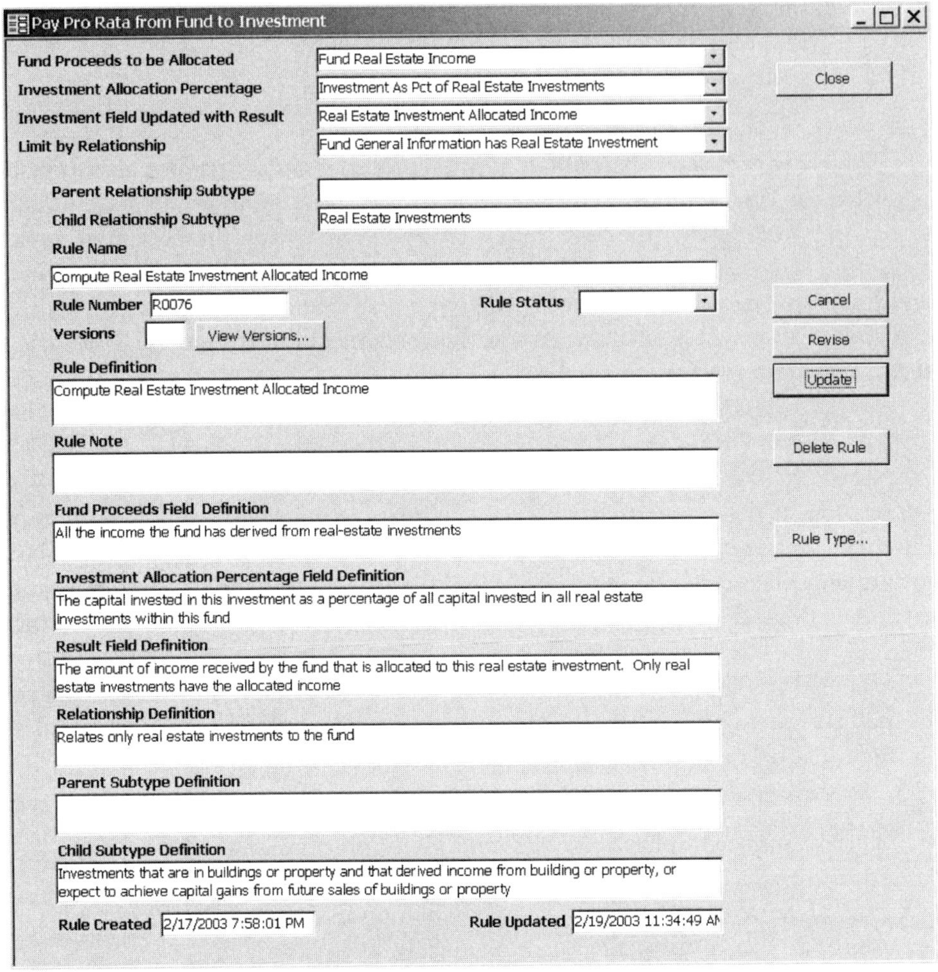

FIGURE 19.6
Using a Relationship with Subtypes

to subtypes is that they are recognized by one value in either an indicator or reference data column. The code generation routine simply needs to pick up the physical name of the column and the associated value and add them to the SQL SELECT statement. This contrasts with trying to use the potentially complex conditions that actually identify the subtype as part of the SQL SELECT statement. Subtypes are recognized by a value in an indicator or reference data code column, but they are identified by a distinct rule.

LISTING 19.2
Generated Code for Rule Using Subtypes

```
' Rule: R0076 / User Rule: R0076
 ' Rule Name: Compute Real Estate Investment Allocated Income
  ' Target Table:
  '    Investment / INV_INVESTMENT_S
  ' Target Column:
  '    Real Estate Investment Allocated Income / INV_REALESTINC_A
  ' Source Columns:
  ' Fund Real Estate Income / FUND_REALESTINC_A
  ' Investment As Pct of Real Estate Investments /
  ' INV_REALESTPCT_A
  strSQL = "SELECT C.*, P.* FROM INV_INVESTMENT_S C, FUND_FUND_S P
"  _
        & " WHERE C.FUND_C = P.FUND_C " _
        & " AND INCT_C = 'REALEST'"
  rstSource.Open strSQL, CurrentProject.Connection, _
      adOpenKeyset, adLockOptimistic, adCmdText
  Do While Not rstSource.EOF
  ' Set Up Default Values
    dblSrc1 = 0
    dblSrc2 = 0
    If Not IsNull(rstSource("FUND_REALESTINC_A")) Then
        dblSrc1 = rstSource("FUND_REALESTINC_A")
    End If
    If Not IsNull(rstSource("INV_REALESTPCT_A")) Then
        dblSrc2 = rstSource("INV_REALESTPCT_A")
    End If
    dblSrc4 = 0
    If dblSrc1 <> 0 And dblSrc2 <> 0 Then
      dblSrc4 = dblSrc1 * dblSrc2 * 0.01
    End If
    strSQL = "UPDATE INV_INVESTMENT_S SET INV_REALESTINC_A = '" _
      & CStr(dblSrc4) & "'" _
      & " WHERE INV_C = '" & rstSource("INV_C") & "'"
    cmd.CommandText = strSQL
    cmd.Execute lngAffected
    rstSource.MoveNext
  Loop
  rstSource.Close
```

Conclusion

This chapter has discussed using relationships, and sometimes these relationships can involve subtypes. Being able to work with relationships is a vital part of any rules engine design, and as has been seen, it is something that arises in a number of different contexts. Subtypes have also been introduced in this chapter, but there are additional concepts that must be understood when subtypes are used. Subtypes can also figure prominently in rules that do not involve relationships. In the next chapter we will continue with the management of subtypes within business rules, but in rules that do not include relationships.

20 RULES WITH SUBTYPES AND BUSINESS METADATA

In the previous chapter subtypes were used in the context of relationships. However, rule types that do not involve relationships can also use subtypes. The components of these rules all come from a single table, and we shall consider an example in this chapter. This again highlights the importance of subtypes when dealing with business rules.

Another aspect of business rules that is not widely appreciated is that if rule types are very specific for the business they support, it becomes possible to associate business-specific metadata with rules. This opens up many new possibilities for managing information within business rules engines that are very difficult to implement in other design approaches.

Calculate A Fee

The rule type that we shall consider in this chapter is called **Calculate A Fee**. Fees are very important to investment partnerships, hedge funds, and all financial vehicles that manage other people's money. They provide a way for the partnership or fund to gather additional income, and they also provide a way for the management of the fund (as opposed to the investors) to earn more money. Thus, these operations tend to charge many different kinds of fees. In general, a fee is computed using the following elements:

- *Fee Base:* This is a sum of money on which a fee is assessed. It can be an invested amount, a flow of funds, or some other amount.
- *Fee Rate:* A percentage that is used to assess the fee.

- *Fee Premium/Discount:* This is a number that is added to or subtracted from *Fee Rate* to adjust it to what the fund manager requires.

Thus, the general calculation of a fee is:

$$Fee = Fee\ Base * (Fee\ Rate + Fee\ Premium/Discount) * 0.01$$

In reality, fees also have one or more time dimensions to them. For instance, they may be annual fees that are paid monthly. Other fees are monthly fees that are calculated on one date and paid on another date. However, to simplify the discussion of fees in this chapter, we shall assume that all the fees we are dealing with are calculated only once and have no time dimensions.

Another issue is that there can be many different types of fees. Some fees are partnership fees, which are charged for just belonging to the partnership. For instance, investors are always charged partnership fees. Servicing fees are another kind of fee, and they are charged for carrying out certain kinds of administrative tasks. For instance, investments require work to service them, such as filing required documents and collecting income streams. Then there are more specialized kinds of fees. For instance, a real estate investment may generate real estate management fees. If the partnership invests in a commercial building, it will charge this fee to the tenants of the building.

Fees are therefore something of the greatest interest to the management of investment partnerships. Management typically categorizes fees into different classes—partnership fees, servicing fees, real estate management fees, and so on. However, from an IT perspective this poses a serious problem. These categories apply to different kinds of fees, but each fee is usually represented by a single column containing an amount. These columns may be found on many different tables in the database. The categorization of fees is a property of the column—it is metadata. It is not usually possible to implement additional tables and columns in a regular business database to classify columns.

Of course, there are ways to get around the problem by changing the design approach. For instance, a **Fee** table could be introduced that has one record for each kind of fee. Then it is a simple matter to categorize each record. A new reference table containing the categorization could then be introduced. However, the fee amounts that were previously on many different tables now have to be placed on the **Fee** table. Some of these fees are paid by investors, and others by investments. It becomes necessary for the **Fee** table to track the primary keys of the records in these tables. This is not at all easy to implement, and it becomes very difficult, if not impossible, to track who or what paid a particular fee amount on the **Fee** table.

This is only one example of a set of problems that involve the business classifying or otherwise grouping the data that it manages. A more common problem is that an amount column in a table may be associated with a particular currency column, but there is no easy way to identify this linkage. Naming conventions can help, but they are not a reliable basis for program logic. Neither do data models appear to have the capabilities to record these groupings or classifications in such a way that they can be used for processing, although data modeling tools do have textual components that can be used for documentation. However, business rules do hold the promise to be able to resolve these issues, if the rule types are specific enough.

Let us now examine a rule definition interface for the **Calculate A Fee** rule type, which illustrates a design approach to these issues.

Setting Up the Rule Type and Selecting a Target Column

Let us suppose that there is a need to calculate a partnership fee for each investment. A new column called *Investment Partnership Fee* can be added to the **Investment** table using the functionality described in Chapter 13. This will use a fee base represented by the existing column *Investment Total Amount*, and a new column called *Investment Partnership Fee Rate* will be the fee rate. The fee rate will be data entered on the Investment Definition screen (though in reality it would be calculated by another rule from other data held for each investment).

The new rule type is set up by directly updating the **Business Rule Type (BRTP_BIZRULETYPE_M)** table. In the new record on this table, *Business Rule Type Code* is set to "CALCFEE" and the *Business Rule Type Definition Function* is "frmRULE_CALCFEE", which is also the name of the Access form that is the definition interface for this rule type. A code generation routine for the new rule is required for batch processes. A new record is added to the **Code Generation Routine (CGR_CODEGENROUTINE_M)** table. The name of the code generation function is BldCALCFEE(). This function is located in the module BuildCode. The user must associate the new rule type with the appropriate business process steps. In the sample application, the rule type has been associated with the business process step "Calculations after Investment Screen Update."

With the required columns set up and the rule type implemented, the user will begin rule definition at the Business Rule Summary Screen described in previous chapters. When the rule type **Calculate A Fee** is chosen and the **Add Rule** button pressed, a list is displayed of all the numeric columns in the base table associated with the selected business process step. Only numeric columns can contain a fee amount. The screen that appears is shown in Figure 20.1.

If the user clicks on a target column that already has its values populated by another rule of any rule type, the rule is displayed in the text box labeled *Rule Name*. If the user presses the **Select** button, the rules engine displays the selected rule. Only if the user selects a target column that is not updated by any rule does the rules engine proceed to the rule definition interface for **Calculate A Fee**.

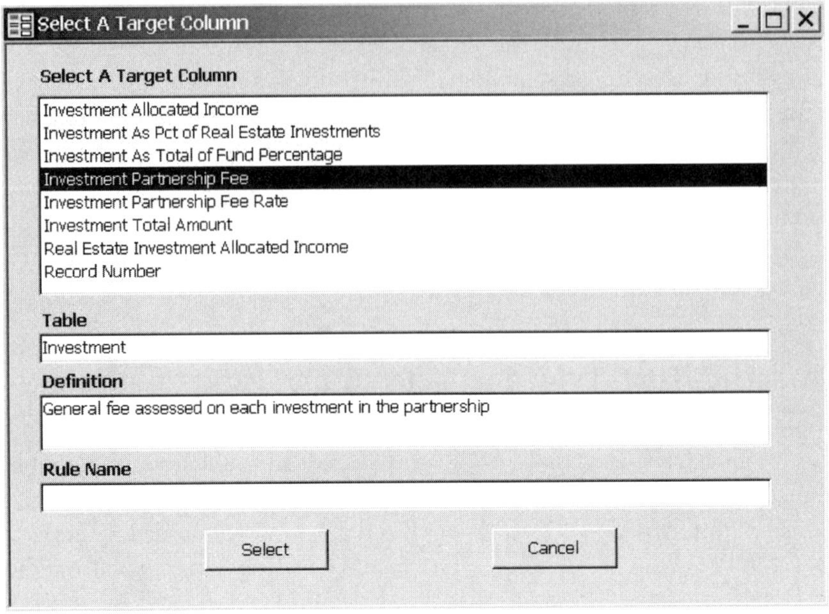

FIGURE 20.1
Select a Target Column

The Rule Definition Interface

The screen where rules of the type **Calculate A Fee** can be defined is shown in Figure 20.2.

The main design points in this screen are as follows:

- The selected target column, and the table it belongs to, are shown at the top of the screen. It is assumed that all columns required to define any rule exist within one table. If this assumption is not correct, the functionality has already been built in previous rule types to deal with additional tables.

- The user selects the columns that represent the *Fee Base* and *Fee Rate*. Only numeric columns in the table where the target column is located are displayed.

- A *Fee Premium/Discount* is data-entered. This must be numeric.

- The *Limit by Subtype* field can be used to select a subtype in the table where the target column is located. This will limit the records that the rule operates on to those belonging to the selected subtype.

- *Fee Type* categorizes the fee that is being defined.

- The remainder of the screen shows metadata that is common to all rules, and definitions of selections made by the user.

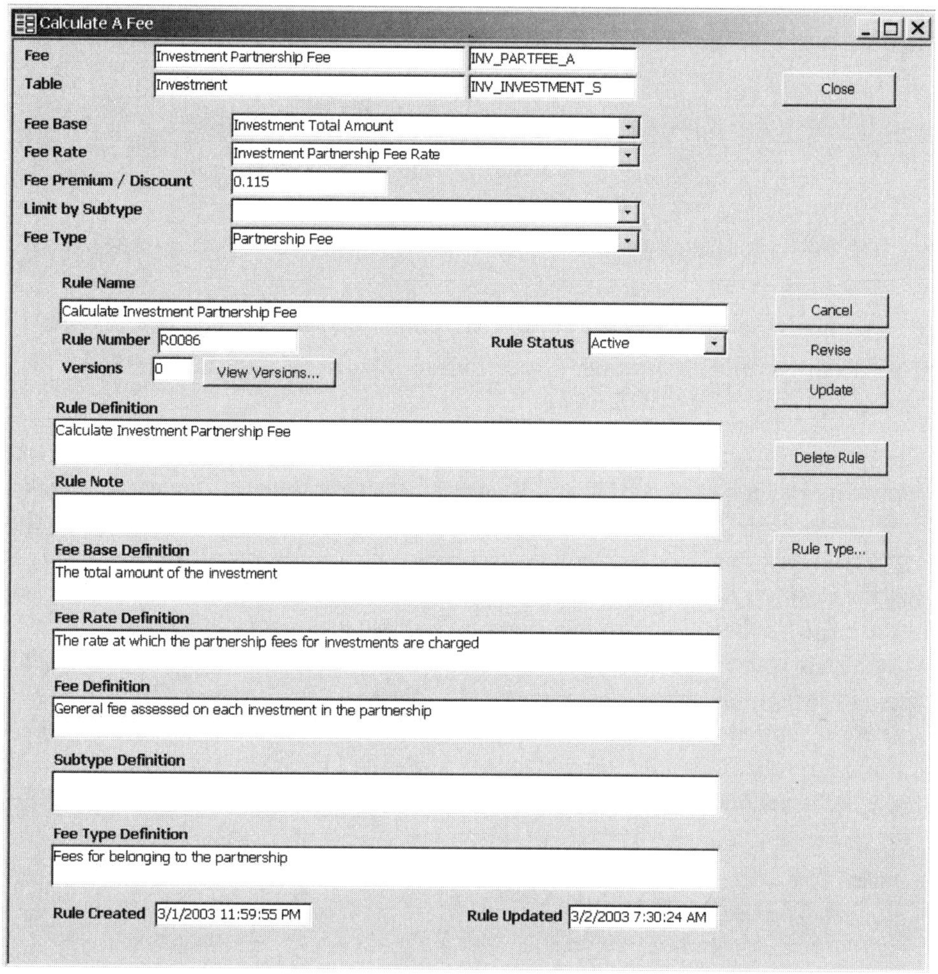

FIGURE 20.2
Rule Definition Screen for Rule Type **Calculate A Fee**

There is no problem with rule duplication in this screen. When the target column was selected, the screen could only be reached if the target was not already populated by a rule, or if it was populated by a **Calculate A Fee** rule.

The rule type definition interface is therefore fairly simple. However, it does have some impact in terms of Repository design that must be considered.

Repository Design Changes

The data entered on the rule type definition screen can all be accommodated in the existing Business Rules Repository with the exception of *Fee Type*. *Fee Type* requires the creation of a new reference data table to hold all the different types of fees that the business needs to manage. This gets us to the point where the user can select a *Fee Type* on the rule type definition screen, but where should the selected *Fee Type* be stored? The design opted for here is to store it on the **Business Rules** table.

Fee Type is metadata that categorizes a set of columns (fees). Actually these columns have other business-relevant metadata, such as:

- The business calls all these columns "fees." They are an important category of data to the business.

- Fees are calculated using a *Fee Base*, a *Fee Rate*, and a *Fee Premium/Discount.*

- There is a standard arithmetic operation to calculate a fee using *Fee Base, Fee Rate*, and *Fee Premium/Discount.*

All these other pieces of metadata are captured by the rule and stored in the Repository tables **Business Rule** and **Business Rule Component**. Therefore, it makes sense to store *Fee Type* there also. Some people may feel uncomfortable that in this way a boundary has been crossed between business data and metadata. The reality is that the Business Rules Repository already contains a great deal of metadata relevant to the business. The design to incorporate *Fee Type* is shown in Figure 20.3.

Another issue in the rule type definition screen is where to store *Fee Premium/Discount*. In the sample application it is stored in the field *Business Rule Component Post Text* in the table **Business Rule Component**. This field was discussed in Chapter 18 and is used to hold data directly entered by the user. However, it is legitimate to ask if the information should be stored here or in a column of a table that stores

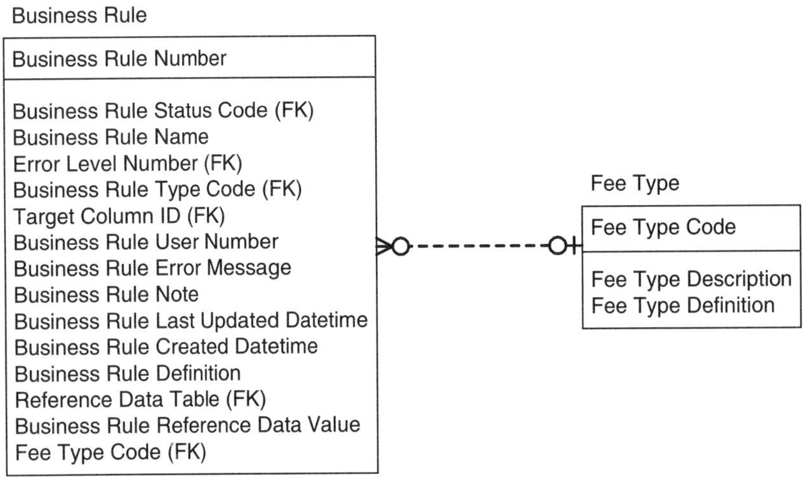

Business Rule

Business Rule Number
Business Rule Status Code (FK) Business Rule Name Error Level Number (FK) Business Rule Type Code (FK) Target Column ID (FK) Business Rule User Number Business Rule Error Message Business Rule Note Business Rule Last Updated Datetime Business Rule Created Datetime Business Rule Definition Reference Data Table (FK) Business Rule Reference Data Value Fee Type Code (FK)

Fee Type

Fee Type Code
Fee Type Description Fee Type Definition

FIGURE 20.3
Design to Accommodate *Fee Type*

business data, such as **Investment**. If *Fee Premium/Discount* is required for additional processing (e.g., additional rules), then it certainly should be stored on a business-relevant database table, and not in the Repository. Also, if it is not a global number, but can change on a record-by-record basis, it should be stored on a business-relevant table. On the other hand, if *Fee Premium/Discount* is a global number that is only used in the execution of the rule, then it is acceptable to store it in the Repository. In this situation, the only other place where it may be used is in reporting, such as in a report about how fees are calculated. However, these kinds of reports are going to have to involve the Repository in any case, because the Repository holds the rules that must appear in the reports.

Dealing with values that are data-entered by users in rule definitions can be a sensitive issue. The rules engine designer must be aware of the requirements for the data values when deciding where to store them.

Subtypes in Calculate A Fee

The rule definition screen shown in Figure 20.2 permits a subtype to be defined to restrict the records that will be processed by the rule. In Figure 20.4, another rule has been defined that restricts the records to real estate investments. This rule calculates *Investment Real Estate Partnership Fee*.

The code that is generated for this rule is shown in Listing 20.1.

The code restricts the operation of the rule to records that belong to the "Real Estate" subtype. Records can potentially change subtype every time the code is run. For instance, a user may change a value on a data entry screen that results in some records no longer being classified as "Real Estate." The rules engine cannot allow values for *Investment Real Estate Partnership Fee* from when the rule was last executed to persist for records that no longer belong to the "Real Estate" subtype. Therefore, the rule begins by setting *Investment Real Estate Partnership Fee* to zero for all records in **Investment**. The issue of records changing subtype between rule executions must be dealt with in any rules engine design, though there are other approaches besides the one illustrated here.

Conclusion

In this chapter the concept of enriching the Business Rules Repository with metadata relevant to the business has been discussed. Business rules offer an ideal vehicle for recording this metadata because rules show how database columns are actually being used. The use of subtypes has also been discussed, especially the need to deal with records that change from one subtype to another.

This is the last rule type that we shall consider in this book. The rule types that have been discussed have illustrated many of the design issues in building a business

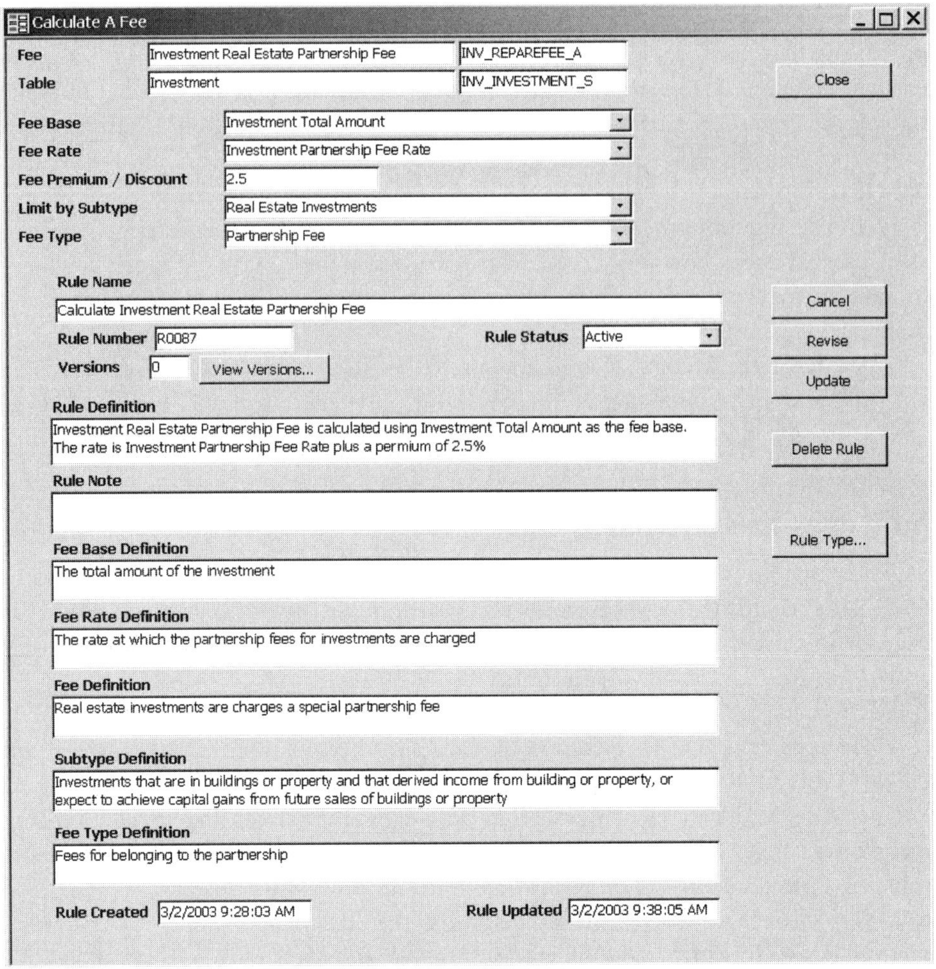

FIGURE 20.4
Using a Subtype in **Calculate A Fee**

LISTING 20.1
Generated Code for **Calculate A Fee** Rule

```
' Rule: R0087 / User Rule: R0087
  ' Rule Name: Calculate Investment Real Estate Partnership Fee
    ' Target Table:
    '    Investment / INV_INVESTMENT_S
    ' Target Column:
    '    Investment Real Estate Partnership Fee / INV_REPAREFEE_A
    ' Source Columns:
```

```
' Investment Total Amount / INV_TOTAL_A
' Investment Partnership Fee Rate / INV_PARTFEERATE_A
'  SubType Used: Real Estate Investments
' —Discriminator Column: Investment Category Code / INCT_C
' —Discriminator Value: REALEST
  strSQL = "UPDATE INV_INVESTMENT_S SET INV_REPAREFEE_A = 0 "
  cmd.CommandText = strSQL
  cmd.Execute lngAffected
strSQL = "SELECT * FROM INV_INVESTMENT_S " _
  & " WHERE INCT_C = 'REALEST' "
rstSource.Open strSQL, CurrentProject.Connection, _
    adOpenKeyset, adLockOptimistic, adCmdText
Do While Not rstSource.EOF
' Set Up Default Values
  dblSrc1 = 0
  dblSrc2 = 0
  If Not IsNull(rstSource("INV_TOTAL_A")) Then
    dblSrc1 = rstSource("INV_TOTAL_A")
  End If
  If Not IsNull(rstSource("INV_PARTFEERATE_A")) Then
    dblSrc2 = rstSource("INV_PARTFEERATE_A")
  End If
  dblSrc3 = dblSrc1 * (dblSrc2 + 2.5) * 0.01
  strSQL = "UPDATE INV_INVESTMENT_S SET INV_REPAREFEE_A = '" &
CStr(dblSrc3) & "'" _
    & " WHERE INV_C = '" & rstSource("INV_C") & "'"
  cmd.CommandText = strSQL
  cmd.Execute lngAffected
  rstSource.MoveNext
Loop
rstSource.Close
```

rules engine, and various solutions to these issues. The rule types have also utilized the infrastructure built earlier for the business rules engine. It is hoped that at this point readers will have a sufficient basis to build whatever rule types their applications require.

In the remaining chapters we will consider the need to debug business rules engines, and the management reporting that they can support.

21

DEBUGGING IN BUSINESS RULES ENGINES

An issue with business rules engines that cannot be dismissed is the problem of what to do if a user suspects something is wrong. In traditional systems development projects there is a team of IT professionals that, in theory at least, can be called upon to help to investigate and correct problems. With purchases of packaged software, there is often a provision for some kind of after-sales support.

Business engines are different. Problems can arise because of the logic that users themselves have defined. Of course, there can also be problems with the core functionality of the engine itself, but these are much rarer because if code generation does not work, it is usually immediately obvious—for example, when the generated code cannot be parsed or compiled by the software environment in which it executes. When users define the rules, there may be no preexisting specification that can be looked at to determine what may be going wrong if problems are suspected, unlike traditional systems development projects (although good, up-to-date specifications are rare). Similarly if a rules engine is implemented in a number of client sites, a knowledge base containing histories of reported problems may not be as helpful as it is for packaged software. What is required is some way for users to at least attempt to debug possible problems. This chapter presents several approaches to this problem. The management of the rules engine, which can be a significant help in avoiding problems, is discussed in the following chapter.

Viewing Data

The way in which data could be viewed directly in the database was discussed in Chapter 13. Now that we have built a number of rules and executed them it is possible to examine the results. In the sample application, the screens where data is

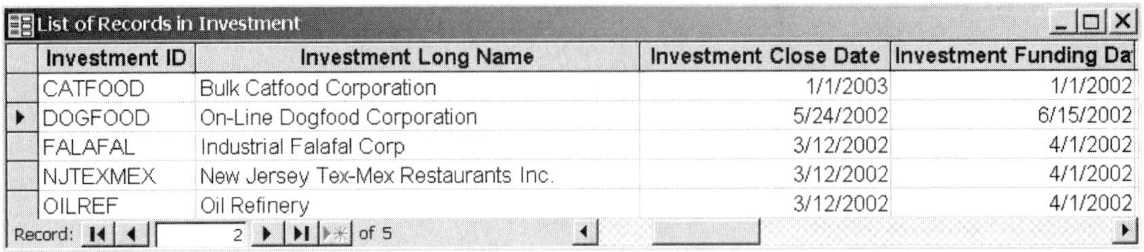

List of Records in Investment

Investment ID	Investment Long Name	Investment Close Date	Investment Funding Da
CATFOOD	Bulk Catfood Corporation	1/1/2003	1/1/2002
DOGFOOD	On-Line Dogfood Corporation	5/24/2002	6/15/2002
FALAFAL	Industrial Falafal Corp	3/12/2002	4/1/2002
NJTEXMEX	New Jersey Tex-Mex Restaurants Inc.	3/12/2002	4/1/2002
OILREF	Oil Refinery	3/12/2002	4/1/2002

Record: 2 of 5

FIGURE 21.1
Browse **Investment** Table

displayed need to be rebuilt every time the underlying tables have their structures changed. Since this has happened several times to the **Investment** and **Fund** tables, the corresponding screens should be rebuilt. This is done in the sample application by selecting **Database Maintenance** from the main menu and then **Build Table List Display**. A list of tables appears. The **Fund** and **Investment** tables should be selected. The data display screens for these tables are then rebuilt.

To view the data in these tables, select **Database Maintenance** from the main menu of the sample application, and then **View Data**. Again, a list of tables appears. Select the **Investment** table. The browse display of this table appears as shown in Figure 21.1.

This display makes it very easy to see what values populate columns that are updated by business rules. The user can, potentially at least, see what the results of business rules are. If displays of the raw data, such as the screen in Figure 21.1, are not available, then the user has to rely on printed reports and screen outputs to find data. These may not necessarily show the required data, and a newly created column may not be included in any screens or reports. Furthermore, screens and reports often show data in an indirect way (perhaps including hard-coded rules that affect the way data is shown), and often for only a selected subset of records in a table. It is also unlikely that such screens and reports will show all the columns in a given table.

However, the screen in Figure 21.1 is rather wide and does not show many columns of a given record in the table within the area viewable on the screen. Double-clicking on this screen leads to the screen shown in Figure 21.2.

This screen permits us to see detailed data a little more easily. *Real Estate Allocated Income* and *Investment Allocated Income* are both updated by rules discussed in previous chapters. These rules are executed when the **Save** button on the Investment Definition screen is pressed. In the sample application, the Investment Definition screen is accessed by selecting **Application Functions** on the main menu, and then **Enter Investment Details** on the popup that appears. Thus, the reader can play with the sample application to alter investment details and can see how the rules run to affect the data in the **Investment** table.

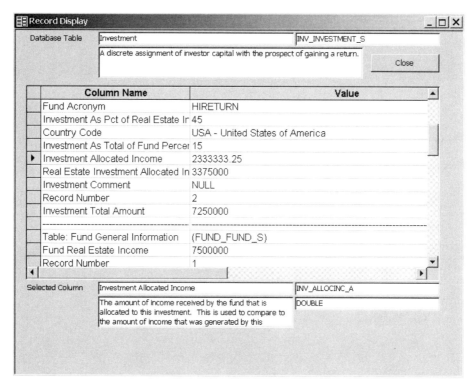

FIGURE 21.2
Detailed Record Display

Users will require some knowledge of the data model underlying the application to make full use of this facility. However, any user placed in the position of defining rules will quickly demand some kind of functionality to visualize what results the rules have created.

The rules engine designer may wish to add more metadata to the screens shown in Figures 21.1 and 21.2. There is certainly a lot more metadata that can be used in the Business Rules Repository. For instance, a column that is updated by a rule could be identified as such, and the rule definition presented to the user.

What the ability to view data gives is one means to detect and investigate errors. However, this is only after rules have executed. A rules engine needs a way to record what happens as rules execute, and this is discussed in the next section.

Logging Rules Activity

In a traditional hand-crafted application, there is usually little that can be done by users to see how control flows through program code. IT staff often have to use aids

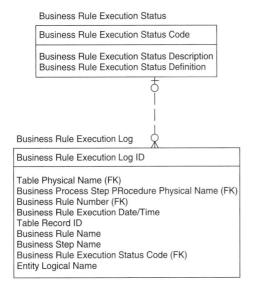

Business Rule Execution Status

Business Rule Execution Status Code
Business Rule Execution Status Description Business Rule Execution Status Definition

Business Rule Execution Log

Business Rule Execution Log ID
Table Physical Name (FK) Business Process Step PRocedure Physical Name (FK) Business Rule Number (FK) Business Rule Execution Date/Time Table Record ID Business Rule Name Business Step Name Business Rule Execution Status Code (FK) Entity Logical Name

FIGURE 21.3
Business Rule Execution Log

that come with the programming language they use, or other specialized tools, to actually watch program execution as it happens. With business rules engines there is a great deal more structure, and it is possible to record how generated code executes and to review what happened at a later time. This capability to log the execution of rules can be used for a number of very useful things. Users can review logs to investigate rules, and rules engine designers can use them to find performance bottlenecks.

A log requires that information be stored somewhere, and this implies that additional database tables are required. The design used in the sample application is presented in Figure 21.3.

The main table for logging business rule execution is **Business Rule Execution Log**. This contains one record for every log event. A *log event* in the sample application is the start or end of processing for a business process step, and the start and end of one instance of a rule firing. An instance of a rule firing is one rule updating or constraining one instance of a column (or other system object), and not a rule processing a set of records at a time. The log events are described by the records contained in the table **Business Rule Execution Status**. The columns of **Business Rule Execution Log** are as follows:

- *Business Rule Execution Log ID*: A system-generated sequential number that identifies a log record.

- *Table Physical Name:* The physical name of the base table that is being updated (or otherwise referenced) by the business rule.

- *Business Process Step Procedure Physical Name:* The physical name of the business process step within which the rules are executing.

- *Business Rule Number:* The identifier of the business rule that is executing.

- *Business Rule Execution Status Code:* A code that identifies a log event.

- *Business Rule Execution Date/Time:* The date and time at which the log event occurs.

- *Table Record ID:* The value of RECORD_ID_C of the base table that is updated by the rule.

- *Business Rule Name:* The full name of the business rule, corresponding to the *Business Rule Number.*

- *Business Step Name:* The full name of the business step, corresponding to the *Business Process Step Procedure Physical Name.*

- *Entity Logical Name:* The full name of the database table, corresponding to the *Table Physical Name.*

The last three of these columns repeat descriptive information that is held in other tables. This is necessary for easier display of the log data.

The physical structure of **Business Rule Execution Log** (**BRX_BREXECU-TIONLOG_M**) is shown in Table 21.1.

ATTRIBUTE LOGICAL NAME	COLUMN PHYSICAL NAME	COLUMN DATATYPE
Business Rule Execution Log ID	BRX_C	Autonumber
Table Physical Name	TAB_PHYSNAME_T	Character (50)
Business Process Step Procedure Physical Name	BPSP_PHYSNAME_T	Character (40)
Business Rule Number	BRULE_NUMBER_C	Character (5)
Business Rule Execution Status Code	BRXS_C	Character (10)
Business Rule Execution Date/Time	BRX_D	Date/Time
Table Record ID	RECORD_ID_C	Long Integer
Business Rule Name	BRULE_NAME_T	Character (120)
Business Step Name	BPSP_NAME_T	Character (120)
Entity Logical Name	TAB_ENTLOGNAME_T	Character (250)

TABLE 21.1 Physical Structure of **BRX_BREXECUTIONLOG_M** (**Business Rule Execution Log**)

Implementing Logging

The way that logging is implemented in the sample application is by having a single routine that records logging events. This routine is called at various points in the execution of business process steps and the rules that are contained within them. The function, LogExecution(), is shown in Listing 21.1.

LISTING 21.1
Function to Update **Business Rule Execution Log**

```
Public Function LogExecution(strStep As String, strRule As String,
_
        lngRecord As Long, strTab As String, strStatus As String)
As String
'*****************************************************************
' Records a log event.  Called by the generated code.  It updates
' the Business Rule Execution Log.
'
' Parameters:
' strStep = The Business Process Step Procedure Physical Name of
'            the currently executing business process step
' strRule = The Business Rule Number of the currently executing
' rule lngRecord = Value of RECORD_ID_C of the record in the
' table currently being updated
' strTab = The able Physical Name of the table currently
'            being updated
' strStatus = A code describing the current log event
'*****************************************************************

Dim cmd As ADODB.Command, strSQL As String, lngAffected As Long
Dim rstRule As ADODB.Recordset, strStepName As String, strRuleName
As String
Dim strTabName As String

   LogExecution = "Y"
   If IsNull(kstrLogNow) Then
     Exit Function
   End If
   If kstrLogNow <> "Y" Then
```

```
      Exit Function
   End If


   Set cmd = New ADODB.Command
   cmd.ActiveConnection = CurrentProject.Connection
   cmd.CommandType = adCmdText
   Set rstRule = New ADODB.Recordset

   strRuleName = ""
   If Trim(strRule) <> "" Then
      strSQL = "SELECT * FROM BRULE_BIZRULE_M   " _
            & " WHERE BRULE_NUMBER_C = '" & strRule & "'"
      rstRule.Open strSQL, CurrentProject.Connection, _
          adOpenKeyset, adLockOptimistic, adCmdText
      strRuleName = Trim(rstRule("BRULE_NAME_T"))
      rstRule.Close
   End If
   strStepName = ""
   If Trim(strStep) <> "" Then
      strSQL = "SELECT * FROM BPSP_BIZSTEPPROC_M   " _
            & " WHERE BPSP_PHYSNAME_T = '" & strStep & "'"
      rstRule.Open strSQL, CurrentProject.Connection, _
          adOpenKeyset, adLockOptimistic, adCmdText
      strStepName = Trim(rstRule("BPSP_NAME_T"))
      rstRule.Close
   End If
   strTabName = ""
   If Trim(strTab) <> "" Then
      strSQL = "SELECT * FROM TAB_TABLE_M   " _
            & " WHERE TAB_PHYSNAME_T = '" & strTab & "'"
      rstRule.Open strSQL, CurrentProject.Connection, _
          adOpenKeyset, adLockOptimistic, adCmdText
      strTabName = Trim(rstRule("TAB_ENTLOGNAME_T"))
      rstRule.Close
   End If

   strSQL = "INSERT INTO BRX_BREXECUTIONLOG_M (TAB_PHYSNAME_T,
BPSP_PHYSNAME_T, " _
            & "BRULE_NUMBER_C, BRXS_C, RECORD_ID_C, BRX_D,
BRULE_NAME_T, " _
            & "BPSP_NAME_T, TAB_ENTLOGNAME_T) VALUES (" _
```

```
              & "'" & strTab & "', '" & strStep & "','" & strRule &
"','" _
              & "'" & strStatus & "', " & CStr(lngRecord) & ", Now(),
"  _
              & "'" & strRuleName & "','" & strStepName & "','" _
              & strTabName & "')"
     cmd.CommandText = strSQL
     cmd.Execute lngAffected

     Set rstRule = Nothing
     Set cmd = Nothing

End Function
```

As can be seen from Listing 21.1, LogExecution() gathers information from several different sources before updating the **Business Rule Execution Log**. Thus, it is likely to have an effect on rules engine performance.

LogExecution() has to be called from the generated code. This means that the code generation routines have to generate the code to call LogExecution() in addition to the other functions they perform. The best way to implement this is to have a special function called by each code generation routine to write the code to call LogExecution(). One reason to have such a central routine is that the role of LogExecution() is likely to grow over time, and it is best to have just one piece of code to change when this happens. The reason that LogExecution() is likely to grow is that new classes of rule type may require additional metadata to be stored about their execution, and new code generation environments may also require additional metadata. For instance, the discussion of logging has so far been confined to rules that update columns and run batch processes. A business rules engine is likely to have to deal with more complexity than this. For instance, rules that validate screen data entry will require different treatment, and thus extensions to LogExecution().

An example of generated code that calls LogExecution() is shown in Listing 21.2.

As can be seen from Listing 21.2, there is a call to LogFunction() when a business process step starts to run, with a *Business Rule Execution Status Code* of "SS" (for "Start Step"). When each rule executes there is a call every time a new record in the base table is read, with a *Business Rule Execution Status Code* of "SR" (for "Start Rule"). If the update operation is carried out, there is another call *Business Rule Execution Status Code* of "ER" (for "End Rule"). Finally, although this is not shown in Listing

LISTING 21.2
Calls to LogExecution() in Generated Code

```
'CalcfrmINV_INVESTMENT_S----Start
Public Function CalcfrmINV_INVESTMENT_S() As String
Dim intErr As Integer, strErr As String, rstSource As
ADODB.Recordset
Dim strSQL As String, strGo As String, strInd As String
Dim strTab As String, strPhysName As String
Dim strSrc1 As String, strSrc2 As String, strSrc3 As String,
strSrc4 As String, strSrc5 As String, strSrc6 As String
Dim dSrc1 As Date, dSrc2 As Date, dSrc3 As Date, dSrc4 As Date,
dSrc5 As Date, dSrc6 As Date
Dim dblSrc1 As Double, dblSrc2 As Double, dblSrc3 As Double,
dblSrc4 As Double, dblSrc5 As Double, dblSrc6 As Double
Dim cmd As ADODB.Command, lngAffected As Long, varMy As Variant,
strMy As String
' Last Generated: 2/19/2003 1:32:39 PM

CalcfrmINV_INVESTMENT_S = "Y"
Set rstSource = New ADODB.Recordset
Set cmd = New ADODB.Command
cmd.ActiveConnection = CurrentProject.Connection
cmd.CommandType = adCmdText
strMy = LogExecution("CalcfrmINV_INVESTMENT_S", "", 0, "", "SS")
  ' Rule: R0076 / User Rule: R0076
  ' Rule Name: Compute Real Estate Investment Allocated Income
   ' Target Table:
   '    Investment / INV_INVESTMENT_S
   ' Target Column:
   '    Real Estate Investment Allocated Income / INV_REALESTINC_A
   ' Source Columns:
   ' Fund Real Estate Income / FUND_REALESTINC_A
   ' Investment As Pct of Real Estate Investments /
   ' INV_REALESTPCT_A
  strSQL = "SELECT C.*, C.RECORD_ID_C AS RECID, " _
        & " P.* FROM INV_INVESTMENT_S C, FUND_FUND_S P " _
        & " WHERE C.FUND_C = P.FUND_C " _
        & " AND INCT_C = 'REALEST'"
  rstSource.Open strSQL, CurrentProject.Connection, _
        adOpenKeyset, adLockOptimistic, adCmdText
  Do While Not rstSource.EOF
```

```
' Set Up Default Values
strMy = LogExecution("CalcfrmINV_INVESTMENT_S", "R0076", _
            rstSource("RECID"), "INV_INVESTMENT_S", "SR")
dblSrc1 = 0
dblSrc2 = 0
If Not IsNull(rstSource("FUND_REALESTINC_A")) Then
    dblSrc1 = rstSource("FUND_REALESTINC_A")
End If
If Not IsNull(rstSource("INV_REALESTPCT_A")) Then
    dblSrc2 = rstSource("INV_REALESTPCT_A")
End If
dblSrc4 = 0
If dblSrc1 <> 0 And dblSrc2 <> 0 Then
  dblSrc4 = dblSrc1 * dblSrc2 * 0.01
End If
strSQL = "UPDATE INV_INVESTMENT_S SET INV_REALESTINC_A = '" _
    & CStr(dblSrc4) & "'" _
    & " WHERE INV_C = '" & rstSource("INV_C") & "'"
cmd.CommandText = strSQL
cmd.Execute lngAffected
strMy = LogExecution("CalcfrmINV_INVESTMENT_S", "R0076", _
            rstSource("RECID"), "INV_INVESTMENT_S", "ER")
rstSource.MoveNext
Loop
rstSource.Close
```

21.2, there is a call when the end of the business process step reached with a *Business Rule Execution Status Code* of "ES" (for "End Step").

The rules engine designer may well decide that there is a need to put additional information into the log. One candidate may be the record numbers of the database tables from which source columns of a rule are taken. On the other hand there is little point in logging information that will never be used. Rules engine designers need to understand the requirements of the environments they work in to decide how far logging should go.

Control of Logging

Logging tends to degrade performance, although the level of degradation tends to depend on how logging is implemented. Given this, and the fact that the log tables

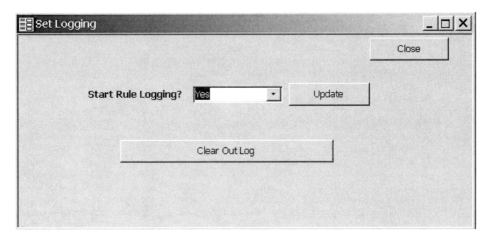

FIGURE 21.4
Logging Activation Screen

can grow very quickly, logging should not be permanently enabled. Therefore, there needs to be a way of switching it on and off. In the sample application, a global variable called kstrLogNow is used to control logging. When this variable has a value of "Y," logging routines will perform logging functions. If the variable has some other value, no logging is performed.

In the sample application, the global variable is switched on and off via a screen shown in Figure 21.4.

In the sample application, this screen is reached by selecting **Application Functions** on the main menu, and then **Start/End Rule Logging** on the popup that appears.

The combo box on this screen will set kstrLogNow to "Y" if "Yes" is chosen. Once set, the global variable remains set for the user's session. When the user signs off, the global value does not persist—it has to be set again when the user next signs on. It should be remembered that the sample application is single-user, not multiuser, and that the logging techniques implemented in it may have to be changed in a multiuser environment.

Viewing the Log

With the infrastructure of the log in place, it is a reasonably easy matter to make it visible to the user. In the sample application a simple screen to view the log has been implemented. It can be accessed by choosing the main menu option **Application Functions** and then **View Log**. A screen like that shown in Figure 21.5 appears.

Rule Nu	Rule	Event	Table	Table Name	Tab	Date/Time
		Start Business Process Step Exec			0	003 1:47:43 PM
R0076	Compute Real Estate Investment /	Start Business Rule Execution	INV_INVESTME	Investment	2	003 1:47:43 PM
R0076	Compute Real Estate Investment /	End Business Rule Execution	INV_INVESTME	Investment	2	003 1:47:43 PM
R0076	Compute Real Estate Investment /	Start Business Rule Execution	INV_INVESTME	Investment	13	003 1:47:43 PM
R0076	Compute Real Estate Investment /	End Business Rule Execution	INV_INVESTME	Investment	13	003 1:47:43 PM
R0076	Compute Real Estate Investment /	Start Business Rule Execution	INV_INVESTME	Investment	16	003 1:47:43 PM
R0076	Compute Real Estate Investment /	End Business Rule Execution	INV_INVESTME	Investment	16	003 1:47:43 PM
R0075	Compute Investment Allocated Inc	Start Business Rule Execution	INV_INVESTME	Investment	1	003 1:47:43 PM
R0075	Compute Investment Allocated Inc	End Business Rule Execution	INV_INVESTME	Investment	1	003 1:47:43 PM
R0075	Compute Investment Allocated Inc	Start Business Rule Execution	INV_INVESTME	Investment	2	003 1:47:43 PM
R0075	Compute Investment Allocated Inc	End Business Rule Execution	INV_INVESTME	Investment	2	003 1:47:43 PM
R0075	Compute Investment Allocated Inc	Start Business Rule Execution	INV_INVESTME	Investment	13	003 1:47:43 PM
R0075	Compute Investment Allocated Inc	End Business Rule Execution	INV_INVESTME	Investment	13	003 1:47:43 PM
R0075	Compute Investment Allocated Inc	Start Business Rule Execution	INV_INVESTME	Investment	15	003 1:47:43 PM
R0075	Compute Investment Allocated Inc	End Business Rule Execution	INV_INVESTME	Investment	15	003 1:47:44 PM
R0075	Compute Investment Allocated Inc	Start Business Rule Execution	INV_INVESTME	Investment	16	003 1:47:44 PM
R0075	Compute Investment Allocated Inc	End Business Rule Execution	INV_INVESTME	Investment	16	003 1:47:44 PM
		End Business Process Step Exec			0	003 1:47:44 PM

Record: |◄ ◄ | 1 ► |►| |►✱| of 72   ◄ |

FIGURE 21.5
View **Business Rule Execution Log**

This screen lets the user quickly see which rules have executed and in which order.

One problem with any kind of log is that it can quickly become very large. There needs to be a mechanism to clean it out, and in the sample application this is implemented in the Logging Activation Screen shown in Figure 21.4. There is a button on this screen that deletes the contents of the log.

Conclusion

The debugging functionality described in this chapter probably represents a minimum set of what is required in a rules engine. However, as noted above, additional logging capabilities and additional richness in the presentation of log information to the user should be driven by requirements for the specific business rules engine being built. One goal should be to present the users with information that they can understand and deal with. It is true that additional functionality of interest only to the builders of the rules engine may be necessary, but users should be shielded from this.

22

MANAGING THE BUSINESS RULES ENGINE

At this point we have covered all the basic functionality that is required to make a business rules engine work. However, there is a management reporting component to a business rules engine that must also be implemented.

As discussed in the Introduction there are many reasons for building a rules engine. The abilities to quickly implement an application in different business environments and to extend an application after it is implemented are key drivers for the adoption of rules engines. Yet there are other important reasons for using business rules engines. These include being able to understand the logic that an application is using when it runs and the assurance that the definitions of business rules matches what is actually being executed. All of these goals require that there be some kind of management reporting, and with rules engines such reports can go far beyond what is possible for traditional hand-crafted program logic.

In this area, it is vital for the rules engine designer to consider the following:

- Does the designer understand the management reporting that must be provided for the rules engine to work successfully in its target business environment? The reports may be oriented more to the business than to the components of the rules engine.

- Can the required management reports be produced from the Business Rules Repository that the rules engine designer has created? If they cannot be produced, there are one or more design shortfalls in the Business Rules Repository, and these must be corrected.

It is worthwhile, therefore, to review reports that are frequently needed and to explore the role they play in the management of the operations of the rules engine.

In the following sections, a number of these reports are discussed. They are also matched with the design of the Business Rules Repository to make certain that they can be produced with the design presented in this book. The reports have not been created in the sample application, but readers with sufficient knowledge of Microsoft Access may wish to make a try at building some of them.

Rules Reports

These reports are needed to monitor what rules have been defined and the situations in which they are executed.

Rule Sequence within Business Process Step

This report lists the rules within each business process step to show:

- The rules that are implemented for the business process step
- The sequence in which these rules fire within the business process step

It is critically important that users review this information and sign off on it before business process steps are run in a production mode. The report must be informative enough that users can understand what logic is running within the business process steps and can easily relate this information to the business as they understand it. If the report fails to provide users with this level of understanding, a black box has been created, and the users cannot be sure of what is going on in the rules engine. Such an outcome would signal a failure in the business rules approach and would be a strong indicator of more difficulties to come.

Users tend to focus on one business process or business process step at a time. The report should therefore ask users to select a business process or business process step and print out only the rules involved in that step. Listing 22.1 shows a SQL SELECT statement that can be used to implement this report.

The rules engine designer may wish to add content from other tables such as **Business Rule Type** to enhance the information provided to the user.

Usage of Business Rules within Business Process Steps

This report lists each rule and shows what business process steps it is used in (if any). One reason why this is important is that if a business rule is never executed, it is worth knowing that and asking why it is kept in the rules engine. In the design approach presented in this book, such orphan rules should not exist because all rules are defined in the context of business process steps. However, in other design

LISTING 22.1
SQL SELECT Statement to Provide Data for Report "Rule Sequence within Business Process Step"

```
SELECT BRULE_BIZRULE_M.*, RBSP_RULESOFSTEP_M.RBSP_SEQUENCE_N,
        BPSP_BIZSTEPPROC_M.BPSP_NAME_T,
    BPSP_BIZSTEPPROC_M.BPSP_LASTCODEGEN_D,
        BPROC_BIZPROCESS_M.BPROC_DESC_M
    FROM ((BRULE_BIZRULE_M INNER JOIN RBSP_RULESOFSTEP_M ON
        RULE_BIZRULE_M.BRULE_NUMBER_C =
    RBSP_RULESOFSTEP_M.BRULE_NUMBER_C) INNER JOIN
        BPSP_BIZSTEPPROC_M ON RBSP_RULESOFSTEP_M.BPSP_PHYSNAME_T =
        BPSP_BIZSTEPPROC_M.BPSP_PHYSNAME_T) INNER JOIN
    BPROC_BIZPROCESS_M ON
        BPSP_BIZSTEPPROC_M.BPROC_C = BPROC_BIZPROCESS_M.BPROC_C
    ORDER BY RBSP_RULESOFSTEP_M.RBSP_SEQUENCE_N;
```

LISTING 22.2
SQL SELECT Statement to Provide Data for Report "Usage of Business Rules within Business Process Steps"

```
SELECT BRULE_BIZRULE_M.*, RBSP_RULESOFSTEP_M.BPSP_PHYSNAME_T
    FROM BRULE_BIZRULE_M LEFT JOIN RBSP_RULESOFSTEP_M ON
        BRULE _BIZRULE_M.BRULE_NUMBER_C=RBSP_RULESOFSTEP_M.
        BRULE_NUMBER_C
    ORDER BY BRULE_BIZRULE_M.BRULE_NUMBER_C,
    RBSP_RULESOFSTEP_M.BPSP_PHYSNAME_T;
```

approaches it may be possible to create rules that are not associated with business process steps.

A second reason is that it is often important to know where a rule is executed. Certain kinds of rules, such as those used to recalculate balances, may need to be executed in a number of business process steps, and users need to make sure that they have been included in every relevant business process step.

Of course there is also the possibility that a rule has been included in a business process step when it should not have been. The design approach in this book provides some protection against this, since it requires every business process step to have a set of permitted rule types associated with it. However, this is not complete protection against erroneous inclusion of a rule in a business process step. A report can help to find instances of rules that should not be present in a business process step.

Listing 22.2 shows a SQL SELECT statement that can be used to implement this report.

This SQL SELECT statement contains an outer join to ensure that all business rules are selected, not just those that are used in business process steps.

Column Reports

Besides business rules, the information that the rules work with is of great interest to users. The primary system objects that rules work with are database columns. There have to be reports to show what database columns are read by rules (source columns) or have their values constrained by rules (target columns).

Columns Targeted by Business Rules

This report shows what database columns are targeted by business rules. Target columns either have their values populated directly by business rules or have their contents validated in some way by business rules. In the Business Rules Repository, target columns are identified in the **Business Rule** table (**BRULE_BIZRULE_M**) by the column *Target Column ID* (COL_C).

Columns can be listed by the table they belong to. Listing 22.3 shows a SQL SELECT statement that can be the basis of this report and that does list columns by table.

Not all rules will appear in this report. Some rules operate on system objects other than columns. For instance, referential integrity rules to detect duplicates target a database table rather than any column. Separate reports are required for these kinds of rules.

LISTING 22.3
SQL SELECT Statement to Provide Data for Report "Columns Targeted by Business Rules"

```
SELECT BRULE_BIZRULE_M.*, COL_COLUMN_M.COL_ATTLOGNAME_M,
TAB_TABLE_M.TAB_ENTLOGNAME_T
FROM (BRULE_BIZRULE_M INNER JOIN COL_COLUMN_M ON
        BRULE_BIZRULE_M.COL_C=COL_COLUMN_M.COL_C) INNER JOIN
TAB_TABLE_M ON
        COL_COLUMN_M.TAB_PHYSNAME_T=TAB_TABLE_M.TAB_PHYSNAME_T
ORDER BY TAB_TABLE_M.TAB_ENTLOGNAME_T,
COL_COLUMN_M.COL_ATTLOGNAME_T;
```

LISTING 22.4
SQL SELECT Statement to Provide Data for Report "Usage of Columns in Rules"

```
SELECT COL_C, BRULE_NUMBER_C, "TARGET" AS COLTYPE
FROM BRULE_BIZRULE_M
WHERE COL_C IS NOT NULL
UNION
SELECT COL_C, BRULE_NUMBER_C, "SOURCE" AS COLTYPE
FROM BRC_BIZRULECOMP_M
WHERE COL_C IS NOT NULL
UNION
SELECT COL_CHILD_C AS COL_C, BRULE_NUMBER_C, "CHILD SOURCE" AS
COLTYPE
FROM BRC_BIZRULECOMP_M
WHERE COL_CHILD_C IS NOT NULL
ORDER BY BRULE_NUMBER_C, COL_C;
```

Usage of Columns in Rules

At some point, a user will need a list of all rules that use a given column, irrespective of whether the column is a source column or a target column. The **Business Rules (BRULE_BIZRULE_M)** table of the repository holds the *Target Column ID* and the **Business Rule Component** table (**BRC_BIZRULECOMP_M**) holds the *Source Column ID* and *Child Column ID* (needed for certain rules using relationships). This is evidently rather a complex set of related data, although the SQL SELECT statement in Listing 22.4 can deal with it.

However, there is one additional way in which columns can be used in rules. This is where a rule uses a subtype, or a relationship that contains a parent subtype and/or a child subtype. It is simply not feasible to have a single SQL SELECT statement to gather all of this data together, and the best solution is to write some program logic to find all of the column information associated with rules and store it in a temporary table from which the report is then produced.

The relationships associated with a rule are stored in the *Relationship ID* (REL_C) column of the **Business Rule Component** table (**BRC_BIZRULECOMP_M**). Information on each relationship is stored in the **Relationship** table (**REL_RELATIONSHIP_M**), which contains the *Parent Subtype ID* (STP_PARENT_C) and *Child Subtype ID* (STP_CHILD_C). The **Subtype** (**STP_SUBTYPE_M**) table contains the *Subtype Discriminator Column ID* (COL_C). This is the column that is indirectly used in any business rule that utilizes subtypes.

Although this navigation through the Business Rules Repository is a little tortuous, the information is at least present and accessible.

It is recommended that this report be presented by listing columns within tables. For each column, a list of the rules in which each column is used should be provided. The role of the column in each rule should be stated—that is, whether it is a target column, a source column, or a subtype discriminator.

Usage of Columns in Business Process Steps

This report is one level of complexity greater than the previous report. Here it is necessary to show what business process steps (and business processes) a given column participates in. The "Usage of Columns in Rules" report provided a list of business rules that utilize each column. What needs to be done is to find which business process steps each of these rules participates in.

Again, this navigation is of a level of complexity that is probably beyond a single SQL SELECT statement in the context of the design of the Business Rules Repository presented here. Thus, some special programming will be necessary. However, the information can be obtained from the Business Rules Repository.

User-Defined Columns Control Report

Users can extend the tables of the database that cover the business domain of the application (as opposed to the tables of the Business Rules Repository). Therefore, a report that lists columns that have been defined by users is a good idea for overall management of the rules engine. In particular, columns that have been added for frivolous reasons and are not utilized in any business rules need to be identified. These are candidates for removal.

The basic SQL SELECT statement to retrieve this information is shown in Listing 22.5. It can be used as is, in which case the columns could be displayed within tables. A better idea is to combine this information with information about rules in order to show what rules the columns are used in. In the preceding sections, ways

LISTING 22.5
SQL SELECT Statement to Provide Data for "User-Defined Columns Control Report"

```
SELECT COL_COLUMN_M.*, TAB_TABLE_M.TAB_ENTLOGNAME_T
FROM COL_COLUMN_M INNER JOIN TAB_TABLE_M ON
     COL_COLUMN_M.TAB_PHYSNAME_T=TAB_TABLE_M.TAB_PHYSNAME_T
WHERE COL_USERDEFINED_I="Y"
ORDER BY TAB_TABLE_M.TAB_ENTLOGNAME_T, COL_ATTLOGNAME_T;
```

in which the usage of columns in rules could be determined were discussed. These approaches should be used here to provide a report showing how user-defined columns are used in rules. The primary reason for users to define columns is to be able to implement additional rules, and so it is important to know how the columns are being used.

Subtype Reports

Subtypes are very important in ensuring that certain rules affect only subsets of records within database tables. Since they are primary drivers for business rules they need to be monitored carefully.

Subtypes without Rules to Identify Them

Every subtype in a given database table is recognized by a certain value in a certain column in that table. The column is known as the *Subtype Discriminator Column,* and the value is known as the *Subtype Discriminator Value.* Each subtype should have one business rule that identifies it. Subtypes that lack such rules will never be identified by the business rules engine, and thus the rules that depend on them will never be executed. Therefore, it is very important to know if there are any subtypes that do not have rules for their identification.

The rule to identify a subtype is stored on the **Subtype (STP_SUBTYPE_M)** table in the column *Business Rule Number* (BRULE_NUMBER_C). The report should find all subtypes where *Business Rule Number* is null, as shown in the SQL SELECT statement in Listing 22.6.

Subtypes and Reference Data Values

Some subtypes will be identified by reference data code values and not indicators. In this case, each reference data code value should identify a separate subtype. In other words, if a reference data table exists, and one of its code values is used to identify a

LISTING 22.6
SQL SELECT Statement to Find Subtypes Without Business Rules

```
SELECT STP_SUBTYPE_M.*
FROM STP_SUBTYPE_M
WHERE BRULE_NUMBER_C IS NULL;
```

subtype in some other table, then all code values in the reference data table would be expected to be used to identify subtypes.

It is not possible to produce this report by a single SQL SELECT statement. It requires program logic to be created as follows:

- All reference data tables that are used in any way to identify subtypes need to be found. This can be done by looking at each value in *Subtype Discriminator Column ID* in the **Subtype** table and finding the parent reference data table.

- Information for each value of *Subtype Discriminator Column ID* can be retrieved from the **Column** table. From this it can be determined if the *Subtype Discriminator Column ID* is for an indicator column or represents a reference data code value. If the latter is the case, the parent reference data table can be found.

- Once a list of all reference data tables used in *Subtype Discriminator Column ID* has been found, this list can be used to produce the report. The report should list each reference data table and then each reference data code value within the table, plus the description of this code value. Within this should be a list of each subtype identified by each reference data code value.

Ideally, there will only be one subtype identified by each reference data code value. More likely there will be gaps where a reference data table has some values used for subtypes, and other values that are not used to identify any subtypes. The user needs to consider whether this is correct, or whether the gaps indicate that there are errors.

The rules engine designer may construct a Business Rules Repository that is quite different from the one discussed here. However, it is very important that any Business Rules Repository be able to link reference data code values (traditionally viewed as data) to the definitions of subtypes (traditionally viewed as metadata).

Use of Subtypes in Rules

Some rules are used to identify subtypes. These rules should be executed unconditionally. Other rules are executed only for certain subtypes. A report should be provided to users so that they can see which rules are conditionally executed for subtypes. Such a report can be constructed using the techniques already described in this chapter.

Relationship Reports

Relationships can be extended by users as described in Chapter 9. Management reports are therefore required so that users can track what relationships have been defined and how they are used in the rules engine.

Lists of Relationships

A complete list of relationships should be provided. Several lists would probably be more appropriate as follows:

- A list of all relationships by table. This will show all relationships in which a given table is involved, irrespective of whether this table is the parent or the child in the relationship. For each relationship the definition of the relationship should be provided and the parent and child tables should be identified.

- A list of relationships by parent table. For each table, only the relationships where that table is a parent table are shown. For each relationship, the definition of the relationship and the child table are shown.

- A list of relationships by child table. For each table, only the relationships where that table is a child table are shown. For each relationship, the definition of the relationship and the parent table are shown.

None of these reports may easily be created using a single SQL SELECT statement. However, all the required information is in the Business Rules Repository.

User-Defined Relationships

The reports described in the previous section can be limited to those that are defined by users. These can be differentiated from relationships that came from the data model by the *Relationship from Data Model Indicator* (REL_FROMDM_I) in the **Relationship** table.

Use of Relationships in Rules

This list should show all rules that involve each relationship. It is a variant of the report "Use of Subtypes in Rules" discussed earlier.

From this report the user can determine if user-defined relationships are not used for any rules, in which case these relationships can probably be removed from the repository. Also, the user can determine what rules do use relationships, and if there are any missing rule types. For instance, there may be a need to aggregate data across particular relationships. If no rules are associated with these relationships, there is a strong probability that someone has forgotten to define them, since aggregation will only occur by means of rules.

Business-Specific Reporting

Throughout this book, one of the themes has been that an advantage of building a business rules engine is that it can be made highly specific to the business domain that the overall application supports. Reporting is no exception. Thus, it should be possible to produce reports from the rules engine that are very specific to the business.

Such reports can be facilitated by capturing business-relevant metadata with rule definitions. For instance, the **Pay Pro Rata from Fund to Investment** rule type discussed in Chapter 19 identified an *Investment Allocation Percentage*. Allocation percentages in general are important things in partnership accounting, and it may be useful to provide a list of them. The rule metadata makes this possible.

Chapter 20 showed how fees could be categorized in the rule type definition screen for the **Calculate A Fee** rule type. From this it is relatively easy to produce a list of all fees in the application, and to show how each fee is calculated. It is even possible to create business-oriented reports that mix data and metadata. For instance, a report showing details of real estate management fee amounts could be constructed as follows:

- Obtain a list of all real estate management fee columns. This is done by finding the target columns for each **Calculate A Fee** rule type that is classified as a real estate management fee.

- For each table in turn where these fees are located, loop through every record. Display the values of the primary key columns. These can be determined from the **Column** table. Also display the contents of any description column. This is recognized by *Column Description Indicator* on the **Column** table.

- Show the real estate management fee amounts for each record processed.

Another piece of metadata that may be found in many rules is the association of an amount and a currency. These are typically represented by two columns in a database table, but it is usually very difficult to know which currency column matches which amount column—data models do not provide for this. Some people try to use naming conventions, but these usually have limited success. In contrast, rules can record which currency field matches a column (e.g., if the rule has to perform currency conversions). This is one example of using rules to identify subtle associations between columns in tables that could not be otherwise recorded. The majority of these associations are likely to make sense only for specific business purposes. It has to be admitted that some extensions to the Business Rules Repository may be required, but this is true in general when new rule types are implemented.

This is but a small glimpse of what is possible in terms of business-specific management reporting from the rules engine. The rules engine designer needs to work with business users to determine exactly what their reporting requirement are. These requirements should all be oriented to helping users be as self-sufficient as possible in operating the rules engine.

Conclusion

Many more examples could be provided of management reports that can be useful in the management of an operational business rules engine. It is hoped that those listed here will assist rules engine designers in considering their reporting needs.

At this point, all aspects of building a business rules action have been touched upon. As stated at the outset, this is a book about design, and not a prescribed solution. The objective has been to introduce design issues, consider them, and propose implementable solutions. The rules engine designer will have to confront many of these same issues that have been discussed, but may face requirements that dictate somewhat different solutions. Part of what is required is to think in a different way about metadata than is commonly needed for a traditional systems development approach. Achieving this is perhaps the best guarantee that a designer will build a successful business rules engine.

USING THE SAMPLE APPLICATION

The sample application is referred to in many of the chapters of this book. It serves as a vehicle for examining how functional elements of a business rules engine may be implemented. Discussing design options can provide a general appreciation of a certain number of the issues involved. Only by going to the level of program code can many of the details involved in these design decisions become apparent. Thus, it is ultimately necessary to examine the program code in the sample application to fully appreciate many aspects of the design of a rules engine. The sample application is not intended to be a functioning rules engine that can be adapted to production use. The philosophy of this book is that if a business rules engine is to be built, its structure and functionality should match the business area in which it is to be deployed.

Readers should therefore look at the sample application within this context and are welcome to change it to experiment with their own design issues. This appendix lists the functionality in the application so that the reader will be better able to utilize it.

Installing the Sample Application

The instructions for downloading the sample application are provided in the Introduction. After the application has been downloaded, the reader should check that it can operate correctly on the PC where it has been placed. This can be done as follows:

1. Open the sample application (the file "bizrules.mdb") with Microsoft Access.
2. On the main database window click in the "Modules" button on the left of the window. The modules of the application will appear, as shown in Figure A.1.

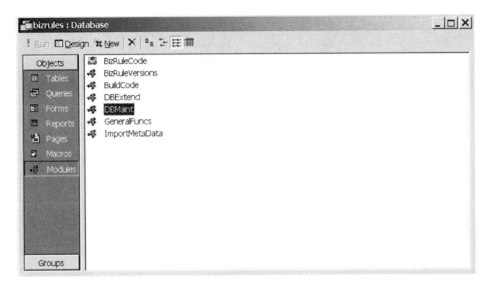

FIGURE A.1
Modules of Sample Application

3. Double-click on the module DBMaint to see the program code. The screen shown in Figure A.2 will appear. This is how all program code in modules is displayed.

4. Click on the option **Tools** in the menu at the top of the screen, and then on the option **References** in the popup that appears. A screen like that shown in Figure A.3 appears.

5. In this screen there are six references that are checked at the top of the screen. The references that the reader sees must match these references, in the order they are listed in Figure A.3. If a reference is not checked, the reader must scroll down, find it, and click on the check box next to it. If the references are not in the sequence shown in Figure A.3, the reader should use the up and down priority arrows to correct the sequence.

Figure A.2 shows how program code can be accessed in modules. There is one other area where program code occurs in the sample application, and this is in the Class Modules of Forms. To view forms, select the **Forms** button on the left of the main database window. The screen shown in Figure A.4 will appear.

To look at the program code behind a form, it is necessary to open it in design mode. To do this highlight the form and click on the **Design** button on the toolbar of the database window (or alternatively, right-click on the form

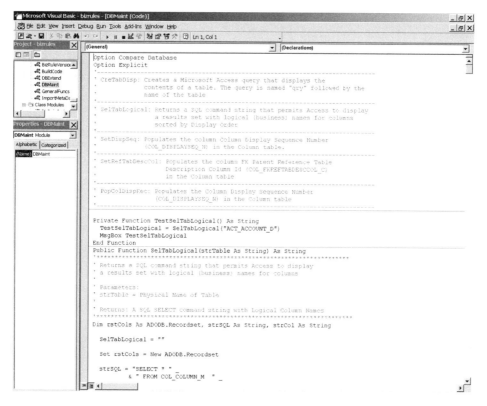

FIGURE A.2
Program Code

name and choose "Design View"). A screen like that shown in Figure A.5 then appears.

To view the code in the form's class module, click on **View** in the top menu and then on **Code** in the popup that appears.

This is all that is required to be able to view the program code. If the reader wishes to learn more about Microsoft Access, there are a number of good books about it, and some are listed in Resources and Further Reading. This is not a book about Microsoft Access and should not be treated as one. Access is only used as a means for implementing design constructs shown here. Other programming languages may be more appropriate for a rules engine to be implemented in a production setting, depending on requirements. The advantage of Access is that it is a stand-alone programming language and database, and it is reasonably easy to follow program code implemented in it. That is why it has been chosen for the sample application.

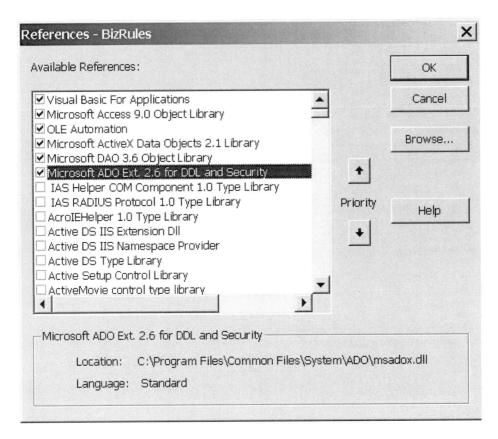

FIGURE A.3
References

The following sections provide details of the structure of the sample application, beginning with the business-relevant tables of the sample application.

Database Tables Relevant to the Business

There are many tables in the sample application. Those that are needed for rules engine functionality are discussed in the body of the book. Some tables are required for the business area that the sample application covers—an investment partnership. These tables, too, are presented at various places in the book to make specific points about design decisions. However, not all of these tables are actively used by the sample application. Those that are used in this way are centered around the **Investment** table. Figures A.6 and A.7 present the logical and physical structures of the tables that hold business data and that are used by the sample application.

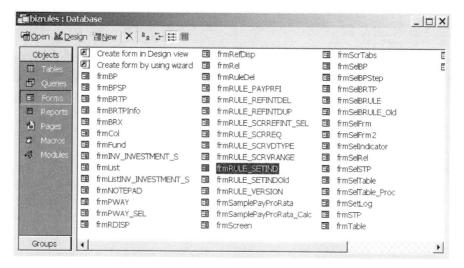

FIGURE A.4
Forms of the Sample Application

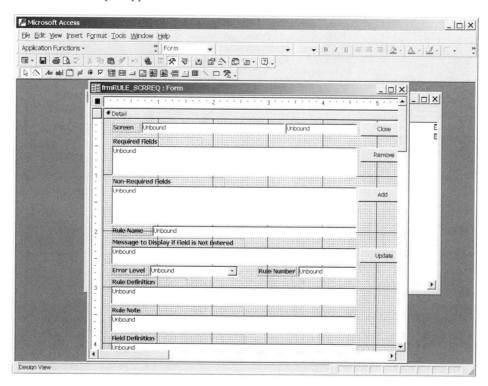

FIGURE A.5
Form in Design View

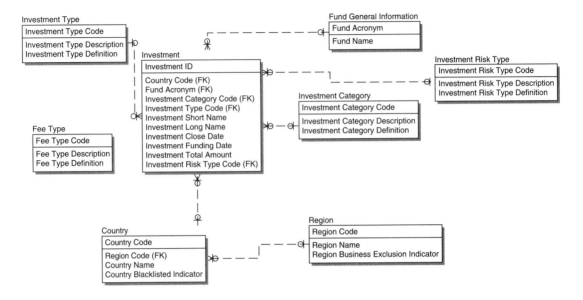

FIGURE A.6
Logical View of Business-Relevant Database Tables

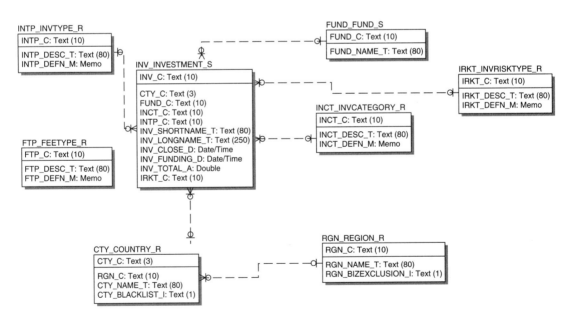

FIGURE A.7
Physical View of Business-Relevant Database Tables

The Menu System

The main menu of the application appears above the main database window. It consists of the options described in Table A.1.

The details of the menu options will now be discussed.

Application Functions

The suboptions that appear when **Application Functions** is selected from the main menu are described in Table A.2.

Database Maintenance

The suboptions that appear when **Database Maintenance** is selected from the main menu are described in Table A.3.

Business Rules

The suboptions that appear when **Business Rules** is selected from the main menu are described in Table A.4.

Repository Functions

The suboptions that appear when **Business Rules** is selected from the main menu are described in Table A.5. The menu structure of the sample application has now been described.

MENU OPTION	DESCRIPTION
Application Functions	Leads to the "business" side of the sample application, as opposed to rules engine functionality. This is needed to view and enter data and to actually execute business rules.
Database Maintenance	The rules engine functionality that enables users to view the tables and columns of the database and to view data within them. It also permits users to change the structure of the database.
Business Rules	The rules engine functionality that enables users to manage and define business rules, as well as to generate their executable versions.
Repository Functions	The rules engine functionality that deals with other aspects of the Business Rules Repository.

TABLE A.1 Main Menu Options in the Sample Application

MENU OPTION	DESCRIPTION
Enter Investment Details	This option leads to the Investment Definition screen. Nearly all examples of rule engine functionality are based on this screen. It updates data in the **Investment** table (see Figures A.6 and A.7). The Investment Definition screen is the Access form **frmINV_INVESTMENT_S**. Pressing the **Save** and **Delete** buttons on the Investment Definition screen executes the code generated for all examples of business rules described in the book.
Enter Fund Details	This option leads to the Fund Definition screen that updates data in the **Fund** table (see Figures A.6 and A.7). There is only one record in the **Fund** table. This screen is needed for a very few examples in the book.
Start/End Rule Logging	This option leads to a screen that enables logging of the running of business rules. Only rules associated with batch processes are logged. The screen also allows the log to be cleaned out.
View Log	This option leads to a screen that shows the log that records the execution of the business rules defined in the system. Only rules running within batch processes are logged.

TABLE A.2 Suboptions below Application Functions in Menu Structure

MENU OPTION	DESCRIPTION
View Data	When this option is selected, a list of database tables is presented to the user. If a database table is selected, the data within it is displayed. If the user changes the structure of a database table, the Build Table List Display option must be executed (see below) before the new structures become visible. The **Investment** table is the primary table that should be viewed.
Edit Database Columns	The user is asked to select a business process and business process step. Then a list of tables associated with the selected business process step is presented. If the user selects a table, then the columns in the table are displayed. The user can add new columns and edit certain information for existing columns. The primary business process that should be selected is "Investment screen validation and processing." Either of the first two business process steps should then be selected. From the list of tables that appears, the **Investment** table is of the most interest.

TABLE A.3 Suboptions below Database Maintenance in Menu Structure

MENU OPTION	DESCRIPTION
Edit Database Tables	This option is similar to the previous one. The user is asked to select a business process and then a business process step. A list of tables is then presented. When the user selects a table, information about it is displayed. The user can edit some of this information. The **Investment** table and all reference data tables are of interest for this screen.
Build Table List Display	This option presents a list of tables. If the user selects a table, then an Access form is build to display the table using the functionality under the suboption View Data (see above). This function should be invoked if a database table has its structure changed.
Add Record Number to Tables	This function adds a *Record Number* column to all business-relevant database tables. The physical name of the column is RECORD_ID_C. It should only be run if new business-relevant tables are added to the database.
Repository Synchronization	This function compares the physical structure of the database with information recorded in the Repository. If errors are detected some can be repaired. The function reports its findings to the user.

TABLE A.3 *Continued*

MENU OPTION	DESCRIPTION
Define Business Rules	When this option is selected, the Business Rule Definition screen appears. The user must select a business process and business process step on this screen. Then all the rules within the selected business process step are displayed. The primary business process that should be selected is "Investment screen validation and processing." Either of the first two business process steps should then be selected. When the user selects a rule the next screen that appears depends on the rule type of the selected rule.
Rule Deletion Controls	This screen permits the user to enforce restrictions on the deletion of business rules.

TABLE A.4 Suboptions below Business Rules in Menu Structure

MENU OPTION	DESCRIPTION
Relationship Editor	This option leads to a screen where a user can select a relationship or copy it to a new relationship. On the next screen that appears the user can edit relationship details.
Subtype Editor	This option allows users to edit subtypes. Users have full control over subtypes.
Pathway Editor	This option presents a screen of all pathways in the application. The user can edit only a couple of data items for any pathway.
Update Repository from Data Model	This option invokes the functionality to update the repository from metadata imported from an ERWin data model. The import of table, column, and relationship metadata must have occurred before this option is run.
Business Processes	When this option is selected a list of business processes is displayed.
	When a business process is selected, a screen appears where details of the business process can be updated. It is possible to select a button to show the business process steps belonging to the business process.
	If a business process step is selected, a screen where the business process step can be edited is displayed. This is important for rule definitions because this screen is where the rule types permitted for a business process step are defined. If a rule type is not permitted for a business process step, then no rules of this type can be defined for the step.
	The primary business process that should be selected is "Investment screen validation and processing." Either of the first two business process steps should then be selected.
Screen Definitions	This option displays a screen where information about all screens in the application is presented. The most important screen is the Investment Details screen.

TABLE A.5 Suboptions below Repository Functions in Menu Structure

Modules of the Sample Application

The modules of the sample application contain program code. At the start of each module are explanations of the functions and subroutines found within it. Overall descriptions of the modules are presented in Table A.6.

Forms of the Sample Application

There are a number of forms in the sample application. These are described in Table A.7.

MODULE	DESCRIPTION
BizRuleCode	This module contains only generated code that represents the executable forms of business rules.
BizRuleVersions	Contains the functionality to maintain different versions of business rules.
BuildCode	Contains all the functions needed to generate code for business rules. This is where the code generation functions for each business rule type are located.
DBExtend	Contains functionality that enables users to extend the database.
DBMaint	Contains functionality to enable users to manage the database.
GeneralFuncs	General functions and subroutines for the sample application.
ImportMetaData	Contains functions that are used when metadata is imported from a data model.

TABLE A.6 Modules of the Sample Application

Tables of the Business Rules Repository

The tables of the Business Rules Repository are discussed in detail in the body of this book. Table A.8 summarizes their logical and physical names.

Steps to Add New Rules for a New Rule Type

The steps to create a new rule type, define new rules for it, and test these rules are summarized below.

1. Analyze the rule type and create a design for a rule definition function and one or more code generation functions.

2. Add a new record to the table **Business Rule Type** table **(BRTP_BIZRULETYPE_M)**. This must be done by directly editing this table in the sample application. An acronym and description must be provided for the rule type. Also, the name of the Access form that will be the rule definition interface for the rule type must be entered.

3. Build the Access form that is the rule definition interface for this rule type.

4. Add at least one new record to the table **Code Generation Routine** **(CGR_CODEGENROUTINE_M)**. This must indicate the name of the code generation function for at least one code generation environment.

5. Build the Access function that is the code generation routine for the selected code generation environment. This should be located in the module

FORM	DESCRIPTION
frmBP	View/edit business process information. Reached from the menu options **Repository Functions > Business Process**.
frmBPSP	View/edit business process steps. Reached from the form frmBP.
frmBRTPInfo	Certain rule type definition screens have a button **Rule Type . . .** Clicking on the button leads to this screen, which displays information about the rule type.
frmBRX	Displays a log of rule execution activity. Reached from the menu options **Application Functions > View Log**.
frmCol	View/edit a database column. Reached from the menu options **Database Maintenance > Edit Database Columns**.
frmFund	View/edit fund details. Reached from the menu options **Application Functions > Enter Fund Details**.
frmINV_INVESTMENT_S	The Investment Definition Screen. Reached from the menu options **Application Functions > Enter Investment Details**.
frmList . . .	All forms that begin with frmList are for displaying data from the database table that appears in the form name following "frmList". These forms are built by the system when the menu options **Database Maintenance > Build Table List Display** are selected. The forms are displayed when the menu options **Database Maintenance > View Data** are selected.
frmNotePad	A utility form used for general sets of information to be displayed to a user.
frmPWAY	Pathway Definition Screen. Reached from the menu options **Repository Functions > Pathway Editor**.
frmPWAY_SEL	Screen to select a Pathway.
frmRDISP	Complete display of a data record. Reached by double-clicking on one of the forms whose name begins with "frmList".
frmRel	View/edit a relationship. Reached from the menu options **Repository Functions > Relationship Editor**.
frmRuleDel	Controls rule deletion. Reached from the menu options **Business Rules > Rule Deletion controls**.
frmRULE_CALCFEE	Rule definition screen for rule type **Calculate A Fee**.
frmRULE_PAYPRFI	Rule definition screen for rule type **Pay Pro Rata from Fund to Investment**.
frmRULE_REFINTDEL	Rule definition screen for rule type **Referential Integrity for Dependent Records**.

TABLE A.7 Forms of the Sample Application

FORM	DESCRIPTION
frmRULE_REFINTDUP	Rule definition screen for rule type **Check for Duplicate Records.**
frmRULE_SCRREQ	Rule definition screen for rule type **Required Screen Fields.**
frmRULE_SCRVDTYPE	Rule definition screen for rule type **Valid Datatypes for Screen Fields.**
frmRULE_SCRVRANGE	Rule definition screen for rule type **Screen Fields Valid Ranges.**
frmRULE_SETIND	Rule definition screen for rule type **Set An Indicator.**
frmRULE_SETREFCODE	Rule definition screen for rule type **Set A Reference Data Code Value.**
frmRULE_VERSION	Displays prior versions of a rule. Reached from rule type definition screens.
frmScreen	View/edit screens. Reached from the menu options **Repository Functions > Screen Definitions.**
frmSelBP	Screen to select a business process. Reached from various points in the application.
frmSelBRTP	Screen to select a business rule type. Reached from various points in the application.
frmSelBRULE	Business Rule Selection Screen. Reached from the menu options **Business Rules > Define Business Rules.**
frmSelIndicator	Select an indicator column from a list of indicator columns. Reached from frmSelBRULE for rule type **Set An Indicator.**
frmSelIndicator	Select a numeric column from a list of numeric columns. Reached from frmSelBRULE for certain rule types.
frmSelRefCodeValue	Select a reference data code column from a list of reference data code columns. Reached from frmSelBRULE for rule type **Set A Reference Data Code Value.**
frmSelRel	Select a relationship.
frmSelSTP	Select a subtype.
frmSelTable	Select a table.
frmSetLog	Controls logging of business rule execution. Reached from the menu options **Application Rules > Start/End Rule Logging.**
frmSTP	View/edit subtypes. Reached from the menu options **Repository Functions > Subtype Editor.**
frmTable	View/edit table definitions. Reached from the menu options **Database Maintenance > Edit Database Tables.**

TABLE A.7 *Continued*

TABLE NAME	TABLE NAME
BPROC_BIZPROCESS_M	Business Process
BPSP_BIZSTEPPROC_M	Business Process Step
BPTP_BIZPROCTYPE_M	Business Process Implementation
BRC_BIZRULECOMP_M	Business Rule Component
BRCV_BIZRULECOMPVER_M	Business Rule Component Version
BRST_BRULESTATUS_M	Business Rule Status
BRTP_BIZRULETYPE_M	Business Rule Type
BRULE_BIZRULE_M	Business Rule
BRV_BIZRULEVERSION_M	Business Rule Version
BRX_BREXECUTIONLOG_M	Business Rule Execution Log
BRXS_BREXECSTATUS_M	Business Rule Execution Status
CGE_CODEGENENV_M	Code Generation Environment
CGR_CODEGENROUTINE_M	Code Generation Routine
COL_COLUMN_M	Column
DBS_DBSERVER_M	Database Server
DBSV_DBSERVVER_M	Database Server Version
DTP_DATATYPE_M	Datatype
DTTP_DTPTYPE_M	Datatype Type
ELVL_ERRORLEVEL_M	Error Level
GCDE_GENCODE_M	Generated Code
NOTE_NOTEPAD_M	Notepad
PWAY_PATHWAY_M	Pathway
PWL_PWAYLEVEL_M	Pathway Level
RBSP_RULESOFSTEP_M	Rules of Business Process Step
RDISP_RECDISPLAY_M	Record Display
RDR_REFDATARULES_M	Reference Data Rules
REL_RELATIONSHIP_M	Relationship
RKEY_RELKEYATT_M	Relationship Key Attribute
RTBS_RULTYPBIZSTEP_M	Rule Types Permitted in Business Process Step
SCR_SCREEN_M	Screen
STP_SUBTYPE_M	Subtype
SYS_SYSTEM_R	System Defaults
TAB_TABLE_M	Table
TBRC_BIZRULECOMP_M	Temporary Business Rule Component

TABLE A.8 Tables of the Business Rules Repository

BuildCode. It is recommended that the batch processing code generation environment be selected.

6. Select one or more business process steps that are allowed to use the new rule type. On the main menu select **Repository Functions > Business Processes**. A list of business processes appears. The business process steps of a process can

then be selected. On the screen to view/edit business process steps, the new rule type can be associated with the selected business process step.

It is recommended that the business process "Investment screen validation and processing" be selected, and then the business process step "Calculations after Investment Screen Update."

7. The rule type has been implemented at this point, and it is possible to begin to define rules. Before doing so, there may be a need to add new columns to the database. To do this select the menu options **Database Maintenance > Edit Database Columns**. Select a table, such as **Investment**, and create the new columns.

8. To define a new rule, select the menu options **Business Rules > Define Business Rules**. Select a business process and business process step. Select the rule type at the bottom of the screen, and then the button **Add Rule**.

    It is recommended that the business process "Investment screen validation and processing" be selected, and then the business process step "Calculations after Investment Screen Update."

9. The rule type definition screen will now appear. Define one or more rules. Code should be generated when the **Close** button is pressed (though some other design approach may also be implemented). Be aware that before code is generated, all programming changes in Access must be saved. If this is not done, Access may not be able to complete the operation.

10. Ensure that the business process step with which the rules are associated can be invoked from the application. For instance, the function for the business process step "Calculations after Investment Screen Update" is invoked when the **Save** button on the Investment Definition Screen is clicked. The designer may want to invoke the function in a different way.

11. Test the new rules. If they are associated with the Investment table, select the menu options **Application Functions > Enter Investment Details**. The Investment Definition screen appears. Edit some data and press the **Save** button to invoke the new rules.

12. If any database table was changed, the screens that permit browsing of data must be regenerated. Select the menu options **Database Maintenance > Build Table List Display**. Select the database targeted by the new rules. Its data display screen will be recreated.

13. Select the menu options **Database Maintenance > View Data**. Select the database targeted by the new rules. Look at the data displayed. This should show the results of the rule execution.

14. The generated code can be found in the module BizRuleCode. It can be examined to determine whether it meets the original design.

RESOURCES AND FURTHER READING

Access 2000 Developer's Handbook, Volume 1: Desktop Edition. Getz, K., Litwin, P., and Gilbert, M. San Francisco: Sybex, 1999.

Business Rules and Information Systems: Aligning IT with Business Goals. Morgan, T. Boston: Addison-Wesley Publishing, 2002.

Business Rules Applied: Building Better Systems Using the Business Rules Approach. Von Halle, B. New York: John Wiley & Sons, 2001.

Business Rule Concepts: The New Mechanics of Business Information Systems. Ross, R. Business Rule Solutions, Inc., 1998.

Business Rules Community (http://www.brcommunity.com)

Designing Quality Databases with IDEF1X Information Models. Bruce, T. New York: Dorset House Publishing, 1992.

Managing Reference Data in Enterprise Databases: Binding Corporate Data to the Wider World. Chisholm, M. San Francisco: Morgan Kaufmann Publishers, 2001.

Principles of the Business Rule Approach, Ronald G. Ross, Addison-Wesley, 2003. Available via www.BRSolutions.com

Reference Data Portal (http://www.refdataportal.com)

The Business Rule Book: Classifying, Defining, and Modeling Rules. Ross, R. Boston: Database Research Group, Inc, 1997.

The Business Rules Group: An Independent Peer Group of I/S Professionals (http://www.businessrulegroup.com)

The Data Administration Newsletter (TDAN) (http://www.tdan.com)

What Not How: The Business Rules Approach to Application Development. Date, C. J. Boston: Addison-Wesley Publishing, 2000.

Object Management Group (OMG) (http://www.omg.org)

INDEX